POLICE
AND
COUNTER
INSURGENCY

POLICE
AND
COUNTER
INSURGENCY

THE UNTOLD STORY OF
TRIPURA'S COIN CAMPAIGN

KULDEEP KUMAR

 SAGE www.sagepublications.com
Los Angeles • London • New Delhi • Singapore • Washington DC

First published in 2016 by

 SAGE Publications India Pvt Ltd
B1/I-1 Mohan Cooperative Industrial Area
Mathura Road, New Delhi 110044, India
www.sagepub.in

SAGE Publications Inc
2455 Teller Road
Thousand Oaks, California 91320, USA

SAGE Publications Ltd
1 Oliver's Yard, 55 City Road
London EC1Y 1SP, United Kingdom

SAGE Publications Asia-Pacific Pte Ltd
3 Church Street
#10-04 Samsung Hub
Singapore 049483

Published by Vivek Mehra for SAGE Publications India Pvt Ltd, typeset in Berkeley 10/13 pts by PrePSol Enterprises Pvt Ltd and printed at Saurabh Printers Pvt Ltd, Greater Noida.

Library of Congress Cataloging-in-Publication Data

Names: Kumar, Kuldeep, author.
Title: Police and counterinsurgency : the untold story of Tripura's COIN
    campaign / Kuldeep Kumar.
Description: New Delhi ; Thousand Oaks : SAGE, 2016. | Includes
    bibliographical references and index.
Identifiers: LCCN 2015041356| ISBN 9789351507475 (hardback : alk. paper) |
    ISBN 9789351507468 (epub) | ISBN 9789351507482 (ebook)
Subjects: LCSH: Police–India–Tripura. | Counterinsurgency–India–Tripura.
Classification: LCC HV8249.T75 K86 2016 | DDC 355.02/18095415--dc23 LC
record available at http://lccn.loc.gov/2015041356

ISBN: 978-93-515-0747-5 (HB)

The SAGE Team: Rudra Narayan Sharma, Sanghamitra Patowary, and Anupama Krishnan

Dedicated to

my dear mother and the loving memory of my father

Thank you for choosing a SAGE product!
If you have any comment, observation or feedback,
I would like to personally hear from you.
Please write to me at **contactceo@sagepub.in**

Vivek Mehra, Managing Director and CEO,
SAGE Publications India Pvt Ltd, New Delhi

Bulk Sales

SAGE India offers special discounts
for purchase of books in bulk.
We also make available special imprints
and excerpts from our books on demand.

For orders and enquiries, write to us at

Marketing Department
SAGE Publications India Pvt Ltd
B1/I-1, Mohan Cooperative Industrial Area
Mathura Road, Post Bag 7
New Delhi 110044, India

E-mail us at **marketing@sagepub.in**

Get to know more about SAGE

Be invited to SAGE events, get on our mailing list.
Write today to **marketing@sagepub.in**

This book is also available as an e-book.

Contents

List of Illustrations

Tables

Figures

List of Abbreviations

AASU	All Assam Students Union
ADC	Autonomous District Council
AFSPA	Armed Forces Special Powers Act
AGP	Asom Gana Parishad
AOR	Area of Responsibility
AQIS	al-Qaeda in the Indian Subcontinent
AR	Assam Rifles
ASER	Annual Status of Education Report
ATTF	All Tripura Tiger Force
BAC	Bodo Autonomous Council
BDO	Block Development Officer
BJP	Bharatiya Janata Party
BKI	Babbar Khalsa International
BLTF	Bodo Liberation Tiger Force
BNCT	Borok National Council of Tripura
BOP	Border Outpost
BPR&D	Bureau of Police Research and Development
BSF	Border Security Force
BTC	Bodo Territorial council
BTF	Bengali Tiger Force
CAPF	Central Armed Police Forces
CD	Community Development
CFM	Counterinsurgency Field manual
CHRI	Commonwealth Human Rights Initiative
CIAT	Counterinsurgency and Anti-Terrorist

CI-CT	Counterinsurgency-Counter Terrorism
CIJW	Counterinsurgency and Jungle Warfare
CI Ops	Counterinsurgency Operations
COB	Company Operation Bases
COIN	Counterinsurgency
CorCom	Coordination Committee
CPI (M)	Communist Party of India (Marxist)
CRPF	Central Reserve Police Force
CT	Counter-terrorism
DAR	District Armed Reserve
DGP	Director General of Police
DGFI	Director General of Foreign Intelligence
DHD	Dima Halam Daogah
DIG	Deputy Inspector General
DLOG	District Level Operations and Intelligence Group
DSP	Deputy Superintendent of Police
ERT	Emergency Response Teams
GAIL	Gas Authority of India Limited
GOI	Government of India
GSAS	Geo-satellite Applications System
HDI	Human Development Index
HDR	Human Development Report
HQ	Head Quarter
HuJI	Harkat–ul-Jihad-al-Islami
IBB	Indo-Bangladesh Border
ICM	Institute for Conflict Management
IDA	Institute for Defense Analysis
IED	Improvised Explosive Device
IETF	Internet Engineering Task Force
IGP	Inspector General of Police
IIPA	Indian Institute of Public Administration
INPT	Indigenous Nationalist Party of Tripura
IPFT	Indigenous People Front of Tripura
IPM	Indian Police Medal
IPS	Indian Police Service
IRB	India Reserve Battalion

IS	Internal Security
ISI	Inter-services Intelligence
IWTT	Inland Waterway Trade and Transit Treaty
JBIC	Japan Bank of International Cooperation
JIC	Joint Intelligence Committee
JKLF	Jammu and Kashmir Liberation Front
JMB	Jamaat-ul-Mujahideen Bangladesh
JWCI	Jungle Warfare and Counterinsurgency
KCP	Kangleipak Communist Party
KIA	Kachin Independent Army
KPLT	Karbi People's Liberation Tigers
KYKL	Kangleipak Yawol Kunna Lup
KLO	Kamtapur Liberation Organisation
KNA	Kuki National Army
KNF	Kuki National Front
LEP	Law Enforcement Professional
LMG	Light Machine Gun
LWE	Left Wing Extremism
MCCI	Maoist Communist Center of India
MHA	Ministry of Home Affairs
MLA	Members of Legislative Assembly
MNF	Mizo National Front
MNRF	Manipur Naga Revolutionary Front
MOU	Memorandum of Understanding
MP	Member of Parliament
MPA	Manipur People's Army
MPF	Modernization of Police Forces
MPLF	Manipur People's Liberation Front
MULTA	Muslim United Liberation Tigers of Assam
NCRB	National Crime Record Bureau
NCRWC	National Commission for Review of Working of the Constitution
NCTC	National Counter-Terrorism Centre
NDFB	National Democratic Front of Bodoland
NEC	Northeast Council
NEEPCO	North Eastern Electric Power Corporation
NER	Northeast Region

NHRC	National Human Rights Commission
NLFT	National Liberation Front of Tripura
NNC	Naga National Council
NORINCO	North Industries Corporation
NPC	National Police Commission
NPCC	National Power Construction Corporation
NPM	New Public Management
NREGA	National Rural Employment Guarantee Act
NSA	National Security Agency
NSCN (IM)	National Socialist Council of Nagaland (Issac-Muviah)
NSCN (K)	National Socialist Council of Nagaland (Khaplang)
NSCN (U)	National Socialist Council of Nagaland (Unification)
NSSO	National Sample Survey Organisation
OC	Officer-in-Charge
ONGC	Oil and Natural Gas Commission
PDP	People's Democratic Republic
PISA	Program for International Student Assessment
PULF	People's United Liberation Front
PLA	People's Liberation Army
POTA	Prevention of Terrorism Act
PPM	President's Police Medal
PPU	Paramilitary Police Unit
PREPAK	People's Revolutionary Party of Kangleipak
PRI	Panchayati Raj Institutions
P.S.	Police Station
PWG	People's War Group
QRT	Quick Reaction Team
ROP	Road Opening Party
RSP	Revolutionary Socialist Party of India
SATP	South Asia Terrorism Portal
SDM	Sub-divisional Magistrate
SDPO	Sub-divisional Police Officer
SECC	Socio-economic and Caste Census
SF	Security Forces

SIRB	Specialized IRBs
SLCC	State-level Coordination Committee
SLOG	State-level Operations and Intelligence Group
SOG	Special Operations Group
SoO	Suspension of Operation
SOP	Standard Operating Procedure
SP	Superintendent of Police
SPG	Special Patrol Groups
SPO	Special Police Officer
SPP	Special Police Picket
SRE	Security Related Expenditure
ST	Scheduled Tribe
SWAT	Special Weapons and Tactics
TADA	Terrorist and Disruptive Activities (Prevention) Act
TNV	Tripura National Volunteers
TOB	Temporary Operating Bases
TRA	Tripura Resurrection Army
TSR	Tripura State Rifles
TTAADC	Tripura Tribal Areas Autonomous Development Council
TUJS	Tripura Upajati Juba Samity
UBLF	United Bengali Liberation Front
UGC	University Grants Commission
U.K.	United Kingdom
ULFA	United Liberation Front of Assam
UN	United Nations
UNLF	United National Liberation Front
U.S.	United States
VR	Village Resistance
ZUF	Zeliangrong United Front

Preface

My professional association with Tripura began in 1986 when I had been allotted this state as my cadre in Indian Police Service (IPS). As a part of practical training, all IPS trainee officers were then required to familiarize themselves with the functioning of various units of police administration of their allotted cadre for a period of six months immediately after completion of initial Phase One of training and then return to Sardar Vallabhbhai Patel National Police Academy, Hyderabad, for the final phase of training and the graduation ceremony. Accordingly, I landed in Tripura in the later half of 1986, and, as luck would have it, this period coincided with one of the most virulent phases of violence unleashed by the Tripura National Volunteers' (TNV) insurgents. The insurgent violence during this phase was marked by large-scale attacks, arson, and ruthless massacre of non-tribal civilians (Bengalis) living in interior tribal-dominated areas to enforce their mass exodus.[1] As a trainee officer in south Tripura district, I went along with troops of the newly raised 1st Battalion Tripura State Rifles (TSR)[2] for long-range patrolling, ambushes, and raids on extremist hideouts, and also accompanied the District Superintendent of Police/other senior officers to interior villages following incidents of insurgent violence. The change from serene and secure environs of police academy to killing fields of Tripura was dramatic and gave me an idea of future challenges that awaited me. However, I was impressed with the professional ethos and élan of TSR troops and felt confident that

---

[1] TNV violence ended in 1988 following the signing of an MOU on August 12, 1988 in Delhi among the Center, the State government, and the TNV.
[2] The passing out parade of 1st battalion TSR was held on April 11, 1986.

with this force it shall be possible to neutralize insurgent groups and restore peace in the state; and in fact, TSR units did lead the counterinsurgency (COIN) campaign that effectively dismantled the insurgent network in quick time from 2000 onward when they were provided proper professional leadership and an unambiguous mandate for offensive operations. My interaction with TSR personnel during my initial years of service (1986–1991) led to a lifelong bonding with them, and I felt proud when I had an opportunity to lead them in future assignments. This field exposure also made me realize the crucial importance of proper training, discipline, and strict adherence to security protocols in COIN operations as even a small mistake—a careless movement, cough, or whisper—could seriously imperil the life of all members of the operational group. The lessons learnt during this early part of my career have always stayed with me and served me well in later assignments.

My next engagement with insurgency in Tripura had started in March 2000 when I returned to the state on completion of my central deputation period and was posted as Deputy Inspector General (DIG)/Armed Police (March 2000–July 2003) charged with the responsibility of overseeing COIN operations by TSR. By sheer coincidence, this time again Tripura was faced with serious breakdown of governance and law and order due to extreme insurgent violence perpetrated by All Tripura Tiger Force (ATTF) and National Liberation Front of Tripura (NLFT) insurgents. However, soon there was a remarkable turnaround in the situation with the assumption of charge by B.L. Vohra as the state DGP in May 2000. During the next few years, the insurgent violence was effectively contained in most parts of the state, leading to gradual restoration of institutions of governance and democratic polity. Since then, peace has been further consolidated in this state and all insurgent groups have been effectively marginalized politically and operationally. My last assignment in the state was as the Additional DGP/TSR (2012–2013). In this capacity, I provided leadership to the force, mentored and coached the officers, and paid special attention to matters related to troops' training, welfare, and morale. In between these assignments, I also had the opportunities to observe insurgency in Assam, Nagaland,

Punjab, and Jammu and Kashmir during my deputation with the Intelligence Bureau (February 1992–February 2000) and Central Industrial Security Force (CISF) (August 2003–July 2008).

Oddly enough, I had to go out of Tripura (and India) to appreciate full significance of these professional assignments and figure out "the method in this madness."[3] During my stint in Leicester University (2005–2006), my study of various COIN campaigns led me to a realization that it was a nuanced understanding of the prevailing situation in Tripura by police and political leadership and judicious application of various COIN strategies and tactics mentioned in the literature that had led to a dramatic decline in insurgent violence. Consequently, I chose Tripura's COIN campaign as the topic for my dissertation (Kumar, 2006). This was a maiden attempt by anyone to analyze Tripura's current COIN campaign. During the next few years, there was more improvement in Tripura's security scenario, which encouraged me to further develop this theme during my stint in Monash University, Australia (2009–2011). Thus, both my academic research and professional experience have combined together to deepen my understanding of COIN strategies and helped me immensely in my subsequent leadership roles.

Aims and Approaches

The purpose of publishing this book is to ensure wider dissemination of research findings to facilitate more positive outcomes of COIN campaigns in other theaters. This book is intended to generate new understandings of police-led COIN in India, concentrating specifically on Tripura's experience for facilitating better understanding of the protracted process of capacity-building and integration of police strategies with an overarching "grand strategy," which has effectively neutralized the main insurgent groups and dismantled their vast network of terror and crime. The

---

[3] The actual line from Shakespeare's *Hamlet* is 'Though this be madness yet there is method in it' (*Hamlet*, Act 2, Scene 2).

national recognition for these efforts has come in the form of the highly prestigious award—President's Colour—to Tripura Police by the Government of India (GOI) in 2011. According to a news item, Tripura is the fourth state in the country after Jammu and Kashmir, Punjab, and Tamil Nadu to receive this rare distinction (Outlook, January 10, 2012).

Since 2000, the previously much-maligned state police have emerged as a credible law enforcement agency to reverse the escalating graph of insurgent, ethnic, and political violence leading to near normalcy in this small northeastern state of India, bordering Bangladesh. This book develops an understanding of how the state police in Tripura have reorganized and reoriented themselves to emerge as a remarkably efficient COIN force and documents the main elements of police response. Second, it identifies the main components of the state government's comprehensive strategy, which has politically marginalized insurgent groups, restored democratic politics, and facilitated implementation of various programs for overall development in Tripura.

The book suggests that police-led initiatives can offer effective strategies and mechanisms for COIN operations even during periods of extreme militant and ethnic violence and that the physical challenges of policing in disturbed areas can be significantly reduced through well-conceived processes of reorganization, reorientation, and modernization of police. Furthermore, the experience of Tripura demonstrates the efficacy of a comprehensive approach to fighting tribal insurgencies based on political accommodation, good governance, and rule-of-law in developing democratic countries.

The key aspects of the state police's transformation have been outstanding leadership, reorientation, and empowerment of first responders through a steady augmentation of resources—manpower, mobility, weaponry, communication, training, and intelligence—and aggressive operations. The police institutions have been revitalized, and a decentralized robust police infrastructure has been built across the state at the police stations (P.S.)/outposts, and armed battalions' company/platoon locations, enabling them to respond effectively and promptly to multifarious challenges in their respective jurisdictions.

Seen against the backdrop of raging insurgencies, ethnic violence, and precarious law and order situation in northeast and other parts of the country, the achievements of Tripura Police have been truly remarkable. A proper appreciation of this campaign could yield a wealth of strategic and best tactical practices and broaden and deepen our understanding about the challenges of COIN. However, characteristically, neither the current success nor the earlier unprecedented violence has received due attention from the international academic community or security professionals outside the country, and even within India this campaign has not been sufficiently analyzed. At the international level, there have been very few studies conducted on strategically less "significant," though more disastrous, conflicts in the developing countries as the concentration of funds and resources favors some selected areas, for example, Northern Ireland or Balkans earlier, and Iraq and Afghanistan in recent years (Schnabel, 2005: 32). The validity of this observation is certainly borne out by the dearth of studies of tribal insurgencies in India's northeast that have proved extremely intractable, impaired human security of millions of people, impeded economic development, and pose considerable threat to national security.

At the dawn of the millennium, Tripura was one of the most violent corners of the country, with over 36 percent of violent crime as against the national average of 13.5 as per the data published by India's National Crime Record Bureau (NCRB). During 1997–2000, the state, which has barely 8 percent of the total population of the northeast region (NER) accounted for over 70 percent of the total abductions, with an average of almost 350 per year peaking at 514 abductions in 2000. The abductions and targeted violence unleashed by insurgent groups caused widespread fear and insecurity among general populace and party cadres, provoked ethnic clashes and retaliatory political violence, leading to breakdown of law and order that further undermined the state government's authority. Despite all this, Tripura was nowhere to be seen on the national radar. Anindita Dasgupta in an incisive analysis of Tripura's insurgent violence in an article "Tripura's Brutal *Cul de Sac*" observed that:

The state has abdicated its responsibility in Tripura. The democratic constitutional process has been subverted, and electoral outcomes are increasingly decided by the overt or covert support of the armed militants.... The fact that Tripura is not visible in the Indian, South Asian or global indices of political violence merely points to the media and scholarly neglect, and it is possible that this oversight itself has fuelled the bloodshed (Dasgupta, 2001).

Examples of such scholarly neglect are two recent edited volumes—*Policing Insurgencies: Cops as Counterinsurgents* (Eds C. Christine Fair and Sumit Ganguly, 2014) and *India & Counterinsurgency: Lessons Learned* (Eds Sumit Ganguly and David Fidler, 2009). Both these books present several cases ranging from insurgencies in Ireland, Malaya, Philippines, Kenya, Iraq, and Afghanistan to insurgencies in Kashmir, Punjab, Mizoram, Nagaland, and Andhra Pradesh in India with a view to distil some useful lessons from these campaigns. However, Tripura's COIN campaign that had successfully contained insurgent violence in large parts of the state by then does not find any mention in these otherwise excellent books. Similar negligence is evident in most other books on Indian insurgencies that usually rehash old and settled cases. Apparently, research in conflict zones is inherently risky and difficult, and the "messy" character of the problem frequently discourages researchers and academicians from "soiling" their hands (Sahni, 2001). In Tripura in the face of security threats, even local academics found it difficult to carry out research as conceded by Mahadev Chakravarti, a well-known political commentator from the state, in a background paper "Insurgency and Human Security in Tripura: Past and Present" written for the *Human Development Report, Tripura, 2007*:

It is also very difficult to find committed investigators to do fieldwork in sensitive areas due to security risk involved. As a result, all the conflict-torn areas of Tripura could not be covered due to volatile situation. Considerable time may be required in confidence-building before starting any research work on the subject (Chakravarti, 2005).

It is in this backdrop of volatile security situation and persistent neglect that I have chosen to analyze and document the comprehensive COIN policies adopted by the federal and the state government since 2000 to defeat the insurgent designs in the northeast state of Tripura.

Main Questions

The focus of this book is on the following main issues:

1. How have the state police in Tripura reorganized and reoriented themselves to emerge as a remarkably efficient COIN force in recent decades and what have been the main elements of police response?
2. What have been the main components of the state government's comprehensive strategy, which has politically marginalized insurgent groups, restored democratic politics and facilitated implementation of various programs for overall development in Tripura?
3. What insights can we gain from this book for resolution of ethnic insurgencies in other democratic developing countries?

K.P.S. Gill, a highly acclaimed police officer credited with defeating Khalistan terrorism in India during the 1990s, while expressing his exasperation over the escalating terrorist violence in the country, had observed:

> In many ways, India, with the largest number and widest variation in the character of terrorist movements and low-intensity wars on its soil, is a paradigm case, an accurate representation of the magnitude of the challenge, the escalating potential of future violence, and of all that has gone wrong in the state's response (Gill, 2001: 10).

However, over the past decade and half, Tripura has made suitable course correction, and this book reveals an almost textbook-like application of various COIN theories and practices available in the literature from "winning the hearts and minds" to the purely tactical and psychological operations. *Almost* because much remains to be done to redress perceived and real grievances of the indigenous people and persuade recalcitrant neighbors to cut the umbilical cord, which ties the insurgent groups to them. In brief, this study reveals how adherence to basic tenets of good policing coupled with a thorough revamping of police for its COIN role and a comprehensive COIN strategy has significantly diminished insurgents' capabilities for indiscriminate violence.

Chapter Outlines

This book is organized in three parts. While Part One (Chapters 1–3) is more of a general nature devoted to conceptual understanding of policing and COIN and an overview of India's COINs, Part Two (Chapters 4–7) comprises an in-depth examination of various aspects of insurgent violence and the government's COIN strategy in NER, particularly Tripura, followed by a concluding chapter which sums up the discussion and distils lessons from the comprehensive political strategy and the policing aspects of Tripura's campaign. The final part, Part Three (Chapter 8), comprises several case studies to illuminate different facets of COIN.

The chapter scheme is as follows: Chapter 1 provides an overview of growth of police from the late-eighteenth century to the present era and traces major trends in modern policing, especially the growth of paramilitary units for domestic policing and international peacekeeping operations and its implications on civil society. It also examines the suitability of police strategies, tactics and technologies for COIN, and their adaptation by the military in some contemporary conflicts. The concluding section underlines the centrality of leadership in COIN and the relevance of research, education, and training in building capabilities of COIN forces. Chapter 2 considers definitions of the key terms of this book—insurgency, COIN, and terrorism, explores the relationship between COIN and counter-terrorism, and the use of terror by various illicit groups to show that traditional distinctions between insurgency, terrorism, and organized crime have become blurred in most modern conflicts, necessitating a fresh appraisal of prevailing COIN strategies. Chapter 3 concentrates on India's failure to develop a coherent Counterinsurgency-Counter Terrorism (CI-CT) policy in the post-independence period and provides an overview of major internal security challenges faced by the country—Naxalite violence and insurgencies in Kashmir and Punjab. It also considers respective roles of police, paramilitary, and the army in COIN, with special reference to India. Chapter 4 presents a thematic overview of insurgencies in northeast India and describes in detail the situation in the three most violence-prone states of Assam, Nagaland, and Manipur. It also unravels links of the main insurgent groups with Muslim fundamentalist organizations, organized crime, drugs, and arms trafficking. Chapter 5 presents salient features of Tripura's comprehensive approach to COIN, and also examines contribution of various policy initiatives of the Union government in building capacities of the state government. It also discusses the emergence and growth of insurgency, violence profile, and internal and external linkages of the two main insurgent groups, that is, NLFT and ATTF. Chapter 6 presents a comprehensive overview of the strategies and tactics adopted by the state police for successfully combating the insurgent violence. It is seen that empowerment of first responders has ensured a rapid response to developing situations, improved intelligence, and police–public interface, leading to enhanced capacities for governance and development by the administration in these areas. Chapter 7 presents the main insights from this research in two clusters that are drawn from policing aspects of COIN and political aspects of COIN, respectively, and concludes with an assessment of Tripura Police's current capabilities for COIN. Chapter 8 comprises various case studies to illustrate the operationalization of the new concept of COIN in different situations. The first case study of Takarjala, a so-called "liberated zone" recovered by police, emphatically illustrates that a comprehensive approach integrating a wide spectrum of policy options and condign and calibrated use of force is highly effective in marginalizing ethnic insurgencies, leading to durable peace and overall development. This is followed by three more case studies that illuminate various facets of a carefully conceived strategy to win "hearts and minds" of local tribal population. The concluding case study of Teliamura police sub-division, which was afflicted with severe insurgent, political, and ethnic violence at the turn of the millennium, presents the main elements of police response to insurgency and various processes related to the transformation of Tripura Police.

This book emphatically suggests that local police forces are fully capable of combating all forms of political violence, including insurgency and terrorism, and functioning as the lead agency in a multi-force environment if they are professionally led and suitably reoriented, retrained, and equipped. Second, a comprehensive strategy that integrates kinetic measures with other political, economic, and social measures designed to address the real or perceived grievances of the affected ethnic groups and overall development is highly effective in weaning away support from insurgent groups and garner support for government policies. Popular endorsement of government policies through periodic free and fair elections exposes the hollowness of insurgent claims and ultimately leads to their political defeat.

Acknowledgments

This book draws mostly on the study and research undertaken by me in Australia and India for the completion of my Masters' (Research) thesis on police-led counterinsurgency operations (CI Ops) in Tripura (India) at Monash University (2009–2011), and also on the fieldwork done earlier during 2006 for a shorter dissertation on a similar topic as a part of my M.Sc. in Security and Organizational Risk Management at Leicester University, United Kingdom. One chapter "Understanding Policing" and some case studies were not part of any previous thesis and have been written specifically for this book, while all the other chapters have been suitably revised. My professional experience of three decades of policing in diverse organizations and conflict theaters, including India's northeast and Jammu and Kashmir has been immensely useful to me in drawing proper lessons from this research.

In this endeavor, I have received generous help from numerous friends, colleagues, institutions, and governments. However, a large number of serving police, paramilitary/military, and security personnel who graciously spared time from their busy schedules to participate in this research and shared their professional experiences and candid views cannot be mentioned for reasons of confidentiality. All the same, their help is gratefully acknowledged and hopefully, they would recognize their contributions.

My gratitude extends to the following persons and institutions for their support:

- Mr Pranay Sahay, IPS, former DGP, Tripura, for granting his approval to the Tripura Police personnel for participation in this research.

- Mr Anish Prasad, then Superintendent of Police, West Tripura District, and Mr Arjun Debbarma, then Commandant, 6th Battalion Tripura State Rifles, for providing voluminous data required for various case studies.
- My two research supervisors, Dr Pete Lentini and Dr Ben McQueen, Director and Deputy Director, respectively, of the Global Terrorism Research Center, Monash University (Australia) for their guidance, encouragement, and more importantly, their faith in me, my ability, and the necessity to write this book.
- Mr B.L. Vohra, IPS (retd.), Mr B.C. Nayak, IPS (retd.), and Dr Paddy Rawlinson, my research supervisor in Leicester University for recommending my application for AusAID scholarship for pursuing research in Monash University.
- Government of India and Government of Tripura for granting me study leave of two years (2009–2011) and the Government of Australia (AusAID) for granting me Australia Leadership Awards (ALA) scholarship and Department of Personnel & Training (DOP&T), Government of India, for partial scholarship to pursue M.Sc. at Leicester University (2005–2006). Without the generous support of these governments and institutions, it would have been difficult for me as a serving police officer to pursue academic courses and research that have led to the publication of this book. However, I must state that the views expressed in this book are my own and not necessarily of the governments/institutions mentioned here.

I am sincerely indebted to the anonymous reviewer for his/her many perceptive suggestions and special thanks to Rudra Narayan Sharma and Sanghamitra Patowary of SAGE Publications for their valuable guidance at all stages of this book.

Finally, on a purely personal note, loving thanks to my wife Sangita for her presence, encouragement, and amazing support in all my endeavors. She and Angad, my younger son, traveled with me to Australia, and we all have fond memories of some excellent Australian and Indian friends and dream destinations. My son Dushyant also encouraged me throughout in this effort.

Introduction

Many developing countries, mostly Africa, Asia, Latin America, and the Middle East, have been facing protracted ethnic or ethnonational insurgencies in the post-Cold War period and India is no exception. Since independence, many states in India—including the cluster of states nestled in India's strategic northeast, popularly known as "the seven sisters"[1]—have been home to myriad insurgencies, civil wars, tribal and ethnic conflicts, and irredentist claims associated with illegal migration. India's northeast is certainly one of the hottest trouble spots of South Asia, with more than 30 armed insurgent groups actively engaged in pushing demands ranging from secession to autonomy and the right to self-determination, and a multitude of ethnic groups and ethnic militias fighting each other and the state over competing homeland demands and scarce resources, and for recognition of their distinct identity. However, northeast insurgencies do not conform to any stereotype, and despite superficial similarities, each insurgency is unique. In many ways, northeast insurgencies have proved to be more intractable due to extremely complex social and political environment, and arguably pose more threat to national security than the internationally much publicized Kashmir imbroglio (Cline, 2006).

Historically, this region has been a meeting ground of many races and communities by virtue of its location on one of the world's greatest migratory routes, cutting across such countries as

---

[1] The expression "the Seven Sisters" of NER of India refers to the states of Arunachal Pradesh, Assam, Manipur, Meghalaya, Mizoram, Nagaland, and Tripura. Subsequently, another state, Sikkim, was added to the North East Council (NEC), the region's apex funding and development agency, in 2002 to expedite its development.

Tibet/China, Nepal, Burma/Myanmar, Thailand, and Bangladesh (Das, 2007). In the earlier stages, the flow of population was almost exclusively from the eastern direction, and majority of the migrant tribes and nationalities belonged to the Tibeto-Burman or the Mon-Khmer stock. However, with the arrival of the British the direction of flow changed as *coolies* (cheaply hired unskilled Oriental labor), traders, clerks, and preachers were brought by them from neighboring Bengal and Bihar to open up Assam's economy. Presently, the NER is home to over 160 Scheduled Tribes (STs) and over 400 other tribal and sub-tribal groups and communities (*Northeast Region, Vision 2020*, Vol. 1:14). Their distinct "Mongoloid" racial features and the fact that these areas had not been conquered or administered for a great length of history gave its people a sense of being different from those in mainland India, and in fact, most of the ethnicities that claim to be autochthons can trace their ancestries and affinities to Southeast Asia (Goswami, 2007).

While it is not possible to put an exact date, the genesis of processes that turned this "melting pot" of migrant communities into a "witches' cauldron" of ethnic trouble and turmoil can be traced to the advent of colonialism to this part of the world in 1826 after the first Anglo-Burmese War (1824–1826), which wrested the territory away from the Myanmar Empire and secured it for the British Raj. The colonial policies of "divide and conquer," large-scale economic exploitation, shuffling of administrative boundaries, and demarcation of new frontiers, which cut across communities and ethnic groups have caused trouble and turmoil in many parts of South Asia, including India (Ezrow and Frantz, 2013: 56–59). The full implications of these colonial policies for NER would be discussed in detail in a subsequent chapter related to northeast insurgencies.

NER, situated in the foothills of the Himalayas, is the physical gateway between India, China, and Southeast Asia. It is strategically important for both India and China, as China also claims the Indian state of Arunachal Pradesh as part of south Tibet. NER is distinguished by several remarkable geo-political features that have implications for COIN strategies. First, the region is virtually landlocked, having less than two percent of its external boundaries contiguous with other states, and the remaining over 98 percent of its porous border—a total of 6,387 km—is international border with Bangladesh (2,700 km), China (1,345 km), Myanmar (1,643 km), and Bhutan (699 km). Furthermore, the NER is tenuously connected to the rest of India through a thin strip of land commonly known as the Chicken's Neck or Siliguri Corridor in North Bengal.[2] This "peripheral" status and geographical isolation has had several deleterious consequences for the region's economic development and emotional integration with the rest of the country. Furthermore, the nature of the polity, economy, and society of the neighboring regions and countries has added a special set of problems. Two developments in particular, that is, the covert and overt support extended by some neighboring countries to northeast insurgent groups and influx of large number of people from Bangladesh across a large and porous international border have posed serious problems for national security and influenced political developments in the region (Dasgupta, 1997).

Second, the NER accounts for one of the largest concentrations of tribal people in the country—constituting about 30 percent of its total population—and three states—Nagaland, Mizoram, and Meghalaya—contain an overwhelming majority of Christians and tribal population. However, post-independence, the large-scale unchecked influx of migrants, both Hindus and Muslims, from across the international borders has transformed the demographic landscape of many northeast states, heightened insecurities of indigenous people, and given rise to many secessionist movements. This is particularly true of insurgency in Tripura, and, in fact, Tripura is the only state in India that has been transformed from a tribal-majority to tribal-minority status in the short span of a few decades post-independence. Even as late as 1941, tribals constituted 50.09 percent of Tripura's total population of 513,010. However, by 1981, the tribal population was reduced to barely 28.44 percent in a total

---

[2] The Siliguri Corridor has an approximate width of 33 km on the eastern side and 21 km on the western side.

population of 2.05 million. Massive displacement of tribal people due to developmental projects is also an important factor fueling discontent among tribals as most of them are not beneficiaries of such projects (Reddy and Reddy, 2007).

Thirdly, terrain in most of the northeast states is rugged, hilly, and under dense forest cover, rendering large parts of rural hinterland inaccessible or difficult to negotiate, conditions generally considered conducive to insurgency (Fearon and Laitin, 2003). According to an official estimate based on satellite images the territory under forest cover constitutes about 64 percent of the total area of the region, thus limiting the availability of arable land (Poffenberger, 2006), and though agriculture accounts for a major share of the economies of all states in the NER, the agricultural productivity is low due to the low usage of high-yielding variety seeds and fertilizers, and inadequate irrigation, infrastructure, and credit (*Northeast Region, Vision 2020, Volume 1*: 48–50). Furthermore, the area is predominantly rural with over 80 percent of the population living outside towns and cities, enhancing the cost of delivering public services to the sparse population. All these factors have implications for the current strife in the region as according to a time-series study conducted by Henrik Urdal (2008) of 27 Indian states for the period from 1956 to 2002, scarcity of productive land is associated with higher risks of political violence, particularly when interacting with high rural population and low agricultural yield

Finally, most of the northeast states and federal government are ruled by different political parties or coalition of parties, leading to difficulties in generating consensus and coordinating state responses to internal security problems. The diversity of COIN approach and different levels of success in COIN is explained by the fact that according to the Indian federal structure, the responsibility for maintenance of internal order and fighting insurgencies is vested in the state governments. Consequently, the state response to insurgency is influenced by their perception of problem, and frequently national interests are sacrificed at the altar of political exigency (Miklian, 2011).

Table I.1:

Security Situation in Northeast Region (2007–2014)

Years	Incidents	Extremists Arrested	Extremists Killed	Extremists Surrendered	Security Forces (SFs) Killed	Civilians Killed
2007	1,489	1,837	514	524	79	498
2008	1,561	2,566	640	1,112	46	466
2009	1,297	2,162	571	1,109	42	264
2010	773	2,213	247	846	20	94
2011	627	2,141	114	1,122	32	70
2012	1,025	2,145	222	1,195	14	97
2013	732	1,712	138	640	18	107
2014	824	1,934	181	965	20	212

Source: MHA, Annual Report, 2014–2015: 10.

Table I.1 provides the profile of insurgent violence in northeast region during 2007–2014. Experience and research suggest that insurgencies in India's northeast have been spurred and sustained by an intricate mix of greed and grievances (Vadlamannati, 2011), aided and abetted by hostile neighbors, and fueled by the proliferation of small arms and light weapons, and narcotics trafficking (Hussain, 2006; Bhaumik, 2007; Singh, 2008). A perception of neglect and inept handling of some sensitive issues by the federal government, an all pervasive political-militant–bureaucratic-contractor nexus at the local level, and a lack of sufficient political clout at the national level has further exacerbated the problems of NER. The northeast states have only 25 members of parliament (MPs), including 14 from Assam, in the 545-member House of the People (Lok Sabha, that is, Lower House of Parliament). The absence of national-level towering political leaders, industrial/corporate lobbies and civil society organizations from the NER has also meant that there are hardly any influential groups that can press popular concerns or project the aspirations of the people at the central level. Consequently, there is (a) widespread alienation, dissatisfaction, and disaffection among large sections of people due to economic deprivation, and persistent political and economic discrimination (Vadlamannati, 2011); (b) proliferation of insurgent groups, ethnic militias, state-backed militias, and massive deployment of the army and paramilitary on almost permanent basis in the region, leading to militarization of the region and brutalization of society; and (c) frequent breakdown of law and order resulting from competitive violence unleashed by political parties, warring ethnic groups and insurgent factions, discouraging investors and impeding economic development (Lacina, 2007, 2009a, 2009b). Taken together all these developments have given rise to conditions of "durable disorder" and severely undermined institutions of governance, eroded people's faith in state's capacity to protect or deliver even basic services to citizens, denting state's claim to legitimacy (Baruah, 2005, 2009).

It is the case that most Indian state governments faced with escalating violence have failed to make correct assessment of the challenges faced by them or lacked the political resolve to commit requisite resources over the protracted period of conflict. They have also failed to revamp their own structures of governance and law enforcement and clamored for deployment of army or federal forces to combat such severe violence. Typically, governments have resorted to a militaristic approach to deal with severe and escalating insurgent violence and terrorism, often with disastrous results. Over the past two decades alone, almost 20,000 people have perished in insurgent violence in India's northeast, and millions displaced from their homes and settled in refugee camps, a living testimony to the failure of state apparatus to protect them from militant depredations.

In the backdrop of this dismal security scenario, the successful COIN campaign of Tripura presents a refreshing change. Tripura, a small state in the NER of the country (area: 10,492 sq. km; population 3.6 million as per *Census of India*, 2011) bordering Bangladesh has been facing tribal insurgency for more than three decades. The current phase of extremist violence that began in early 1990s assumed a particularly virulent form toward the later part of the decade, and police, administration, and the political establishment were hard-pressed to come up with suitable responses to contain rising insurgent, ethnic, and political violence. However, starting in 2000 a well-conceived process of reorganization, reorientation, and capacity-building has led to a radical transformation of Tripura police from a weak and largely passive force into an extremely effective, capable, and confident one (*The Telegraph*, 2000). In their new avatar, police have successfully led the COIN campaign to neutralize insurgent threats and created space for political and developmental initiatives. Following the improved security scenario, many Indian public sector units and foreign countries have shown interest in setting up industries or providing financial assistance and technology to fund poverty alleviation programs for local communities. Japan Bank of International Cooperation (JBIC) has been funding a project since 2007–2008 for poverty reduction of the people dependent on forest resources, while German Development Cooperation (KfW) is funding a "Participatory Natural Resource Management Project" since 2008–2009 to assist local farming communities dependent on forest resources. Apart from these externally aided projects, other major projects include a 726 MW Palatana thermal power project commissioned in June 2013 with the help of Oil & Natural Gas Corporation (ONGC) and another 104 MW gas-based thermal power project at Monarchak in Sepahijala district taken up by North Eastern Electric Power Corporation Ltd. (NEEPCO). The state government has also cleared a joint venture of ONGC and Chambal Fertilizers and Chemicals to set up a gas-based urea manufacturing plant in Unakoti district with an investment of ₹5,000 crore. The execution of this project would go a long way in meeting fertilizer requirement of Bangladesh and other states in India's northeast, east and south. The proposed extension of rail line from Agartala to the southernmost town of Sabroom would further boost economic development within the state and facilitate trade and commerce with neighboring Bangladesh.

The partition of India had been an unmitigated economic disaster for northeast states as it had severed NER's major arteries of communication by inland water, road, and railway through East Pakistan, and blocked access to its traditional markets as well as Chittagong port in East Pakistan/Bangladesh. The central government's "Look East" policy—now renamed "Act East" policy—and *North Eastern Region Vision 2020* document released in July 2008 envisage a central role for NER as the gateway to

Southeast Asia. However, some observers have argued that more than the "Look East" policy, it is the Bangladesh policy that is more relevant for the region (Ghosh, 2006a). In this context, the return of Awami League's Sheikh Hasina as Prime Minister of Bangladesh in 2009 augurs well for Tripura, and Manik Sarkar, the Chief Minister of Tripura, has been making concerted efforts to further consolidate friendship with Bangladesh. Following the visit of prime minister of Bangladesh and her trade delegation to Agartala in January 2012 and the recent visit of prime minister of India to Bangladesh in June 2015, the prospects of bilateral trade between India and Bangladesh and economic development in Tripura have improved considerably. A notable achievement during PM Modi's visit to Bangladesh was the *Land Boundary Agreement*, which is aimed at comprehensive settlement of complex boundary issues through exchange of enclaves and a fixed demarcation of boundary in all un-demarcated segments. Besides this, more than 20 agreements were also signed with a view to strengthen bilateral diplomatic, security, trade, and cultural relations. Indian ships have now been allowed access to Chittagong and Mongla ports, new bus routes connecting Agartala–Dhaka–Kolkata and Guwahati–Shillong–Dhaka have been started, and more border *haats* (local markets) have been opened up to provide trading opportunities for local people. Memoranda of Understanding (MOUs) have been signed on cooperation in human trafficking, fake currency and narcotics smuggling. The Inland Waterway Trade and Transit Treaty (IWTT) has been renewed. Identification of locations for border trade posts, signing of extradition treaty and bilateral trade agreements, and concessions by Bangladesh to transit goods and machinery through its territory are all steps in the right direction. In brief, Tripura is now well poised to reap the "peace dividend" after decades of turmoil and geographical isolation.

The COIN campaign of Tripura is notable for many reasons. First, Tripura has bucked the general trend of over-dependence on military and joined Punjab and Andhra Pradesh as the only two other states that have thoroughly revamped, reorganized, and reoriented their police in recent decades to lead COIN operations and successfully neutralized insurgent/terrorist threats in their respective jurisdictions. Second, unlike many other cases, Tripura's COIN campaign is distinguished by a steadfast adherence to human rights of the insurgents and scrupulous observation of the rule of law. Third, though the methods and tactics of insurgencies—terrorism, subversion, propaganda, and guerrilla warfare—have served insurgents of all hues for centuries, during the Cold War period, insurgencies were usually associated with the communists, and, in fact, soon after India's independence the undivided Communist Party of India (CPI) had spearheaded the first armed rebellion against the state in 1948–1950 in Tripura, before deciding to join the electoral democracy. The key demands of CPI were political, social, and economic reforms, and "liberation" of India from its ruling class. In Tripura, tribal leaders like Dasarath Debbarma and Aghore Debbarma resorted to guerrilla warfare to press their demands.[3] Therefore, some observers have argued that the recent insurgency is a legacy of that movement. Most interestingly, the present phase of COIN campaign that has effectively neutralized insurgent threats and restored peace to large parts of Tripura has also been overseen by the Left Front government, of which CPI is a constituent party. This ability to coordinate state responses and subordinate parochial interests to larger national interests across political boundaries signifies strengths of Indian democracy as also wisdom and maturity of political leadership at the federal and state level, in stark contrast to many other states in the country.

Internationally, the role of local police, administration, and government in contemporary conflicts has been receiving increased attention following conflicts in Iraq and Afghanistan. The criminalization of insurgent networks coupled with a growing nexus of warlords and drug lords and porous borders in many conflict theatres has also bolstered the case for good policing. An improved understanding of these issues could significantly reduce violence in many conflict theatres through better restructuring of police forces, and more effective crime

---

[3] Dasarath Debbarma became an MP in 1952 and served as the Chief Minister of Tripura from 1993 to 1998.

control strategies and conflict management policies. This research brings an empirical focus on the role of police in combating ethnic insurgencies through concurrent documentation of the present conflict, including some case studies of a police sub-division and armed police battalions to illuminate different aspects of COIN. It also spells out the elements of integrated approach to COIN adopted successfully in Tripura. This research emphatically suggests that the combination of local forces and a comprehensive approach to COIN for restoration of rule-of-law, governance, and development in violently divided societies can be an effective and politically salient response to defeat insurgencies, as well as build the prospects for long-term post-conflict social harmony.

PART ONE

1

Understanding Policing

Introduction

The endless succession of "small wars" interspersed with the "long war" and two World Wars over the past century has caused tremendous loss of life, displaced millions, and severely tested the polity and economies of many nations. According to the International Council of Red Cross' *People on War Report,* the last hundred years have been the "mega death" century with an estimated 110 million deaths in various conflicts (*Small Arms Survey,* 2001). Furthermore, while prior to the twentieth century, an estimated 90 percent of the conflict casualties were combatants, in the 1990s the proportion of civilian casualties had soared to around 80 percent worldwide (*Human Security Report,* 2005). A cursory look at the current flash points would reveal several zones of intense violence in Asia, Africa, Middle East, and Latin America. Apparently, war is everywhere (Gregory, 2011) and the battlefield has been extended to "everyone, everything, and everywhere" (Liang and Xiangsui, 2002). These developments suggest that the nature of conflict has undergone transformation, blurring the lines between civilian and military (Manwaring, 2002) and, in fact, "human terrain" has become the new battlefield in this "war among people." Moreover, not only is conflict one of the major factors shaping the modern world (Hill, 2010), but the coming decades are predicted to be still more anarchic as the problems caused by "scarcity, crime, over-population, tribalism, and disease" are expected to aggravate and destroy the social fabric of our world (Kaplan, 1994). These deepening socio-economic divisions have already caused serious upheavals within many nations, leading to a marked global shift from inter-state wars to intra-state wars since the mid-twentieth century that has considerable implications for international political system and calls for a reassessment of prevalent strategies for conflict management and conflict resolution.

Policing is one of the primary methods of conflict management during peace times. However, during conflict, policing may be seriously impaired due to weakness of state authority or overwhelmed by widespread severe violence (Hill, 2010). The consequent lack of general law enforcement has been considered a strong contributor to conflict (Jones et al., 2005). Therefore, re-establishment of state authority in contested spaces and augmentation of police capacities and capabilities are essential for reduction of violence and restoration of peace. However, this is an extremely complex and protracted process that requires a nuanced understanding of insurgency, conflict policing, and building state capacities (Sobek, 2010; Ward et al., 2010).

Hill (2010) has surveyed the current literature on conflict and concluded that while we have gained some insights into how conflict can impact justice systems and police organizations in the post-conflict period, there remain significant gaps in our understanding of how police cope with conflict or "what police *do* during conflict" or the relationship between conflict, crime, and policing. An improved understanding of these issues could be helpful in framing more effective conflict management policies and facilitate better decision-making regarding restructuring and nurturing, instead of supplanting, police during conflict or the timing/necessity of intervention, or devising suitable crime control strategies to assist upon intervention, leading to significant reduction in violence. This research is a modest attempt to fill some of these gaps in our understanding of conflict policing through concurrent documentation of how police have successfully coped with insurgent, ethnic, and political violence in one of the states in India's turbulent northeast.

This chapter is divided into four sections to facilitate better conceptual understanding of policing and its role in COIN. The introductory section provides an overview of growth of modern police from late eighteenth century till the present era, followed by the second section on policing. The third section comprises of a discussion of the suitability of police strategies, tactics, and technologies for COIN. The centrality of leadership in COIN is well documented in the literature. The chapter concludes with some insights into strategic and tactical leadership development for COIN gleaned from latest research and the relevance of training and education in preparing future leaders. It will be seen that (a) the fusion of internal and external threats to national security has tended to blur the boundaries between the police and military in most contemporary conflicts, necessitating radical changes in these organizations' learning, development, and operational strategies; and (b) soldiers and law enforcement personnel need more advanced skill base to adapt to the complexities, ambiguities, and uncertainties that are hallmark of contemporary conflicts. In nutshell, nations need more rounded soldiers who are proficient in both combat and COIN, and law enforcement personnel who are equally adept in community policing and offensive policing, and professionally competent to effectively respond to multiple challenges facing modern police forces.

Policing: Then and Now

The word "police" was borrowed by the English from the French and originally meant "the regulation of the city or country, so far as regards the inhabitants" (Johnson, 1806: ii, "police"). According to J.C.P. Lenoir (1779: 34), a noted French General, police is "the science of governing men and to do them good." Thus, originally, "the police" was an abstract notion synonymous with governance, and did not refer to an agency or individuals (Brodeur, 2007). However, over the course of centuries, this distinction was gradually lost and policing became what the police do. But it is useful to distinguish between the ideas of "police" and "policing":

> "Police" refers to a particular kind of social institution, while "policing" implies a set of processes with specific social functions. "Police" are not found in every society... Policing is arguably a necessity in any social order, which may be carried out by a variety of different processes and institutional arrangements (Reiner, 2000, quoted in "Policing and the Police" by Ben Bowling and Janet Foster, in Maguire, Mike, Morgan, Rod, and Reiner, Robert [Eds], The Oxford Handbook of Criminology, 3rd edition, pp. 981).

Ordinarily, the main function of police is to maintain formal and informal social control by "policing" of the society, achieved through crime management, order management and security management (IW, 2006). However, contemporary policing is not restricted to public police alone, but carried out through multiple agents such as private security agencies, citizens in a voluntary capacity working with or without public police, vigilantes, and, increasingly by paramilitary or military personnel when deployed for internal security duties or peacekeeping operations. But these other forms of policing are not considered conducive to sustainable, democratic policing as practiced in Anglo-American societies (Manning, 2005).

Contrary to popular perception, modern police history originated not in Britain, but in Ireland with the passing of the Irish Preservation Act in 1814, which authorized the Lord Lieutenant of Ireland "to establish police in any area in which he saw it fit to proclaim a state of disturbance" (Jeffries, 1952). This was followed two decades later by the Constabulary (Ireland) Act of 1836, which established the Irish Constabulary that became the model for police development in several parts of the world (Stead, 1985). Interestingly, in stark contrast to the colonial model, the home variety of policing envisaged in the Metropolitan Police model introduced by Sir Robert Peel in 1829 laid emphasis on crime prevention, winning the trust and cooperation of the people, integrating itself into the neighborhoods, and restrained use of force. Gradually, this 1829 Peel version of democratic policing diffused to Canada, New Zealand, Australia, and the U.S. (Manning, 2005).

Historically, the character of police institutions has been shaped by the interests of dominant elites (Emsley, 1999). Thus, during the eighteenth and nineteenth centuries, policemen were deployed to control plebeians, vagrants, and casual laborers as it was believed that criminals, rioters, and revolutionaries existed largely among these marginalized groups. Unsurprisingly, business frauds and various forms of corruption that flourished in those times were not registered as "crime." And just as the establishment of colonial police was guided more by the commercial interests of an expanding capitalism rather than the interest of the governed people (Brogden, 1987), there are reasons to believe that current exercise of reshaping indigenous police into "democratic" policing in both Iraq and Afghanistan is also designed to serve the dominant interests of the U.S. and its allies at the expense of host nations (Manning, 2005).

In an insightful essay, Kelling and Moore (1988), while discussing the evolution of American policing, have divided the history of policing in the U.S. in three different eras, based on the dominance of a particular strategy: the political era (1840s–early 1900s), the reform era (1900s–1970s), and the community problem-solving era that commenced in the 1980s. Due to paucity of space, the discussion here is restricted to elaboration of defining features of only the third era that is marked by broadening of police function to include provision of services, conflict resolution, problem-solving through community to achieve better quality of life and citizen satisfaction through reduction of fear and insecurities. At the organizational level, this strategy is marked by increased participative planning and management, decentralized task forces and matrices, and executive involvement in developing, articulating, and monitoring strategy. Though Kelling and Moore (1988) have described developments in North America, their analysis is largely applicable to other developed Western nations in Europe, Canada, and Australia also. In brief, the "new policing order" is distinguished by dismantling of the rigid bureaucratic order, introduction of New Public Management (NPM) principles and practices to bring greater professionalism and accountability, and deliver high-quality services to citizens (Choudhary, 2009: 42).

However, the challenges of policing the post-modern "risk" society in the twenty-first century have led many governments and police leaders to seriously reflect upon the developments that are shaping the field of policing and security, and articulate a new vision of police through a number of policy reports such as the report of Independent Commission on Policing for Northern Ireland, 1999, the report of Law Commission of Canada, 2006 and the report of Dutch Police titled "Police in Evolution" (Project Group Vision on Policing 2006). Post-9/11 policing has now shifted into an "era of uncertainty" and several new and unanticipated threats to external security and internal security have given rise to problems that are beyond the capacities of traditional policing (Ransley and Mazerolle, 2009). Furthermore, the emergence of these new and unforeseen security threats has blurred boundaries between police, military, and security agencies, and shifted the focus from responding to crime to a new mood of prevention, pre-emption, and precaution. The current environment combines the tensions and blurring of boundaries between "high" and "low" policing accompanied by rise of plural policing, with non-state actors effectively eroding the state monopoly of policing by expansion of private security and community policing networks (Shearing and Marks, 2011). These trends have been further accentuated by neo-liberal economic policies and ideological triumph of market models across the world (Zedner, 2009). Consequently, despite significant advances in policing, the harsh reality remains that the poor, disadvantaged, and marginalized groups in all countries continue to be the main victims of violence and injustice (Clegg et al., 2000). It has been argued that the global phenomenon of Al-Qaida, the endurance of Maoist insurgencies in India, and even the recent popular uprising across the Arab world are all indicative of a manifest failure to understand phenomenon of marginalization and the complex ways in which poverty, under-development, and exploitation drive cycles of organized crime, rebellion, and terrorism (Zala and Roger, 2011). Therefore, addressing underlying drivers of insecurity and resolving deep tensions between elites and non-elites must be accorded priority over military solutions. It has also been recommended that police should forge inclusive local partnerships with government, non-government organizations, and citizens to enlist their support as "co-producers" of public safety and security (Clegg et al., 2000). Many police forces across the world have heeded this advice to successfully reinvent themselves. The Nexus Policing Project in Victoria, Australia is a fine example of such an initiative by police to relocate themselves in modern communities to deliver effective policing service to local communities (Shearing and Marks, 2011).The goal of this project, which commenced in 2004, was to link the knowledge and capacities of the Victoria Police and the non-police agencies and groups in a coordinated approach to delivering increased community safety through seven pilot projects. The police joined up with local groups to diagnose social problems and mobilized all existing capacities, skills, and resources in resolving these problems. Crucially, by empowering other social networks, police position themselves as a specialized resource to be called upon as a last resort, not as a first port of call. The Belgian police are also reported to have effectively integrated components of community policing, intelligence-led policing and management to devise an excellent model of policing (Choudhary, 2009: 42). The London Metropolitan Police have sought to address public concerns of fear, insecurity, and incivility in public places through Police Community Support Officers (PCSO).[1] Significantly, this initiative has also succeeded in attracting hard-to-reach black and ethnic minorities into policing (Blair, 2007). The success of these partnerships confirms the findings of earlier U.S. research that public perceptions of legitimacy are shaped

---

[1] The PCSOs are civilians recruited, trained, equipped, and vetted by the Met to assist the beat constables and provide presence in public places. Further, PCSOs do not have the power of arrest, and they do not police public order or go to court. However, they have the power to issue fixed penalty notices for minor offenses, to demand the name and address of the offenders, and to detain for 30 minutes if that name and address is refused and to use reasonable force to do so (Blair, 2007).

by personal assessments of how police treat people, particularly when they are in distress and need help, rather than objective assessments of declining crime rates or response time (Bayley and Perito, 2010: 102).

To conclude, this section has traced the changing contours of landscape of policing, highlighted the gravity of the challenges facing the police, and also listed a few initiatives by various police departments across the world that have succeeded in meeting these challenges by forging partnerships between police and other stakeholders in society. However, it must be remembered that there are no universal ready-made "best practices" in policing and the development of appropriate solutions would be specific to countries, localities, and culture between national regions and between urban and rural areas (Clegg et al., 2000).

Adapting Police Strategies, Tactics, and Technologies for COIN

An insurgency in its initial stage is usually manifested in an increase in subversive activities and violence—murder, extortion, arson, robbery, and kidnapping—primarily directed against government officials, facilities, and civilians to weaken the government control, erode popular support for the regime, and garner resources for own struggle (Epstein, 1968). Most commentators agree that police are best suited to deal with such criminal acts by virtue of the nature of their responsibilities and skill sets. In COIN mode, police tasks include intelligence collection; arrest and prosecution of insurgents; resource and population control; intensive and aggressive patrols in affected zones, particularly semi-rural and rural areas; and effectively dealing with the riots instigated by the insurgents to discredit the government (Epstein, 1968).

Clearly, police and law enforcement are inextricably linked with COIN—both as a potent tool available to the governments as principal responders and as prime target of insurgent violence. As principal responders, police and law enforcement have usually provided the bulk of forces in successful COIN campaigns, and massively expanded to further augment the force levels during the course of campaigns (Caleski, 2009). The requirement of good policing in contemporary conflicts has been further bolstered by a growing nexus of warlords and drug lords, criminalization of insurgent networks, and difficulties in regulating movements of men and materials across porous borders in several conflict theaters. Furthermore, it is well established now that the police are the key component that connects security, the economy, and peace and order with civil administration (Jackson and Lyon, 2002). In view of all these developments, increasing numbers of police personnel are being drafted now for COIN and various stabilization and reconstruction missions (Caleski, 2009: 41).

Historically, though, COIN doctrine has been more inclined in favor of military operations and its "heavy imprint", with limited role for police and law-enforcement agencies. However, the stalemate and fiascos of the U.S. and allied forces in Iraq and Afghanistan have led several observers to recommend that comprehensive planning and resource allocation for policing tasks, at par with combat planning, shall be made an integral part of COIN strategy to buttress legitimacy (Caleski, 2009; Bayley and Perito, 2010; Kilcullen, 2010).Interestingly, unlike governments, the insurgents have never been in doubt of the pivotal role of police and law enforcement in COIN and systematically targeted police patrols, police stations, police recruiting and training institutions, and families of police personnel in a bid to eliminate or marginalize their principal adversaries. According to General Joseph Peterson, the U.S. commander in charge of training in Iraq, 12,000 Iraqi police were killed by insurgents during 2003–2005 and an estimated 900 Afghan police died in 2007 (Bayley and Perito, 2010: 74–75). In India, annual SF casualties in insurgent/terrorist violence have averaged over 450 between 1994 and 2014, which is extraordinarily high for any nation during peacetime and indicative of the sustained severity of targeted violence in internal conflicts.

In view of their specialized professional skills, the armed forces of many nations including the United States (U.S.) and the United Kingdom (U.K.) have evinced keen interest in learning from law enforcement prior to deployment in conflict zones. For example, 70 marines were attached in 2010 from Camp Pendleton for a week with Los Angeles police for learning the basics of anti-gang investigations, police professionalism, and community policing in preparation for deployment in Afghanistan. Calese (2005) has drawn a correlation between insurgent organizations and organized criminal groups and identified five areas spanning the cultural, technical, conceptual, and training domains in which military can benefit from law enforcement's expertise in dismantling criminal organizations. Briefly stated, these areas include (a) a major change in the mindset of combat troops from "kill" to "capture" to exploit the intelligence available from the insurgents, and prevent fresh recruitment of insurgent groups; (b) exploitation of the technology available to law enforcement for identity verification and disrupting criminal intelligence networks; and (c) community policing orientation, proficiency in inter-personal skills, and specialized training for gaining "street knowledge" and dealing with criminal gangs, drugs, and human trafficking. Considering that the ultimate aim of COIN is to win "hearts and minds" of the affected communities, a community policing doctrine has been recommended for military in view of its positive impact on public perceptions of crime and safety; and enlistment of popular support for government by directly addressing many popular concerns to prevent alienation and dissatisfaction with the government (Beers, 2007).

The specialized skills of law enforcement professionals (LEPs) have been found particularly useful to the military units in Afghanistan in collecting, refining, data-mining, and extrapolating intelligence as the result of raids or cache, collecting actionable and incriminating evidence, and interrogation of suspects (Hsia, 2008). The LEP individuals who serve at the brigade level are mostly FBI agents, Drug Enforcement Agency agents, or Secret Service agents focusing on crime analysis, including targeting and tracking of insurgents; while those LEP individuals who are embedded in battalions are seasoned policemen having expertise in working street gangs, large-scale criminal enterprises and undercover operations.

Many domestic police programs/technologies have also been adapted by U.S. forces in Iraq. These include a computer network and biometric identification system—the Snake Eater Kit—which comprises mobile fingerprint, iris and retina scanners, a digital camera, a GPS system, and a laptop computer linked to a database of local population (Gonzalez, 2009)[2]; and deployment of biometric readers at military checkpoints in Baghdad to control movement between ethnic enclaves (Graham, 2010). Some other police innovations that have been found suitable for military application by COIN theorists are: the Neighborhood Watch, embedded video, computerized intelligence files, and statistical analysis (Celeski, 2009; Libicki, 2007; Calese, 2005).

In the Indian context, K.P.S. Gill (2001a) has mentioned a long list of inexpensive and innovative optical, electrical, and electronic devices and bullet-proofing materials that were developed by Punjab police in the early 1990s to crush Khalistan terrorism. These included dragon lights with toughened glass coated with a combination of dyes to check the visible light and allow the filtration of infrared radiation for unobtrusive observation of terrorist movements at night up to 250 meters with the help of night vision goggles. Similar treatment of airplane landing lights increased visibility up to 700 meters, while coating of headlights and parking lights of police vehicles-enabled policemen to drive safely at night; Parabolic Sound Enlarger that amplified sound of terrorists' movements at night in water bodies and forested areas through the directional focusing of a parabola; mechanical clock detector and electronic timer detector to detect concealed timer devices; and development of country-made bulletproof jackets, bulletproof mobile firing posts, improvised bullet-proofing of vehicles, and polycarbonate riot control shields. Crucially, all these devices were made in real time at a fraction of cost of similar imported devices and in the face of strong opposition from bureaucracy and government auditors (Gill, 2001a). A similar exercise was undertaken in Tripura also during 2000–2002 to

---

[2] The Snake Eater is a variation of the system developed for the Chicago police and adapted by Lockheed-Martin for the U.S. Marines in Iraq (Libicki, 2007: 25).

suitably equip police for their COIN tasks by forging improvised bulletproof vehicles and bullet-proof sentry posts in a TSR battalion's workshop to provide physical security to troops and enhance their confidence and morale.

Notwithstanding the obvious advantages of police deployment, historically, governments have deployed regular military units to take forceful action against the insurgents due to their failure to recognize the true nature of insurgent activities early enough and deploy commensurate police and other national resources to defeat incipient insurgencies (Celeski, 2009: 12). This is because in absence of determined action from the governments, incipient insurgencies rapidly transform into full-blown insurgencies, and overwhelm police capacities. Therefore, conventional wisdom holds that once the insurgent violence has crossed a certain threshold, police shall not be deployed as the lead agency for COIN operations. Most recently, this position has been stated forcefully by Bayley and Perito (2010: 76–77) who have argued that local police should not be used as offensive COIN force for four reasons: it blurs the distinction between police and military, distracts police from their core function of serving and protecting civilians in their daily life, erodes their legitimacy as collateral damage to civilian population mounts, and creates problems of command and control as these COIN police forces often become "a force within a force, operating according to their own priorities and stretching the limits of their legal authorization" (Hansen et al., 2006). The Core Policing paradigm restricts the role of police and law enforcement in COIN to intelligence collection, disabling support networks through arrest and prosecution of insurgents and their collaborators, maintenance of public order, VIP protection, convoy escorts, and guarding of facilities and borders (Bayley and Perito, 2010: 78).

However, a competing view posits more confidence in police capabilities for neutralizing insurgent groups and envisages a lead role for it in COIN:

> Once provided an enhanced capability to deal with insurgents, police and law enforcement agencies can take the lead, augment,

support or replace military forces during all phases of campaign (Caleski, 2009: 15).

The offensive policing actions which help neutralize insurgents include paramilitary operations, counter-guerrilla patrolling, pseudo operations and raids, and cordon and search operations. This research also supports the views of Caleski (2009) regarding suitability of police as lead agency in COIN and further suggests that there is no binary between "offensive policing" and "core policing." In fact, all policemen engaged in COIN are simultaneously required to be proficient and ruthless in taking on insurgents and be extremely respectful and courteous in their interaction with the indigenous populations in their jurisdiction. This is borne out by my personal experience of policing in Tripura where respect for human rights of local people has not been compromised in the fight against insurgents. Modern research also supports the view that "fairness and effectiveness are not mutually exclusive, but mutually reinforcing" (Skogan and Frydl, 2004).

The narrative (as mentioned earlier) has attempted to highlight suitability of police and law enforcement personnel, methods, and technologies in COIN and their adaptation by military in some contemporary conflicts. However, such influences work in both directions and many COIN techniques have found their way into domestic law enforcement arena, undermining democratic governance of civil society. Some observers have taken a critical view of these developments and argued that the massive police–military intelligence networks which gather information about not only subversives or terrorists, but also routinely collect data on whole populations spawn a culture of repression in society at home and abroad (Williams, 2011). The specific mechanisms for collecting such broad-based information include: tracking cell phone use, conducting a national-registry census, installing video cameras, and analyzing internet sites (Libicki, 2007: 9). Presently, massive controversy is going on following details of warrantless electronic surveillance revealed by National Security Agency's whistleblower Edward Snowden in the U.S. Earlier, U.S. government's mapping of the American Muslim population in 2002 and 2003 through Department of Homeland Security,[3] and instructions of FBI director Robert Muller in February 2003 to prepare "demographic profiles" by all Bureau field units had raised concerns about the status of civil liberties of the affected groups (Markon, 2010). Hocking (1988) has drawn attention to the social and political implications of applying colonial COIN practices for countering domestic unrest and argued that these have been used "to quell the unemployed, the never employed, the socially deprived, and the politically active." The policing of global justice protesters in the "Battle of Seattle" and the S11 protests against the World Economic Forum in Melbourne and Genoa in which police in riot gear used chemical weapons, plastic and rubber bullets, and, in the case of the latter, even live ammunition to defeat protesters has been cited as an apt example of such political repression (McCulloch, 2001a). Recently, there have been riots in several cities in the U.S. following repeated incidents of shooting of black men by police officers. The cover of *Time* (2015) put it most eloquently: "Black Lives Matter. This Time the Charge Is Murder." Here, it may not be out of place to mention that as per current instructions troops of Tripura's armed battalions when detailed for such law and order duties to augment law enforcement numbers are under strict orders not to carry arms, and deployed with only a cane, shield, and helmet under close supervision of civil police officers from local P.S. to avoid excessive use of force on civil protesters.

To conclude, in post-modern era a marked trend toward convergence of police and military roles is discernible, leading to "transfer of theory, strategy, and techniques from domestic police to the military—and back" (Williams, 2011). While the deployment of law-enforcement personnel strategies and technologies employed by them for crime control has been helpful in ensuring a more nuanced application of force and targeted action by counterinsurgents and prevented popular backlash, critics have cautioned that indiscriminate application of COIN

---

[3] The statistical data on people who identified themselves as "Arabs" in the 2000 census was sorted by zip code and nationality by the Department of Homeland Security.

techniques in domestic arena is fraught with serious implications for civil liberty and most likely to lead to repression.

Creating Capacities for COIN: Role of Leadership and Education, Training, and Research

In the COIN literature, the two main approaches to COIN have been usually described as "population-centric" (hearts and minds/ soft approach) and "enemy-centric" (hard approach). However, in view of the critical role of leadership for success in COIN, it would be perhaps apt to describe COIN as "leader-centric" warfare (Moyar, 2010). Research conducted by Mark Moyar, a professor of national security affairs at the U.S. Marine Corps University, on recent Iraq and Afghanistan wars and seven other nearest historical precedents indicates that effective COIN campaigns have usually focused simultaneously on both the population and the enemy, and that variations in the effectiveness of COIN have correlated closely with changes in leadership quality rather than changes in methods. Furthermore, besides identifying main leadership attributes for success in COIN,[4] his research also suggested that senior leaders could enhance the leadership attributes of their junior commanders by providing right types of training and education, coaching and inspiring them through personal example.

Challenges before COIN Leadership

The main challenges before the top leadership include an accurate assessment of the situation and formulation of COIN strategy, timely mobilization of requisite resources to meet present and emerging

---

[4] The 10 most important leadership attributes for success in COIN identified by this research are: initiative, flexibility, creativity, judgment, empathy, charisma, sociability, dedication, integrity, and organization. This article has been adapted from a recent book of Professor Mark Moyar titled *A Question of Command: Counterinsurgency from the Civil War to Iraq* (Yale University Press, 2009).

threats, and a clear articulation of vision for success; while the junior leadership is charged with the responsibility for physically securing territory and people from insurgent violence, facilitating development tasks and administration, and winning popular support for government campaign by exemplary conduct even when under fire. Notwithstanding enormous differences in their responsibilities, the shifting nature of COIN campaign requires leadership at all levels to be highly adaptable, resourceful, and possess a high degree of emotional intelligence and cultural sensitivity to perform well. It is a tall order and the difficulties of COIN forces are compounded manifold if they are required to conduct operations abroad in a vastly different culture (Petraeus, 2006).

Moreover, unlike conventional wars, today's "hybrid conflicts" are marked by complexity, ambiguity, and uncertainty (Kiszely, 2007), and require highly versatile soldiers equally proficient in combat and COIN. The following extract gives some idea of the high professional standards expected of the troops in COIN:

> Soldiers and Marines are expected to be nation builders as well as warriors. They must be prepared to help re-establish institutions and local security forces and assist in rebuilding infrastructure and basic services. They must be able to facilitate establishing local governance and rule of law (*U.S. Army/Marine Corps Counterinsurgency Manual no. 3–24*, 2007, pp. xivi).

There is a close relationship between development and security for durable peace; and for performing the non-military tasks, the COIN leaders need to have knowledge of governance, economic development, public administration, and rule of law so that they can help subordinates understand "challenging, unfamiliar environments and adapt more rapidly to changing situations" (CFM, 2007: liv). Confronted with the urgent task of adapting organizations from one mode of war fighting to another in COIN, some organizations emphasize doctrine and training at the expense of education which is misplaced:

> Training is preparing people, individually or collectively, for given tasks in given circumstances; education is developing their

mental powers and understanding. Training is thus appropriate for the predictable; but for the unpredictable and for conceptual challenges, education is required (Kiszely, 2007).

John A. Nagl (2002), a noted American soldier-scholar and author of *Learning to Eat Soup with a Knife: Counterinsurgency Lessons from Malaya and Vietnam*, has conducted extensive research on the role of learning environment and organizational culture in COIN performance of some leading militaries and concluded that the relatively poor performance of the U.S. military as compared to the U.K. in various COIN campaigns could be attributed to its slow pace of institutional learning and inability to adapt its war-fighting mode to ever-changing environment of conflict. Following comprehensive assessments of its training and education requirements to produce flexible and adaptable leaders, the US military has been making concerted efforts during the last decade to transform itself into a flexible and learning organization. As part of this exercise, in line with the recommendations made in *Learning to Adapt to Asymmetric Threats* (IDA, 2005), the U.S Army has encouraged more frequent exchange of ideas between professional soldiers and academics, instituted new training courses and methods for professional military education, expanded graduate/post-graduate school opportunities for officers in civilian universities and sponsored numerous research programs. These collaborative efforts have culminated in publication of a radically different (and hugely popular)[5] COIN manual titled *The U.S. Army/Marine Corps Counterinsurgency Field Manual* (2007) in an unclassified form by the Chicago University Press for professional guidance of its troops in Iraq and Afghanistan. It is so well written that in my view this should be made compulsory reading for everyone engaged in COIN campaigns. Efforts have been made, in varying degrees, by several other nations also to reorient and retrain their military and police for COIN.

---

[5] This *Counterinsurgency Field Manual* was downloaded more than 1.5 million times in the first month after its posting on the Fort Leavenworth and Marine Corps websites (CFM, 2007: xvii).

Attributes of Leadership

Success in COIN demands exceptionally high standards of physical, mental, and intellectual vigor from those in leadership positions, whether military, police, or civil. Apart from being highly adaptable, flexible, and professionally competent, effective leaders displayed tremendous initiative to invigorate all COIN programs—military as well as non-military; exhibited absolute integrity in all their personal and professional dealings; and worked fearlessly and dedicatedly day and night through insecure areas defying threats of assassination (Rowe, 2006). The boldness exhibited by senior leaders who had acquired considerable operational experience during their service especially motivated their juniors (McClellan, 1996).[6]

The irregular nature of warfare places a huge premium on the attributes of adaptability and flexibility. An important study by Institute for Defense Analyses, Department Of Defense, USA titled "Learning to Adapt to Asymmetric Threats" (2005) reviewed the literature and identified adaptability as the central, overarching meta-skill necessary for success in COIN, and observed that "confronting the unexpected and new is considered routine" in contemporary conflicts (IDA, 2005: 2–3). This study also identified intuition, critical and creative thinking, social awareness, and social skills as crucial for developing future leaders and teams who could respond effectively to the asymmetric threats of the twenty-first century. Significantly, this study also concluded that the traditional distinction between training and education was no longer relevant for preparing soldiers for asymmetric threats because the soldiers would have to be capable of performing traditional tasks as well as demonstrate resourcefulness, initiative, creativity, and inventiveness on the modern battlefield. This confluence of training and education as learning describes training as *field learning* and education as *institutional learning* (emphasis in original). A fine example of such integration is provided by the New

---

[6] McClellan was Commissioner of Police, RCMP, who rose from the ranks and later served as Vice President of Interpol.

South Wales police in Australia that have required their recruits and constables to complete university-based associate degrees in policing practice to integrate skills training with education over the past 15 years (Bradley and Nixon, 2009).

A more recent study "Growing Strategic Leaders for Future Conflict" in the U.S. has attempted to identify salient characteristics, educational experiences, and assignments, which could help in developing future strategic leaders for asymmetric warfare by interviewing senior military officers with rich operational experience (Salmoni et al., 2010).[7] The recommendations of this study included diverse educational experience to include civilian institutions and institutionally rewarding those who take advantage of these non-traditional developmental opportunities, recurrent joint assignments and exposure to the interagency processes and norms, assignments on theater and strategic level staff in proximity to senior military and civilian leaders, and repeated exposure to foreign cultures and their militaries. It has been argued that this need for officers to broaden horizons beyond the tactical and operational is essential, so that services do not start having generals who think like battalion commanders (Salmoni et al., 2010).

However, despite all this compelling research evidence highlighting an imperative and urgent need for changing the mind-set and warrior ethos of the U.S. forces, the task remains far from easy due to "profound institutional and political obstacles" (Sewall, 2007: xliii), the vested interests of the "iron triangle" of defense contractors, military establishments and governments that have profited from the flawed "doctrine of firsts" in the past, and the rigid, bureaucratic structure of uniformed forces that impedes change (McMaster, 2008).[8] Apparently, "the only thing more difficult than getting a new idea into the military is to get an old

---

[7] The sample included 37 interviewees of which a third were at the three- or four-star level; more than 40 percent were at the one- or two-star level; while 25 percent were colonels or Navy captains. As for service, nearly 60 percent were soldiers and 25 percent Marines, 11 percent were Navy SEALs, and the remaining two were Air Force special operation senior leaders (Salmoni et al., 2010).

[8] McMaster (2008) has mentioned that military's fascination with the army brigade organization that could "see first, decide first, act first, and finish decisively" has not undergone any significant change.

one out" (Liddel-Hart, 1943: 115). The same observation holds true for criminal justice system also including police. Despite some changes in the areas of management, accountability, and operational strategies introduced in a few police departments, police research has not led to wide spread operational changes even when it has been accepted as true:

> We have known from the 1970s that random patrol, rapid response, and reactive investigation do not prevent or control crime. We also know that they remain the central activities of police departments, usually, for all practical purposes to the exclusion of all else (Kennedy, 2010).

Paterson (2011) has reviewed the international literature on the role of higher education in police training and concluded that higher education promotes a flexible value system which is more attuned to the needs of community-oriented policing, enhances ethical and professional behavior, and is directly linked to perceptions of police legitimacy and fairness. This has direct relevance to policing in COIN where popular perceptions of legitimacy and fairness are considered crucial for government's success. Presently, in most developed countries, substantial financial resources and time are devoted to improve the standard of police education and training which is continually being refined and updated to meet the needs of a changing society, focusing on "technological advances, appropriate responses to social change, and ensuring human rights" (Kratcoski, 2004).

Along with education and training, social science research has also provided useful inputs to the COIN leadership by flagging important issues pertaining to contemporary conflicts, peacekeeping and peace-building, leadership, and organizational culture etc. In most developed countries, substantial resources are now devoted to study of terrorism, insurgencies and political violence by governments, universities, Think Tanks, and other research institutions. Besides this, significant contribution to police professionalization is being made by the growing tribe of "trained academics," that is, police officers who have completed

PhD/research degrees and chosen to continue to serve with the police organization (Knutsson, 2010). A similar trend is true of the military also as seen from large number of excellent books and articles published by several soldier-scholars including Lieutenant General David Petraeus, Lieutenant General Sir John Kiszely, Brigadier Nigel R.F. Aylwin-Foster, Lieutenant Colonel John Nagl, Lieutenant Colonel David Kilcullen, and Lieutenant Colonel Mark O'Neill.

Another promising development in this field is a small, but growing, trend toward a close and continuous partnership between police and the university system well illustrated by Australia's "Linkage" program of industry-university partnerships (Bradley and Nixon, 2009).[9] Victoria police in Australia have used the Australian Research Council's "Linkage" funding stream[10] for securing full collaborative partnerships between police and researchers to cover policy and practice regarding a wide range of police problems including CT and policing multi-faith communities, network policing, integrity, and high performance policing.[11]

However, it may also be pertinent to mention that much of the recent impetus for the shifting of some police training responsibility from the police service to the colleges and universities in many developed countries has been driven by current economic downturn to shift the cost of training onto individuals rather than the government (Cordner and Shain, 2011). Already, in many states in the U.S., individuals pay all their expenses to attend basic police academy before searching for police employment.

---

[9] David Bradley, a leading academician in the field of police professionalization, became a Victoria Police Research Fellow in 2002 and has worked closely with Christine Nixon who became the Chief Commissioner of Police in Victoria. Both Bradley and Christine have collaborated closely on several projects.

[10] Under the "Linkage" scheme, for every dollar spent by police in cash and kind (the latter being salaries and cost of collaborating police managers and members), the Australian Research Council offers multiple amounts of cash to pay for the salaries of research staff (Bradley and Nixon, 2009).

[11] Till 2009, Victoria Police had secured grants for 18 research projects in partnership with more than 20 universities both in Australia and elsewhere, with over 120 academics and 25 doctoral students (Bradley and Nixon, 2009).

Surprisingly, such concern for professionalism and education is not reflected in training missions of indigenous forces that are led by the U.S. and allied forces in Afghanistan and Iraq or other United Nation's (UN) missions. A comprehensive review by Bayley and Perito (2010) revealed that training of law enforcement personnel in both these countries was grossly under-funded and conducted in an extremely haphazard manner for short durations ranging from two to 10 weeks by mostly private contractors with little understanding of local language or culture. Furthermore, almost 60–80 percent of training was related to force protection and officer safety, leaving little scope or time for training in democratic policing, human rights, communication skills, leadership, and team building. Consequently, the local police ended up as "little soldiers," with few skills for devising crime prevention strategies, investigation or delivering justice. The poor standards of police training and insufficient allocations for development by the U.S. and its allied nations in Iraq and Afghanistan suggest that despite all their rhetoric there is little political will for genuine nation-building to rebuild these countries into vibrant nations as was done in the case of European nations after the World War II through the Marshall Plan.

The UN department of peacekeeping missions has also failed to develop any standard model of training for indigenous police and programs vary immensely among missions. Considering the pivotal role played by local police in COIN/CT and the complete lack of relevant training and education imparted to them, it is easy to understand the reasons for continuing lawlessness and "troubles" in countries fighting insurgencies/civil wars despite presence of sizable number of foreign troops provided by the UN/allied forces.

2

Understanding Insurgency and Counterinsurgency

Introduction

Insurgency is typically a form of internal war with some elements of civil war that challenges existing socio-political order with a view to reallocate power within the state or to secede and form an autonomous entity or ungoverned space that insurgents can control (CFM, 2007: 3). In the post-World War II period, internal wars have been more prevalent and caused far greater deaths, destruction, and displacement of populations across the world than interstate wars. According to an estimate, between 1945 and 1999, at least 16.2 million people were killed in 127 civil wars as against about 3.33 million battle deaths that occurred in 25 interstate wars (Fearon and Laitin, 2003), and the early decades of the twenty-first century have not seen any dramatic improvement in the security scenario or reversal of this trend.

The growth of insurgency was fueled and facilitated by nationalist movements and the process of decolonization from the 1940s through the 1970s that led to emergence of large number of financially, bureaucratically, and militarily weak states, which were marked by endemic state weakness in the form of poverty, instability, a large population, and limited administrative control of their peripheries. The conventional wisdom had it that a greater degree of ethnic or religious diversity and broadly held grievances made these countries more prone to civil wars. However, recent research suggests that (a) ethno-nationalist struggles over access to state power, rather than ethnic or religious diversity, have played a more important part in the dynamics leading to the outbreak of civil wars in roughly half of the conflicts fought in the post-World War II era; and (b) exclusion of large ethnic groups from state power or their under-representation in government coupled with a history of previous conflict or a loss of power in recent history significantly increases the likelihood of violent conflicts (Cederman et al., 2010). Esteban et al. (2012) have examined ethnicity–conflict nexus by scrutinizing data from 138 countries from 1960 to 2008 and concluded that (a) civil conflicts are associated with, and possibly driven by, public payoffs such as political power; (b) ethnic markers are frequently used as a means to restrict political power or economic benefits to a subset of the population. The veracity of these observations is borne out by the analysis of various insurgencies in India in the succeeding chapters of this book.

This chapter is organized into five sections. The first section provides an introduction to insurgency and its development. The second section considers some definitions of key terms of this book—insurgency, counterinsurgency, and terrorism—and critically examines the use of terrorism by various illicit groups and relationship between COIN and CT. The third section presents an overview of guerrilla warfare and identifies the main trends in the past and contemporary insurgencies to understand the complex and evolving nature of insurgency. The fourth section examines the two main approaches to COIN—the military approach and the political approach, and recommends a historically grounded model of successful COIN that is considered suitable for successful resolution of insurgencies. It would be seen that globally the character of insurgency has changed significantly due to increased salience of traditional motivators such as religion and ethnicity as well as impact of modern trends of globalization, urbanization, and diffusion of modern technologies of communication and warfare, necessitating more creative approaches to COIN. The concluding section gives an idea about the difference in COIN practices adopted by India and the Western world. This chapter builds the argument of this book that a comprehensive approach encompassing political, economic, and social dimensions is more likely to earn legitimacy, promote stability, and lead to durable peace, while indiscriminate use of overwhelming force usually condemns the society to endless cycles of guerrilla warfare and repression.

Definitions: Insurgency, Counterinsurgency, and Terrorism

Like many other concepts in social sciences, the meaning of some key terms of this book—insurgency, counterinsurgency, and terrorism—is also heavily contested, and neat definitions have remained elusive though tomes have been written on these subjects. Definitional constructs have ranged from those developed by governments, agencies within governments, private agencies, and academics, depending on their perspective and world-view. It is also a fact that governments are usually reluctant to confer status of insurgents on rebels as this gives them a certain amount of legitimacy, while labeling them as terrorists enables governments to deal with rebels as common criminals within the framework of law. In this respect, labeling plays a crucial role in civil conflicts. Historically, the "politics of naming" indulged in by the global media, academics, and policy makers in the developed countries has obscured or ignored the actual nature of armed conflicts or insurgencies waged against them by branding opponents or dissenters as terrorists, bandits, or rebels and by ascribing motives such as greed, grievances, or fanaticism, while ignoring the complex array of factors and events that drove these conflicts (Bhatia, 2005).

Prior to the twentieth century, insurgency was regarded as a purely military affair (Beckett, 2001: vii), but most modern definitions of insurgency recognize the protracted nature of the struggle and its politico-military dimensions. This multidimensional

nature of insurgency is well described by Mao in his highly influential book, *On Guerrilla Warfare*:

> Revolutionary warfare is never confined within the bounds of
> military action... any revolutionary war is a unity of which the
> constituent parts, in varying importance are military, political,
> economic, social and psychological (Mao, 1961: 9).

In the same vein, Robert Taber (2002: 16) in his classic study of
guerrilla warfare *The War of the Flea* has also observed that:

> Essentially, then, the guerrilla fighter's war is political and social,
> his means are as political as they are military, his purpose is almost
> entirely so.... *Guerrilla war is the extension of politics by means of
> armed conflict* (emphasis in original).

According to the *U.S. Army/Marine Corps Counterinsurgency
Field Manual* (2007: 2):

> An insurgency is an organized, protracted politico-military struggle
> designed to weaken the control and legitimacy of an established
> government, occupying power, or other political authority while
> increasing insurgent control.

These definitions make it clear that insurgency connotes
a political legitimacy crisis of some kind between a non-ruling
group and the ruling authorities in which the non-ruling group
consciously uses political resources and violence to alter various
aspects of politics—integrity of the borders, the political system,
the authorities in power, and the policies that determine who
gets what in society (O'Neill, 1990: 13). Therefore, resolution
of insurgencies depends on the government identifying which
dimension, military or political, is most crucial at any given
time, followed by a coherent COIN strategy based on a rigorous
assessment of the goals, strategies, and forms of warfare adopted
by the insurgents (O'Neill, 1990: 154).

R. Scott Moore (2007), a highly respected American soldier–
scholar, has presented a dynamic model of insurgency that reflects

a complex, three-dimensional web of competing beliefs, catalytic actions, and unacceptable structures that lead to violence, especially during political, economic, and social instability.[1] A proper understanding of the interaction of these three dimensions could be helpful in identifying the causes and the cures for insurgency.

Acknowledging this complex and multi-dimensional nature of modern insurgencies, current definitions of COIN also factor in a wide spectrum of policy options. For example, the *U.S. Army/Marine Corps Counterinsurgency Field Manual* (CFM, 2007: 2) defines COIN as the "military, paramilitary, political, economic, psychological, and civic actions taken by a government to defeat insurgency." However, this definition is not adequate as it does not indicate the end state or purpose of COIN efforts.

R. Scott Moore has addressed these issues in his article "The Basics of Counterinsurgency" (2007) and offered a more comprehensive definition:

> Counterinsurgency is an integrated set of political, economic, social and security measures intended to end and prevent the recurrence of political violence, create and maintain stable political, economic and social structures, and resolve the underlying causes of insurgency in order to establish and sustain conditions required for lasting stability.

This definition addresses the complex dynamics of insurgency, places the security operations in their wider social and political context and clearly states the ultimate objective of COIN. The COIN strategy for establishing lasting stability involves, among other things, establishing and maintaining security, providing essential services, establishing governance, sustaining development, supporting reconciliation, and fostering social change (Moore, 2007). From this perspective, the object of war is not victory by destruction of the enemy, but "a better peace—'better' in the sense

---

[1] In Moore's model, the Competing Beliefs may concern issues related to identities and culture, historical narratives, and symbols; Unacceptable Structures include ineffective authority, military occupation, poverty, modernization, urbanization, and social stratification; and Catalytic Actions include state violence, intervention, repression, deprivation, corruption, discrimination, and crime (Moore, 2007).

of being more secure, prosperous, or advantageous to any given side" (Kilcullen, 2010: 12). In the present context, this definition is useful because Tripura government's COIN strategy recognizes that the goal of the COIN campaign has been the reestablishment of a secure environment for governance and development, and not just a victory over, or the elimination, of the insurgency.

However, some more critical accounts of Western COIN hold that there is a hidden political agenda as these concepts (insurgency and COIN) have been carefully crafted by proponents of COIN to mask true nature of their interventionist foreign policy in the uplifting guise of the "civilizing mission" and justify these to domestic populations (Porch, 2011). *The Selected Writings of Eqbal Ahmad*, (edited by Bengelsdorf et al. and Foreword by Noam Chomsky) published posthumously in 2006 also offers a nuanced critique of COIN establishment from the perspective of developing countries. In his seminal article *Counterinsurgency*, written in 1971, Ahmad has analyzed the nature of the U.S. COIN operations in Vietnam and other countries and observed that:

> Counterinsurgency involves a multi-faceted assault against organized revolutions.... It serves to conceal the realty of a foreign policy dedicated to combating revolutions abroad and helps to relegate revolutionaries to the status of outlaws. The reduction of a revolution to mere insurgency also constitutes an *a priori* denial of its legitimacy (Ahmad, 2006: 36–37).

Apparently, this lack of unanimity surrounding COIN concepts stems from the diverse nature and adaptability of those who wage insurgency and the overlapping traits of these types of conflicts, as also divergent perspectives of the authors. However, from the earlier discussion, it is clear that political power is the central issue in insurgencies and counterinsurgencies; and each side aims to get the people to accept its governance or authority as legitimate (CFM, 2007: 2). With this basic understanding of insurgency and COIN, we now proceed to understand the concept of terrorism and its relationship with other forms of political violence and crime.

Though there are over hundred definitions of this term, a standard definition of terrorism still remains elusive as the term "terrorism" evokes strong emotional responses leading to moral judgments clouding understanding of the concept. According to the *Oxford Advanced Learner's Dictionary*, terrorism is "the use of violent action in order to achieve political aims or to force a government to act" (2000: 1342). According to Bruce Hoffman (1998: 43), a noted American expert, the essence of terrorism is "the deliberate creation and exploitation of fear through violence or the threat of violence in the pursuit of political change." Paul Wilkinson (1977: 49), a British academic and expert on terrorism, has defined political terrorism as:

> The systematic use of murder and destruction, and the threat of murder and destruction to terrorize individuals, groups, communities or governments into conceding to the terrorists' political aims.

From this perspective, terrorism is a particular method of perpetrating violence used by non-state actors in pursuance of their political aims to force a government to act in a particular fashion. Terrorism is also distinguished by its preference for targeting non-combatants as noted in the following definition of the U.S. government:

> Premeditated, politically motivated violence perpetrated against non-combatant targets by sub-national groups or clandestine agents, usually intended to influence an audience (Section 2656f [d] of Title 22 of the U.S. Code available at http://www.state.gov/s/ ct/rls/crt/2006/82726.htm)

According to Bard E. O'Neill (1990: 24):

> Terrorism is a form of warfare in which violence is directed primarily against non-combatants (usually unarmed civilians), rather than operational military and police forces or economic assets (public or private).

These definitions make it clear that political terrorism has two main features: (a) creating an atmosphere of fear to facilitate political change; (b) deliberate targeting of non-combatants by non-state actors. Terrorism is also distinguished from other forms of violence by the fact that acts committed are legitimized to a degree by their political nature (Kiras, 2007: 175). The following discussion examines uses of terrorism by various illicit groups, which would facilitate better understanding of modern conflicts that are a complex amalgam of insurgency, terrorism, and organized crime.

Relationship between Terrorism, Insurgency, Guerrilla Warfare, and Criminal Organizations

Historically, terrorism has been used as a useful auxiliary weapon by insurgent leaders who recognize that terrorism alone is insufficient to achieve strategic goals, and may even prove counterproductive by alienating potential domestic and international supporters if it becomes indiscriminate (O'Neill, 1990: 79–80). However, there is no universal pattern so far as the decision to use terrorism is concerned. Some guerrilla leaders and theoreticians, such as Che Guevara and Mao-Tse-Tung opposed the use of terrorism against the civilian population, while others such as Carlos Marighella believed that terrorism was a weapon the revolutionary could never afford to relinquish.

The essence of distinction between terrorism and guerrilla warfare lies in their targeting preferences and operating methods. Historically, guerrillas have attacked small regular military units, isolated outposts, police, and paramilitary forces, while terrorist attacks target the general population (Mockaitis, 2008: 6). Guerrillas operate more like military units requiring extensive logistical support and base camps, and operate in numbers that are much larger than the typical terrorist cells. The insurgent groups who favor urban–warfare strategies usually have small closely knit secretive organizations, while those who adopt protracted-popular war strategies require more complex structures and systems as they anticipate long struggle and substantial military activity. Finally, while the guerrillas attempt to achieve their goals by depleting the government's physical resources over time, terrorists seek to erode government's psychological support.

However, acts of terrorism do not inevitably lead to a wider insurgency and the vast majority of groups using the tactic of terrorism remain locked in a cycle of individual, usually spasmodic, acts of bombing, assassinations, hostage-taking, and others. The crucial difference between terrorism and insurgency is the scope and scale of violence (Kiras, 2007: 175). The key factors that determine whether a terrorist campaign expands into a wider insurgency are: its capacity to win substantial popular support, inspirational leadership, availability of sufficient weapons, and repressive actions by government, and its security forces that lead to an increase in popular support for an insurgency (Wilkinson, 2001: 17).

Furthermore, insurgent organizations cannot remain static. If the insurgency grows and the insurgents pursue a coherent strategy, the movement may succeed by seizing power or extracting concessions from the government. However, if the support does not grow but the insurgents persist in their pursuit of violence, then they have become mere terrorists. Insurgencies may also degenerate into mere criminality. As most insurgent organizations resort to extortions, racketeering, kidnapping, and narcotics trafficking to fund their campaign, this transition may occur quite easily. According to some estimates, al-Qaeda, Taliban, and various criminal groups control nearly 10 percent of the world's total turnover of US$ 400 billion of narcotics trade (Heickero, 2014). Clearly, such huge financial assets have been of immense help to these terrorist organizations to finance their operations worldwide.

The objectives of various illicit groups who use terrorism differ significantly. According to Bard E. O'Neill (1990: 24–25), insurgent terrorism is purposeful, rather than mindless violence unleashed by insurgents for achieving their specific long-term, intermediate and short-term goals, which may range from changing political system (long-term), erode government's psychological support by instilling fear among public, officials, and their international supporters (intermediate) or extracting particular concessions such as release of prisoners or payment of ransom (proximate). Criminal organizations generally make selective use of terror to eliminate rivals, punish traitors within their own organization, and intimidate witnesses from testifying against them or targeting judicial and law-enforcement officers perceived hostile to their operations. This is done with a view to avoid unwanted attention from the government. However, an exception to this rule may occur when legitimate authority becomes so weak that criminal organizations may gain control of whole sectors of an economy or even territory. For example, drug cartels in Columbia are powerful enough to control entire provinces and heroin traffickers exercise similar control over the Golden Triangle region of Southeast Asia.

It would be seen from the earlier discussion that, in theory, there is clear difference between insurgency and terrorism. However, in the context of contemporary trends in violence against the state, such neat distinctions are not always discernible as most contemporary "irregular" conflicts are a conflation of insurgency and terrorism and seamlessly integrate insurgent and terrorist paradigms. Therefore, some leaders and COIN experts have argued that a proper response to these conflicts demands a comprehensive Counter Terrorism-Counter Insurgency (CT-CI) strategy. However, such CT-CI strategies need to be crafted carefully with due regard for the inherent complexities involved in relationship between these two concepts.

Relationship between COIN and Counterterrorism

Counterterrorism (CT), like COIN, is a catch-all term, which includes all offensive measures—political, legal, diplomatic, financial, and military—undertaken to prevent an adversary from employing terrorism. Over the past decade, the fusion of threats from terrorism and insurgency in many conflicts has blurred distinctions between COIN and CT, leading to attempts by policy makers to chalk out a comprehensive CI-CT policy, which addresses their national security concerns stemming from twin threats of global insurgencies and domestic terrorism. The decision to use the term "Overseas Contingency Operations" in 2009 by the Obama administration instead of the "Global War on

Terror" represents a certain blending of the two techniques of CT and CI in U.S. military's large-scale deployment overseas (Ford, 2012). In many contemporary conflicts such as Afghanistan, Pakistan, and Iraq, CT operations are being run concurrently with COIN missions.

However, despite some overlap between these two concepts there remain significant differences between CT and COIN and some components of one strategy may not support, or even nullify, the objectives of other strategy. For example, some components of the CT strategy which inhibit the international movement of selected terrorists, track cells operating in otherwise peaceful countries or target hardening of vulnerable prominent people and facilities may not contribute much to the COIN effort (Byman, 2006). Therefore, there is a need for a more nuanced understanding of these two concepts by the political leaders to avoid costly stalemate and failures. The following excerpt brings out political risks of conflating the two concepts of CI and CT:

> At the political level, the conflation of counterterrorism and counterinsurgency risks producing an overly interventionist foreign policy which distracts and exhausts the US and UK as they treat an ever-increasing number of localized insurgencies as the incubators of future terrorist threats (Boyle, 2010).

Traditionally, law enforcement and intelligence instruments have been more salient in CT, and military force has been used selectively in support of policing/COIN operations, hostage rescue, or retaliatory air strikes. This is so because the local police are better placed to learn about the emerging local terrorist threats and identify vulnerable targets, and coordinate the first response to attacks. In their CT role, police are primarily responsible for (a) protecting vulnerable people and places (target hardening); (b) disrupting terror networks by intelligence operations; and (c) investigating, arresting, and prosecuting terrorist suspects. In this context, community policing has been found more advantageous than traditional methods by police in gaining crucial intelligence and public confidence as it does not undermine community trust by compiling unsubstantiated lists of suspects; avoids charges of profiling, phone tapping and their legal/political consequences; and does not resort to covert intelligence operations and costly surveillance of suspects and places (Clarke and Newman, 2007).

However, the "Global War on Terror" has militarized CT and given rise to practices that have made CT as a distinct model of warfare that relies overwhelmingly on Special Forces, air power, drone strikes, sophisticated communication, and computer networks to gain crucial intelligence required to kill enemy and disrupt terror networks (Boyle, 2010). Post-9/11, in Australia, the U.S., and the U.K., radical new legislation has given unprecedented powers to security/intelligence agencies to conduct covert surveillance, and detain and interrogate people suspected to have information related to terrorism (Epifanio, 2011). Therefore, it has been argued sometimes that citizens' physical security and liberty as well as stability and democratic nature of the state faces greater risk from threat of CT than terrorism (Wolfendale, 2006).

Jenny Hocking in an article "Counterterrorism as Counterinsurgency: the British Experience" (1988) has argued that domestic CT measures have been heavily influenced by COIN thought in five main elements: exceptional legislation, intelligence, pre-emptive controls, military involvement in civil disturbances, and media management. These measures have led to an increase in the penetration of state in civil society and militarized urban policing, leading to a marked tendency to find a military solution to the intractable economic and social problems of Western capitalist nations. Some recent attempts to contain, curtail, or control growth of social media and expression of dissent by governments in many countries, including the U.S. and India, are grim reminders of the dangers faced by civil society groups across the world (India Today cover, 2012; The Economist, 2013). The U.S. National Security Agency (NSA) documents leaked by Edward Snowden since June 2013 have further reinforced such misgivings about the global surveillance carried out by the U.S. in the name of CT. It has now transpired that the NSA infiltrated the Internet Engineering Task Force (IETF) and other standard-setting bodies to weaken encryption standards, install backdoors in firewalls, servers, and hard drives; snooped on Google and Yahoo servers by tapping into their private links; subverted major undersea cables to tap into global internet traffic; and also tapped phones of many prominent world leaders (Bajaj, 2014). These acts are over and above the PRISM program that authorizes the US government to legally tap telecom companies for all metadata. In view of these developments, one is inclined to agree with the view that liberal democratic response must be based on a commitment to uphold and maintain the rule of law and all efforts shall be made to ensure that liberal principles of legitimacy are not distorted or abrogated in the desire to defeat terrorism by resorting to institutionalized and bureaucratized terror (Chalk, 1995).

An Overview of Insurgent Warfare

The violent aspect of insurgency is manifested in many forms of warfare—terrorism, guerrilla warfare, and conventional warfare. However, notwithstanding the upsurge of terrorism since the 1970s, the most familiar kind of violence used by insurgent groups has been guerrilla warfare that acquired prominence during the early nineteenth century when these harassing tactics were used by Spanish irregulars fighting Napoleon's forces in the Peninsular War. At that time, guerrilla warfare was regarded as a purely military form of conflict and seldom treated in detail or accorded much importance by classical war theorists. In fact, Clausewitz, who was among the first to deal with concept of popular uprising in his classic *On War*, accorded them a role in "strategic defense" as an auxiliary to regular military forces to resist an invading army (Clausewitz, 1976). In such warfare, the role of guerrillas was restricted to harassing the enemy by launching surprise attacks at the periphery instead of confronting enemy forces in a frontal attack as they could be crushed by regular enemy forces. Clearly, it was not visualized that irregular warfare could be decisive in shaping the outcome of wars and it was Mao-Tse-Tung who demonstrated that guerrilla warfare could be effectively employed to defeat much larger conventional forces through political mobilization of people.

Mao's theory of protracted people's war and its tremendous success during the Chinese revolution captured the imagination of many revolutionaries and it became the blueprint of many other insurgencies during the Cold War. However, the harassing "hit and run" tactics of guerrilla warfare described by Mao (1961), Taber (2002), and Guevara (2007) have remained largely unchanged:

> Hit and run, wait, lie in ambush, again hit and run, and thus repeatedly, without giving any rest to the enemy (Guevara, 2007: 11).

> When guerrillas engage a stronger enemy, they withdraw when he advances; harass him when he stops; strike him when he is weary; pursue him when he withdraws (Mao, 1961: 34).

One of the more significant contributions of Mao to the insurgent warfare was his stress upon the integration of military, political, economic, social, and psychological elements and mobilization of popular support as crucial elements of success in revolutionary war. According to Mao:

> Because guerrilla warfare basically derives from the masses and is supported by them, it can neither exist nor flourish if it separates itself from their sympathies and cooperation (Mao, 1961: 33)

An important school of thought on insurgency warfare that differed significantly from Mao's theory of protracted people's war is associated with Che Guevara and Regis Debray who developed the strategy of "guerrilla foco" in Cuban revolutionary strategy. While Mao stressed the leading role of the party and substantial preparation before the military struggle, these revolutionaries did not believe that the vanguard had to be a Marxist-Leninist party; contended that beginnings of revolutionary warfare must be developed by armed action; and argued that guerrilla force was the political embryo from which the party could rise. According to Debray (1967: 106):

> Under certain conditions, the political and military are not separate, but form one organic whole, consisting of the people's army, whose nucleus is the guerrilla army. The vanguard party can exist

in the form of guerrilla foco itself. The guerrilla force is the party in embryo.

Consequently, their approach mainly involved violence in the form of small to moderately sized guerrilla attacks and limited political organization. However, despite these significant differences, Guevara, like Mao, recognized that guerrillas could not succeed without wholehearted help from local population and requirement of regular army for the final victory:

> The guerrilla band is an armed nucleus, the fighting vanguard of the people. It draws its great force from the mass of the people themselves.... Triumph will always be the product of a regular army, even though its origins are in a guerrilla army (Guevara, 2007: 9, 12).

But Guevara's failed attempt to replicate the Cuban experience in Bolivia-led insurgent intellectuals to reassess their strategies and emergence of theory of urban guerrilla warfare associated with Brazilian Carlos Marighella, author of the *Handbook or Minimanual of Urban Guerrilla Warfare*. Like other insurgents, those engaged in urban warfare also seek to erode a government's will to resist and mobilize popular support, but their process is quite different. The strategy of urban terrorist is to turn political crisis into armed conflict by performing violent actions such as kidnappings, ambushes, assassinations, attacks on fixed targets, and sabotage of economic assets with a view to undermine the confidence of the government and provoke repression, which would alienate the masses from the government (O'Neill, 1990: 46). Significantly, Marighella was also of the view that terrorist operations though crucial, were not decisive because the struggle must eventually be transferred to countryside (Marighella, 1969).

The overwhelmingly central focus on revolutionary warfare during most of the Cold War resulted from the ideological predispositions and global struggle for power and influence between the Western and Eastern Blocs, which pitted insurgents in many Third World countries against colonial regimes or their pro-Western post-colonial successors. Though the concept of insurgency has been generally associated with the communists, the fact remains that its tactics have served well diverse groups ranging from Islamic fundamentalists and ethnic nationalists to "rebels" primarily interested in looting diamonds or coca. In his "Introduction" to the special edition of *Australian Army Journal* titled "Counterinsurgency," the Chief of Australian Army Lieutenant General Peter Leahy has rightly argued that despite introduction of modern digitization, precision, and stealth technology, the character of war in the post-Cold War period has not undergone any *fundamental* transmutation, and war continues to remain an innately social and political activity (emphasis in original, Leahy, 2008). Successful insurgency still stems from the existence of valid popular grievances, sharp social divisions, an unsound economy, an oppressive government, and most crucially, existence of a revolutionary organization capable of articulating and exploiting popular dissatisfaction with the *status quo* (Taber, 2002: 151). The following discussion highlights features of insurgency that have remained constant over the centuries.

Constant Features of Insurgency

Features of insurgency that have remained fairly constant over the years have been insurgent groups' preference for difficult terrain, hit-and-run tactics and a degree of local popular support. The availability of "rough and inaccessible terrain" such as swamps, mountains, and forests has been one of the main factors contributing to the success of guerrilla operations as it neutralizes the operational advantages of regular forces by hampering their mobility and artillery. Favorable topography also provides isolated strategic base areas for insurgents that allow the insurgents to plan, train, rest, recuperate, and marshal equipment and to organize the people in relative security (O'Neill, 1990: 56). At the tactical level, guerrillas conduct hit-and-run operations and ambushes to loosen state control over territory and the population, and erode the enemy's will and capability to govern (Ibrahim, 2004). In view of all these advantages, guerrilla tactics have been frequently adopted by strategically weak irregulars to fight a superior invading army or as an auxiliary to regular military forces. Some other factors that have remained constant over the years include the primacy of politics, the significance of psychological operations, the resort to protracted war, and the employment of unconventional forces and tactics (Sloan, 1999: 67–80). Additionally, insurgents possess cultural understanding and ingenuity, and can constantly adapt into ever more sophisticated organizational structures (Hoffman, 2005).

Contemporary Insurgencies

In the post-Cold War period, insurgency has become more common and strategically significant due to mounting global discontent arising from globalization and growing inequities; the collapse of traditional political, economic, and social orders; weak regimes; organized crime; population pressure; and the widespread availability of armaments (Metz and Raymond, 2004). As mentioned earlier, one of the constant features of insurgency has been its ability to constantly adapt to the new circumstances with great agility and speed. This adaptability is amply manifested in its remarkable evolution from a purely military form of conflict before the twentieth century to the protracted political, social, and economic warfare waged by Mao and the contemporary "hybrid wars" comprising terrorism, insurgency, propaganda, and economic warfare (Kilcullen, 2009: 5–38). The events in Iraq and Afghanistan have clearly demonstrated modern insurgents' ingenuity to adapt guerrilla tactics to frustrate the modern armies of superpowers by waging fourth-generation and fifth-generation warfare (Sahni, 2009e). The other distinguishing feature of contemporary insurgencies is their transnational character, which is different from the single country focus of previous era. Consequently, insurgent groups such as Islamic State often espouse goals that transcend national boundaries and engage in real-time cooperation between insurgents spread in many countries. Furthermore, in earlier insurgencies, a key component of strategy was creation of local, regional, and main force components able to make transition from defensive to offensive warfare and mount decisive conventional operations. By contrast, modern insurgents employ "diffuse, cell-based structures" and "leader-less resistance," which enables them to create mass movements without mass organization, rendering traditional COIN strategies ineffective (Kilcullen, 2006).

According to Lieutenant General Sir John Kiszely, a highly decorated British officer who saw action in Falklands, Bosnia, and Iraq, the post-modern asymmetric conflicts are characterized by their "complexity, ambiguity, uncertainty, and volatility," and pose considerable intellectual challenge to the modern forces because the nature of "war" and "peace," and "victory" and "defeat" is not easily comprehensible as the contest does not take place in the battlefield, but in a complex civilian environment, and success depends not on physical destruction of the enemy but on denying popular support to the enemy and winning it for oneself (Kiszely, 2007). The complexity and peculiar character of such contemporary conflicts is well brought out in the following "Paradoxes of Counterinsurgency Operations" (CFM, 2007: 47–51):

Paradoxes of Counterinsurgency Operations

1. Sometimes, the more you protect your force, the less secure you may be;
2. Sometimes, the more force is used, the less effective it is;
3. The more successful the counterinsurgency is, the less force can be used and more risk must be accepted;
4. Sometimes, doing nothing is the best option;
5. Some of the best weapons for counterinsurgency do not shoot;
6. The host nation doing something tolerably is normally better than us doing it well;
7. If a tactic works this week, it might not work next week;
8. Tactical success guarantees nothing;
9. Many important decisions are not made by generals.

(CFM, 2007: 47–51)

There is no doubt that waging COIN warfare is incredibly harder and counter-intuitive for forces accustomed to conventional warfare or neutralizing traditional insurgents. Some other factors that have considerable bearing on contemporary insurgencies include increased salience of religion and ethnicity, phenomenon of "failed/failing states," urbanization, and revolution in modern communications technology.

Religion and Ethnicity

A prominent feature of most contemporary insurgencies is the replacement of Marxist revolutionary ideals with the extremist forms of religion and ethnic identities. Radical Islam, in particular, has emerged as a new ideological imperative behind insurgency and strongly influenced numerous conflicts in the Middle East, Asia, and Africa. However, religious fundamentalist organizations such as Hezbollah and Hamas often have an implicit political agenda also behind armed conflicts waged in the name of religion. Apart from religion, ethnic identity has also played an important role in contemporary conflicts and, in fact, ethnic or ethno-national insurgencies have become the predominant form of insurgency following the decolonization process and end of the Cold War. In such conflicts, the aim of many non-state actors is not so much control of population but population exclusion or expulsion based on group identities.

In India, these twin factors of ethnic identity and religion are seen at work in many insurgent movements across the country. Aggressive engagement with "identity politics" by sub-national groups leading to severe violence has become a common feature of India's NER. This form of ethnic violence inspired by insurgency is designed largely to foster "identity" as well as advance standard political goals. Many commentators have noted the salience of ethnicity and observed that the various movements in the northeast for secession or autonomy have more to do with identity than ideology as the multiple tribal and sub-tribal groups struggle to safeguard their ethnic, linguistic, and religious identity from the large-scale influx of people into the region (Bhaumik, 2004; Verghese, 2004). However, it is also pertinent to mention here that identities and ethnic solidarities are not rigid or permanent but remain fluid with tribes and clans oscillating from one group to another, influenced by a host of factors (Ngaihte, 2014). For example, when the Naga Club submitted a memorandum to the Simon Commission in 1929, the Kuki tribes were represented in it, but the Tangkhul tribes were not. However, right now the Tangkhul tribes are an important part of the Naga movement while the Kuki tribes are not only excluded but are also the most vocal in opposing the demands.

Foreign intelligence agencies such as Pakistan's Inter-Services Intelligence (ISI) and Bangladesh's Directorate General of Forces Intelligence (DGFI) have been quick to exploit these fears and insecurity of ethnic groups and succeeded in raising more than one dozen fundamentalist organizations, most of them in Assam, working to destabilize the region (Upadhyay, 2009: 70). The emerging linkages of prominent northeast insurgent groups with foreign Islamist extremist groups have further added to the complexity of tribal insurgencies. The Jamaat-ul-Mujahideen Bangladesh (JMB) and Harkat-ul-Jihad-al-Islami (HuJI), a major terrorist group of Pakistan with an affiliate in Bangladesh, have come to notice for establishing terror modules in many northeast states. The involvement of hostile foreign agencies and fundamentalist organizations in this troubled region is a cause of serious concern and renders the resolution of northeast's tribal insurgencies still more intractable.

Failed/Failing States

There has been a marked rise in the emergence of non-state actors and their capacity to control large geographical areas due to the breakdown of the international bipolar system and weakening of central authority in many states. Consequently, the terrorist organizations and trans-national criminal organizations have often moved in to take advantage of the power vacuum in the failed or failing states. The use of Sudan and Afghanistan by Osama bin Laden and al-Qaeda to create a global terrorist organization is an apt example of this phenomenon. More recently, taking advantage of political instability in Iraq and Syria, heavily armed Islamic State extremists have moved in to take control of many cities defeating regular troops. Thus, a combination of state failure and modern terrorism poses a serious threat to the international security as failed or dysfunctional states can become harbor sites and potential breeding ground for modern terrorists, or serve as a catalyst for interstate conflicts (Hoffman, 2005).

While India is definitely not a "failed" state, it has been called a "flailing state" as the state administration appears unable to effectively discipline the field-level agents such as the policemen, teachers, engineers, health workers, and so on, and compel them to deliver even routine services to the citizens as it is plagued by rampant corruption, incompetence, indifference, and absenteeism (Pritchett, 2009). This observation is largely true of the country's NER also as state weakness, though localized, is endemic in the NER, with Manipur considered to be perilously close to the threshold of "failed" state. In Nagaland too, there has been a retreat of state from the crucial areas of governance, emasculation of several public institutions including police, and subversion of politics, leading to morbid fratricidal violence and a fragmented and fractious society (Ravi, 2014). This "crisis of governance" is considered to be the single biggest obstacle to peace in the NER as the level of corruption remains extraordinarily high and the ties between mainstream political parties and ethnic militias give rise to conditions of "durable disorder" (Baruah, 2005: 16).

Some commentators (Becket, 2005; Metz, 2007) have also observed that the failed/failing states with rich natural resources are particularly lucrative to criminal activities and give rise to "commercial insurgencies" in which the profits from drugs or mineral resources are the main prize in countries such as Colombia, Somalia, and Liberia. The significance of drugs or mineral commodities in sustaining insurgencies has increased as the absence of Cold War compels insurgent groups to purchase arms, raising the economic cost of insurgency (Beckett, 2005; CFM, 2007: 19). Apparently, the imperatives of economics of insurgency have prompted many insurgent groups in India's northeast to trade arms for drugs to generate huge profits to finance their operations and also supply a secure financial base to pursue their separatist agenda. In this regard, economist Paul Collier (2000) has argued that globally the most significant factor of civil conflicts is the ability of rebel organizations to be financially viable. Collier has also observed a strong correlation between the insurgent violence and a specific set of economic conditions such as a region's dependence on exports of primary commodities and low national income.[2] In this context, it is striking that India's northeast is both poor and a primary commodity-exporting region, factors which facilitate illegal tax collection and contribute to persistence of armed conflicts in the region (Baruah, 2005: 72). Clearly, in India's northeast the transition of "freedom fighters" to "warlords" to "drug lords" has corrupted the insurgent movements and exposed the hollowness of these "liberation struggles" launched ostensibly to protect and promote ethnic interests (Bhaumik, 2009: xxii; Dasgupta, 2001).

Urbanization

While the classic guerrilla warfare setting was the mountainous terrain, the rapid growth of urbanization in the developing world has led to a marked shift from rural- to urban-based operations as the modern guerrillas seek security, lucrative targets, and broader support among the population of modern mega-cities (Hoffman, 2005). The ongoing global trend toward urbanization means that future insurgencies will continue to form in cities rather than rural areas, and pose significant challenges to developing countries struggling with myriad socio-economic-political problems resulting from globalization, modernization, rapid population growth, urbanization, poverty, and corruption (Beckett, 2005). On all these counts, modern India scores high with a population of over 1.2 billion, pervasive corruption and poor governance, and likely

---

[2] According to Collier (2000), primary commodities are highly lootable, primary production centers located in conflict zones are easily accessible and cannot be moved elsewhere, making their owners vulnerable to extortion. Second, low national income is correlated with armed civil conflicts, because poverty and unemployment make it easier for the insurgents to recruit new members quite inexpensively.

to suffer significant levels of insurgent violence in the foreseeable future. Tactically, there has been a noticeable shift from the more traditional rural ambush to the use of Improvised Explosive Devices (IEDs), particularly suicide bombs. This has enabled the modern insurgents to overcome the "lethality self-limit" imposed by rifle-based tactics, which entail more risk and require more fighters to generate greater lethality (Kilcullen, 2006).

While the security analysts have generally presented urban insurgency as a distinct variant, insurgents themselves have been far more pragmatic and employed a deadly rural–urban synthesis of field approaches and doctrine to exploit the specifics of each situation (Marks, 2003). This trend of combining rural and urban action is noticeable in India also and even in the predominantly rural NER, the insurgent groups have frequently used major cities, mostly state capitals, for taking shelter, extortions, and perpetrating violence through use of bombs and IEDs.

Diffusion of Technology

Contemporary insurgent groups have been quick to exploit modern information and warfare technologies, even as they continue to draw sustenance from classic motivations such as ethnicity and religion. The revolution in communications has led to "the revolution of rising expectations" among poor masses and disadvantaged sections of society and provided a revolutionary base for launching struggles against repressive regimes worldwide (Taber, 2002: 184). The new social media and technologies were effectively employed by protesters in recent uprisings in many Arab countries, most notably Tunisia and Egypt (Omotola, 2012).[3] Furthermore, these technologies have ushered a revolutionary transformation and conflation of insurgency and terrorism through major changes in organization, strategy and conduct of operations. Consequently, minor states, sub-national groups, and even individuals possess offensive capabilities formerly reserved solely for nation states.

---

[3] In Egypt, 80,000 protesters were able to coordinate online through a social networking site on Facebook, April 6 Youth, and launched a mass protest on January 25, the national police day holiday.

More specifically, internet communication and technology have provided insurgents a worldwide audience for instant publicity; an "electronic sanctuary" for financial transfers, recruitment, intelligence, and other operational purposes; and reduced their dependence on formal organizations by facilitating operations through diffuse, cell-based structures (Kilcullen, 2009: 5–38). The modern technologies and proliferation of weapons have also enabled insurgent groups to create situations of "disruptive dominance," which are enormously disproportionate to their actual strength or support base and increased influence of sub-state actors. The Islamic State insurgents and the al-Qaeda possess extraordinary command of latest media technologies and use social media sites for spreading their messages of jihad and wide publicity of brutal terror tactics for recruitment, propaganda, and "networking" (Heickero, 2014). According to the Washington-based U.S. Institute of Peace (USIP), the terrorist network controlled more than 5,000 websites in 2006 and every year hundreds of new sites are added (Weimann, 2006). It is believed that there are more than 4,500 sites that have helped al-Qaeda to develop into a truly global ideological movement (Atwan, 2006).

This discussion highlights the complex nature of contemporary conflicts, which involve multiple actors, motives, and conflict theaters spread across the globe and in the "virtual world." Therefore, it is vitally important that a proactive comprehensive strategy is evolved by the governments based on an accurate assessment of the existing and emerging insurgent challenges and a more nuanced understanding of modern communication technologies and realities governing these conflicts. The following discussion analyzes various approaches to COIN and their implications for the governments and the insurgents.

Counterinsurgency

The renewal of interest in COIN in recent years has been attributed to predicament of the U.S. and its allies in Iraq and Afghanistan, leading to re-evaluation of strategies to fight irregular conflicts, particularly insurgencies. It has been rightly observed that the state response to insurgencies is the most crucial variable in deciding the course of the conflict (O'Neill, 1990: 125), and also that the nature of state response depends to a large extent on the nature of that state as "counterinsurgency mirrors the state" (Kilcullen, 2010: 10). In response to widespread insurgency, the state may choose from several policy options: it may seek to subdue the insurgents militarily; capitulate and seek to appease insurgents by offering concessions; or address the "root causes" of insurgency and explore non-military options also for political resolution of the problem (Wilkinson, 2001). While totalitarian states are relatively unencumbered by restraints on their power to crush insurgencies, democratic countries refrain from deploying the full range of coercive resources at their disposal as they operate under numerous legal, constitutional, and moral constraints (Inbar, 2003: viii–ix). Thus, in response to a long-term insurgency, liberal democracies may choose to resolve the problem by coming to some sort of accommodation with insurgent groups, usually in the form of power-sharing agreements. However, it has also been argued that group grievances may not matter much as even 500–1,000 men under right conditions can make for a long-running, destructive war, and what matters is the capability and reach of police and military to distinguish active rebels from non-combatants in rural areas (Fearon and Laitin, 2003).

A more critical view of Western COIN holds that it takes a bureaucratic and managerial view of revolutionary movements and is largely concerned with devising strategy and tactics to nullify military advantages of guerrillas; fails to acknowledge the illegitimacy of incumbent regimes; and despite rhetoric of "winning hearts and minds" utterly fails to win over people's allegiance and gain legitimacy (Ahmad, 2006). Apparently, there is no standard bundle of COIN practices, and the word "counterinsurgency" may mean completely different things in different contexts. In brief, COIN is "whatever governments do to defeat rebellions" (Kilcullen, 2010: 2).

Different Approaches to COIN

The Military Approach

In literature, there are two distinct approaches to COIN— "annihilating versus turning the loyalty of the people" (Nagl, 2002: 26). While the former approach treats unconventional war much like a conventional war and focuses on the military defeat of the guerrilla fighters by overwhelming power, the latter seeks to divide the people from the insurgents and win popular support for counterinsurgents. However, the asymmetric nature of conflict in insurgencies poses severe difficulties for militaries of great powers that exhibit a rigid adherence to big-war paradigm as the training and orientation of the army predispose it to use overwhelming force and the military frequently ends up alienating the very population it seeks to protect (Toft, 2001).

Rich and Stubbs (1997: 7–8) while reviewing the use of military for COIN in the Third World after World War II have noted that the use of military to dissuade people from supporting guerrillas usually backfires as military tend to use excessive and indiscriminate force in dealing with public, leading to alienation among large sections of people that swells the ranks of guerrillas and their sympathizers. However, a review of some recent operations in Iraq and Afghanistan would indicate that major powers seem habituated to use overwhelming power and suffer unintended consequences. The use of overwhelming firepower during the November 2004 "Operation Phantom Fury" in Fallujah, Iraq reignited the insurgency. Furthermore, the U.S. policy of pre-emptive strikes and "direct intervention" in various Muslim countries has tended to alienate large sections of Muslims worldwide, created a crisis of confidence among Western allies in the Muslim world, and boosted al-Qaeda recruitment and support (Kilcullen, 2009: 20). Similarly, an exclusive focus on big war paradigm, the scorched earth method, and "migratory genocide" badly hurt the Soviet efforts in Afghanistan (Cassidy, 2008).

Notwithstanding these setbacks suffered by major powers from use of overwhelming force, there is no denying that force does have an obvious and crucial role in COIN, especially in the initial phases, as some insurgents have to be killed and suitable conditions created in the conflict zone. In fact, it has been rightly argued that "there is no oppositional dyad: politics versus use of force" and force is one of the many options available within the political spectrum (Sahni, 2010a). But the utility of military force is circumscribed and it can have mostly a tactical role to play in contemporary insurgencies, guided by the overall strategic considerations of the campaign (Duyvesteyn, 2008). In line with this thinking, the new U.S. doctrine marks a significant dilution in the emphasis on use of force and recognizes that the military operations must be guided by the overall strategy and tightly integrated with all other instruments of national power for success.

But there is some skepticism whether in the absence of explicit government endorsement of this doctrine and the prevailing military culture, it would be possible to effect changes on the ground by the U.S. forces (CFM, 2007: xxxiv–xxxv; Sewall, 2007). This skepticism gains strength from the fact that the U.S. budgetary and other resource allocations continue to favor the creation of huge military capabilities, thus hampering capacities for stabilization and reconstruction required for COIN.

The Political Approach

Making a radical departure from the military approach, the political or "comprehensive" approach organizes COIN around "people-centric" policies instead of conventional "enemy-centric" policies and recognizes that safety, security and support of the masses is crucial for the success of COIN. The cardinal principle of this approach is the recognition that the primary threat posed by all insurgencies is political rather than military. Insurgencies are directed to undermine the legitimacy and credibility of the state and, therefore, the state response should also focus on the political resolution of the issues rather than physical annihilation of the enemy (Pimlott, 1988: 19–20).

This approach is best represented by the British theory and practice which has been greatly influenced by their colonial campaigns in Malaya, Cyprus and Kenya, and finds eloquent expression in works of Galula (1964), Thompson (1967), and Kitson (1971). Robert Thompson, who had extensive experience in Malaya and South Vietnam, was among the most ardent advocates of this nuanced approach. In his classic, *Defeating Communist Insurgency,* he laid down five basic principles, which predominantly address the political rather than military aspects of the conflict:

Basic Principles of COIN

1. The government must have a clear political aim;
2. The government must function in accordance with the law;
3. The government must have an overall plan;
4. The government must give priority to defeating the political subversion, not the guerrillas;
5. In the guerrilla phase of insurgency, a government must secure its base areas first.

(Thompson, 1967: 50–57)

In consonance with this political approach, some commentators have recommended that in Iraq and Afghanistan conflicts, the U.S. would be well advised to follow a comprehensive approach that builds government effectiveness and legitimacy, integrates civil and military efforts and a population-centric security policy founded on local community partnerships, self-defending populations, and small-unit operations that keep the enemy off-balance (Kilcullen, 2009: 265). Clearly, a grand strategy that addresses the root causes of the problem that have given rise to insurgencies in Iraq and other countries is essential to ensure lasting peace and victory (Bowman, 2007: 48–51). R. Scott Moore (2007) has presented a historically grounded model of successful COIN based on his analysis of over 60 COIN campaigns, which resonates with our analysis of Tripura's COIN campaign. According to this model, the ultimate goal of successful COIN is lasting stability, which is provided by rebuilding social, political, and economic structures to peacefully address issues that may continue to arise, and transforming beliefs that gave rise to insurgency so that hatred and distrust no longer dominates. Lasting stability is achieved, over time, by sustained actions that neutralize insurgent capabilities through targeted actions, provide basic needs of civil population on daily basis, and address the underlying causes of insurgency (Moore, 2007).

Another significant aspect of the political approach is the strengthening of indigenous police and armed forces, which not only augments COIN force levels, but also diminishes the enemy's recruiting base and builds partnerships with local communities. This was an important objective of the British approach and has been recognized as an important principle of COIN policy by the American and other allied forces. In Malaya, the British hugely expanded the local police force; weeded out the corrupt and incompetent personnel; reformed and retrained the entire police force in investigation, intelligence, and leadership; and progressively turned the war over to the Malayans for successful COIN operations. In a similar vein, Beers (2007: 75–85) has also argued in favor of recruiting and training large number of locals as law enforcement personnel in Iraq and Afghanistan to enhance security, reduce insurgents' recruitment base, and put local communities on the side of counterinsurgents.

However, many observers have noted that frequently the British have departed from their professed policy of the minimum use of force and adopted extremely brutal measures to suppress local rebellions, for example, in South Africa and Kenya (Beckett, 1988: 10–11; Gray 2008; Sewall, 2007: xxxiv). The tactics adopted by both the British and Americans in their COIN campaigns abroad are ill-suited for resolving problems connected with indigenous ethnic insurgencies in the developing world (Jafa, 2001: 222). In his incisive analysis of the Western COIN concepts and campaigns in *Counterinsurgency* (1971), Eqbal Ahmad has shown how the U.S. policies led to massive destruction in Vietnam, Latin America and several other countries due to their failure to acknowledge "the illegitimacy of incumbents, the finality of broken political and social links, and the forging of new ones" (Ahmad, 2006: 47). He has argued that Western COIN concepts are not suitable for developing countries because these are

> ... ultimately concerned with order more than participation, control more than consent of the governed, obedience more than title to authority, stability more than change. To them, the people are objects of policy, a means rather than an end, a manipulable, malleable mass whose behaviour towards the government is ultimately more important than their feelings (Ahmad, 2006: 59).

It is also seen that in striking contrast to their operations in the Third World, developed countries have generally adopted far more accommodative mechanisms in dealing with their own citizens. In this context, the use of referendum for deciding the issue of secession by Scotland in the United Kingdom in 2014 is an apt example of this accommodative approach. Apparently, there are significant differences in governments' approach to "domestic" COIN and "expeditionary" or third-country COIN (Kilcullen, 2010: 11).

As regards India, the Indian government has generally avoided use of air strafing or heavy artillery against the rebel groups and its army doctrine emphasizes low-profile and people-friendly operations rather than high-intensity operations related only to body and weapon counts. The Indian approach to COIN emphasizes a highly flexible policy marked by a deliberate restraint in the use of power, and seeks to reintegrate "misguided" citizens into the national mainstream through various means including granting political autonomy, amnesty, signing of accords, ceasefires, and suspension of hostilities. The space for accommodation, resource transfer, and power-sharing has prevented insurgent groups from launching desperate "do-or-die" offensives and helped the Indian state to manage insurgent movements by co-opting insurgent leadership to resolve insurgencies (Bhaumik, 2009: xv). Research conducted by Mason (1996) also suggests that accommodative and non-coercive COIN strategies are more effective in enlisting popular support for government, and total reliance on firepower is usually counterproductive, given the calculus of fear by which non-elites choose between regimes and rebels. From this perspective, introduction of enlightened political and socio-economic reforms designed to address popular concerns and grievances by successive governments appears to be the best antidote against large-scale violent conflicts in liberal democracies (Wilkinson, 2003: 79).

Conclusion

Religious extremism, ethnic intolerance, acute socioeconomic inequities, and rapid urbanization have given birth to fanatical movements in many parts of the world demanding radical political and social change. The problems for counterinsurgents have been compounded by the rapid proliferation of modern weapons and diffusion of modern telecommunication and warfare technologies which enable diverse militant groups to network effectively across widely separated conflict theaters and mobilize popular support worldwide.

In this scenario, conventional responses have limited applicability, necessitating a fresh appraisal of conventional doctrine and discovery of new paradigms of COIN. In recent years, a vast literature concerning "best practices" in COIN has emerged (Cassidy, 2004, 2006, 2008; Long, 2006; Kilcullen 2009) which can be useful if it is kept in mind that not all insurgencies are alike and "flawed causal beliefs can engender flawed policies, and flawed policies can obviously lead to failed COIN" (Greenhill and Staniland, 2007). The developing countries also need to be aware that most COIN ideologies have been developed by Western nations in response to revolutions occurring in the non-Western world. Therefore, these policies should not be mechanically manufactured or imported, but adapted to local culture and values. Moreover, as the "best practices" COIN literature is almost always produced by the wealthy and strong nations, it fails to recognize the defects of "basic institutional weakness, state structure, and excessive influence by elite" in middle-power nations such as India (Haines, 2009).These constraints severely limit the application of proposed strategies in developing world. Therefore, each country needs to work out its own specific measures to counter a particular insurgency, and be alert to make necessary changes quickly to effectively respond to insurgents' evolving strategy and tactics.

In the Indian context, the success of COIN operations in three widely dissimilar theaters in Punjab, Andhra Pradesh, and Tripura reinforces the importance of generating local COIN strategies for indigenous insurgencies and terrorism. The operational strategy of these campaigns was mounted within the templates of "police-primacy, intelligence, and police-led operations" (Sahni, 2010a) instead of the more usual practice of army-led operations in the country. A close study of these successful campaigns suggests that the paradigm of an "emergency responses" approach to terrorism and internal security threats must be rejected; and a tremendous effort of robust capacity-building has to precede any attempts to deal effectively and proactively with existing and emerging challenges (Sahni, 2009b). It is also a fact that India's COIN experience has not been uniformly successful and that the army has not always strictly adhered to its official doctrine as it has been sometimes accused of adopting extremely harsh methods in COIN operations in Mizoram, Manipur, Nagaland, Punjab, and Kashmir. Moreover, effectiveness of India's COIN policy has been frequently compromised by institutional weaknesses, rampant corruption, partisan politics, and lack of strategic vision as discussed in detail in Chapter 3.

3

India's Counterinsurgencies:
A General Overview

Introduction

In the twenty-first century, impressive economic growth coupled with substantial political and military power has already established India as a rising global power (Mohan, 2006). Most contemporary assessments suggest that India would be the fifth largest economy in the world sometime during the first half of this century, and, in fact, a study by the Central Intelligence Agency estimated that India is projected to possess the fourth most capable concentration of power by 2015 after the U.S., the European Union, and China (Tellis, 2005: 29–30).[1] Paradoxically, even as its power and clout have continued to rise in the international arena, the country's internal security scenario has progressively worsened since independence as localized insurgencies in the past have been replaced with chronic separatist, ethnic, and communal violence that have spread to all corners of the country. Comparatively speaking, in recent decades, India has suffered hugely from domestic terrorism, insurgent movements, and widespread political violence. According to the *Global*

---

[1] The study ranks countries by composite measures of national power, that is, weighted combinations of gross domestic product, defence spending, population, and technology growth.

Terrorism Index 2014, that measures the impact of terrorism on individual countries based on a 5-year weighted average.[2] India globally ranked sixth with a score of 7.77, behind only Iraq (12), Afghanistan (9.39), Pakistan (9.37), Nigeria (8.58), and Syria (8.12) and ahead of Bangladesh, Libya, Somalia, and Yemen.

According to an assessment in 2013, 205 districts of the country's 640 districts were affected by varying degrees of chronic subversive, insurgent, and terrorist activities, including 120 districts affected by the Maoist violence, 65 districts in northeast states, and 20 districts in Jammu and Kashmir (SATP 2). The magnitude of the violence can be gauged from the fact that from 1994 till 2008, annual civilian fatalities in terrorist/ insurgent violence in the country have been well over 1,000, and the number of security personnel killed averaged over 450 every year from 1994 to 2014 (SATP 3). This is an extraordinarily high casualty rate of security personnel during peacetime by any standards, and comparable to the annual average of 480 casualties suffered by coalition forces in Iraq from 2003 to 2012, and much higher than the annual average of 270 casualties suffered by the Coalition forces in Afghanistan between 2001 and 2012.[3]

In this context, Prakash Singh (2012), a former director general of paramilitary Border Security Force (BSF), who also served as the Police Chief of Assam and Uttar Pradesh, has noted that since independence, India has faced a new major security threat every decade, and its security problems have continued to multiply instead of getting resolved, and right now the nation faces serious threat from international terrorism, Maoist insurgency, terrorist/ insurgent violence in Jammu and Kashmir and northeast, and ethnic and communal violence in several states all over the country. These problems have been further compounded by a fresh wave of agitations in many parts of the country by various ethnic groups demanding homelands resulting from central government's recent decision to create a new "Telangana" state by dividing Andhra

---

[2] The indicator weights used for calculating country scores in a given year are: total numbers of fatalities (weight 3), sum of property damage measures (2), total number of incidents (1), and total number of injuries (0.5).

[3] For coalition forces casualties in Afghanistan, see http://icasualties.org/oef/ accessed on July 21, 2013.

Pradesh. Internationally, India is perceived as a "soft" state, lacking an unambiguous counter-terrorism policy despite escalating violence by terrorist groups (Subramaniam, 2012). Furthermore, there are several potentially disruptive possibilities in India's sociopolitical profile and inadequate appreciation of multiple security threats that find their epicenters in the environment—demography, health, ecology, economics, culture, and society (Ghosh, 2006a). The Indian media and elite tend to focus on issues and concerns of privileged sections of society, ignoring the parlous state of the domestic realm (Dreze and Sen, 2013). An apparent lack of governance, or misgovernance, characterized by corruption, lack of accountability, policy paralysis, and a pervasive sense of insecurity has frustrated large sections of society (Bajpai and Pant, 2013: 6). *India Today,* a popular national news magazine put "The Angry Indian" on its cover as the newsmaker of 2012 (*India Today,* 2013). The popular disenchantment with the ruling United Progressive Alliance (UPA) government manifested itself in sweeping victory of the Bharatiya Janata Party (BJP) led by the Prime Minister Narendra Modi in 2014 General Elections and the rout of the Congress-I. Since then, the pervasive pessimism has been replaced somewhat by a general optimism, and people do hope that the country will register higher growth and make all-round progress under the new dispensation ("Mood of the Nation" Poll 2014, *India Today Group*). However, the harsh reality remains that there has been no fundamental change in the nature of politics or politicians at the ground level. The public representatives at both federal and state levels are perceived as selfish and solely concerned with plundering national resources and amassing personal wealth with impunity, flouting all norms of legality and governance (Mahajan, g *files* 2012). According to this report, India's 543 MPs had collective assets worth ₹30,000 million with over 60 percent of them being millionaires and the assets of 304 MPs who re-contested in 2009 grew 300 percent in five years; proof that it pays to be in office. These reports also gain credence from the fact that over one-third of the MPs and Members of Legislative Assemblies (MLAs) were reported to have criminal cases against them (*The Times of India*, 2012).[4] Meanwhile, there have been several instances of physical assaults and transfer/suspension of upright IAS/IPS officers in many states recently for opposing vested interests (*The Asian Age*, 2013). All these developments raise serious doubts about the *bona fides* of political rulers in the country, and may potentially lead to "popular uprisings" as triggered by legitimacy deficit in several countries across North Africa in recent years (Omotola, 2012). Therefore, it has been rightly observed that notwithstanding some reduction in terrorist/ insurgent violence in the country recently, India's vulnerabilities have not diminished as India's capabilities remain seriously deficient to effectively tackle external and internal threats (Bajpai and Pant, 2013a: 12).

This chapter addresses two main issues: (a) Why has India as a nation failed to formulate a coherent CI–CT policy despite having a wide experience of such political violence over the past more than six decades? (b) What are the roles of the military, paramilitary, and police in COIN? Accordingly, this chapter has been divided into three sections. The first section provides a brief overview of some major insurgencies, while the second section deals with the factors inhibiting a coherent response to the insurgent and terrorist violence. The concluding section examines the roles of police, paramilitary, and the army in combating insurgencies, and the implications of increasing trend of militarization of police and growth of paramilitary forces to combat insurgencies. The intensity and spread of insurgent violence in the country has been facilitated by: lack of a coherent (CT–CI) strategy; crippling deficiencies in governance, administrative, and law-enforcement capacities, a range of demographic factors creating vast opportunities for extremist mobilization; and an institutional failure to learn from the past failures or successes. It would be argued that over-reliance on federal military and paramilitary forces in internal security duties in the country is a consequence of persistent neglect by the state

---

[4] According to this news item, 1,450 MPs and MLAs have declared criminal cases pending against them in sworn affidavits filed with the Election Commission in recent elections. Furthermore, of these tainted elected representatives, 641 MPs and MLAs have serious criminal cases, such as rape, murder, attempt to murder, kidnapping, robbery, and extortion against them.

governments in building their own core capacities for effective response, and not indicative of any inherent weaknesses in police.

Causes of Insurgency and Modus Operandi of Indian Insurgent Groups

In the post-World War II period, several Asian countries have been ravaged by intense and protracted conflicts that have come in the form of civil wars, armed insurgencies, revolutions, and coups d'état, with far-reaching domestic and international consequences. The civil war in Pakistan led to the breakup of that country in 1971; political uprisings in Thailand (1973 and 1991), the Philippines (1986), South Korea (1986), Taiwan (1991), Bangladesh (1991), and Indonesia (1998) resulted in dramatic political change in these countries; separatist struggles pose significant challenge in India, China, Indonesia, and Burma; and Pakistan, Indonesia, and Bangladesh are threatened by radical Islam. These conflicts have claimed millions of lives of combatants and non-combatants, forcibly displaced tens of millions, and caused indirect deaths due to disease and malnutrition. The causes of internal conflicts in these countries range from contestations over political legitimacy, national identity, state building, and distributive justice that are often interconnected. Some observers have viewed class struggle or economic inequality as the main driver of social conflict in industrial or semi-industrial societies (Dahrendorf, 1959; Sen, 1973), while others have contended that civil conflicts frequently represent an "ethnic backlash" generated by intense resentment among ethnic minorities over the postcolonial states' desire to produce a pulverized and uniform national identity (Ganguly, 2012).

As noted earlier, a study by Cederman et al. (2010) suggests that in the post-World War II era quest for political power rather than ethnic or religious diversity have played a more important part in the dynamics leading to the outbreak of civil wars in roughly half of the conflicts. Using India as an illustration, Lacina (2005) has argued that low-intensity armed conflicts can be best understood as political lobbying by the insurgent groups. In a country like India, insurgent groups often use low-grade violence to articulate political demands that resonate with their constituents as they are aware that democratic societies frequently eschew use of coercive powers and are willing to make political concessions to preserve peace. There is also considerable evidence suggesting that onset of large-scale ethnic violence is a direct result of political elites' efforts to retain or grab power (Fearon and Laitin, 2000). This analysis certainly applies to many insurgencies in India. While the Naxalites have clearly articulated their aim to seize political power through protracted armed struggle (Ahluwalia, 2012),[5] it would be seen that tussle for political power or dominance has been a significant contributory factor in many other conflicts also.

Punjab

Table 3.1:

Trends of Terrorist Violence in Punjab (1983–1993)

Years	Civilians	SF Personnel	Terrorist	Total
1983	75	20	13	1,08
1984	359	20	77	456
1985	63	8	2	73
1986	520	38	78	636
1987	910	95	328	1,333
1988	1,949	110	373	2,432
1989	1,168	201	703	2,072
1990	2,467	476	1,320	4,263
1991	2,591	497	2,177	5,265
1992	1,518	252	2,113	3,883
1993	48	25	798	871
Total	11,668	1,742	7,982	21,392

Source: South Asia Terrorism Portal/SATP1.

---

[5] The Maoist roadmap for revolution is found in an elaborate document "Strategy and Tactics of the Indian Revolution" which was conceived by the joint central committees of the People's War Group (PWG) and the Maoist Communist Center of India (MCCI) prior to their merger in 2004 (Ahluwalia, 2012).

Since 1994, there has been a sharp reduction in terrorist violence, and during the two decades from 1994 to 2014, there have been only 89 civilian casualties and four SF casualties as per data maintained by SATP. The recent terrorist attack on July 27, 2015 on a police station in Gurdaspur district of Punjab in which four policemen and three civilians were killed is suspected to be carried out by Pakistan-based terrorist outfits and has nothing to do with the imaginary return of Sikh militancy in Punjab.

The Sikh separatist movement started in the early 1980s, peaked in the decade between 1984 and 1993 and was decisively defeated by resolute police action by the mid-1990s (Table 3.1). According to K.P.S. Gill (1997), this movement was a rebellion of a privileged quasi-feudal caste-based orthodoxy that saw its privileges shrinking and perceived a threat to its various political and economic interests, rather than any government repression.[6] Most of the prominent leaders in this agitation were prosperous rural Jat Sikh landlords who hailed from the Malwa region in Punjab.[7] It is also a fact that the bitter struggle for power between the two major political parties, that is, Congress and Akali Dal, rather than Sikh nationalism, played a major role in fueling insurgency in the late 1970s. In this tussle for political power both these parties resorted to unscrupulous politics, competitive communalism, and political brinkmanship, culminating in a spiral of terrorist violence that consumed over 20,000 lives before it was finally crushed in early 1990s. The Akali Dal exploited the long-standing fears of Sikhs about threats to Sikh identity and their resentment against government policies and launched agitations to press for various territorial, economic, and religious

---

[6] The underlying tensions of this Akali Dal agitation were: The Akali Dal's frustration at being out of power, Jat Sikhs' feelings of receiving inadequate remuneration for their farm output, the frustration caused by petering out of the Green Revolution, the fear of both the Sikh fundamentalists and apprehensions of being pushed into a minority status within Punjab by immigration of Hindu migrant laborers and emigration of Sikhs to foreign countries (Singh, 1984: 42–47).

[7] The most prominent leaders of Akali Dal and SGPC, such as Prakash Singh Badal, Gurucharan Singh Tohra, Sant Harcharan Singh Longowal, and Sant Jarnail Singh Bhindranwale, were all Jat Sikhs hailing from Malwa region (Singh, 1984: 42–47). Malwa is the region of Punjab that lies south of the Sutlej river.

demands.[8] In response, the Congress also attempted to divide the Sikh community on caste and class lines and created a Sikh Frankenstein in the form of Sant Jarnail Singh Bhindranwale, who unleashed a reign of terror in Punjab from the hallowed precincts of the Golden Temple. The Khalistan movement also gathered momentum due to marginalization of political moderate leaders by the Center's dismissal of the Akali Dal governments and direct attempts by some Congress leaders at the center to control the political affairs in Punjab (Marwah, 2009: 89–95); crude manner of police search of all Sikh passengers by Haryana police to stop terrorists or their associates from reaching Delhi during the Asian Games (1982); the army's disastrous Operation Blue Star that massively damaged the Golden Temple in an attempt to evict and neutralize Bhindranwale and other terrorists, followed by the army's Operation Woodrose launched to mop up surviving terrorists and clear all religious places of terrorists across Punjab (1984); and the gruesome anti-Sikh riots that followed the assassination of Prime Minister Indira Gandhi by her Sikh security guards in Delhi, Punjab, and many other states. All these events infuriated the Sikh masses, particularly the Sikh youth, who became more vulnerable to extremist propaganda and joined terrorists to avenge real and perceived injustices. The Pakistan ISI exploited this opportunity by providing arms, explosives, training, and sanctuaries to Sikh extremists who now began talking of secession and forming of an independent Sikh state. It is also a fact that Punjab police was ill-prepared to handle a full-blown insurgency in the early 1970s, and this also contributed to the growth of insurgency. The police weaknesses were further compounded by lack of an unambiguous anti-terrorist policy and political brinkmanship by various parties at the center and state, leading to frequent release of large number of hardcore terrorists who resumed their murderous terrorist activities as soon as they were released. Soon after coming to power in 1985, the Akali Dal government led by Barnala ordered

---

[8] After independence, the Union government created many new states along linguistic and ethnic lines through reorganization of states. However, the Sikhs had to wait till 1966 for creation of a Punjabi-speaking state within the Union, and even this did not guarantee the Akali Dal political power in the state as they had to cobble coalitions to form government.

release of over 2,000 extremists *en masse,* while 40 high-profile terrorists—"the Jodhpur Detenues"—were released as part of another compromise with the terrorists, leading to a sharp spike in civilian and police casualties.

As regards their tactics, between 1978 and 1988, Sikh terrorists extensively used Sikh *gurudwaras* (Sikh shrines) for taking shelter, storing weapons, gaining access to congregations and the Sikh youth, for mobilization and recruitment purposes, and control of substantial human, material, and financial resources (Fair, 2009: 112). The *gurudwaras* also helped terrorists in acquiring a certain religious legitimacy as historically, these have been the rallying places for Sikh martial campaigns. However, the meticulously planned and executed Operation Black Thunder (April 1988) led to apprehension of many hardcore terrorists and exposed their nefarious activities within sacred precincts of the Golden temple, leading to public disillusionment and loss of popular support to extremist groups. Consequently, the Sikh terrorists now increasingly resorted to indiscriminate killings through use of remote-controlled IEDs and sophisticated Kalashnikov assault rifles (the AK-47) and depended more on criminal elements and foreign support for survival. The modus operandi of the terrorists included moving around in towns and countryside on motorcycles and tractors (Marwah, 2009: 93), retaliatory targeted killing of large number of police personnel and their family members after liquidation of any major terrorist leader to demoralize security forces,[9] attacks on "soft targets" such as government officials, migrant industrial workers, elected political representatives, and party workers who defied their diktats to boycott elections and indiscriminate killing of civilians, particularly Hindus, to fan communal violence. Furthermore, terrorists coerced common people to paralyze administration through violent demonstrations against senior police officers and observance of strikes and blockade of roads and railway tracks, and mobilization of massive crowds

---

[9] For example, following the death of Sukhdev Singh Babbar, Chief of the Babbar Khalsa International (BKI) in an encounter with police on August 9, 1992, terrorists killed 37 policemen and another 63 family members of policemen in retaliation during that month.

through hundreds of trucks and trolleys at the "martyrdom" ceremonies of slain terrorists.

The Punjab campaign saw gradual transformation of an initially weak, demoralized, and ill-prepared local police into a highly effective force suitably reoriented, motivated, trained (or retrained), and equipped for its new CI role. The Punjab police succeeded in neutralizing terrorists' threats by devising suitable counter measures in real time, and launching well-coordinated and intelligence-led operations that were supported by army and other security forces. The insurgency was crushed when state police was given a clear mandate by the political leadership to launch offensive operations and provided requisite resources for this purpose. The inspirational leadership of Police Chief K.P.S. Gill was crucial in this effort and he succeeded in motivating his junior colleagues and constabulary to take the fight to terrorists and defeat them despite heavy odds (Chima, 2014: 270–286).

Kashmir

The insurgency in Kashmir developed in the mid-1980s that witnessed intense political turmoil and tussle for power between the National Conference, the dominant political party in the state, and the Congress government at the center following the death of Sheikh Abdullah, the then Chief Minister in 1982. The clumsy dismissal of two state governments in 1984 and 1986 further charged the political atmosphere.[10] This was also a period of simmering discontent and anger among large sections of public, particularly youth, due to rampant corruption, nepotism, high levels of unemployment, and other economic and political failures of the government (Patankar, 2009: 67). However, the immediate trigger for insurgency in Kashmir was provided by the flawed state elections of 1987, which were commonly perceived to be rigged by the National Conference and Indian National Congress alliance

---

[10] The government of Farooq Abdullah (son of Sheikh Abdullah) was dismissed in 1984, and the successor Ghulam Mohammad Shah government was dismissed in 1986.

to defeat the local conglomeration of political parties represented by Muslim United Front, leading to strikes, protests, and sporadic terrorist violence (Ganguly, 2009: 79). In 1988, the Jammu and Kashmir Liberation Front (JKLF) began staging attacks on government officials, offices, and other public institutions with a view to achieve independence for Kashmir, including the parts occupied by Pakistan. As the local police was unable to handle the situation, paramilitary Central Reserve Police Force (CRPF) and BSF were deployed to quell the insurgency. However, these forces were not properly oriented or trained for COIN and their lack of cultural sensitivity, poor knowledge of local customs, and harsh methods further worsened the situation. The release of five JKLF activists in Indian custody to secure the release of Rubiya Sayeed, the daughter of Union Minister for Home Affairs, Mufti Mohammed Sayeed, kidnapped by JKLF in December 1989 also emboldened the insurgents. It is also a fact that initially the central government failed to gauge the depth of people's anger and frustration and treated it as a routine law and order problem. The harsh methods of Governor Jagmohan Malhotra (1984–1989), who was appointed to deal with the crisis, further infuriated the people who now resorted to an armed struggle as all other avenues of civil protest were blocked.

Over the years, insurgency in Kashmir has endured due to extensive support of Pakistan to separatist political and terrorist outfits, and mutated into protracted proxy war and into an important struggle for the global *Jihadi* movement (Patankar, 2009: 77–78). The insurgent tactics in Kashmir have included mass demonstrations by frenzied mobs led by separatist leaders, targeted attacks against security forces and massacres of minority Hindu and Sikh community leading to their exodus from the valley, abduction of high-profile Indians and foreign tourists, siege of holy shrines such as Hazratbal (1993) and Charar-e-Sharif (1995), cross-border infiltration and employment of foreign mercenaries and *Jihadi* elements. The main terrorist groups in Kashmir are Hizb-ul-Mujahideen (militant wing of the Islamic organization Jamat-e-Islami), Harkat-ul-Ansar, and Lashkar-e-Taiba.

Table 3.2:

Trends of Terrorist Violence in Jammu and Kashmir (2005–2014)

Years	Incidents	SFs Killed	Civilians Killed	Terrorists Killed
2005	1,990	189	557	917
2006	1,667	151	389	591
2007	1,092	110	158	472
2008	708	75	91	339
2009	499	78	71	239
2010	488	69	47	232
2011	340	33	31	100
2012	220	38	11	50
2013	170	53	15	67
2014	222	47	28	110

Source: MHA, *Annual Reports*, 2013–2014: 6 and 2014–2015: 5.

According to an estimate, since its inception, the insurgency in Kashmir has claimed 43,765 casualties including 14,713 civilians, 6,163 security personnel, and 22,889 terrorists (till June 14, 2015: SATP 4). It is also seen that the decline in extremist violence since 2008 (see Table 3.2) has been accompanied by a dramatic increase in the number of massive street protests, cut-throat electoral competition, and assertion by indigenous intellectuals writing against the *status quo*, reflecting a broader shift in the Kashmiri resistance from militant violence to "contentious politics" (Staniland, 2013). D. Suba Chandran, Director, Institute of Peace and Conflict Studies, New Delhi, during his extensive travels in Kashmir observed that common people were more concerned with everyday problems and frustrated by corruption and bad governance. For a majority of them the issues of employment, electricity, water, and freedom from harassment by security forces take precedence over demand for independence (Chandran, 2012).

India's COIN strategy in Kashmir has been marked by government's commitment to political resolution of insurgency, use of steady and substantial force against insurgents, holding of largely free and fair elections to devolve power to local authorities. The Assembly elections in 2002 and 2008, which returned the People's Democratic Republic (PDP) and National Conference respectively to power have been generally perceived to be free from central government's interference and representative of popular mandate (Mahadevan, 2009). The Assembly elections in 2014 leading to formation of a coalition government of BJP and PDP have further strengthened the democratic process and the ability of this government to deliver good governance and address local grievances satisfactorily would have a tremendous bearing on the resolution of the political problem. At the tactical level, the main features have been (a) creation of a special force for COIN, that is, the Rashtriya Rifles; (b) deployment of forces in a COIN grid; (c) use of *ikhwans* or captured militants; (d) deployment of road-opening parties; and (e) the "covert apprehension technique" (Ganguly, 2009: 83). All these strategic and tactical measures have succeeded in substantially containing the insurgency; however, the situation remains challenging in the foreseeable future due to involvement of Pakistan and global *Jihadi* groups.

Naxalism/Left Wing Extremism/Maoist Violence

The origins of Naxalite movement are commonly traced back to an incident of police firing into a crowd on May 25, 1967 in a remote village called Naxalbari in the Darjeeling district of West Bengal, which was the site of nascent agrarian revolution sponsored by the Communist Party of India (Marxist) (CPI [M]). Since then, this movement has traversed and spread through the tribal and backward areas of many states of central and eastern India, its class war has turned into caste war in some cases, and in many areas the movement has been criminalized and sustained by extortion, sale of illicit drugs and looting of security camps and police stations (*Report of the Commission on Center-State Relations*, Volume V, 2010: 70). At present, the worst affected states are Chhattisgarh,

Jharkhand, Odisha, and Bihar, while the Maoist problem also exists in certain pockets of Maharashtra, Madhya Pradesh, Andhra Pradesh, and Telangana (see Table 3.3). The estimates of CPI (Maoist) armed cadres in the country vary from 10,000 to 20,000, with many more supporters and sympathizers (Mazumdar, 2013). The merger of the People's War Group and the Maoist Communist Center of India in 2004 to form a unified entity called the CPI (Maoist) has made the Naxalite challenge even more formidable, and during the last decade alone, the Maoist violence has claimed 2,775 civilians and 1,764 security personnel, while security forces have killed 2,221 Maoist insurgents (till June 14, 2015, SATP 5). The central government has adopted a multi-pronged strategy and identified 106 districts in 9 states for special and focused attention to address security; development and governance deficits in these Left Wing Extremism (LWE)-affected areas (MHA, *Annual Report*, 2013–2014).

The social base of Maoist movement consists overwhelmingly of the landless and small peasants with marginal landholdings, mostly from the lower and intermediate castes (Bhatia, 2005: 1536–1549). The Maoist ideology and propaganda has resonated with these marginalized sections of population as post-independence they have continued to suffer persistent economic and political discrimination, social indignities, and sexual exploitation at the hands of feudal landlords (Verma, 2014: 296–98). The government's failure to establish credible institutions of local governance and enforce rule of law, lack of development, abysmal levels of poverty, and pervasive corruption and collusion between bureaucrats-contractors-politicians to extract rich mineral and other resources in the vast rural hinterland has further reinforced popular perceptions of neglect and exploitation. Finally, lack of firm political resolve and consensus, and weak policing in most states has hampered evolution of common political strategy and execution of well-coordinated anti-Maoist operations across states.

Table 3.3:

State-wise Details of Naxal Violence (2009–2014)

State	2009		2010		2011		2012		2013		2014	
	Incidents	Deaths	Incidents	Deaths	Incidents	Deaths	Incidents	Deaths	Incidents	Deaths	Incidents	Deaths
Andhra Pradesh	66	18	100	24	54	9	67	13	36	11	18	4
Bihar	232	72	307	97	316	63	166	44	177	69	163	32
Chhattisgarh	529	290	625	343	465	204	370	109	355	111	328	111
Jharkhand	742	208	501	157	517	182	480	163	387	152	384	103
Madhya Pradesh	1	0	7	1	8	0	11	0	1	0	3	0
Maharashtra	154	93	94	45	109	54	134	41	71	19	70	28
Odisha	266	67	218	79	192	53	171	45	101	35	103	26
Uttar Pradesh	8	2	6	1	1	0	2	0	0	0	0	0
West Bengal	255	158	350	258	92	45	6	0	1	0	0	0
Telengana										4	14	5
Others	5	0	5	0	6	1	8	0	7	0	7	0
Total	2,258	908	2,213	1,005	1,760	611	1,415	415	1,136	397	1,090	309

Source: MHA, Annual Report, 2014–2015: 20.

At the ideological and strategic level, their operations have been influenced by Mao's policy of guerrilla warfare with a focus on rural areas to create "guerrilla zones" and then eventually transform them into "liberated zones" by taking advantage of hilly terrain and inaccessible thick jungles (Mazumdar, 2013). The Maoists' operations are characterized by careful selection of vulnerable targets, thorough reconnaissance of area, innovative methods to trap police, and use of remotely controlled IEDs and explosives to deadly effect. The Maoists have also introduced and executed the "swarming tactics" to deadly effect in their operations. In this mode, large number of heavily armed Maoist cadres numbering 500–1,000 participate in each operation to lay siege and attack an entire town or several prominent targets, such as police stations, paramilitary posts, armories, and other vital economic or government targets.

So far, only Andhra Pradesh has succeeded in neutralizing the Maoist threat effectively by adopting a broad-based approach by undertaking a thorough overhaul, reorientation, and up-gradation of its police capabilities, backed up by firm political resolve and resources provided by the state government. The Greyhounds, a special anti-Maoist police unit, has earned well-deserved reputation for its professionalism and is a model for other police forces. The police efforts have been complemented by several developmental and administrative measures designed to address their perceived and real grievances. Recently, Odisha police has also notched up many operational successes by improving its police capabilities and leadership in the most affected areas (Subramanian, 2014). Meanwhile, COIN operations have continued to flounder in most other states, despite substantial deployment of central paramilitary forces, due to their policy of political expediency and other structural and systemic weaknesses. To overcome these problems, the present central government has resolved to wipe out LWE extremism during the next 3 years through a uniform anti-Maoist policy and substantially strengthening the police capabilities in the worst affected states and augmenting deployment of paramilitary forces for anti-Maoist operations (*The Economic Times*, 2014). While the impact of these fresh initiatives and policies remains to be seen, the fake Naxal surrender scam of over 500 poor and innocent Jharkhand men, mostly tribals, lured to pay bribes and pose as Maoists for CRPF jobs in 2011–2012 has laid bare the exploitative nature of security establishment in its interface with the poor tribals and suggests that such misdirected COIN efforts are unlikely to usher durable peace anytime soon.

The investigation carried out by *India Today* magazine reveals that the job scam was scripted by some elements within CRPF and Jharkhand police in collusion with civilians, leading to prolonged detention of these innocent men in old Ranchi jail campus where CRPF's elite CoBRA battalion was stationed. The State government has recommended a CBI probe (*India Today*, 2015).

Factors Impeding Effective Response to Insurgent/ Terrorist Violence

There are some recurring themes in contemporary "best practices" COIN literature: rule of law, focus on population, their needs and security, prioritizing of political solutions over security-based solutions, intergovernmental coordination and cooperation, effective population control and border control measures, police primacy and intelligence-led operations, supported by military as per requirement, and establishment of a stable electoral state (CFM, 2007: 51; Sepp, 2005). However, it has been argued that many of these western COIN strategies have limited applicability in contemporary medium-powered multi-ethnic countries such as India that simply do not have a responsible political environment, refined organization, institutions, or extensive resources essential for this purpose, and suffer from crippling deficiencies in three critical areas: basic institutional weakness, state structure, and excessive influence by an elite (Haines, 2009). In the absence of capable institutions, it is difficult for the socially, ethnically, and religiously diverse groups to articulate their grievances through legitimate channels and get them redressed within the political system. This is certainly the case in India, and the countrywide turmoil and collective dissatisfaction with the state authorities is reflected in staggering number of 75,991 agitations during 2013 in which 14 civilians were killed and 427 injured in police action, and 10 policemen were killed and 1,249 were injured due to actions of riotous mobs (BPR&D, 2014: 121).[11] A total of 460 state police/Central Armed Police Forces (CAPF) personnel were killed on duty in 2013–2014 (1 September–31 August) while engaged in tackling serious law and order and internal security problems (BPR&D, 2014: 165). The political violence unleashed by these large numbers of agitations, terrorist incidents, and insurgent movements across the length and breadth of India certainly suggests some fundamental flaws in prevalent political structures, institutions, and policies.

As noted earlier, "counterinsurgency mirrors the state" (Kilcullen, 2010:10–11), that is, the choice of methods and policies adopted by a government depend, to a considerable degree, on the nature of the state. Therefore, it may be proper at this stage to consider some salient features of India's polity that have bearing on its COIN responses. India is a union of states, and its constitution provides for a parliamentary form of government of the British type with an executive responsible to parliament, and an indirectly elected president as the head of state. The basic apparatus of governmental administration inherited from colonial period—a small elite cadre of all-India services, civil and criminal law, and a professional army strictly under the control of the political administration—has been retained with some minor changes. The constitution also provides for a federal structure with distribution of powers between the Union and the states that is heavily inclined toward the Union. According to the 7th Schedule (Article 246), responsibility for "public order" and "police" is vested in the states, while the Union government is responsible for military and national security. There are several other constitutional provisions (Article 352–356) that back central government's supremacy should it choose to intervene in case of "national emergency" or to protect the states from "internal

---

[11] In 2013, of the total 75,991, a majority of them were political agitations (31.94 percent), followed by agitations by government employees (15.82 percent), labor (10.80 percent), students (10.78 percent), and communal (6.26 percent), while 24.40 percent were categorized as "others" (BPRD, 2014: 122).

disturbance." However, there is some ambiguity as to who should respond to internal insurgencies, and there are significant differences between constitutional guarantees and political realities. Many times central government has failed to enforce its writ to protect larger national interests in the face of determined opposition from the state governments. For example, presence of a large contingent of federal government's paramilitary CRPF failed to protect the Babri mosque from demolition on December 6, 1992 as the state government ruled by opposition BJP did not requisition the assistance of CRPF (Subramanian, 2007). Similar politically expedient and self-serving policies pursued by elites have marred the state response to Maoist violence in the country. More nefariously, political elites and Maoists in many states, for example, Chhattisgarh and Jharkhand have used the conflict to mask mineral extraction by private mining corporations in a mutually beneficial arrangement (Miklian, 2011). Selective enforcement of laws to perpetuate the established order with all its inequities has also been considered an important contributor to Naxalite violence or LWE (Verghese, 2008: 8). The fact that political parties in India are not federal and are fragmented also exacerbates terrorist activity and hampers their ability to enact coherent and effective counterterrorism measures (Piazza, 2010). Atul Kohli's (1997) analysis of three ethnic movements in India— those of Tamils in Tamil Nadu during the 1950s and the 1960s, of Sikhs in Punjab during the 1980s, and of Muslims in Kashmir during the 1990s—suggests that persistently unaccommodating policies and postures of national leaders and leaders of ethnic movements exacerbate political problems, leading to escalation of violence.

Crisis of Conviction

The national discourse on insurgent/terrorist violence has been marked by a lack of coherent strategy and vacillation between responses dictated by "developmental solutions," "root causes," "political solution," and immediate imperatives of containment of violence, resulting in a pattern that displays "the consistency of a pendulum, swinging with insistent regularity from one extreme to another" (Sahni, 2003 and 2009d). Frequently, the gains secured by a government through tactical or policy innovations have been squandered by successor regimes for political reasons. Such pandering and concession to insurgent causes by politicians has caused immense problems to the security forces. For instance, in Punjab just when the police had begun to commit itself for the first time in anti-terrorist operations, 40 high-profile prisoners were released in March 1988 as a "good-will gesture," leading to immediate unprecedented violence in the state (Gill, 1999).[12] Again, in Andhra Pradesh in 2004, soon after its formation, the new state government halted the COIN operations against Maoist insurgents throughout the state and allowed the ban on the PWG and six other Maoist outfits to lapse, leaving them free to carry out their activities (Mishra, 2007: 150). The subsequent COIN successes in both Punjab and Andhra Pradesh owe a great deal to a firm political resolve and support of their respective governments, which allowed the security forces (SFs) to carry out their job without political interference. In Assam, the government has released several top United Liberation Front of Assam (ULFA) leaders, and initiated the process of "peace talks," after the CI operations and concerted actions by the Bangladesh government had neutralized most of their top leadership.

The spread of Maoist violence in the country can be attributed to the lack of a coordinated and coherent COIN strategy by the federal and state governments. Such examples can be multiplied manifold from virtually every state facing insurgency in the country. The inconsistency of the Indian response is also explained by the fact that under the Indian Constitution, Schedule Seven, List II-"State List," public order is a state subject, and as these states are ruled by different political parties, their vision of the problem is colored by their political interests (Mishra, 2007: 11). An example would be helpful in unraveling the implications of this lack of political consensus for national security. Between 2005 and 2015 (till June 14, 2015, SATP 6), the Maoist violence in the country claimed

---

[12] According to Gill (1999), an unprecedented 288 people, including 25 policemen were killed in March, 1988 and another 259 including 25 policemen were killed in April, soon after this "good-will gesture."

6,760 casualties, which is much higher than the combined total of 6,043 casualties in *all* northeast states and 5,658 casualties in Jammu and Kashmir during the same period. Currently, the states that are worst affected by Maoist violence are Chhattisgarh, Jharkhand, Bihar, and Odisha. Chhattisgarh and Jharkhand are ruled by the BJP, the national ruling party; Bihar is ruled by a coalition government comprising Janata Dal (United), Rashtriya Janata Dal (RJD) and Congress and Odisha is ruled by Janata Dal (Biju). Besides this, Maoists are also active in certain pockets of Maharashtra, West Bengal, Andhra Pradesh, and Telengana, which are ruled by different parties. Even as the Maoist movement continues to spread rapidly across the nation, political parties have failed to evolve any common approach to this problem. In this scenario, the difficulties in coordinating a national response across over a dozen of Maoist violence-affected states can be well imagined. In the northeast "inter-state rivalries and turf wars" have prevented the formation of any trans-regional body to coordinate COIN strategies despite obvious threats to national security in this highly strategic region (Bhaumik, 2009). In yet another example of partisan politics, state chief ministers have virtually vetoed a federal proposal to constitute National Counter -Terrorism Centre (NCTC) two years after it was first conceived after the Mumbai terror strike (Kanwal, 2012). Frequent squabbles among country's premier investigative and intelligence organizations such as the Intelligence Bureau, National Investigation Agency, and Central Bureau of Investigation have further hampered effective coordinated responses to terrorist threats (*The Asian Age,* 2013).

The counter-terrorism efforts have also been hampered by lack of a suitable legal framework to deal with acts of terrorism. Following allegations of widespread abuse of earlier counter-terrorism laws like the *Terrorism and Disruptive Activities Act* (TADA) and *Prevention of Terrorism Act* (POTA) and its unpopularity among sections of the minority communities, there has been a clear lack of political will and political consensus to legislate effective counter-terrorism legislation in the country. Amazingly for a nation that has suffered thousands of casualties, kidnappings, and destruction of property in terrorist violence in recent years, the acts of terrorism are still dealt with under the *Unlawful Activities (Prevention) Act, 1967* (Gordon, 2008). This is in stark contrast to the prompt legislative response of the liberal democratic western nations following the terrorist attacks of September 11, 2001. A study conducted by Epifanio (2011) of the 20 western democracies revealed that these countries had no hesitation in enacting effective anti-terrorist laws which, *inter alia*, "reduced civil freedom, limited procedural rights of terror suspects, and made immigration laws far more restrictive."[13] These countries have further tightened anti-terrorism security measures following a spate of terrorist incidents in many European cities in recent months. Clearly, North America and Western Europe countries have been highly pragmatic and proactive in framing national security policies to deal with the risk of terrorist incidents in their respective jurisdictions.

A similar inconsistency is also apparent in India's responses to frequent provocations by inimical neighboring countries, particularly Pakistan, who has been aiding insurgent and terrorist groups in the country (Paul, 2006). Consequently, there has been an "endless succession of 'peace initiatives' at the highest level—regularly interrupted by escalating violence, military mobilization, coercive diplomacy, and belligerent political rhetoric..." (Sahni, 2009d). In this context, underlining the crucial importance of strong and consistent government policy, W.C. Sonderlund (1970) has rightly noted that once the insurgent challenge is in the open, the "success of the operations depends not primarily on the development of insurgent strength, but more importantly on the degree of vigor, determination, and skill with which the incumbent regime acts to defend itself." Clearly, such "vigor, determination, and skill" have been usually lacking in the country's response to both the domestic and international threats to national security. The three major reasons for deteriorating internal security scenario in the country have been

---

[13] The study also mentions that the number of restrictive regulations in the sample 20 countries went up from 3.8 before September 11, 2001 attacks to 16.6 in 2008. In some countries, there was substantial increase in restrictive regulations, that is, in Germany it went up from 4 to 16, in Spain from 12 to 23, and in the United Kingdom from 3 to 28 (Epifanio, 2011).

identified as lack of strategic vision among political leaders, low priority to national security as political expedient considerations override everything else, and poor state of law enforcement apparatus, which is just not geared to meet the challenges confronting the nation (Singh, 2012). A recent study (Mahadevan, 2012: 10–11) has identified four major constraints to explain India's poor response to escalating terrorism threats to the nation: (a) lack of political consistency, (b) lack of political consensus, (c) lack of operational capacity, and (d) lack of operational coordination. Consequently, even as India's strategic environment continues to deteriorate steadily, national security system in the country remains archaic and dysfunctional in the absence of any meaningful reforms since independence (Prakash, 2012).[14]

Crisis of Capacities

Though precise definition of state capacity has been elusive, recent research suggests that economic development, bureaucratic capacity, and political institutional coherence and quality are important components of state capacity and go together (Hendrix, 2010). State capacities and structures also play a critical role in deciding the course of social revolutions (Skocpol, 1979: 32), and the lack of governing capacity has been cited as the most critical factor in the rise of political violence in developing countries (Huntington, 1968). Research conducted by Thyne (2006) suggests that states providing public goods (for example, medical services and education) have a lower risk of civil war onset. However, the poor delivery of basic services and maladministration has landed India the dubious distinction of being a "flailing" state (Pritchett, 2009). Over the past many decades, India has also suffered serious

---

[14] Admiral Arun Prakash (retired) was the Chief of Naval Staff of India and also served as the member of National Security Task Force, 2001, and the Naresh Chandra Committee to review the challenges to national security and make recommendations set up in 2011 by the Government of India (GOI). The Committee gave its report in May 2012, but no worthwhile action for implementation of its recommendations seems to have been taken so far. Also see Anit Mukherjee's article "Failing to Deliver: Post-crises defence reforms in India, 1998-2010" in Bajpai and Pant, (Eds) *India's National Security*, (Oxford: India, 2013).

erosion of security, governance, and administrative capacities in large parts of the country creating vast opportunities for extremist mobilization. Therefore, restoration of the authority and functions of governance across the country, but particularly in the vast rural hinterland, must constitute an integral part of any comprehensive approach to COIN and CT.

Policing: There is an acute deficit of police leadership across the country, which is reflected in as many as 1,045 posts in IPS lying vacant out of total sanctioned strength of 4,554 as on January 1, 2014, yielding over 20 percent vacancies among the officers who are assigned senior positions in the state police and federal paramilitary forces (BPR&D, 2014: 104). Furthermore, the growth of police has not kept pace with the rising population, crime or violence in the country, and the total sanctioned police-population ratio (per 100,000 population) stands at 185 in 2013 (BPR&D, 2014:29), which is much less than the ratio of 220 recommended by the United Nations for "peacetime policing," or the ratio maintained by most western countries that confront much less violence as compared to their Indian counterparts.[15] The actual number of policemen available for duty per 100,000 gets further reduced to only 140 due to large number of vacancies (BPR&D, 2014: 29). The CAPF also carry large number of vacancies with an actual strength of 927,369 against sanctioned strength of 1,007,630 in all ranks (BPR&D, 2014:67).

Furthermore, mere availability of larger number of policemen in a state does not necessarily translate into better policing in the absence of effective government policies and strategies as the example of Nagaland and Manipur would indicate. In 2013, Nagaland had only 96 people per policeman and Manipur had 102 people per policeman against the all-India figure of actual 716 people per policeman due to relatively larger size of police force in these two states (BPR&D, 2014: 15). However, the security scenario in both these states remains highly disturbed due to presence of large

---

[15] The UN recommended ratio is 222 policemen per 100,000 population and the police–population ratio in some western countries is as follows: Italy: 559, U.S.: 315, Portugal: 465, Belgium: 358, Germany: 291, South Africa: 277, Australia: 209, France: 205, and U.K.: 205 (Sahni, 2009b).

number of insurgents, poor quality of policing, and weaknesses in government policies and governance. The shortages of manpower at the national level are exacerbated by poor quality of the police, which is "primitive, ill-trained, and ill-equipped force, and, in most States, has little capacity or orientation to handle full-blown insurgency" (Sahni, 2010). Furthermore, the police have a feudal mindset and the entire criminal justice system is almost on the verge of collapse. The prosecution of terrorism cases takes decades in India's courts due to clogging of cases, and the conviction rate is less than 10 percent as against 80 percent or more in Western countries (Kanwal and Manoharan, 2009).

These problems of law enforcement are compounded by the country's poor capacities for generation, utilization and integration of intelligence; lack of an integrated apparatus for financial intelligence and enforcement; and poor technical capabilities for electronic counter-intelligence and economic intelligence. Regrettably, successive governments at the federal and state levels have shown little interest to implement comprehensive recommendations made by the National Police Commission (NPC) (1977–1981), the Ribeiro Committee (1998), the Padmanabhaiah Committee (2000) or made necessary allocations to radically transform and empower police to meet these high expectations (CHRI, 2011).[16] Consequently, police forces across the country have largely remained "neglected, under-resourced, and abandoned to the mercy of an obstructive bureaucracy and a manipulative political executive for decades," and critical deficiencies persist in manpower, equipment, and operational infrastructure (ICM, 2007: 28).[17] An example would be helpful in understanding the pathetic state of policing in some parts of the country. According to a news item, a public function was held in Bihar to celebrate the martyrdom anniversary of a freedom fighter. The police contingent deputed at the venue of function was to fire

---

[16] For critique of Police reforms in India, see "Commonwealth Human Rights Initiative 2011," http://www.humanrightsinitiative.org/publications/police/PRDebatesInIndia.pdf accessed on October 9, 2012.

[17] For relevant police data, see *Crime in India*, 2012, Chapter 17 "Police strength, Expenditure and Infrastructure," Tables 17.1 to 17.12.

21 rounds in the air to pay gun salute as a mark of respect to the martyr. However, despite repeated attempts, not a single round could be fired by police as both the guns and ammunition were over 25 years old (*The Times of India*, 2013)!

The condition is particularly bad in militancy-affected NER where many militant groups have far more modern weapons and equipment than the state police; a large number of police stations and outposts do not have proper buildings and lack even minimal housing for constabulary. Many state police forces also suffer from poor mobility due to acute shortage of transport resources. Nationwide, 629 police stations do not have any vehicle, 327 police stations do not have telephone facility, and 118 police stations are without wireless (BPR&D, 2014: 96). The problems of policing have been further aggravated due to rampant corruption, politicization, and criminalization prevalent among sections of police, and the subversion of loyalty of the force in many states (Ghosh, 1992: 20–21). The total number of deaths in police custody/lockup from 2011 to 2013 has been rising: 2011 (104), 2012 (109), and 2013(118). In many cases judicial enquiry or magisterial enquiry was conducted into such custodial deaths, but very few policemen were charge-sheeted and hardly anyone was convicted (*Crime in India*, Compendium 2013: 151). The present status of police in India has been accurately summed up by Gordon (2008):

> Essentially, policing in India is under-resourced and morale is low. Corruption is endemic. Manipulation by the incumbent political party is the norm. The relationship of the police to the public is often one of power and misuse of power rather than of "community policing." Legislation to protect human rights is not especially strong and is often ignored.

All these developments have combined together to undermine the efficiency and effectiveness of the local police station, which is the center of all operations, and which as first responder has the primary responsibility of tackling all challenges within its jurisdiction, including terrorism and insurgency.

Governance: Successful government campaigns to undermine insurgencies are closely associated with "both a program to address the needs of the people and administrative competence and capability" (O'Neill, 1990: 143). However, in India, the basic capacities for governance have been degraded to such an extent that even the most rudimentary tasks of routine maintenance cannot be executed with a minimal efficiency. The spread of Maoist insurgency in the country has been attributed to persistent and pervasive poverty, exploitation, and inequality in rural areas for centuries and the fact that the policies followed by the post-independent Indian state have led to a further polarization between the rich and poor and the urban and rural areas (Ahuja and Ganguly, 2007). The pattern of capitalist development pursued by the federal government has further exacerbated the regional economic inequalities inherited from the colonial period and impacted the national politics, leading to creation of two Indias—one developing fast and the other languishing (Ghosh, 2006a). Noble-laureate Amartya Sen and Jean Dreze have critically examined India's development record in their recent book, *An Uncertain Glory: India and its Contradictions* and noted that in absence of "growth-mediated" development over the past two decades, India's performance has actually deteriorated on a wide range of basic social indicators despite impressive economic growth. Their study reveals that *"living conditions in the poorer half of India are not much better, if at all, than in the poorer half of Africa"* (emphasis in original, Dreze and Sen, 2013: 77). Overall, India had the best social indicators in south Asia (except Sri Lanka) in 1990, but now stands *second-worst*, ahead of only Pakistan. According to World Bank data, only *five* countries outside Africa (Afghanistan, Bhutan, Pakistan, Papua New Guinea, and Yemen) have a lower "youth female literacy rate" than India; only *five* countries (Afghanistan, Cambodia, Haiti, Myanmar, and Pakistan) do worse than India in child mortality rate; only *three* have lower level of access to improved sanitation (Bolivia, Cambodia, and Haiti); and none (anywhere—not even in Africa) have a higher proportion of underweight children (Dreze and Sen, 2011). Large sections of India remain extremely poor due to inequalities in income distribution, and only 16 countries outside Africa had a lower "gross national income per-capita" than India in 2010 (*World Development Indicators,* 2011). The influence of the corporate sector on public policy has grown considerably, and some state governments have been implicated in deliberately provoking Maoist violence to facilitate exploitation of huge mineral reserves in central India by private mining corporations (Azam and Bhatia, 2012). Apparently, these developments reflect a general pattern of pervasive imbalance of political and economic power and a massive neglect of the interests of the disadvantaged sections of the society (Dreze and Sen, 2011), leading to frustration, unrest, and agitations. Millions of poor undertrials continue to languish in jails for years while the rich and powerful manage to secure bail, parole, and other privileges with ease. An effective grievance redress system mechanism is an integral part of good governance. However, according to a news item, nearly 120,000 grievances lodged by citizens on an online central portal remain unattended by states, resulting in overall 80 percent pendency and almost 90,000 complaints have been pending for over one year (*The Economic Times,* 2015).

The poor capacity for governance is also reflected in abysmal ratios of government employees to population (per 100,000). India's federal government has a ratio of only 295 per 100,000 as against 889 in the U.S. and 1,408 in Canada (Sahni, 2009b). Similarly, the number of state and local government employees in the country is nowhere near the level of developed countries, despite the fact that these nations focus primarily on "core" functions, and allocate several welfare and developmental tasks to the private sector.[18] Moreover, an overwhelming number of these employees are in lower cadres, and the administrative skills, training, and technological competence of those in higher echelons is less than satisfactory. There are more than 4,200 vacancies in district and subordinate courts against the sanctioned strength of 19,700 judges, leading to huge pendency of 18.9 million criminal cases in these courts.

---

[18] For instance, the State and local government employees in the U.S. account for another 6,314 per 100,000; in sharp contrast, Uttar Pradesh has 352; Bihar, 472; Orissa, 1,007; Chhattisgarh, 1,067; Maharashtra, 1,223; Punjab, 1,383; Gujarat, 1,694 (Sahni, 2009b).

However, absolute numbers are only one aspect of the problem. Even in several northeast states that have ratios, which are substantially larger than all-India figures, the quality of governance and security apparatus remains highly suspect. A multi-disciplinary study conducted by Indian Institute of Public administration (IIPA) in association with NEC has identified lack of an effective delivery system as the most important reason for under-development of the northeast (Reddy and Reddy, 2007: 4). These critical shortages in the country's security and administrative structure cannot be met easily due to poor quality of its human resources and extreme poverty, which limit its "capacities for capacity generation" (Sahni, 2010).

While India has achieved near universal enrolment and enhanced hard and soft infrastructure, the overall standard of education is well below global standards: Program for International Student Assessment (PISA) 2009+ results ranked Tamil Nadu and Himachal Pradesh (two of our better states) 72 and 73 out of 74 participants, ahead only of Kyrgyzstan and way behind the OECD average. India did not participate in PISA 2012. Annual Status of Education Report (ASER) findings have been reporting low levels of learning among the 5–16 years age groups in rural India since 2005. A recent countrywide annual survey conducted recently by Pratham,[19] an NGO, indicated that three years after introduction of Right to Education, learning outcomes and skills in reading and arithmetic of India's school children had declined from an already poor level, despite government's claims of improvement in infrastructure in primary schools (*The Telegraph*, 2013). The nation is awash with a plethora of institutes issuing fake degrees and certificates for all sorts of courses. In June 2015, the University Grants Commission (UGC) released a list of 21 fake universities, of which as many as five were based in the national capital, Delhi. More disturbing revelations are coming from Madhya Pradesh where the officers of Professional Examination Board (Vyavsayik Pareeksha Mandal or Vyapam) have been found involved in

---

[19] This 2012 survey by Pratham covered 596,000 children from 14,591 primary and upper primary rural schools—90 percent of them run by the government—in 567 districts all over the country (*The Telegraph*, 2013).

rigging a variety of eligibility tests for courses and recruitment including medical entrance and government employment. The Vyapam Vyavsayik scam has been going on for more than six years with the alleged involvement of many highly influential senior politicians and bureaucrats. The police have already arrested more than 2,000 persons, and over 40 witnesses and accused involved in this case have died so far. The state government under intense pressure has handed over investigation of this case to CBI.

Consequently, the overall standard of higher education remains poor despite substantial increase in the number of universities, colleges, and diploma-level institutes. As per the *Labor Bureau Report 2014,* the current size of India's formally skilled workforce is only two percent, which compares poorly with other countries like South Korea (96 percent) and Japan (80 percent). All these factors make it impossible to conceive and implement "developmental solutions" in the immediate future as the time frames of development and COIN are different and cannot be reconciled.

Demographic Factors

India's population is already huge and has grown fairly rapidly from 1.04 billion in 2000 to 1.21 billion in 2011, and is further projected to grow to 1.37 billion in 2020. Worse, almost 63 percent of the growth between 2000 and 2020 would come from some of the most backward states in the country. The urban population of 285 million in 2000 is projected to almost double to 540 million in 2020, which would be almost 40 percent of the total population. India also has a large young population, which can potentially increase conflicts if their energies are not channelized productively. According to projections, the total labor force aged 15 and above is likely to rise from 354 million in 1991 to 627 million by 2021 and to 692 million by 2031 (Ghosh, 2006a). However, employment growth has been sluggish, particularly in rural areas. A large number of workers are self-employed and engaged in low-income-generating activities. A revealing analysis of the economics of farmers based on data collected by National Sample Survey Organisation (NSSO) in 2012–2013 shows that the marginal farmers who make up 75 percent of all agriculturalists with less than 1 hectare of land are all in the red (*The Times of India*, 2015). The consequent poverty and distress leading to suicide of many farmers during 2015 has become a highly emotive political issue in India.

A large number of people in India live in extreme poverty, and the inequities have not been reduced despite economic growth in recent decades, severely straining the nation's social and political systems. The top 10 percent Indians own nearly three-quarters (74 percent) of the country's wealth, and the share of India's super-rich (top 1 percent) who owned 37 percent of India's personal wealth in 2000 has increased to 49 percent in 2014 (*Global Wealth Report 2014*, Credit Suisse). On the other hand, the share of the poorest quintile in terms of the monthly per capita consumption expenditure in total consumption actually declined from 8.0 during 1993–1994 to 7.3 in 2004–2005 and 7.1 in 2009–2010 in urban areas indicating growing inequities (*Millennium Development Goals: India Country Report, 2014*: 22). Furthermore, as per the report of the federal government's *Socio-Economic and Caste Census* (SECC), more than 50 percent of the nearly 180 million rural households own no land or any other asset, and have to depend on casual, manual work for survival. But perhaps the worst sufferers are India's 10.43 crore tribal people who constitute 8.6 percent of the total population. Official data on all indicators of development reveal that India's tribal people are the worst-off in terms of income, health, education, nutrition, infrastructure, and governance. Around 40 percent of the 60 million people displaced following development projects in the country are tribals. A study by Sanchita Bakshi et al. (2015) shows that more than three quarters of tribal population is concentrated in only 15 percent sub-districts in India, and usually these "enclaves" are pockets of intense backwardness even within the most developed districts. Nationwide 92 districts have sub-districts or blocks that figure in the list of both the top 20 percent and bottom 20 percent of India's sub-districts. India ranked 135th position in the *UN Human Development Index 2014*, much below than other BRIC countries and even lower than neighboring Sri Lanka. The *Global Hunger Index 2014* puts India at 55th rank, below Nepal and Sri Lanka and its hunger status remains classified as "serious." Clearly, policy interventions in the last six decades have not been very effective in reducing poverty and ameliorating the plight of poor people in the country.

A study made by the CIA of the U.S. indicated that the two periods of serious insurgent challenges to the Sri Lanka state from the JVP in the 1970s and the Tamil insurgency in the 1980s coincided exactly with the years when the 15–24 "youth bulge" in those communities exceeded 20 percent of the total population (Fuller, 1995). More recently, the involvement of youth in "popular uprisings" in several North African countries such as Tunisia, Egypt, and Libya has been associated with large-scale unemployment estimated at around 20–30 percent in these countries (Omotola, 2012). A time-series study of 27 Indian states for the period from 1952 to 2002 conducted by Henrik Urdal suggests that "youth bulges" increase the risk of all three forms of political violence, that is, armed conflicts, political violence events, and Hindu–Muslim riots, particularly in states with great male surpluses (Urdal, 2008). Given the present pattern of economic development and demographic scenario, widespread youth unrest can be predicted in less developed states, many of which are in the border regions of India. This calls for more attention and sensitive handling of developments in northeast states as all of them have international borders, and several ethnic insurgent groups enjoy safe havens and sanctuaries in neighboring countries (Ghosh, 2006a).

Historically, those nations have tended to do well economically that have promoted participatory development and invested massively into public services, particularly, quality education and health, for expansion of human capabilities (Dreze and Sen, 2013: X–Xi). A dispassionate analysis of India's present socio-economic-political scenario leads one to the sobering conclusion that the country needs to get its act together without further delay; otherwise it could be consumed by the growing domestic unrest.

Lack of Institutional Learning

Since its independence, India has faced a succession of insurgencies and ethno-nationalist conflicts in several parts of the country. Many of these internal conflicts have been inspired by Maoist extremism or tribal visions of exclusive ethnic homelands, fueled by religious zealotry and manipulated by inimical foreign powers. However, the literature on these internal wars is miniscule, and "a historical amnesia" afflicts much of the Indian security establishment (ICM, 2007: 8).[20] There has been no serious effort on the part of academics, establishment, or security professionals to subject these campaigns to serious scrutiny or learn from a synthesis of experiences of various administrators and counter-terrorism practitioners who have worked in these situations. Consequently, the governments, civilians, and the security forces have failed to learn from past campaigns and continue to make the same mistakes time and again. This failure to pass on the wisdom and best practices of COIN to future leaders imposes a special strain on commanders on the ground who are forced to reinvent the wheel and muddle along, learning slowly "on the job." The government policies discouraging declassification from sensitive ministries like defense, home, and external affairs have also contributed to the present situation (Mukerjee, 2013: 440). This is in stark contrast to the practice in many developed countries where police/army officers routinely share their observations. For example, Lt. General David H Petraeus,[21] a distinguished U.S. military officer, has observed that writing down observations and lessons learned was a time-honored tradition of soldiers and the process of collection, evaluation and dissemination of observations had

---

[20] This lack of institutional learning afflicts other sectors too. For example, Dreze and Sen (2013: 72–80) have noted that India could learn much from the success of Kerala, Tamil Nadu, and Himachal Pradesh in laying foundations for growth through participatory development, well-conceived social support systems, and actively promoting expansion of human capabilities through investments in quality education and health.

[21] Lt. General Petraeus commanded the 101st Airborne Division during the first year of U.S. invasion of Iraq and also served as the first commander of the Multi-National Security Transition Command-Iraq and the NATO Training Mission-Iraq.

been institutionalized through formation of the "Center for Army Lessons Learned" (http://call.Army.mil) in the U.S. more than two decades ago (Petraeus, 2006).

Policing Insurgencies—Roles of Police, Paramilitary, and Military

Traditionally, the primary responsibility of civil police has been maintenance of public order and social control through enforcement of federal and local laws, while the military handles external threats. However, customary police efforts have been overwhelmed by increasing politically inspired violence, terrorism, illegal immigration, narcotics and organized crime that have blurred distinctions between internal and external threats, and thus, between police and military responsibilities (Beede, 2008). This blurring of distinctions has led to two noticeable trends: the militarization of police and police-ization of the military, manifested in increased deployment of military in internal security duties; a close operational relationship between police and military in crime control, particularly drug control and terrorism control efforts; and technology transfers and cross-training in the area of special weapons and tactics (SWAT), COIN, and anti-terrorism exercises (Kraska, 2007). However, extensive and frequent deployment of the military in internal security duties diverts them from their main task of protecting the country from external aggression, undermines their efficiency by neglecting training and leads to severe strain and stress. Moreover, their deployment is usually not very effective as they lack necessary training and orientation and are prone to overreact in confrontations with the public (Arnold, 1986: 15). Military commanders in many countries also resist such deployment for internal security duties, apprehending that such operations may split the military vertically by making troops subject to the same tensions and cleavages dividing the civilians (Enloe, 1976).

Therefore, to reduce the involvement of the military in civilian affairs and meet the escalating threats to internal security, governments have increasingly turned to paramilitary forces or created special paramilitary units within the police. Though the U.S. has never had a specific paramilitary force at the national level, such forces have been common in other countries. The most famous of these include the French Gendarmerie, the Italian Carabinieri, and the Spanish Guardia Civil. These troops comprise a significant proportion of each nation's respective police forces and report to their ministries of defense.

In contrast, paramilitary police personnel in Anglophone countries such as the U.S., the United Kingdom, and Australia usually operate as paramilitary police units (PPUs) under the authority of their respective civil police organizations.[22] These PPUs are deployed for high-risk assignments involving hostages, sniper, or terrorists, conduct raids for contrabands (drugs, guns, and money), and patrol crime "hot-spots" (Kraska, 2007). However, the proliferation of PPUs over the past few decades has been a cause of concern to some observers who have argued that it undermines democratic policing by ignoring norms of transparency, accountability and human rights, criminalizes social problems, and frequently leads to use of coercive power in handling non-violent political and social protests (Muzzatti, 2005: 120).

In culturally and religiously diverse societies, particularly, the use of paramilitary and "hard-power" responses carries a significant risk of alienating sections of population and escalating tensions through which terrorism is generated and sustained. To counteract such consequences of militarized responses in multi-cultural societies, community policing has been projected as an alternative strategy. Pickering et al. (2008) have reviewed a three-year-study conducted by Monash University and Victoria police in Australia, which suggests a radical transformation of role of police in counter-terrorism by conceptualizing it within the gamut of community policing. Instead of specialized response

---

[22] These PPUs are known by different names such as SWAT, Emergency Response Teams (ERT), and Special Patrol Groups (SPG).

units, this approach seeks to build a trusting relationship with local communities through "culturally literate policing that has *wide* community engagement in daily policing practices as well as *deep* community engagement through intermediate and long-term relationship building" (emphasis in original).

Internationally, during the last two decades an increasing trend toward deployment of gendarmeries in peacekeeping missions has been discernible owing to a growing recognition of their crucial role in restoration of law and order and reluctance or inability of the military to undertake policing tasks. This has also been necessitated due to expanded role of multilateral peacekeeping missions from the narrow focus on SMART operations (supporting, monitoring, administering, reporting, and training) in the 1990s to involvement in operations that involve "three R's—reform, restructuring, and rebuilding"— requiring greater depth and breadth of skills, and the lack of sufficient expeditionary capabilities with the civil police for diverse security tasks such as riot control, border patrolling, countering organized crime, protection role, and COIN (Dziedzic and Stark, 2006). Furthermore, the dual affiliation of gendarmeries with military and civil commands provides for their interoperability and enables them to perform as an ideal interface between police and military forces involved in peace missions (Lutterbeck, 2004).

The purpose of raising such paramilitary forces is well described in one European Union report as follows:

> Paramilitary forces offer, above all else, the capability for the restoration of public order where the absence of any state legitimacy reigns. They have the required expertise and capability to engage in deteriorated situations as a component of armed forces (Quoted in *Statewatch*, 2000).

The professional skills and other advantages of these gendarmes have led to their proliferation in both domestic and international policing. However, some observers have cautioned that unchecked growth of this "paramilitary policing juggernaut" actively promoted by the U.S. in international peace-keeping operations has facilitated militarization of policing in post-conflict societies that may create difficulties in reconciliation and democratization. Moreover, the experience of Israel indicates inherent dangers of such paramilitary policing to democratic norms, underlining the need to proceed with caution before this trend becomes irreversible (Hill and Beger, 2009).

In keeping with the international trends, India has also seen frequent deployment of army and paramilitary forces for COIN operations, as also the creation of special units within the police. As mentioned earlier, though "law and order" is the responsibility of the state governments, there is a clamor for central forces as soon as the violence level crosses a certain threshold. Consequently, the army and paramilitary forces have been frequently engaged in COIN operations in many "disturbed areas" such as Jammu and Kashmir and some northeast states. It has been argued that the heavy and almost permanent deployment of federal forces in these areas has created democracy-deficit (Baruah, 2005: 25), undermined civilian policing and beat patrolling, which are essential to crime control and service provision, and sometimes strained relations between the federal government and the states (Subramanian, 2007: 116).

Therefore, to reduce states' dependence on paramilitary forces and build local capacities for COIN and other challenges, the concept of India Reserve Battalions (IRBs) was introduced by the federal government. Under this scheme, the federal government has sanctioned 145 battalions, including 60 during the last five years (MHA, 2010–11: 155). These battalions are an integral part of the armed police of the state for which they are sanctioned by the GOI, and the cost of their initial raising is substantially met by the federal government. More recently, the GOI have also sanctioned 10 Specialized IRBs (SIRB) in LWE states for providing security to development projects, roads, schools, and health centers (MHA, 2014–15: 22). The GOI have also approved additional central assistance of INR 30 million to raise two commando Coys in each IR battalion raised after 2007–2008.

This brief overview reveals some commonalities among India's insurgencies and Indian democracy's responses. First, it is seen that in most cases the genesis of insurgency can be traced to dysfunctional state governments that failed to redress popular grievances or infuriated people through their inept handling of sensitive situations. The unscrupulous and divisive policies adopted by politicians to aggregate votes by inflaming religious or ethnic passions have also contributed to emergence of insurgencies (Ganguly, 2009: 227–228). Apparently, it is the quest for political power, rather than religious or ethnic diversity or ideology, which has been driving the contest between insurgents and counterinsurgents. It is also a fact that over the time most insurgencies have either lost their ideological moorings or become criminalized, and are sustained by the greed motivation of rebel groups and material support from inimical foreign powers. There is ample evidence of collusive arrangements between insurgents, politicians, bureaucrats and contractors for promoting their vested interests. At the same time, the strength of India's democracy is reflected in successful resolution or containment of many insurgencies through political accommodation, that is, by holding free and fair elections to reflect popular mandate, making sincere efforts to address real or perceived grievances, creating new states or co-opting insurgent leaders in government.

Second, the performance of police is inextricably linked to the fortunes of counterinsurgents. Generally, weak, corrupt, dysfunctional, or predatory police forces have contributed to insurgency, while a neutral, reliable, and professionally competent police force has been instrumental in winning over the loyalties of common people for government. Therefore, the reformation of police and a massive upgrade of its capabilities for meeting *all* challenges in its jurisdiction including law and order disturbances, ethnic, political or political violence, has been an important component of successful COIN strategy. Certainly, this has been the case in Punjab, Tripura, and Andhra Pradesh. The specialized forces such as Greyhounds of Andhra Pradesh police and other commando units have been effective only in an environment of all-round dominance of general police.

The Indian experience would suggest that a massive augmentation of state police capacities, rather than the deployment of army or paramilitary forces, has been the key to the success of COIN operations in the three states of Punjab, Andhra Pradesh, and Tripura. The success of anti-terrorist operations in Punjab during 1992–1994 was facilitated by substantial augmentation of manpower, and enhanced military capabilities of police, particularly SWAT teams, set up with the help of the Indian Army, which eventually grew to a total strength of over 10,000 personnel, or just over one-sixth of the total police force (Mahadevan, 2008). In Andhra Pradesh, the specially raised "Greyhounds" commando units have been highly effective in dealing with the Maoist insurgents (Oetken, 2009: 149). The success of COIN operations in Tripura has been mainly due to its armed battalions which have been explicitly raised, trained, and equipped on the paramilitary pattern. However, it is important to note that such special forces have been effective only in an environment of general force domination, which was made possible by a thorough overhaul of police strategies and sustained building-up of decentralized capacities for police response at the P.S. levels, and the battalion's company and platoon posts (Sahni, 2009d). This has enabled the police to function as the "lead agency" in COIN operations and also enabled them to respond effectively to *all* challenges within their respective jurisdiction. Therefore, the formation of a "Special anti-Naxal force" in the most troubled states of Bihar, Jharkhand, Orissa, and Chhattisgarh on the pattern of "Greyhounds" of Andhra Pradesh approved by the federal government may not yield positive outcomes unless supplemented by comprehensive improvements in policing infrastructure, policies and procedures in the affected states (*Zee News*, 2013).

PART TWO

4

A Thematic Overview of Insurgencies in India's Northeast

Introduction

India's NER is home to the earliest and longest lasting insurgency in the country–since 1952, in the Naga Hills, and over the years, many parts of the region have been convulsed by violence perpetrated by a large number of armed insurgent groups pursuing a multitude of demands ranging from outright secession to more autonomy within the constitution for the ethnic entities they claim to represent. Summarizing the reasons for secessionist movements in the northeast, Prakash Singh (2000), a renowned police officer and an astute observer of the national scene, has identified the following factors: a feeling of neglect and inept handling by the central government, alienation of tribals, changes in demographic patterns caused by the influx of people from across the border, and the availability of sanctuaries and other facilities by countries inimical to India. This is certainly a fair assessment. The Mizos did not pursue any secessionist agenda initially and their demands were mainly related to full autonomy within the state of Assam, special financial assistance, and adequate representation in the bureaucracy. But poor administration and neglect of all-round development, fears of losing their distinct ethnic identity and culture within the state of Assam and the perceived callousness of Assam's government in redressing their hardships resulting from a severe famine, which erupted in the early 1970s, led to feelings of bitterness and subsequent armed insurrection by the Mizo National Front. In Manipur, the perceived insensitivity of the Indian government to Manipuri culture, language, and distinct identity as reflected in the delay in granting full statehood and inclusion of Manipuri language in the Eighth Schedule of the Constitution played a significant part in generating a sense of alienation. In Assam and Tripura, the continuous influx of illegal immigrants from Bangladesh and consequent changes in the demographic, linguistic, and religious profile of these states have provided triggers for insurgency.

A recent study (Vadlamannati, 2011) that analyzed the panel data pertaining to armed rebellions in the northeastern states of India from 1970 to 2007 to answer the question "Why Indian men rebel?" identified persistent economic and political discrimination of marginalized groups and relative deprivation as the major causes of rebellion in NER.[1] This research also suggests that while legitimate grievance-based issues might have provided the initial impetus to northeast insurgencies, it is the greed motivation of rebel groups that has sustained these movements, leading to the conclusion that "greed and grievances in practice are entwined and difficult to unravel" (Vadlamannati, 2011).

The sheer number of militias in India's northeast is extraordinary and, at times, the number of groups has exceeded more than a hundred. Presently, over 30 militias of varying sizes and strength are operating in the region.[2] Among them, there are as many as 18 groups that have been listed as major militant/insurgent groups and

---

[1] According to Vadlamannati (2011):

My findings show that the two dimensions of deprivation (an absolute dimension covered by absolute poverty rate within a state and a relative dimension, captured by the relative poverty rate of the state) along with discrimination comprising two facets (economic and political discrimination of marginal groups in these regions) are positively related to conflict outbreak. These results hold after controlling for income, population pressures, ethnic affiliations, forest area, state capacity, peace years, neighboring conflict events, and distance to New Delhi.

[2] This includes the active insurgent groups operating in the NER and also various factions of ULFA, NSCN, and other groups engaged in peace talks/ceasefire with the government (SATP). However, the number of groups does not always correspond to the strength of insurgency in a particular state. For example, the small number of groups in Nagaland only means that insurgent movement is consolidated and power is concentrated among a few groups only.

all of them except two factions of the National Socialist Council of Nagaland (NSCN) have been declared as "Unlawful Associations" under the *Unlawful Activities (Prevention) Act, 1967* by the GOI. In addition, the listed groups active in Assam, Manipur, and Tripura (except the two NSCN factions) have also been listed as "terrorist organizations" in the schedule to *Unlawful Activities (Prevention) Act, 1967* (MHA, 2014–2015: 265).[3]

The proliferation of armed groups in the northeast has been attributed to the demonstration effect of the "success" of other such groups in the past in making huge money through widespread criminal operations and extortion, and the availability of generous financial benefits through rehabilitation package like the Tripura National Volunteers (TNV) members received after their surrender in 1988.[4] From this perspective, the mushrooming of these insurgent groups is primarily driven by the personal agenda of disgruntled members of erstwhile insurgent groups rather than any concern for tribal causes.[5]

The security situation in NER has shown mixed trends over the past decades, and periods of relative peace have been interspersed with intense violence. Recently, India's northeast has emerged as the most unsafe conflict theater for the SFs with 41 deaths already reported this year (till July 19, 2015). In one of the deadliest attacks on Indian SFs, the NSCN Khaplang (K) insurgents killed 18 army men and injured 11 others in an ambush in Manipur's Chandel district on June 4, 2015. There was a sharp escalation in the number of casualties of civilians in Assam also due to violence unleashed by anti-talk faction of National Democratic Front of Bodoland (NDFB/ Songbijit group). In Assam, 168 civilians were killed in 2014 as

---

[3] Since then, the Government of India has banned the Khaplang faction of NSCN in September 2015 for their role in the deadly ambush of army personnel in Manipur in June 2015 and other violent activities

[4] Since then this package has been substantially improved in 2009 and includes enhanced monthly payment of ₹3,500 for a period of one year and a grant of ₹150,000. For Manipur, the monthly payment has been increased to ₹4,000 per month and a grant of ₹250,000 since December 1, 2012.

[5] In a study conducted by Khan and Mangathai (2003) of human rights in Tripura, less than 10 percent mentioned "tribal development" as one of the factors for joining the insurgent groups.

compared to only 35 in the previous year. However, the overall security situation in NER has improved and civilian casualties have averaged less than 100 annually from 2010 to 2013. According to GOI statistics, in the NER, during 2014, there were 212 civilian casualties and 20 SF casualties, which is a significant improvement over the situation in 2007 when the total number of civilian and SF casualties was 498 and 79, respectively (MHA, 2014–2015: 10). During the first six months of 2015, there were 24 civilian casualties in northeast states. However, the pattern of violence in the NER is highly complex, and it would be simplistic to interpret it in terms of direct confrontation between the governments and their agencies and insurgent groups. In most northeast states, collusive arrangements exist between the insurgent groups and the legitimate power elites, facilitating transfer of massive resources that sustain and fuel insurgency in the region. Furthermore, notwithstanding their public postures of waging "freedom struggles" against the Indian government and its agencies, most rebel groups fight as much or more against each other over conflicting homelands demands and scarce resources—mainly land, than against the Indian state. This is certainly borne out by the changing pattern of extremist violence in northeast since early 1990s, with increasing attacks on civilian targets, internecine clashes, close ties to organized crime, and obstruction of normal democratic politics (Lacina, 2007). Furthermore, most of the insurgent groups have degenerated into criminality and exist solely to profit through their nexus with politicians, bureaucrats, and organized crime. Finally, the emergence of numerous Muslim fundamentalist organizations in the region and their linkages with militant Islamist outfits abroad, particularly Bangladesh, has added another dimension to the existing challenges to national security. In view of all these developments, some commentators have questioned the validity of federal government's conventional security and political interventions which are more suitable for quelling a rural insurgency with a grassroots base in northeast (Lacina, 2007).

Considering the strategic location of northeast Indian states, and seriousness of the existing and emerging challenges to national security in this region, the need for a comprehensive

COIN policy integrating all elements of national force—political, economic, social, diplomatic, and military is obvious. However, the government responses have been frequently compromised by collusion and the nexus between politicians, bureaucrats, contractors, non-governmental organizations, and insurgent groups, each seeking a pie of the "insurgency dividend" (Baruah, 2005: 18).[6] About three decades ago, the NPC, in its report "Policing in the North-East" (May 1981), had observed that severe insurgent violence in northeast posed a grave threat to the security and stability not only of this region but of the whole country. The NPC also mentioned that the problems of policing in the northeast were far too complex and varied and required "a highly professional, well-organized, and trained police force, which is at the same time aware and responsive to the needs of the tribals." However, there is little evidence of such a professional force in many northeast states even after a lapse of three decades since the publication of this report. The police in most northeast states remain ill-equipped or unresponsive to the all-encompassing lawlessness and violence in the absence of firm political resolve and clear mandate. Substantial military and paramilitary units have been deployed in the region, but coordination between federal and state forces and administration remains less than satisfactory, hampering COIN efforts.

In addition to the weak law-enforcement structures, the northeast also suffers from an acute "crisis of governance" and "crisis of development," which is reflected in poor capacities and competence to undertake core tasks of governance and development. Consequently, despite having large number of state government employees, the level of governance in the region is abysmal. These diminished capacities for governance are further aggravated by an extremely thin presence of all-India cadre officers, emanating from their reluctance to serve "punishment postings" in the region. As per *Census of India*, 2011, the literacy rate in most northeast states ranges from 66.9 percent (Arunachal Pradesh) to 91.5 percent (Mizoram), which is not too far from the national

---

[6] Baruah (2005: 18) has used the term "insurgency dividend" to mean leakage of governmental developmental funds allocated to the region into the "black economy" in northeast India.

average of 74 percent. However, the quality of education is marred by acute shortage of trained teachers and high dropout rates. Active student politics, the culture of protests, blockades, and atrocities by terrorists have caused further deterioration of education standards. In 2010–2011, the number of trained teachers at primary level was very poor in Arunachal Pradesh (7 percent), Nagaland (24 percent), Manipur (35 percent), Mizoram (42 percent), and Meghalaya (45 percent) against the national average of 90 percent (*Human Development Report of Northeast States*, 2014: 33). A similar dismal situation prevailed at upper primary school in these states. However, even in some other states such as Tripura where the percentage of trained teachers was 82 percent, the quality of education imparted to scheduled tribe (ST) students and the performance of ST students at high school and higher secondary level was extremely poor as we shall see in the subsequent chapters.

The High Level Commission appointed by the Prime Minister in its report submitted in 1997 had identified four basic deficits confronting the northeast in its report: a basic needs deficit, an infrastructure deficit, a resource deficit, and a two-way deficit of understanding with the rest of the country (Planning Commission, 1997).The development strategy pursued by the governments, both state and federal, has failed to propel economic growth in the northeast, and their economies are characterized by weak industrial sectors, underdeveloped agrarian societies, and inflated service sectors (Sachdeva, 2013). The state-sponsored industrialization—sugar mills, jute mills, paper mills, or food processing—has not been successful. Furthermore, small-scale industries have not been viable, and there is large-scale industrial sickness. Consequently, the economy remains primarily agricultural, and marked by low productivity due to primitive farm practices. Non-utilization of government funds for productive purposes and underutilization of natural resources like land, water, and forests has further weakened the economic growth in this region (Roy and Dastidar, 2011).

The creation of small-sized, unviable states has caused structural retrogression to a patronage-dependent economy from the center and government-spending propelled economic growth.

In most northeastern states, except Assam, the contribution of own revenue was between 10 and 20 percent of state's total revenue and the remaining was received as tax devolution and grants from the central government. It is also a fact that while the state governments in the region have been reluctant or unable to collect taxes from their citizens, a much larger percentage of people's income is taken by armed insurgent groups as "taxes" and extortions. A top-down development planning strategy has robbed the people of the sense of belonging and led to an inefficient and wasteful resource allocation on one hand and lack of social accountability on the other (NER, Vision 2020, volume 1: 7). However, contrary to popular perceptions, there has been no dearth of funds to northeast states. According to an estimate, the cumulative net devolution from the federal government to the northeast during the period between 1990–1991 and 2002–2003 has been about ₹92,000 crores, of which the grant portion was about ₹65,000 crores (Sachdeva, 2013: 118).

In this scenario, the key to restoration of normalcy in the northeast is a comprehensive approach focusing on the re-establishment of the rule-of-law, good governance, and democratic politics, rather than heavy military or paramilitary deployment. A clear enunciation of a coherent COIN strategy coupled with firm political resolve and concerted actions to build own capacities for security, governance, and developmental functions are the key to restoration of peace in the region.

This chapter addresses two main issues: (a) post-independence, what have been the main characteristics of northeast insurgencies, particularly links between the main insurgent groups and Muslim fundamentalist organizations, organized crime, drugs and arms trafficking? (b) How have the federal and state governments responded to these insurgencies in northeast India? This chapter is organized into three sections. The first section presents an overview of insurgencies in the three most violent states in the region—Assam, Nagaland, and Manipur, followed by section two, which discusses the broad pattern of insurgencies in the region, and the concluding section examines the government's COIN policy in the northeast.

The Northeast Region

Table 4.1 provides information regarding some key indicators concerning population and police in the northeast states relevant to our study. Northeast is India's ethnically most diverse region, home to around 45 million people belonging to hundreds of tribes and sub-tribes. Broadly speaking, there are three distinct groups of people—the hill tribes, the plain tribes, and the non-tribal population. But contrary to general perception, northeast is not dominantly tribal-populated region, and ST population constitutes less than one-third of the total population (*Census of India*, 2011). However, the distribution of ST population is skewed. In four states—Arunachal Pradesh, Mizoram, Nagaland, and Meghalaya—the ST people are in majority;[7] and in Assam, Sikkim, Manipur, and Tripura, ST people are moderately present. Interestingly, the maximum number of ST people—3.8 million out of total ST population of 12.4 million in northeast, reside in Assam where they form 12.4 percent of total population. About two-thirds of the area is hilly terrain, and the rest comprises valleys in Assam and Manipur and some flatlands in between the hills of Meghalaya and Tripura.

Historical Background

In the colonial times, the vast tract of land comprising Assam and two princely states of Manipur and Tripura was commonly referred to as British Assam, and it was only after the reorganization of the region and liberation of Bangladesh that the term "North East" gained currency. The court chronicles of the Kacharis (1515–1818), the Jaintias (1500–1835), and the Manipur Kings (1714–1949) suggest that they had historically retained varying degrees of freedom well into the nineteenth century. In fact, this region became part of India only after the first Burmese War

---

[7] The percentage of ST population is as under: Mizoram (94.4 percent), Nagaland (86.4 percent), Meghalaya (86.1 percent), and Arunachal Pradesh (68.7 percent).

Table 4.1:

Population and Police Data of Northeast (as on January 1, 2014)

State	Capital	Area (sq. km)	Population October 1, 2013 (000)	Total Police Strength (Actual)	Police Stations	No. of Policemen per		Total Police Expenditure (₹ in crore)	Unit cost per Policemen (₹ per annum)
						100 sq. Km of Area	100,000 Population		
Arunachal Pradesh	Itanagar	83,743	1,274	9,873	101	11.8	775	371.32	376,096
Assam	Dispur	78,438	31,445	54,435	340	69.4	173	1,499.54	275,474
Manipur	Imphal	22,327	2,516	25,674	86	115.0	1,020	574.54	223,783
Meghalaya	Shillong	22,429	2,692	11,197	39	49.9	416	295.83	264,205
Mizoram	Aizawl	21,081	1,032	9,326	38	44.2	904	311.07	333,551
Nagaland	Kohima	16,579	2,310	10,003	72	60.3	433	639.21	639,018
Sikkim	Gangtok	7,096	629	4,279	28	60.3	680	167.56	391,587
Tripura	Agartala	10,486	3,714	23,619	73	225.2	636	658.94	278,987
Total Northeast		2,62,179	45,612	1,48,406	777	636.1	5,037	4,518.01	2,782,701

Source: BPR&D, 2014; M inistry of Home Affairs, 2013 and 2014.

(1824–1826) that wrested the territory away from the Myanmar Empire and secured it for the British Raj.

The British policies of progressive segregation of tribal populations into "non-regulated," "backward," or "excluded" areas and the Inner Line system implemented between 1874 and 1935 systematically undermined the "connectedness" of the region with rest of the country (Jafa, 1999). These policies excluded tribal areas from the pattern of administration, codes of civil and criminal procedures, and many other laws that prevailed in other parts of India and created a "frontier within a frontier" by severely restricting access to all "outsiders." Apart from these policies, the proselytizing efforts of the Christian missionaries also served to create a distinct group identity among the tribal people different from the mainly Hindu and Muslim population of mainland India and added a religious dimension to their resistance (Sinha, 2007: 229–232).

The political ramifications of these exclusionary policies were far-reaching as tribal communities remained distanced from the gradual "democratization" that was taking place in the rest of the country through the nationalist (and eventually independence) movement and this accentuated the political and cultural schism between tribal areas and the plains. The dichotomous administrative system also produced wide variations between the pace of development in the hills and plains, with the latter dominating the economic profile of the region, and the tribal areas lagging far behind. As the British departure became imminent, demands for separation from India began to be raised by different sections of tribals.

However, isolationist policies have continued in the post-independence period under the mistaken notion of "protecting" the tribal population against exploitation by "outsiders." The operation of the principle of "protective discrimination" under the Indian Constitution (Article 342) further complicates the situation by deepening the fissures between tribal and non-tribal populations. For example, the Sixth Schedule which provides for the administration of tribal areas in Assam does not provide equal protection to all the tribes. A notable exclusion is the Plain Tribes, which include the Bodos, Misings, and Tiwas communities. Even the Tea Tribes of Assam whose forefathers were brought as indentured labor to work in the tea plantations of Assam have been denied "ST" status, although in their original habitats in states of Jharkhand, Chhattisgarh, Madhya Pradesh, Bihar, and Orissa they are designated as "ST." Many of them call themselves *adivasis* or indigenous people and have formed ethnic militias to press their demand for ST status, for example, Adivasi Cobra Force, Birsa Commando Force, and Adivasi Suraksha Samiti (Indigenous Protection Committee) in Assam.

With a majority of the ethnic groups being designated as "ST," economic rights in regard to land ownership, trade licenses, businesses, and even elected offices are restricted. In the states of Arunachal Pradesh, Meghalaya, Mizoram, and Nagaland, there is near total reservation of seats for ST. Unequal economic and political opportunities coupled with unequal access to resources aggravates perceptions of being deprived among the disadvantaged and have triggered numerous insurgencies in the NER. In view of such discriminatory policies in the northeast, many ethnic groups have come to believe that only violence can bring rewards and increase their share of the developmental cake.

There has been a long history of linguistic and religious revivalist movements in NER. Apart from the alienation of land and other economic resources, cultural pressure and linguistic suppression by the Assamese people alienated the Bodos, the Miris, and the Mishings who launched agitations for preservation of their distinct cultural identity. The Ahom, Meitei, Seng Khasi, and Zomi communities have all felt threatened by the near extinction of their original language and religion (Das, 2009). In Manipur, the Meitei revivalist leaders demanded that the Manipuri language be named "Meeteilon," and in Meghalaya, the Seng Khasi organization led the process of revivalism and reformation of the Khasi religion when it felt that prevalence of Christianity was eroding their traditional socio-religious practices. The Zeliangrong People's Conference agitated for protection of ethnic identity of their people spread in contiguous

110 Police and Counterinsurgency

areas of Manipur, Nagaland, and Assam. In Tripura, the socio-political–cultural marginalization of tribals and domination of Bengalis threatened the distinct ethnic identity of the aborigines who formed various sociopolitical organizations to preserve their interests.[8] Post-1970s de-sanskritization became the focal point for tribal society. In a conscious bid to distance themselves from Bengali culture, the tribals started using their mother tongue Kokborok in speech and writing, worshipping of tribal gods and goddesses, and acceptance of Christianity, and emphasizing on their women to wear traditional *richa-pachara* (traditional attire).

However, while analyzing the relationship of insurgence and institutional development in India's northeast, some observers have given a different perspective on northeast insurgencies and argued that an excessive preoccupation with narratives of unrest, insurgence, and violence[9] and a narrow reading of implications of insurgent violence on the part of scholars, security analysts, and national media has been responsible for substantial misunderstanding of northeastern political processes, leading to an inadequate appreciation of long-term constructive implications of anti-authority struggles and underestimation of positive aspects of community formation, political reconciliation, democratic participation, and innovations in institution-building, and sustenance in the region. It has been argued that successful processing of ethnic demands, which encourages new demands need not be always construed as a danger to national integrity but instead may be interpreted as a signal of social mobility and a manifestation of growing political and social consciousness among a heterogeneous but hitherto "dormant" mass that enables them to seek their space of dignity in the wider system (Dasgupta, 1997; Verghese, 2004: xvii–xix).

According to a noted political commentator Atul Kohli (1997), democracy and democratization in a multicultural

---

[8] Jana Mangal Samity (1936), Jana Shiksha Samity (1945), Tripura Proja Mondal (1946), Tripura Rajya Gana Mukti Parishad (1948), and Tripura Upajati Juba Samity (1967).

[9] A comprehensive study made by Reddy and Reddy (2007: 4–5) has found that like other regions, violence in northeast was concentrated only in pockets, and that contrary to public perception, a large number of villages (more than 71 percent) were crime-free for the last five years.

nation, such as India, are expected to encourage emergence of ethnic self-determination movements that typically follow the shape of an inverse "U" curve and are resolved properly when the state authority is well institutionalized and national leaders and leaders of ethnic movements act in a firm but accommodative manner. However, problems surface when in absence of such favorable conditions the demands are not properly accommodated, and a sense of injustice and exclusion may push some of the demanding groups toward militancy. Therefore, resolution of ethnic conflicts places a premium on "democratic leaders with inclusionary, accommodating strategies" on the part of all contending parties (Kohli, 1997).

An Overview of Insurgencies in Assam, Nagaland, and Manipur[10]

In India's northeast, there are three states—Assam, Manipur, and Nagaland—which have been facing significant levels of insurgent violence for many decades. The insurgency in Tripura has been substantially contained and the situation in Arunachal Pradesh and Mizoram remains largely peaceful (see Table 4.2 and Figure 4.1). However, situation in Meghalaya has turned bad recently with 36 civilian casualties in 2012, 30 civilian casualties in 2013, and 24 civilian casualties in 2014. For comparison, it may be noted that the figures of civilian casualties were 11 (2012), 15 (2013), and 28 (2014) in Jammu and Kashmir, while all northeast states combined (except Assam and Meghalaya) recorded 20 civilian casualties in 2014 (MHA, 2014–2015: 263–264).

The following discussion presents an overview of the insurgencies in Assam, Nagaland, and Manipur, while the situation in Tripura is discussed in a separate chapter.

---

[10] There are several sources which provide an excellent overview of northeast insurgencies. For instance, see Chadha (2005), Verghese (2004), Bhaumik (2009), and Upadhyay (2009).

Table 4.2:

State-wise Violence Profile in Northeast Region (2007–2014)

State	Incidents	Extremists Arrested	Extremists Killed	Extremists Surrendered	SFs Killed	Civilians Killed
Arunachal Pradesh	285	294	108	278	6	35
Assam	2,126	2,634	712	3,788	104	839
Manipur	3,467	9,728	1,149	1,302	106	458
Meghalaya	423	487	95	173	19	105
Mizoram	6	24	6	15	4	3
Nagaland	1,160	1,760	379	31	4	156
Tripura	237	171	35	1,057	12	36

Source: MHA, Annual Report, 2014–2015, Annexure III.

Figure 4.1:

Map of Northeast India and its Neighbors

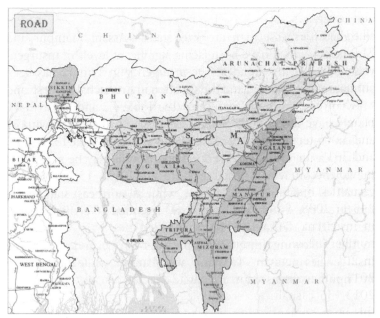

Source: http://www.nelive.in/north-east/news/earthquake-shakes-parts-north-east-India

Disclaimer: This figure is not to scale. It does not represent any authentic national or international boundaries and is used for illustrative purpose only.

Assam

Introduction

Assam is the most prominent state in the northeast with a population of 31.2 million (*Census of India*, 2011) spread over 78,438 sq. km, which gives it a density of population of about 398 per sq. km. The rural population constitutes about 85.9 percent with an average literacy rate of 69.3 percent as compared to average literacy rate of 88.4 in urban areas. About 34 percent of working population was engaged in agriculture. The prominent tribes are the Kachari, Karbi, Koch-Rajbongshis, Dimasas, Mishing, Mishmi, and Rabha. An analysis of sectoral percentage contribution of GSDP at constant (2004–2005) prices from 2004–2005 to 2013–2014 indicates that other than services sector, the contribution of agriculture and allied sectors and industry sector has been declining steadily (*Economic Survey, Assam 2013–2014*). In 2013–2014, the percentage contribution of services sector was 57.5 percent, while the agriculture and allied activities sector and the industry sector contributed 17.8 and 21.2 percent, respectively.[11] In 2013–2014, the state's own revenue was about 42.8 percent of the total budget, while the federal government provided the rest as share of Central taxes and grants.

According to data maintained by SATP 7, a total of 8,141 people have died, including 4,253 civilians, 823 SF personnel, and 3,065 terrorists in violent incidents in Assam between 1992 and 2015 (up to June 14, 2015). There was a sharp escalation in violence in 2007 and 2008 when the number of civilian casualties rose sharply from 96 in 2006 to 287 in 2007 and 245 in 2008. Since then, there has been significant reduction in insurgent violence, and for the first time since 1992, the number of annual civilian fatalities remained less than 60 in 2010 (53 civilian casualties). This trend was maintained in 2011 (18 civilian casualties), 2012 (27 civilian casualties), and 2013 (35 casualties) (see Table 4.3). A significant reason for this improvement has been change in attitude of the regime in

---

[11] The major contribution toward the growth of services sector in northeast states is due to the increase in public administration expenditure (Srivastav, 2006).

Bangladesh, improved operational outcomes, and also because several groups have simply succumbed to exhaustion and entered into dialogue with the government. However, there has been a sharp escalation in violence in Assam since last year mainly due to violent incidents committed by NDFB/Songbijit against Muslim settlers and *adivasis*. The problems for SFs have been further compounded by the emerging nexus between local groups, CPI/Maoists, and some Jihadi groups such as Harkat-ul-Mujahideen and Jamaat-ul Mujahideen Bangladesh (JMB). Some other major active groups in the state are ULFA-I, NDFB, Karbi People's Liberation Tigers (KPLT), Kamtapur Liberation Organization (KLO), and Muslim United Liberation Tigers of Assam (MULTA).[12] The entire state of Assam has been declared as "Disturbed Area" under the Armed Forces (Special Powers) Act, 1958. Clearly, insurgency is far from over in the state and insurgent groups still retain sufficient strength to challenge SFs. The strength of insurgent groups (and surrendered extremists) is also evident from the large number of abductions and rampant extortion in the state.

Table 4.3:
Violence Profile in Assam (2007–2014)

Years	Incidents	Extremists Arrested	Extremists Killed	Extremists Surrendered	SFs Killed	Civilians Killed
2007	474	408	122	229	27	287
2008	387	403	110	724	18	245
2009	424	359	194	616	22	152
2010	251	370	109	547	12	53
2011	145	378	46	789	14	18
2012	169	412	59	757	5	27
2013	211	348	52	92	05	35
2014	246	319	102	102	04	168

Source: MHA, 2014–2015: 263.

---

[12] For a comprehensive list of terrorist groups in Assam, see SATP, "Assam, Major Terrorist/Insurgent Groups," http://www.satp.org/satporgtp/countries/india/states/assam/terrorist_outfits/index.html (accessed on November 30, 2015).

Background

The roots of the problem of insurgency can be traced to a continuous influx of population into Assam since early part of the twentieth century, which has dramatically altered its demographic, linguistic, and religious profile. The shortfall of labor for tea plantations, oil refineries, rice cultivation, and building up rail, road, and inland waterways networks was made up by cheap labor from Sylhet and Mymensingh in present-day Bangladesh and from Bihar, Bengal, Orissa, the Central Provinces, the United Provinces, and Madras. Since then, the illegal migration has continued unabated in the absence of any forceful action for reversing this trend and apparently, as time passed the immigrant population became a powerful vote bank, which was difficult to ignore (Chadha, 2005: 235). While no authentic figures are available on the actual number of illegal immigrants in Assam, in 1997 the Union Home Ministry estimated their number to be around 4 million, out of total 10 million illegal migrants in the country.

This influx has caused significant changes in the religious demography of the state. Over the last decade, the Muslim population in Assam has grown from 30.9 percent in 2001 to 34.2 percent in 2011, out of a total of 31.1 million—the second highest among Indian states, after Jammu and Kashmir. The rate of growth has been the highest among the districts that share a border or lie close to Bangladesh. As a result of this influx from Bangladesh, minorities are said to be a deciding factor in almost one-third of the total 126 Assam Assembly constituencies. Many districts, such as Dhubri, Bongaigaon, Goalpara, Nagaon, Hailakandi, Karimganj, and Barpeta, have already become Muslim-majority districts. Besides this, demographic pattern has also been changing in Kokrajhar district, the heart of Bodoland, leading to conflicts between the Bodos and the Muslims. As elsewhere in the northeast, the influx created pressure on the land, caused unemployment to the native Assamese people, and generated social tensions. Popular sentiments against the "foreigners" led to a mass movement by the All Assam Students Union (AASU) in 1979 seeking detection of illegal immigrants, their deletion from the voters' list, and their deportation to Bangladesh. By all accounts this agitation launched by AASU was a genuine mass movement and an expression of ethnic Assamese fear of their identity being lost by the relentless migration from Bangladesh. The agitation ended in August 1985 with the signing of Assam Accord between the GOI and the AASU. Its leaders formed the Asom Gana Parishad (AGP) and participated in the electoral politics. However, the Accord failed to resolve the issue as the task of identifying "foreigners" proved extremely difficult.

The militant outfit ULFA was established in April 1979 and maintained a low profile initially, focusing on building its organization, support base, training, and linkages with other terrorist outfits in the region and across the borders. It built contacts with the Inter-Services Intelligence (ISI) of Pakistan, NSCN, and the Kachin Independence Army (KIA) of Myanmar. During the regime of AGP (1985–1990), the ULFA created terror in the state by disrupting communications, abducting businessmen for ransom, and killing civilians and government officials. As the government lost its control over the situation, the state was brought under President's Rule on November 28, 1990 and ULFA was proscribed under the *Unlawful Activities (Prevention) Act, 1967.* The army launched major operations in 1990 and 1995 that led to the capture of several top-ranking leaders and hardcore cadres as well as millions of rupees.

Over the years, ULFA has established a vast network of extortion, criminal and quasi-legal operations to fuel and finance militancy and its collusive nexus with government officials and political leaders, which have severely impeded the developmental activities in the state. However, there has been a steady erosion of popular support of ULFA following growing "lumpenization" of its rank and file, a complete turnaround over the issue of illegal migration, targeting of state's assets such as oil refineries and tea plantations, and media reports regarding total capitulation of top leadership to security agencies of Bangladesh and their lavish lifestyle in safe camps abroad. The victory of the Awami League in 2008 elections and again in January 2014 general elections in Bangladesh has resulted in closer cooperation between India and

Bangladesh after years of Bangladeshi support to insurgent groups active in northeast.

Here, it is also pertinent to mention that while the ULFA agitation challenged the federal government, recent insurgencies by other aggrieved communities—the Bodos, the Hmars, the Karbis, and the Dimasas—have been against the regional powers, that is, state government. The Bodos, the largest plain tribe of Assam, have been long articulating demand for ethnic homeland to preserve their distinct linguistic and cultural identities and secure their economic assets, most notably land. More than 90 percent of Bodos depend on agriculture as their main source of income; however, a majority of them are landless as the land has been usurped by non-tribals. Consequently, they have been reduced to abject poverty, and a plethora of tribal welfare schemes launched by the government have failed to alleviate their conditions. The Sixth Schedule of the Constitution which covered the Naga tribes, and the tribal population of Meghalaya, Mizoram, and Tripura left out the Bodos who lived in the plains of Assam. Furthermore, since the Fifth Schedule did not cover Assam, the Bodos were left with nothing (Basumatary, 2014). The 1960 Act, that had made Assamese the official language, further alienated the Bodos. Since then, two ethnic accords have been signed between the government and the Bodos, one in 1993 and the other in 2003, to grant them autonomy through Bodo Autonomous Council (BAC) and Bodo Territorial council (BTC), respectively. However, there are many skeptics who believe that these accords are an exercise in futility. NDFB and Bodoland Liberation Tigers (BLT) have been the most dreaded militant outfits, and over the years committed many rounds of "ethnic cleansing" in Bodoland areas. In retaliation, the non-Bodo communities such as Santhals, Koch Rajbongshis, and ethnic Bengalis have formed their own militant outfits such as the Bisa Commando Force, the KLO and the Bengali Tiger Force (BTF). There have been several rounds of large-scale violence between Bodos and the immigrant Muslims in the BTC areas in which hundreds of lives have been lost and tens of thousands have been displaced. The federal government's decision to form a new Telangana state has revived long-standing demands of the Bodos, Karbi, Dimasas, and Koch-Rajbongshis groups for four new states by carving Assam, leading to several rounds of large-scale violence and curfew in various parts of Assam (*The Times of India*, 2013). The police have failed to effectively respond to multiple challenges of insurgent violence, communal conflagrations, and law and order disturbances despite a sizeable deployment of over 55,000 policemen of which more than 27,000 are armed.

The root cause of problem in Assam is the progressive land alienation of tribals, particularly Bodos, over many decades and the failure of successive governments to clearly identify and disenfranchise illegal migrants due to cynical political calculations (Gill, 2012). The problem has been further compounded by aggressive Islamist politics, with some political parties seeking to mobilize the principal illegal migrant community in Assam, the Bangladeshi Muslims, as it has become increasingly difficult for any party to form government without their support. No permanent solution to chronic problems in Assam is possible without a comprehensive settlement of the twin issues of the transformation of land ownership and demographic destabilization (Gill, 2014).

Presently, 13 insurgent groups are under "Suspension of Operation" (SoO) agreements with the government. Tripartite talks are being held by Central government's Interlocutor with representatives of ULFA (Pro-talk faction) and NDFB (Progressive/ Ranjan Daimary). Here, it is pertinent to mention observations of R.N. Ravi, the present Joint Intelligence Committee (JIC) Chairman who summed up the existing SoO mechanism in an article published on May 8, 2014 as follows:

> They (militants) summarily remove any resistance to their writs by demonstrative killings. They control contracts for Government works and dominate the lucrative trade in legal and illicit forest assets. Besides, the Government gives them hefty cash every month in the guise of maintenance of their cadres and sustenance of "political" activities of their leaders.... They are allowed to retain

their military hardware and continue their military operations with a rider that they must not attack the security forces. In this paradigm of peace the militias and the security forces of the state are at mutual peace while the people remain at the receiving end of both (Ravi, 2004a).

Overall, it would be fair to conclude that there has been a failure of political and police leadership and the security situation is likely to remain complex in the foreseeable future due to insurgent violence and problems related to illegal immigration, tribal land alienation, ethnic polarization and resentment among various ethnic groups over the territorial autonomy granted to other groups.

Nagaland

Nagaland is a small northeastern state with a population of 1.9 million (*Census of India,* 2011) and area of 16,579 sq. km. It shares international borders with Myanmar on the eastern side, and with the states of Manipur, Assam, and Arunachal Pradesh. Nagaland has 86.48 percent tribal population. There are 16 different tribes in Nagaland, which are further divided into as many as 20 clans. Each tribe has its distinct customs, attires, languages, and dialects. Some of the major tribes are Angami, Chang, Konyak, Lotha, Rengma, Sema, Pochury, and Zeliang. The state has literacy rate of 80 percent. The forest cover is about 80 percent of the total land area and the economy of the state benefits from the rich minerals such as iron, limestone, cobalt, coal, nickel and chromium, petroleum, and natural gas. However, Nagaland is a financially stressed state, unable to raise finances (beyond an average of ₹535 crore per annum) and perennially dependent on the federal government for grants to fund more than 90 percent of its annual expenditure. The government spends a huge amount on salary of its employees, numbering more than 100,000 or 5 percent of the total population, thus draining its resources for development and public investment. The ongoing conflict and rampant extortion by insurgent groups has discouraged private investment and industries (Sen, 2013).

Table 4.4:

Violence Profile in Nagaland (2007–2014)

Years	Incidents	Extremists Arrested	Extremists Killed	Extremists Surrendered	SFs Killed	Civilians Killed
2007	272	98	109	4	1	44
2008	321	316	140	4	3	70
2009	129	185	15	6	–	16
2010	64	247	5	12	–	–
2011	61	267	8	–	–	7
2012	151	275	66	4	–	8
2013	145	309	33	1	–	09
2014	77	296	12	–	–	01
Total	**1,220**	**1,993**	**388**	**31**	**4**	**155**

Source: MHA, Annual Report, 2014–2015.

According to data maintained by SATP 8, during 1992–2015 (June 14, 2015), there have been a total of 2,478 casualties in Nagaland, which includes 794 civilians, 255 SF personnel, and 1,429 insurgents. Since 2010, there has been relative peace in Nagaland and the casualties of civilians and security personnel have been in single digits (Table 4.4). However, fratricidal clashes between various factions of NSCN have risen sharply, and during 2012 as many as 43 incidents of fratricidal clashes between Naga factions took place within Nagaland resulting in 53 casualties, which was a significant increase over the figure of seven casualties in 2011, and only two in 2010 (SATP 9). According to an estimate, over 1,800 Nagas have been killed in about 3,000 fratricidal clashes since the beginning of "ceasefire"(1997–2013), as compared to some 940 casualties in clashes with SFs in the 17 years preceding the "ceasefire" (Ravi, 2014). Recently, clashes between the SFs and the Naga militant factions have also escalated following breakdown of talks between GOI and NSCN (K). On June 4, 2015, 18 Indian army men were killed in an ambush by NSCN (K) in Manipur and in a retaliatory attack on insurgents' camps in Myanmar on June 8, an unspecified number of these insurgents were killed by army commandos. Earlier in May 2015 eight Assam Rifles personnel were killed and several others injured in an ambush laid by NSCN (K) in Mon district along the border with Myanmar. NSCN (K) had unilaterally abrogated the ceasefire agreement with the Union government in March 2015.

Background of Insurgency

The roots of Naga separatism precede Indian independence when the "Naga Club," an organization of 20 Nagas, submitted a memorandum to the British administration in 1926, demanding that Naga sovereignty be restored when the British withdrew from India. In subsequent years, the British policies of progressive segregation of tribal areas and arrival of Christian missionaries proved to be a critical factor in creating an idea of a single Naga community. A few months before independence, the Naga National Council (NNC), a representative body of Nagas, signed a Nine-Point Agreement with the Indian government on June 29, 1947 which, among other things, provided for a review of the political status of the Naga Hills after 10 years. However, there were differences in their interpretation and while the Nagas interpreted it as their right to self-determination, the GOI felt that Nagas had the freedom to suggest revision of administrative pattern only after 10 years, which was not acceptable to the NNC (Sinha, 2007: 53). Following this divergence in perceptions, the NNC leader Phizo declared independence on August 14, 1947 and formed an underground Naga Federal Government in March 1956 and a Naga Federal Army of around 3,000 armed guerrillas. The Indian Army was inducted in the state in April 1956, and Phizo fled to Pakistan and thereafter to London in June 1960.

Political Initiatives

In order to find a peaceful solution to the problem, the GOI has taken a number of steps to meet the legitimate demands of the

Nagas. In July 1960, an agreement was reached with the moderate section of the Naga leadership, and the state of Nagaland was formed on December 1, 1963. Immediately after the declaration of statehood, elections to the state legislature was held with an impressive turnout of 76 percent, thereby endorsing the election process; 60 legislators were elected. On November 11, 1975 the Shillong Accord was signed to end hostilities between the GOI and Naga groups that gave insurgents an opportunity to integrate peacefully back into the Indian political mainstream. However, the Accord was denounced by the more radical elements, including Isak Swu and T. Muivah, who later formed the NSCN on February 2, 1980. The NSCN split in 1988, resulting in the formation of NSCN (K) under the leadership of K.K. Khaplang. Since then, both groups have indulged in worst kind of internecine clashes resulting in killing of their own cadres.

The most active insurgent/terrorist groups at present are: Federal Government of Nagaland–Non-Accordist (FGN-NA), Federal Government of Nagaland–Accordist (FGN-A), NSCN (K),NSCN –Reformation (R), Naga National Council–Accordist (NNC-A), and Non-Accordist faction of Naga National Council (NNC-NA). The GOI signed ceasefire agreements with the NSCN (IM) on July 25, 1997 and so far more than 70 rounds of inconclusive talks between the GOI's representatives and the NSCN (IM) have been held at various locations, both within and outside the country (Ngaihte, 2014). A ceasefire agreement was signed with NSCN (K) also in 2001. However, the insurgent groups have routinely flouted the conditions of ceasefire. Heavily armed cadres of NSCN factions openly move out of designated camps in uniform and indulge in road blockades, extortions and other crimes.

During the ceasefire period, more than 1,000 persons have died in militant violence in Nagaland as a result of factional clashes. The fratricidal violence has vitiated the security scenario in neighboring Arunachal Pradesh also where the Assam-based ULFA and the Manipur-based UNLF have reportedly aligned with NSCN (K) in its fight against NSCN (IM) for area domination. Some observers have noted a vested interest of militant outfits in stretching these talks indefinitely because it allows them to remain armed, enables them to indulge in massive extortions, intimidation and other criminal activities and build up their respective outfits for another round of violent confrontation with the government (Shekatkar, 2009: 25). In a meeting on law and order held at Kohima on July 29, 2009, the Chief Minister and the Home Minister both conceded that the ceasefire had enabled the armed groups to indulge in large-scale extortion, intimidation and other anti-social activities and mentioned that the officers were running the government under the threat of AK rifles and even colony leaders and village elders were forced to work for the militants (SATP 10).

The annual extortion by the Naga factions of NSCN is reported to be ₹13 billion each year, and "taxes" are imposed on all state government employees, private businesses, and general population (Khangchian, 2011). Exorbitant "taxes" are levied on all vehicles and goods entering the state and insurgent groups have started distribution of "dealerships" for many commodities. The income from extortion was estimated at over ₹2 billion in Dimapur alone, Nagaland's commercial capital (Dash, 2008). Significantly, this is much higher than the annual plan outlay of Nagaland for 2008–2009, which was pegged at ₹1.2 billion. The non-Naga traders are specially targeted, and in 2008 more than a dozen traders were murdered and over 100 abducted for ransom and extortion. Some commentators have alleged that the successive Nagaland State Governments have been patronizing different factions of militant factions for their vested interests and made no efforts to resolve this long-standing conflict (Routray, 2008b). The role of the state police leadership has also drawn criticism for their lack of will and professionalism in curbing the insurgency. Despite having more than 20,000 police personnel and receiving significant central assistance under the "police modernization" scheme, there has been no augmentation of its capacities for COIN tasks (Routray, 2008a). More specifically, crime investigation, training, and intelligence are neglected, and the near absence of rural policing means that the movement of insurgent cadres and their criminal activities remain virtually unchallenged by police. The presence of army and paramilitary forces also does not hinder insurgent operations as these forces are prohibited by the ceasefire agreement from conducting operations. Arms smuggling remains a serious issue in Nagaland, and at least 25 arms dealers, including two NSCN (IM) cadres, were arrested in 2013. In a major breakthrough, on 30 August 2013 one Thai national was arrested by Bangkok police while arranging for supply of Chinese arms to NSCN (IM), including 1000 assault rifles and an unspecified number of rocket-propelled grenades (SATP 11). NSCN (IM) maintains offices in several countries including the U.S., U.K., Germany, Netherlands, China, Thailand, Japan, and Philippines, and has camps in Bangladesh from where arms are supplied to its cadres.

R.N. Ravi, the current Chairman of the JIC and the interlocutor for talks with Naga groups since August 2014, in an article (*The Hindu*, 2014) had observed that the peace process in Nagaland was flawed because crucial stakeholders—the popularly elected state government, the traditional Naga bodies, and other active militias had been excluded from the processes. According to Ravi, NSCN-IM was essentially a militia of the Tangkhul tribe of Manipur which had little acceptance among broader Naga family, and that the reckless "ceasefire" agreement between the GOI and the NSCN (IM) was pushing the Nagas into a state of civil war, and led to retreat of the state from crucial areas of governance and subversion of democratic politics.

Conclusion

Despite Central government's "peace talks" with NSCN factions and other initiatives to resolve the vexed Naga issue, the prospects of durable peace in the state are not good due to emasculation of important institutions of governance and dominance of heavily armed Naga insurgents, rampant corruption and a reported nexus between rebels, local politicians and bureaucrats. The present impasse in Indo-Naga talks is likely to persist due to determined opposition of the governments of Manipur, Assam, and

Arunachal Pradesh and some non-Naga ethnic groups to the proposed Nagalim. The escalation of violence against SFs, and twin demands—for a separate "alternative arrangement" for the Naga tribes living within Manipur pending final resolution of the Naga issue and the demand for carving out a separate Frontier Nagaland State out of the present Nagaland state—have further complicated the problem (Ngaihte, 2014).

Manipur

Introduction

Manipur is a small northeastern state with a population of 2.5 million (*Census of India,* 2011) and an area of 22,327 sq. km. It shares border with Myanmar, Assam, Mizoram, and Nagaland. Manipur is inhabited by three major ethnic groups—the Meitei, the Nagas, and the Kuki-Chin-Mizo. The ST population constitutes 35 percent of the total population. The people are predominantly Mongoloid and speak Tibetan-Burmese languages. Manipuri is the lingua franca of the state, and English is the official language. About 90 percent of the state is hilly and more than 60 percent of the total land area is covered with natural vegetation. The rural population constitutes 67.5 percent of total population. Almost half of the workers, 49 percent, are engaged in agriculture and allied activities (*Census of India,* 2011). Manipur remains one of the most backward states with regard to the economic development in the country. The main constraints impeding its development are common to many other northeastern states: Geographical and location disadvantage, poor infrastructure, lack of industry and private investment due to insurgency and law and order problems, poor agricultural productivity, corruption and lack of good governance. During the past decade, the central assistance as percentage of approved outlay has been between 75 and 90 percent.

Table 4.5:

Violence Profile in Manipur (2007–2014)

Years	Incidents	Extremists Arrested	Extremists Killed	Extremists Surrendered	SFs Killed	Civilians Killed
2007	584	1,217	219	7	39	130
2008	740	1,711	364	37	16	137
2009	659	1,532	336	28	19	81
2010	367	1,458	108	60	06	33
2011	298	1,365	28	284	10	26
2012	518	1,286	65	350	8	21
2013	225	918	25	513	5	28
2014	278	1,052	23	80	08	16
Total	3,669	9,239	1,387	1,305	111	472

Source: **MHA,** *Annual Report,* **2014–2015.**

In Manipur, from 1992 to 2015 (till June 14, 2015), there have been a total of 6015 casualties including 2,248 civilians, 1,002 SF personnel and 2,765 insurgents (SATP 12). Violence took a sharp turn for worse in 2005 when terrorist related civilian fatalities escalated from 88 in 2004 to 158 in 2005 following the alleged rape and custodial death of a female insurgent Manorama Devi at the hands of Assam Rifles personnel in July 2004. Since then Manipur has continued to be inflicted with severe violence, despite operations by police and SFs. However, there have been some tentative gains for the SFs since 2010 in COIN leading to reduction in civilian casualties (see Table 4.5). But it is a matter of concern that despite the sizable number of state police forces, their role in COIN operations remains marginal in absence of any coherent political strategy to engage militant outfits on a sustained basis and the poor operational preparedness of the force to combat heavily armed insurgent groups.

Background of Insurgency

The landmass of Manipur comprises 90 percent hilly area exclusively reserved for "tribals" —Nagas and Kukis—and the remaining 10 percent constitutes the Imphal Valley inhabited by the Hindu Meiteis and Muslim Meiteis-Pangals who together constitute more than 50 percent of the total population of the state (Sahni, 2002a). One of the main reasons for "internal conflicts" between these tribes results from the fact that while the hill tribes are classified as "ST," the Meiteis have been denied this status resulting in a lack of positions for them in government jobs and education. Further, in another instance of "protective discrimination", the *Manipur Land Revenue and Land Reform Act, 1960* provides that while the hill tribes may settle in the Valley, the Meiteis are prohibited from buying land or settling in the hills. An added complexity is provided by the large Naga population residing in the four hill districts of Manipur, a long and hostile border with Nagaland and the demands of *Nagalim* seeking unification of all Naga majority areas in Manipur, Assam, Arunachal Pradesh, and Myanmar. The Manipuris fear that they would be left with only Imphal Valley, if the GOI concedes this demand and hands over the four hill districts to Nagaland (Phanjoubam, 2002). Other factors fuelling insurgency include the perceived insensitivity of the Union government toward Manipur's culture and heritage, and several accumulated historical grievances relating to Manipur's merger with India, including the delay in granting statehood to Manipur, and official recognition to Manipuri language (Upadhyay, 2009: 40). Manipur was merged fully with the Indian Union on October 15, 1949 but attained full statehood only in 1972 after a long and violent struggle, and it was only in 1992 that the Manipuri language was included in the Eighth Schedule of the Indian Constitution.

Militant Groups[13]

Presently, over a dozen major insurgent groups are active in the state. These include the United National Liberation Front (UNLF), People's Liberation Army (PLA), People's Revolutionary Party of Kangleipak (PREPAK), the Kangleipak Communist Party (KCP), the Kanglei Yawol Kunna Lup (KYKL), Coordination Committee (CorCom), comprising six valley-based groups, Manipur Naga

---

[13] SATP, "Terrorist/Insurgent Groups-Manipur,"http://www.satp.org/satporgtp/countries/india/states/manipur/terrorist_outfits/index.html accessed on October 28, 2012.

Revolutionary Front (MNRF), People's United Liberation Front (PULF), Zeliangrong United Front (ZUF), and the NSCN (IM) and NSCN (K).

In 1964, the state's first Meitei separatist group, the UNLF was formed, followed by the Revolutionary People's Front (RPF) and its military wing, the PLA on July 25, 1978. The RPF believed in Marxist-Leninism, opposed sectarian politics based on ethnic or religious appeal, and received help from the Chinese. Despite receiving major setbacks in the 1980s from the SFs, both the PLA and the UNLF emerged stronger in the late 1990s and have more than 6,000 armed fighters. A significant development has been the formation of CorCom (a coordination committee) that brought together several Meitei rebel groups on one platform in 2011. Faced with the growing strength of Meitei insurgent groups, the Indian government authorized the army to sign an SoO agreement with eight Kuki and Zomi tribal insurgent groups in 2005. Some observers have alleged that these groups were then used by the army in its operations against the Meitei insurgent groups (Bhaumik, 2007: 17–18).

The ethnic conflict between the Nagas and the Kukis since 1992 is a disturbing development in Manipur. A number of Kuki organizations including Kuki National Army (KNA) and Kuki National Front (KNF) have been fighting for a separate state since the 1980s. The roots of the Naga-Kuki conflict lie in the NSCN's attempt to drive out the Kukis from, and control the lucrative drug trafficking and smuggling of contraband through Moreh, a trading center on the Myanmar border. These conflicts have resulted in the death of more than 1,000 persons and an enormous loss of property (Sinha, 2007: 120–121).

Militant-politician Nexus

Citing specific instances of the nexus between politicians, bureaucrats, and contractors, intimidation and murder of honest officers and levying of "taxes" by militant outfits, Rammohan (2002) has observed that the insurgency had become a widespread extortion racket, which has affected every aspect of politics, administration, and the social life of the state. It has been alleged that both politics and militancy are rooted in ethnicity in the northeast, and as the politicians and the militants share a common support base, they tend to collaborate to serve their own vested interests (Routray, 2007b). An instance of this nexus came to light on August 7, 2007 when a police raid on the residences of three politicians (MLAs) in Imphal netted 12 militants of various groups, besides some arms and ammunition. Many politicians have been accused of buying or attempting to buy peace with militant groups.

The dominance of the insurgents is also reflected in their ability to extort huge sums from government offices, local self-government and educational institutions, health centers, commercial establishments, and the general population (Routray, 2007a).The developmental works and civil governance efforts have been badly hampered due to intimidation and extortion by the militant groups who demand up to 30 percent of the funds allocated for various projects (Dash, 2009). In recent years, the militants have been targeting non-local Hindi and Bengali speaking people—mainly comprising migrant laborers and petty traders—to build their own support base among the indigenous population.[14]

Notwithstanding some recent successes of SFs, the situation in Manipur continues to be a cause of serious concern due to sustained high level of violence from insurgent groups. The alienation of Meiteis, the ethnic clashes between Nagas and Kukis, the effect of narco-terrorism, and the nexus between politicians and insurgents has further exacerbated the situation. The activities of almost 10,000 militant cadres of about 15 insurgent groups compound the endemic failure of state administration, taking Manipur to the threshold of "failed" state within the Indian Union. The role of the state police in COIN remains marginal, and in the absence of any coherent COIN strategy by the state government, there is little hope of any fundamental transformation in the situation in near future. The coming days are likely to see more violence as Kukis have decided to intensify their agitation for a separate state following announcement by the federal government to form a new Telangana state (*The Times of India*, 2013).

---

[14] Of the 64 civilians killed in 2009, 28 belonged to this category who were killed in 23 attacks distributed across all the four valley districts.

Broad Pattern of Insurgencies in the Northeast

In recent years, the term "contentious politics" has gained wider currency to describe situations where the actors use disruptive techniques to make a political point, or to change government policy. This approach also recognizes that movements are shaped by interpretation of political agents' perception of how structures affect them based on their own understanding of their identity and changing relationship to others in society. Or in other words:

> ... agents are socially embedded and constituted beings who interact incessantly with other such beings and undergo modifications of their boundaries and attributes as they interact (McAdam et al., 2001, quoted in Pampinella, 2012).

This perspective goes beyond the stereotyped notions of combatants in civil conflicts and can be certainly useful in understanding ground realities of NER where rebel groups are embedded in the workings of northeastern civilian politics (Lacina, 2009). The coexistence of resilient rebel organizations, intermittent complicity of civil society with them, an over-reliance on exceptional legislation and coercive force on almost permanent basis suggest a chronic, though localized, crisis of legitimacy, underlining the fact that "democratic politics and the world of armed rebellions intersect in complex ways" (Baruah, 2009: 11). The following discussion seeks to facilitate better understanding of prevailing situation in NER by unraveling underlying commonalities and broad patterns that are discernible in these insurgent movements.

Terrorism as a Criminal Enterprise

The maintenance of a terrorist enterprise in India's NER, run by large number of insurgent groups, is a costly affair that demands an uninterrupted supply of enormous funds as salaries to cadres, arms procurement and training, both within and outside the country, travel and propaganda entail huge expenditure (Upadhyay, 2009: 58). Considering the narrow support base of ethnic groups, the majority of these funds are required to be mobilized from within the region in absence of any support from diasporas. This compelling need to generate revenues locally explains the existence of a thriving "parallel economy" funded by extortions, kidnappings for ransom, drug and gun running, and "tax collection." To facilitate this, there exist complex collusive arrangements between various legitimate power elites and terrorist groupings in every single terrorism-affected state in the NER, which facilitate transfer of resources into the underground economy of terrorism (Sahni, 2001a). And in contrast to the common perception of terrorist activity as violent confrontation with the government, these groups exhibit a strong preference toward "systemic corruption" rather than violent destruction of the established political order as a result of which a large proportion of the state's revenue gets distributed illegally among politicians, bureaucrats, and banned militant organizations. Elaborating further on the terrorist economy in India's northeast, Sahni (2001a) has noted that almost all government contracts in insurgency-affected states are controlled by insurgent groups who manage to siphon off as much as 70 percent of funds, resulting in poor execution of approved projects with all its attendant evil consequences for state's economy. The locally powerful militant outfits, such as the ULFA, manage to earn millions of rupees per month through the diversion of funds from the lucrative sectors such as "rural development" and "public distribution system." Till very recently, the states of the northeast were categorized as "special category states," which meant that 90 percent of the plan assistance was grant and only 10 percent loan, and the Central devolution to the states in northeast accounted for over 80 percent revenue receipts in the region.[15] Thus, much of the developmental package ended up financing militancy. The fear of terrorist violence results in exodus of capital from the NER, inhibits the emergence of legitimate economy, and an evident lack of commitment and initiative is seen among local administration. Many times the administration is compelled to leave developmental projects mid-way as it is unable to cope with the intimidation and pressure from insurgent groups. The revenue receipts of militant

---

[15] The 12th Finance Commission has recommended that "special category" status of northeast states be withdrawn.

groups, running into hundreds of millions dollars every year, are compounded manifold through a massive network of extortions, "taxes" and enterprises (Bhaumik, 2009: 252–258). The vehicles plying on the major routes in the region are forced to pay "toll tax" at several places as they pass through the dominant terrorist group's area of influence. In Nagaland, the Nationalist Socialist Council of Nagaland—Isak-Muivah (NSCN-IM) reportedly collects a "house tax" from every dwelling unit (Sahni, 2001a). The hold of the militants on every illegal trade and business—including drugs and arms—is well established. According to Prakash Singh (2002), the northeast's proximity to the two large drug-producing regions—the Golden Crescent and the Golden Triangle countries—makes it highly vulnerable to drug trafficking operations of the militant groups such as the ULFA and NSCN, which maintain a nexus with rebel groups across the border in Myanmar.[16]

The criminal activities of insurgent groups have undermined the nation's health and fragile eco-system. The prevalence of Acquired Immune Deficiency Syndrome (AIDS) in the region, particularly in Manipur, Nagaland, and Mizoram from drug abuse has become a serious health issue. An astonishing 30 percent of intravenous drug users reside in the NER alone, which has only 3.8 percent of India's population. The insurgency has also impacted the fragile eco-system as militants establish their hideouts in wildlife parks and sanctuaries and SFs conduct their operations leading to denudation of forest cover. Assam's world famous Kaziranga Sanctuary, Manas Reserve Forest, and Manas Game Sanctuary in Lower Assam have been particularly targeted by insurgents as they provide easy access into the contiguous border areas of Bhutan.

These armed groups are able to operate with impunity most of the time because of their clout in the local politics as they cut political deals and influence elections. In fact, in all the states of the region, electioneering and militancy have become synonymous, though degrees may differ. This is particularly evident in Assam, Nagaland,

---

[16] Explaining the modus operandi, Prakash Singh (2002) mentions that Myanmar rebels bring drugs right up to Tamu and hand them over to local syndicates for dispatch to various destinations in the northeast and further on to the hinterland of India. In fact, a lot of clashes between the Nagas and Kukis were mainly over control of this drug route from Tamu to Imphal.

Manipur, and Tripura. A statistical study which analyzed the pattern of rebel attacks in these four states during 2003 and 2004 established that political events were powerful predictors of insurgent activity and the largest increase in the probability of an insurgent attack comes on election days (Lacina, 2009a: 33). In many states, the insurgent groups have flourished due to patronage extended by mainstream political parties, though this is routinely denied by the parties concerned. Most observers of the Tripura scene have commented that the NLFT shares its political objectives with the Congress, while the ATTF was floated by the Communist Party of India (Marxist) as a rival group to protect its tribal base (Chadha, 2005: 372).

A major factor contributing to the persistence of inter-communal and insurgent violence in NER has been the federal government's strategy of supporting localized autocracy and tolerance of erosion of democracy and law and order in exchange for protection of its critical vital installations, infrastructure, and security personnel (Lacina, 2009b). The generous distribution of federal financial and coercive resources also facilitates consolidation of power and domination of selected local ethnic autocrats over other competing groups in their struggle for scarce resources. The changing pattern of violence in NER with relatively few targeted attacks against federal structures/personnel and prevalence of internecine clashes and inter-communal violence lends support to this argument. Apparently, in many states of the NER, alternative structures of governance are emerging in areas characterized by a high level of disorder or anarchy.

Arms Supply and Drug Trafficking

The acquisition of illegal small arms and light weapons by insurgent groups is a vital factor in the conduct and duration of the conflicts the world over (Louise, 1995)[17] and India's northeast

---

[17] Light weapon is a generic term used to describe all conventional munitions that can be carried by an individual combatant or by a light vehicle. It includes small arms, bazookas, rocket-propelled grenades, light anti-tank missiles, light mortar, shoulder-fired anti-aircraft missiles, and hand-placed landmines. Small arms is a sub-category consisting of automatic weapons up to 20 mm including sub-machine guns, rifles, carbines, and handguns (Louise, 1995: 1).

is no exception. Over the years, there has been a remarkable upgrade of the militants' arsenals. When the Nagas first started armed struggle in 1950s, they had access to weapons left by the Japanese and Allied Forces after the Second World War. Over the years, major insurgent groups such as the NSCN, ULFA, NDFB, and other groups from Manipur and Tripura have collected a formidable arsenal of weapons through various sources, including purchases from friendly Burmese rebel groups, Thai black market, Chinese mafia groups, Pakistan's ISI, and theft and pilferage from Indian SFs (Bhaumik, 2009: 185). The scale of their arsenals can be easily gauged from a massive arms consignment of ULFA, which was seized by Bangladesh police in April 2004.[18]

Mizoram has become an important center for both gun running and narco-terrorism as it provides easy access to Bangladesh's Cox Bazaar and the infamous Golden Triangle—Burma, Thailand, and Laos. All kinds of weapons, from small handguns to rocket launchers, AK-47s and rifles of Russian, American, Chinese, and German make are freely available in the thriving underground market of Mizoram (Nepram, 2001). More recently, China's state-owned weapon manufacturing company, The China North Industries Corporation (NORINCO), has emerged as the largest supplier of arms to northeast insurgent groups through Myanmar and Bangladesh.

The militant outfits, particularly NSCN, use money from arms sale to finance drug trafficking and earn huge profits.[19] Along the border that northeast India shares with Myanmar, several illegal plants have come up to refine opium into heroin. This is facilitated by the fact that India is the largest producer in the world of acetic anhydride, the main chemical needed to produce heroin. The influence of powerful Burmese drug cartels, such as the UWSA

---

[18] The seized weapons included 690 7.62 mm T-56-1 SMGs; 600 7.62 mm T-56-2 SMGs; 150 40 mm T-69 rocket launchers; 840 40 mm rocket launchers; 400 9 mm semi-automatic rifles; 100 "Tommy Guns"; 150 rocket launchers; 2,000 launching grenades; 25,020 hand grenades; 7,00,000 rounds of SMG cartridges; 7,39,680 rounds of 7.62 mm caliber and 4,00,000 cartridges of other weapons (Bhaumik, 2009: 189).

[19] The average retail price of one gram of heroin in India was $5.2, while that in Netherlands was $42.5, in Canada $187.3, and in the US$ 475 (UNDCP World Drug Report, 2000 quoted in Sinha (2007: 242).

and Khun Sa, runs deep into government circles and ensures protection for rebel groups of the northeast. The involvement of serving military and paramilitary personnel, bureaucrats, monks, and priests in drug trafficking and laxity on the part of courts and police in enforcing anti-narcotic laws has led to a strong nexus of rebels, drug-lords and local officials has seriously undermined functioning of state institutions in the region. However, the flow of illicit small arms and drugs in NER is unlikely to be checked in foreseeable future due to absence of "superior intelligence, massive resources, and incorruptible enforcement agencies" required for this purpose (Markowski et al., 2008).

Illegal Migration from Bangladesh and Islamic Militancy

The demographic transformation of the NER in terms of changed ethnic, linguistic, and religious profile is a direct result of the large scale influx of people from across its borders, mainly from Bangladesh, posing a serious threat to India's national security. The magnitude of the influx in Assam can be seen from the fact that the population of four geo-strategically positioned districts—Dhubri, Goalpara, Barpeta, and Hailakandi—has become Muslim majority and five others have Muslim populations in excess of 35 percent.[20] And the situation is becoming alarming in some other states of the northeast as well, particularly Nagaland, Meghalaya, and Tripura. The Task Force on Border Management, headed by Madhav Godbole, a former Union Home Secretary, had estimated the number of Bangladeshi immigrants in India to be 15 million in 2000, which is now expected to have gone up to around 20 million in 2012 (Singh, 2012). India's Supreme Court in its landmark judgment in Sarbananda Sonowal case (2005) had observed that the state of Assam was facing "external aggression and

---

[20] According to a report submitted by the then Governor of Assam, Lt General (retd.) S.K. Sinha to the President of India in November, 1998 the total volume of this infiltration stood at six million (quoted in Lakshman and Jha, "India–Bangladesh: Restoring sovereignty on neglected borders," *Faultlines,* Vol. 14, July 2003. http://www.satp.org/satporgtp/publication/faultlines/volume14/Article7.htm accessed on March 11, 2010.

internal disturbance" on account of large-scale illegal migration of Bangladeshi nationals and quashed the *Illegal Migration (Determination by Tribunal) Act* and directed the government to take necessary steps under the *Foreigners Act*. However, the problem continues to persist and aggravate in absence of a firm decision due to vote-bank politics taking precedence over national security, (Mahapatra, 2012). During July–September 2012 and November 2012, Assam was convulsed with several rounds of large-scale violence between Bengali immigrant Muslims and Bodo/Assamese Hindus and the army had to be called to control the violence. The law and order situation was again disturbed in Assam in 2014 due to a series of attacks NDFB/Songbijit insurgents against *adivasis* and Muslim settlers, leading to massive army operations.

There have been several reports in the regional and Western media of Bangladesh emerging as an important theater for the activities of al-Qaeda and other Islamist fundamentalist organizations since the late 1990s (Lintner, 2002; Saikia, 2004). Though it is difficult to categorically state that there is any "hidden agenda" of engineering large-scale migration of Bangladeshis into the northeast, some analysts have taken serious note of statements made by prominent Bangladeshi persons to justify the ongoing large-scale influx of migrants in India.[21] In northeast India, Islamic militancy spearheaded by fundamentalist groups gained a fillip after the Global War on Terror" when active remnants of al-Qaeda and the Taliban entered Bangladesh and were used by the intelligence agencies like the ISI of Pakistan and the DGFI of Bangladesh to expand their terror network in the region (Saikia, 2009: 156–58). Over the years, more than one dozen fundamentalist organizations have emerged in the region, most of them in Assam. While the ostensible purpose of these outfits was to protect and defend Muslim interests against sustained violent

---

[21] While making a case for *lebensraum* in early 1990s, Sadeq Khan, a former Bangladesh diplomat, stated:

 ·· The natural trend of population overflow from Bangladesh is towards the sparsely populated lands in the Southeast, in the Arakan side and *of the Northeast in the seven Sisters side of the Indian sub-continent'* (emphasis added) *Holiday*, Dhaka, October 18, 1991 cited by Lakshman and Jha (2003).

campaigns over the issue of illegal migration from Bangladesh, gradually the agenda expanded to the "Islamization" of the region, aimed at creating an independent living space for the Muslims. As a strategy, they avoid direct confrontation with the SFs and work to polarize society by engineering religious riots and propaganda. They do not face any resistance from the local ethnic groups and serve as conduits between rebel groups and their patrons across the border. The growth of fundamentalism is facilitated by large number of mosques and madrassas (Islamic theological schools) that have mushroomed in the 10 km belt on both sides of Indo-Bangladesh border (see Table 4.6), even in those stretches where there is negligible population of the Muslim community. The medium of instruction in these schools is Arabic, rather than Urdu, and young children are indoctrinated with fundamentalist theology in these institutions (Singh, 2008).[22] The results of a government survey conducted by the government in 2000 are given in Table 4.6.

Table 4.6:

Mosques and Madrassas in the 10-km Belt on Either Side of Indo-Bangladesh Border

State	Indian Side		Bangladesh Side	
	Mosques	Madrassas	Mosques	Madrassas
West Bengal	458	208	523	302
Assam	236	157	204	38
Meghalaya	17	2	103	38
Tripura	194	72	130	71
Total	905	439	960	469

Source: Singh (2008: 57).

The Islamist militant movements in the region have gained sustenance from the illegal migrant population whose ideology and socio-religious commitments continue to be informed by experiences across the border. Another worrying development has

---

[22] On this point, see Singh (2008), "External Factors: Stoking the Flames," pp. 53–61.

been the recent formation of al-Qaeda in the Indian Subcontinent (AQIS) with Assam as its specific target (along with Gujarat and Jammu and Kashmir) and reports indicating network of JMB in different parts of West Bengal, Assam, and Jharkhand.

Cross-border Linkages of Northeast Groups

A key aspect of the insurgency in the northeast has been support from the neighboring countries—especially China, Pakistan, Bangladesh, and Myanmar. The cross-border linkages of insurgent groups have been greatly facilitated by the over 6,000 km long and porous international borders of India and the culture of "proxy wars" in South Asia.[23] The foreign support has manifested itself in financial and organizational support, weapons supply, training, operational cooperation and smuggling of arms and drugs. The motives behind China's support to Naga insurgents included its displeasure with India's perceived support for the Tibetan resistance movement and sheltering of refugees from Tibet as well as its desire to foment trouble to force the Indian government to remain preoccupied with its domestic matters, leaving China a freer hand to be the dominant power in the region. Similarly, both Pakistan and Bangladesh supported northeast insurgent groups to destabilize India for its attempts to foster rebellion in East Pakistan and Chittagong Hill Tracts in Bangladesh, respectively.[24]

There have been reports of Pakistan's ISI operating training camps in Bangladesh for the northeast insurgent groups. These groups include the NSCN, PLA, and ULFA. The activities of the ISI in Assam have covered a wide spectrum ranging from: sabotage of railways,

---

[23] While the Nagas, the Mizos, and the Manipuri militant groups received support from China and Pakistan, almost all northeast militant groups have enjoyed support from Bangladesh. On the other hand, India's external intelligence, Research and Analysis Wing (RAW) has extended support to many rebel groups in Burma, Bangladesh, and Tibet (Bhaumik, 2007: 25–32).

[24] The total number of Naga militants trained by China and Pakistan is estimated to be around 5,000 by Indian military intelligence. In subsequent years from 1967 to 1971, almost 3,000–4,000 Mizo militants were trained by Pakistan in Chittagong Hill Tracts (Bhaumik, 2007: 28).

roads, communication lines and oil pipelines, and other vital installations; promotion of fundamentalism and militancy among local Muslim youths; accentuating communal cleavages through disinformation campaigns; and the creation of new insurgent outfits on ethnic and communal lines, and provision of necessary logistic support including arms and explosives (Saikia, 2000).

Until very recently, the role of Bangladesh in providing sanctuaries to insurgent groups from the northeast has been causing serious concern to India. The issue of rebel camps in Bangladesh has prominently figured in official Director-General level talks, which Bangladesh routinely denied every time. However, during the past five years, Bangladesh authorities have arrested at least 17 top leaders of insurgent groups active in northeast reflecting a change in attitude of the current regime in Bangladesh. The arrested insurgents include ULFA's Chairman Arabinda Rajkhowa and Deputy Commander-in-Chief Raju Baruah (December 2, 2009), Foreign Secretary Sashadhar Choudhary, and Finance Secretary Chitraban Hazarika on November 1, 2009. In January 2014, a court in Bangladesh awarded death penalty to Paresh Barua, Chief of the breakaway faction of the ULFA, and 13 others in connection with smuggling of arms in 2004 (*The Hindu*, 2014).

India has also received cooperation from Bhutan and Myanmar in COIN operations. In June 2015, the Indian army reportedly attacked NSCN (K) camps inside Myanmar territory with cooperation of Myanmar government following the death of 18 army men in an ambush in Manipur. Earlier, in April 1995, a joint Indo-Myanmar operation—Operation Golden Bird —was launched to intercept insurgents who were returning to their bases in India after procuring huge arms consignment from Bangladesh. In this 44 day-long operation, up to 60 ULFA and other northeastern rebels were killed and several others arrested (Hussain, 2006). Some years later, Bhutan's co-operation was again instrumental in neutralizing insurgent threats operating from its soil. ULFA had set up camps in Southern Bhutan in the wake of the Indian Army's Operation Bajrang in Assam in November 1990. From these camps in thick wooded jungles strategically located close to the Assam border, the militants were able to carry out attacks in Indian territory and return to their bases. However, Royal Bhutan Army's crackdown Operation All Clear in December 2003 dismantled all these camps and led to the killing of 90–120 insurgents and the surrender of over 500 insurgents, while many insurgents managed to flee away through porous borders to Bangladesh, Burma, or Arunachal Pradesh (Hussain, 2003).

India's COIN Policy in Northeast

India's COIN strategy has been profoundly influenced by the philosophy of its first Prime Minister, Jawaharlal Nehru, who had a firm belief in democracy and insisted that internal conflicts be resolved predominantly through political processes. As regards the tribals of the NER, Nehru preferred granting them as much freedom and autonomy as possible so that they could live their lives according to their own customs and desires. This political approach has been amply evident in India's handling of the northeast conflicts as it has deliberately avoided the use of overwhelming force to score military victories against rebels and shown great political flexibility in searching for solutions to local grievances fuelling insurgency by all possible means, excluding secession. The salient features of India's COIN strategy to improve the situation in the NER include:

> Peaceful dialogue with insurgent outfits, deployment of central police forces, raising of India Reserve battalions, reimbursement of Security Related Expenditure, Modernization of Police Forces and implementation of Surrender-cum Rehabilitation Scheme (MHA, 2005–2006: 34).

Political initiatives to resolve ethnic insurgencies in the northeast have included the creation of new states or autonomous territories based on ethnicity, peace negotiations, ceasefires and suspension of hostilities, and acceptance of former insurgent leaders as officials in post-conflict civilian governments. However, the success of these political measures has been limited. A number of "ceasefire" agreements are already in place between the government and the militant groups, and others are being negotiated. However, peace agreements with some groups in the past have led to escalation in violence by other groups. Moreover, in most cases such agreements or ceasefires have not meant decline in extortions or other criminal activities, though there has been significant reduction in targeted killing of SF and government personnel. Swarna Rajagopalan has carried out a comprehensive study of all peace accords in the NER signed over the past six decades and identified the following reasons for the failure of most peace-accords in northeast: pre-accord talks have not been inclusive and important stake-holders have been left out; the provisions agreed upon with one group have patently conflicted with the grievances of another; core conflict issues have not been dealt comprehensively or not dealt at all; and finally, no responsive and political infrastructure has been created for conflict resolution, or even for governance (Rajagopalan, 2008).

For an ethnic group in the Indian Union, three kinds of recognition are possible: cultural recognition by inclusion of their language in the Eighth Schedule of the Indian Constitution which lists national languages, recognition as an ST or caste which carries with it access to special quotas for education and employment, and creation of a territorial unit. The tribal communities in northeast have been resentful of the economic exploitation, subjugation, and imposition of outside culture and religion on their traditional way of life, and launched agitations for ethnic homelands to safeguard their interests. The Center has responded by reorganization of this frontier region, mainly along ethnic lines. Between 1960 and 1987, six new states were created around Assam, and over the years many other territorial and non-territorial councils have been formed in many states. However, this has sharpened hostilities and violence between ethnicities and communities as newer and newer ethnic formulations keep cropping up to reap benefits granted by over-generous state (Goswami, 2007). The reorganization of the northeast states has also been held responsible for intensification of the idea of exclusive homelands which is responsible for much of the violence in this region. The absurdity of exclusive homelands demanded by some insurgent groups is apparent from a description of the overlapping cartographies which draw mostly from legendary, mythical or pre-colonial memories, with little or no reference to the present. Furthermore, in the process of reorganization, the state boundaries have not been defined clearly enough in many cases leading to border disputes and large-scale violence and internal displacement. There have been sporadic violent incidents on the Assam–Meghalaya, Assam–Nagaland, Nagaland–Manipur, and Assam–Mizoram border.

In NER there has been a heavy military and paramilitary deployment on almost permanent basis and "draconian" special laws have been enacted giving sweeping powers to the SFs to secure long and porous international borders and deal effectively with the insurgent violence directed against Indian SFs and communities from the "mainland" Indian states as well as internecine clashes among various ethnic militias. In addition to the army and paramilitary units, the federal government has also sought to build local capacities through its scheme of Modernization of Police Forces and reimbursement of security related expenditure. However, despite considerable augmentation of manpower and other resources, usually police have not been able to play a crucial role in COIN operations in northeast states in absence of firm political resolve and lack of a decentralized robust police infrastructure empowering police stations and dispersed field formations of armed battalions. Since 1997–1998, a Unified Command structure for COIN has been in existence in Assam;[25] however, the coordination mechanisms between federal and state forces have not been very efficient and frequently created friction (Baruah, 2005: 65; Cline, 2006). Moreover, "inter-state rivalries and turf-wars" have stalled the establishment of a trans-regional coordinating body for conducting COIN across all states of NER (Bhaumik, 2007). In 2014 another "Unified Command" has been set up in Arunachal Pradesh on the lines of Assam to deal

---

[25] The Unified Command is headed by the state's chief civilian administrator, but gives sufficient powers to the army in operational matters and coordinates the use of all military and paramilitary forces, and also provides a platform for sharing of intelligence between the army, paramilitary, intelligence agencies, and police.

with the insurgent violence, particularly in Tirap, Changlang, and Longding districts and also 20 km belt bordering the state of Assam.

Conclusion

In recent years there has been a significant decline in militant violence in the region and the SFs have been able to neutralize large number of militants. An insurgency fatigue seems to have set in some groups and the federal government has already signed cease-fire agreements or commenced negotiations with many of them, including ULFA and NSCN factions. The arrest or surrender of several senior cadres of NLFT and ATTF in recent years has further crippled these weak insurgent outfits of Tripura. Unfortunately, many northeast states have not taken advantage of this opportunity to strengthen and modernize their police forces and build robust decentralized capacities to respond effectively to challenges in their respective jurisdictions. Consequently, army has been tasked again to lead the charge against insurgent groups both within and outside the country. However, it also bears repetition that there are no military solutions and SFs can only create ground conditions for political, administrative and developmental initiatives (Verghese, 2004: 308). The flare-up of large scale inter-communal violence in Assam, fratricidal clashes among Naga factions and abrogation of ceasefire by NSCN (K) have raised fresh concerns about the efficacy of current political strategies, and capabilities of intelligence and law-enforcement apparatus. Commenting on the large-scale recurring Bodo-Muslim violence in Assam, K.P.S. Gill has observed that in addition to insurgency and terrorism, Indian administrators, politicians, and law-enforcement agencies need to evolve more effective strategies and policies to deal with challenges of communal and ethnic violence, public protests and other low-grade violence, and keep themselves abreast of national and international trends impinging on perceptions and motivations of people in their respective jurisdictions (Gill, 2012).

The issue of economic development of NER has also significant bearing on the insurgency problem. It is generally agreed that there is dual casualty between insurgency and development, that is, insurgency and terrorism and poor economic development feed on each other. The current official position on the long-term approaches to the problem of insurgency favors rapid economic development. The development in NER has been hampered by: low industrialization, subsistence nature of agriculture, poor infrastructure, and utilization of most government funds for consumption purposes rather than further income generation, and insurgency (Roy and Dastidar, 2011). In this context, India's recent diplomatic efforts to improve relations with neighboring countries, particularly Bangladesh and Myanmar, and a new resolute policy to deal firmly with insurgent groups is likely to have far-reaching consequences. The federal government has also accorded high priority to development of infrastructure, particularly roads, in border areas by creation of the National Highways & Infrastructure Development Corporation Limited (NHIDCL) with sufficient allocation of funds. The government has identified critical road projects that will connect India's South East Asian neighborhood, which will be funded by Asian Development Bank (*The Economic Times*, 2015). Consequently, the prospects of economic development, trade, and commerce in NER have greatly improved now. At the state level, the governments need to have a firmer grip on the law and order and ensure good governance, including governance at the grass-roots through institutions of local self-government, as without a reasonably efficient government, no programs or projects, in the context of COIN, will produce the desired results (Thompson, 1967: 51). Politically, the government should shift its focus from peace accords and seek to strengthen the peace processes by taking a more inclusive and broad-based approach to the issues. Efforts should be made to create multiple platforms for dialogue at every level and facilitate involvement of civil society for participation in peace process, and imagining non-territorial solutions as territorial concessions usually ratchet up demands of other groups (Rajagopalan, 2008). For peaceful and harmonious co-existence of ethnic communities in a country as diverse as India, robust institutional mechanisms are required for protecting and promoting their identity through meaningful power sharing by way of effective decentralization (Mukerjee, 2014: xxii). The formation of autonomous councils and district councils is certainly a right step in this direction, but needs more effective delegation of powers to ensure that these institutions can serve the purpose for which these have been created. To conclude, in the medium and the long-term, only political dialogue and initiatives which are based on mutual trust and flexibility, not exclusivity, which accommodate a range of concerns, and promote good-will among large sections of society, can lead to durable peace (*NER, Vision 2020*). While many northeast states struggle to work this out, the next section of this book provides ample guidance on the comprehensive COIN strategy adopted by Tripura to translate this vision of peace into reality.

5

An Overview of Insurgency and Counterinsurgency in Tripura

Introduction

Tripura is a small landlocked state in India's NER with an area of 10,492 sq. km and a population of 3.6 million as per 2011 *Census of India*. As much as 856 km of its boundary of 1,018 km (almost 84 percent) lies along the international border with Bangladesh, while it shares a 53-km-long border with Assam and 109-km-long border with Mizoram. Keeping in view the infiltration routes of insurgent groups, Tripura's border with Bangladesh the international border of Mizoram with Bangladesh is of strategic importance for Tripura. As mentioned earlier, the partition of Indian sub-continent was an unmitigated economic disaster for Tripura as it had lost all its rail-heads to the west, south, and north that fell in East Pakistan, and the state was cut-off from India's railway network. The distance by road from Kolkata was less than 300 km before partition. After partition, the route to Kolkata via the Siliguri land corridor became 1,700 km long. Presently, Tripura is connected to the rest of India by a National Highway 44 (NH-44), which runs through the hills to Cachar district in Assam and a meter gauge railway line. However, NH-44 is a single-lane highway of sub-standard quality, and a precarious link due to frequent landslides during the rainy season, while flow of goods through railway line is highly limited due to difficulties in transshipment from broad gauge to meter gauge at Lumding (Assam).

The terrain of Tripura is predominantly hilly and forested, and almost two-thirds of the geographical area of the state is covered with hills, forests, and swamps, leaving only 27 percent of the total area suitable for cultivation. The principal hill ranges of Tripura have altitudes varying between 50 and 2,000 feet above sea level, and run parallel to each other from north to south with an average distance of 12 miles between two ranges. The main hill ranges are the Jampui, Sakantang, Longtarai, Atharamura, Baramura, and Devtamura. The state has a tropical monsoon climate with a long rainy season of over six months, and an average annual rainfall of 225 cm (*Tripura: Human Development Report,* 2007: 3–5). These geographical disadvantages have been compounded by an almost total absence of industry, inadequate exploitation of natural resources, poor infrastructural facilities, and low capital formation (*Economic Review of Tripura,* 2013–2014: 8). Consequently, there is widespread poverty and unemployment in Tripura, particularly among the tribal people who live in rural areas. According to the Government of Tripura estimate, more than 55 percent of the population fell below the poverty line in 2001–2002 and the problem of unemployment among youth is alarming (*Tripura: Human Development Report,* 2007: 59). As per records, the total number of unemployed persons registered in the Live Register was 6,41,313 as on March 31, 2014, of which almost 23 percent belonged to the ST category (*Economic Review of Tripura,* 2013–2014: 85). Furthermore, while the average annual registration of ST people between 2000–2001 and 2009–2010 was 8,016, the employment exchanges could find placement for only 398 applicants annually on an average during the same period (*Statistical Abstract 2010–2011,* Government of Tripura: 128–130).

There are 19 STs in the state—Tripuri, Reang, Jamatia, Chakma, Lusai, Mog, Garo, Kuki, Chaimal, Uchai, Halam, Khasia, Bhutia, Munda, Orang, Lepcha, Santhal, Bhil, and Noatia. The population distribution among these tribes is as given in Table 5.1.

Table 5.1:

Distribution of Tribal Population in Tripura¹

Sl. No.	Names of the Tribes	Population (Census Years)			
		1981	1991	2001	2011
(i)	Tripuri/Tripura	3,30,872	4,61,531	5,43,848	5,92,255
(ii)	Reang	84,003	1,11,606	1,65,103	1,88,220
(iii)	Jamatia	44,501	60,824	74,949	83,347
(iv)	Noatia	7,182	4,158	6,655	14,298
(v)	Uchai	1,306	1,637	2,103	2,447
(vi)	Kuki	5,501	10,628	11,674	10,965
(vii)	Halam	28,969	36,499	47,245	57,210
(viii)	Lushai	3,734	4,910	4,777	5,384
(ix)	Bhutia	22	47	29	28
(x)	Lepcha	106	111	105	157
(xi)	Khasia	457	358	630	366
(xii)	Chakma	34,797	96,096	64,293	79,813
(xiii)	Mog	18,231	31,612	30,385	37,893
(xiv)	Garo	7,297	9,360	11,180	12,952
(xv)	Munda/Kaur	7,993	11,547	12,416	14,544
(xvi)	Santhal	2,726	2,736	2,151	2,913
(xvii)	Orang	5,217	6,751	6,223	12,011
(xviii)	Bhil	838	1,754	2,336	3,105
(xix)	Chamal	18	26	226	549
(xx)	Generic	0	0	7,098	48,356
	Total	**5,83,770**	**8,53,345**	**9,93,426**	**11,66,813**

Source: Economic Review of Tripura, 2012–2013: 307.

The economy of the tribal people is built around agriculture, which is mostly characterized by rain-fed cultivation and shifting cultivation. Most of the tribal land holdings are small or marginal and have low productivity. As per *Agriculture Census 2010–2011*, the percentage of marginal and small holdings of ST people in Tripura was 69.16 percent and 18.48 percent, respectively. Consequently, there is a widespread problem of poverty, indebtedness, and chronic

---

¹ The special characteristics of tribal people in Tripura such as sex ratio, literacy and educational level, work-participation rate, marital status, and religion as per data highlights (Census, 2001) are given in Annexure A.

unemployment. The situation was still more pathetic for tribals during the decades from 1960s to 1980s leading to discontent, disaffection, and insurgency. The percentage of people below the poverty line for rural people (mostly tribals) in Tripura went up from 66.1 percent in 1969–1970 to 85.5 percent in 1977–1978, while the corresponding figures for urban people (mostly non-tribals) declined from 52 percent to 44.2 percent during the same period (Bhattacharjee, 1989: 101). A micro-study on the problems of indebtedness among the tribal people in Sadar subdivision published in 1982 revealed that 66 percent of the total families of the survey blocks were in debt (Adihikari, 1982). The tribal people were also poorly represented in higher category of government posts (Bhattacharjee, 1989: 96). In December 1982, category-wise ST representation in government service was Class I (3.33 percent), Class II (7.46 percent), Class III (17.13 percent), and Class IV (20.56 percent). The literacy rate of ST population in India was very poor during 1960–1980, which further limited their chances of employment. As per *Census of India,* literacy rate of ST population in India was as follows: 1961 (8.5 percent), 1971 (11.3 percent), and 1981 (16.3 percent) (Statistical Profile of Scheduled Tribes in India, 2013:13). Considering all these statistics, it is easy to understand that their deteriorating economic conditions, exploitation, and powerlessness to change their material conditions compelled tribal people to take arms in the 1970s and 1980s.

The distribution of the population in Tripura is skewed and uneven, with only 26 percent of the population living in urban areas and nearly 25 percent of the total population concentrated in the newly constituted west district. The percentage of population living in undivided west Tripura district was still higher at 48 percent (*Tripura: Human Development Report, 2007:* 5). In urban Tripura, more than one in five young men are unemployed and in rural areas there is limited availability of work, occupational choices are restricted, and income is precarious. Further, there is overwhelming dependence on the federal government for revenues to the extent of 80–85 percent of the state's revenues (*Economic Review of Tripura,* 2012–2013: 17). During the past decade, however, there has been significant decrease in poverty in the state, as per federal government estimates. As per the figures released by the Planning Commission, poverty in Tripura declined from 40.60 percent in 2004–2005 to 14.05 percent in 2011–2012. The corresponding figures for all India were 37.20 and 21.90, respectively (*Economic Review of Tripura*, 2013–2014: 78).

Each one of these geographical, demographic, and economic features has important implications for the growth of insurgency and the COIN policies adopted by the government. The rugged hilly terrain, dense jungles, and porous international borders are ideally suited for the movement of insurgent groups and ambush of security forces, while the long rainy season and prevalence of malaria in interior areas adversely affect security operations. The COIN operations are also hampered by poor transport and communication network, and lack of proper medical facilities and other basic amenities for troops in interior areas, while the widespread poverty and underdevelopment in interior areas facilitate the recruitment drive of insurgent groups who find it easy to lure poor tribal youth.[2] Henrik Urdal (2008) has conducted a time-series analysis of 27 Indian states, including Tripura, for the period from 1956–2002 and found that scarcity of productive land coupled with low agricultural yield and high rural population growth was associated with higher risks of political violence. The fact that Tripura suffers from all these disadvantages to a considerable degree goes some way in explaining persistent political violence in the state and also suggests areas where improvements in governance and policies have potential for mitigating political violence.

Most observers of the Tripura scene agree that the insurgency in the state has its roots in demographics, as this is the only state in India's northeast that has been transformed from a predominantly tribal to a predominantly non-tribal state during the past few decades (Chadha, 2005; Sahni, 2002a; Bhaumik, 2002). The tribal population in Tripura was 52.89 percent in the 1901 Census and remained relatively stable until the 1940s,

---

[2] This has been corroborated by a study of human rights in Tripura (Khan and Mangathai, 2003), which mentions that 84 percent respondents gave "unemployment" and "economic reasons" for joining the insurgent groups.

when communal clashes in British-ruled East Bengal (later East Pakistan and present Bangladesh) resulted in a steady migration into this state. The communal riots during and after the partition further increased the influx of refugees, and by 1951, the tribal population had declined to 36.85 percent. Thus, in just two decades, the tribals were reduced to a decisive minority. Since then, there has been further decline, and the 2011 population census puts the tribal population at 31.8 percent. There is a general perception that massive internal and external migration in Tripura has been overlooked and even encouraged by vested political interests to reinforce a perceived vote bank as no political party could secure power in the state without the non-tribal vote. Many tribal people have lost their land and reduced to work as landless laborers, while others have become pauper paying exorbitant interest to *Bengali* moneylenders. Simple tribal communities have not been able to cope up with the transition from barter economy to money economy, loss of control over forests, and impact of modernization and globalization on their traditional ways of life and livelihood. This has generated tensions, frustration, and discontent among them and fueled the insurgency.

This chapter considers the main components of Tripura's comprehensive approach to COIN, which has successfully marginalized insurgent groups, both politically and militarily, over the past decade. The introductory section outlines the unique demographic, geographical, and economic factors of Tripura and their impact on the growth of insurgency and COIN in the state. This is followed by a discussion of the COIN strategies of the Union government and how these have been astutely used by the state government to build its own capacities for effective policing and governance. The concluding section analyzes the full spectrum of policies employed by the Tripura government to defeat insurgent designs and create secure environment for governance and development.

It would be seen that the marginalization of local tribals resulting from massive influx of non-tribal people leading to demographic destabilization, the politics of vote bank, and the political–militant nexus have all fueled insurgency in the state. However, starting in 2000, a radical reorganization, reorientation, and rapid expansion of police in the state coupled with astute political moves and economic development have re-established the legitimacy and authority of the state and significantly eroded the militant capacities for indiscriminate violence. The growing cooperation between India and Bangladesh since the return of Awami League to the power in Dhaka in January 2009 has further brightened the prospects for peace in Tripura. This consolidation of peace leading to the restoration of civil governance and development in Tripura is all the more significant in the backdrop of continuing violence, corruption, and lawlessness in many other northeast states in the region that have failed to take full advantage of policies of the Union government and neglected their own efforts to build capacities for COIN efforts.

Historical Background

The early history of Tripura is a complex blend of history with mythology and the long lineage of tribal kings stretching back many centuries, is mentioned in the "Rajmala," the state chronicle, which is not supported by independent archaeological, epigraphic, and numismatic evidence. However, it is generally agreed that by the fifteenth and sixteenth centuries, the Tripura kingdom had expanded considerably and included major parts of present-day Bangladesh such as Sylhet, Comilla, and Chittagong and extended up to the eastern limits of Arakan, which is in present-day Myanmar and Cachar, which is now in Assam (Goswami, 1996). In olden days, the territory of Tripura was divided into two parts—the hilly area and the plains. While the king enjoyed complete independence in the hilly "Tipperah," in the plains, known as "Chakla Roshnabad," he was an ordinary zamindar (landlord) under the Nawabs of Bengal.[3] This arrangement was followed by

---

[3] The name of the state continued to be "Independent Tipperah" till 1866 when it was changed to "Hill Tipperah" by the GOI, but on the appeal of the Tripura Durbar, the ancient name of "Tripura" had again been adopted.

the British too and the king used to pay revenue to the British government, but for all practical purposes he was independent so far as the hill areas were concerned. The king depended on revenues from this plain Chakla Roshnabad area for running his administration and incurring other expenses as the hilly area was mostly covered with jungles and inhabited by tribals who practiced shifting cultivation (locally known as *Jhumia*). In the pre-independence times, Tripura was thinly populated and its population density was only 17 in 1901, which gradually rose to 22 (1911), 29 (1921), 36 (1931), and 49 in 1941. In the subsequent decades, there has been exponential growth due to influx of immigrants, mainly *Bengali* Hindus, from neighboring Bangladesh (earlier East India) and other parts of the country, and the present density of population is 350 as per *Census of India, 2011*.

Interestingly, the roots of present-day problems can be traced to the policies of tribal kings who encouraged high-caste *Bengali* Hindus, Muslims, and other menial jobseekers to settle in Tripura to run the administration, execute development projects, and improve agriculture and trade. It is said that Ratna Manikya (fifteenth-century ruler) settled thousands of high caste *Bengali* Hindu families in the tribal areas of Tripura. This policy was followed by his successors too and gradually most important positions like the ministers, the advisers, and even clerical and subordinate staff in departments of judiciary, forestry, education (almost all the teachers were *Bengali* plain landers) were filled up by immigrants. No serious attempts were made by the *Maharajas* (rulers) to educate tribal people. The Bengal Administration Report for the year 1874–1875 shows that with an estimated population of 75,000 people, there were only just over 100 students studying in two schools. In 1879, the number of students was 700, of which only 52 were Tipperah, 388 *Bengali* Hindus and Muslims, 30 sons of "Thakurs" or royal families, and 232 Manipuris (Bhattacharya, 1992: 86). A year before independence in 1946, the number of total pupils was just over 5,000 which clearly indicates total neglect of education by the rulers of Tripura. Land revenue formed the major part of royal income from the early decades of twentieth century. The lure of money led the tribal kings to allot large tracts of plain land to *Bengali* Hindus for agriculture, and gradually ownership of sizable land passed from tribals to non-tribals who became permanent "settlers" of Tripura, while the indigenous people retreated into the interiors to pursue uneconomic shifting cultivation or join the crowd of agricultural laborers for survival. The laborers constituted 8.93 percent (1941–1951), which increased to 19.26 percent (1961–1971) to 23.91 percent (1971–1981), and 23.38 percent (1981–1991) , while cultivators declined inversely from 62.94 percent in 1941–1951 to 38.09 percent in 1981–1991 (Chakraborty, Dipannita, 2004: 48).

In the nineteenth and early-twentieth centuries, there was substantial immigration of tribal communities such as the Chakmas, Mogs, Manipuris, Garos, Bodos, Khasis, and Kukis from neighboring areas who came in pursuit of agriculture or jobs. More land was diverted for tea plantations by the *Maharajas*. The first tea plantation was started in Tripura in 1916 in Kailasahar division of the state for which laborers of Munda, Oraon, Bhil, Santhal, Bhutia, and Lepcha tribe from Bihar, Orissa, and Madhya Pradesh were employed. Thus, in pursuit of additional revenue for the royal treasury, the tribal kings unwittingly set in motion the processes that had adverse consequences for generations of native tribals and the land and employment opportunities were passed from tribals to non-tribals with disastrous results for tribal communities (Bhattacharyya, 1992: 100–115).

There have been many uprisings by tribal communities even during the reign of maharajas. The earliest instance of insurrection dates back to the sixth decade of the eighteenth century when Samser Gazi led a revolt against the zamindar of Dakshinik Pargana, defeated the royal force and gradually became ruler of Chakla Roshnabad. The oppressive policies of zamindar, cruel exaction of exorbitant revenue, and misrule were the main factors that moved the poor peasants and other common people to revolt. In subsequent years, tribal uprisings took place in 1857, 1860, and 1863 when people revolted against the oppression, exploitation, and cruel exaction of revenue by the Maharaja. After this, there were no more revolts by tribal people till 1942, when the Reang community revolted against forcible recruitment, cruel exaction, and over-taxation by the Maharaja.

Most kings of Tripura were also great patrons of *Bengali* literature, learning, and Hindu religion. In fact, the Rajmala or the chronicles of the kings of Tripura was composed in *Bengali* language during the reign of Dharma Manikya (1431–1462). The tribal kings constructed Hindu temples and employed *Bengali* artists for making images of Hindu deities. Most significantly, by fifteenth century the *Bengali* language had established itself completely in the Tripura court and it was made the state language. Thus, over many centuries, traditional tribal culture came into close contact with materially superior and advanced *Bengali* culture, which led to gradual assimilation of the Hindu culture and ways of life by the tribes of Tripura. By all accounts, this process was not coercive, and tribal people co-existed peacefully with other communities till the pressure became unbearable in the second half of the twentieth century (Bhattacharya, 1992).

After the partition of the Indian sub-continent, this princely state formally acceded to the Union of India in August 1947,[4] became a Union Territory in November 1956 and a full-fledged state in January 1972, with a 60-member Legislative Assembly. As the political reorganization of the NER was done primarily with a view to counter secessionist movements and pacify ethnic unrest in the region, the criteria of financial and administrative viability were not applied to the creation of new states. Consequently, despite massive transfer of funds from the federal government, most states in the northeast remain underdeveloped and suffer from a severe crisis of governance and development. In this context, it is pertinent to mention that the whole state of Tripura was only one district until September 1970 when it was divided into three districts, that is, the west district, South district, and North district. Dhalai district was added in 1995, and in a major administrative reorganization done in 2011, four new districts and many sub-divisions and rural development blocks have been added to make government machinery more accessible to people in remote areas (Figure 5.1). The present administrative set-up is shown in Table 5.2.

---

[4] For details, see "Tripura Merger Agreement, 1949," at http://www.satp.org/satporgtp/countries/india/states/tripura/documents/papers/tripura_merger_agreement_1949.htm accessed on November 29, 2015.

Figure 5.1:

Map of Tripura

Source: http://tripura.gov.in/districtmap

Disclaimer: This figure is not to scale. It does not represent any authentic national or international boundaries and is used for illustrative purpose only.

Table 5.2:

Administrative Divisions in Tripura

Districts	Sub-Divisions	Blocks	Panchayats	Revenue Villages	Tripura Tribal Areas Autonomous District Council (TTAADC) Villages	AMC/NP
West Tripura	3	9	90	96	77	4
Sepahijala	3	7	112	119	52	3
Khowai	2	6	55	78	58	2
Gomati	3	8	70	134	95	2
South Tripura	3	8	99	138	70	3
Dhalai	4	8	41	146	96	2
Unakoti	2	4	59	78	28	2
North Tripura	3	8	69	89	51	2
Tripura	**23**	**58**	**595**	**878**	**527**	**20**

Source: Economic Review of Tripura, 2012–2013: 9.

Politically, the year 1967 may be regarded as a watershed in Tripura in many ways as the changes in the state's demographic profile brought about by an influx of *Bengali* Hindu refugees from erstwhile East Pakistan (now Bangladesh) in the wake of communal riots had a major impact on state's politics. With a continuous decline in tribal population, the Communist Party suffered a severe setback in the Parliament as well as in the Assembly elections held in 1967, losing both the Parliament seats to Congress and securing only three of the 30 seats in the Legislative Assembly. In another significant development, a new tribal political party— Tripura Upajati Juba Samity (TUJS)—was launched to protect and promote the interest of the indigenous population. Its main demands included establishment of an autonomous district council, restoration of alienated lands, and protection of tribal culture. The formation of TUJS marked the beginning of ethno-centric politics and ethnic polarization between tribals and non-tribals. Finally, severe demographic imbalance between tribals and non-tribals gave rise to separatist tribalism, which found expression in the form of the first armed militant movement in the state, known as "Sengkrak" (Clenched Fist).

After the formation of Tripura state, there has been intense competition between the main political parties, that is, the Congress, the Communists, and the TUJS to capture the power. In the first Assembly elections held in 1972, after Tripura became a full-fledged state, the Congress secured a two-third majority and formed the government, while in the next elections in 1977, it was routed due to internal differences, and the Left Front formed the government.[5] The Left Front again emerged victorious in 1983 Assembly Elections, though with reduced majority, and in 1988 Assembly Elections, the Congress–TUJS alliance emerged victorious, partly due to severe violence unleashed by TNV insurgents against the *Bengali* people to discredit the government.

---

[5] The Left Front is dominated by the CPI (M), and also includes CPI and RSP. In the 2013 Assembly elections, the Left Front won 50 out of 60 seats (CPI/M-49, CPI-1, and INC-10). In the 2008 Assembly elections, the Left Front won 49 out of 60 seats (CPI/M-46, RSP-2, and CPI-1). In the 1983 Assembly elections, the Left Front won 39 of the 60 Assembly seats (CPI/M-37 and RSP-2) (*Tripura Year Book*, 2013: 79–100).

Soon after the elections, following an agreement with the federal government,[6] 447 TNV extremists surrendered in September 1988, leading to allegations of a nexus between Congress and TNV extremists. As per this agreement, the TNV agreed to deposit all arms and ammunition, and cease underground activities, while the government promised to initiate suitable measures for (a) resettlement and rehabilitation of surrendered TNV cadres, (b) restoration of alienated lands of tribals, (c) stringent measures to check infiltration from across the border, (d) reservation of 20 seats for tribals in 60-member state Legislative Assembly, and (e) economic empowerment of tribals through greater opportunities for skill formation, self-employment, and jobs in police and paramilitary forces. However, the Congress–TUJS government was affected by internal bickering and soon lost the confidence of the people. The Left Front again came to power in the 1993 Assembly Elections and since then has consolidated its hold and continues to remain in power. The "covert" and "overt" tactical alliances of underground insurgent groups and the main political parties have played a significant role in the electoral fortunes of all the main political parties in the state (Bhaumik, 2009: 208–209).

Post-independence, the influx of the large number of *Bengali* immigrants put a tremendous strain on the already scarce land resources, alienated them from their lands and resulted in their general pauperization due to devious ways of clever traders. Between 1947 and 1971, 609,998 Bengalis displaced from East Pakistan, arrived in Tripura and were settled on land under various government schemes. The magnitude of this influx can be gauged from the fact that the total population of Tripura in 1951 was only 645,707. An area of 777 sq. km was de-reserved by the government in 1948 to solve the mounting rehabilitation problem of *Bengali* refugees immediately after the partition. In another move, the government amended *The Tripura Land Revenue and Land Reforms Act, 1960* in 1974 ostensibly to restore tribal lands but instead it validated all tribal lands alienated before January 1,

---

[6] For details, see Memorandum of Understanding with Tripura National Volunteers (1988) at http://www.satp.org/satporgtp/countries/india/states/tripura/documents/papers/memorandum_understanding_tnv_1988.htm accessed on November 29, 2015.

1969. Worldwide, aspiration toward ownership of land has been held to be the main economic cause of insurgencies, irrespective of ideological aims of the fight (Guevara, 2007: 10). In Tripura too, a direct correlation between land alienation and tribal insurgency has been observed, and in some settled agricultural areas in Khowai and Sadar sub-divisions, between 20 and 40 percent of the tribal lands had been alienated by the end of the 1970s, when tribal insurgency gathered momentum (Bhaumik, 2009: 297–298).

Emergence and Growth of Insurgency

The tribal discontent and frustration resulting from this grave demographic and economic imbalance first found expression in the form of an organized anti-*Bengali* armed struggle *Sengkrak* (Clenched Fist) in 1967 in the northern hilly parts of the state bordering Mizoram. The insurgents were assisted by the Mizo National Front (MNF) and Pakistan's Inter-Services Intelligence (ISI). However, the movement could be easily controlled by the government and fizzled out around 1968 as it was not broad-based and lacked any well-conceived strategy or ideology. The second major tribal insurgent outfit, the TNV, emerged a decade later in 1978 to cause unprecedented ethnic and political violence in the state before signing a tripartite agreement with the Union Home Ministry and the Tripura government in 1988. Some TNV cadres who were not happy about laying down arms and dissatisfied with the slow pace of the implementation of the 1988 Accord formed the NLFT in March 1989,[7] followed by a rival ATTF in July 1990.[8] Over the years, 28 insurgent groups have come to

---

[7] Profile of the NLFT at SATP, available at http://www.satp.org/satporgtp/countries/india/states/tripura/terrorist_outfits/nlft.htm accessed on November 30, 2015.

[8] Profile of the ATTF at SATP at http://www.satp.org/satporgtp/countries/india/states/tripura/terrorist_outfits/attf.htm accessed on November 28, 2015.

notice in Tripura, but most of them have been neutralized and are no longer active now.[9]

The NLFT was formed on March 12, 1989, with Dhananjoy Reang (former Vice President of the TNV) as its "Chairman" with a view to establish an "independent" Tripura free from "Indian neo-colonialism and imperialism" through armed struggle and furtherance of a "distinct and independent identity." However, since its formation, the NLFT has suffered several splits along vertical lines on tribal affiliations, religious, and sectarian considerations and due to personal ambitions for power and pelf of top leaders. Dhananjoy Reang, who had been the President of NLFT, formed Tripura Resurrection Army (TRA) on February 11, 1994 following an attack on him by a splinter group of NLFT in his hideout in CHT, Bangladesh on July 10, 1993 as per direction of Bishwamohan Debbarma and Joshua Debbarma. However, though Dhananjoy Reang could manage to escape with a quantity of arms and with some of his followers, he was not able to sustain the struggle for long and surrendered before the government in 1997. Another split occurred in September 2000, following differences between the Halam and Debbarma tribal members of the NLFT, leading to formation of Borok National Council of Tripura (BNCT) by Joshua Debbarma. Personal ambitions of the leaders and parochial religious considerations between its Christian members and the Hindu tribes are believed to have caused yet another split in 2001 when Nayanbasi Jamatia and Bishwamohan Debbarma parted ways from the parent outfit to have factions of the NLFT under their respective leaderships. In yet another development in June 2003, Bishwamohan Debbarma was replaced by "General Secretary" Mantu Koloi, allegedly at the behest of NLFT's patrons inside Bangladesh. Debbarma is reported to have subsequently set up separate camps on the Tripura–Bangladesh border with his followers. While the Debbarma faction had an estimated strength of 550 cadres, the Nayanbasi faction comprised approximately 250 cadres. Other leaders of the undivided NLFT included

---

[9] Complete list of insurgent/terrorist groups in Tripura is available at "Terrorist/Insurgent Groups-Tripura," SATP, available at http://www.satp.org/satporgtp/countries/india/states/tripura/terrorist_outfits/index.html accessed on November 30, 2015.

Vice President Kamini Debbarma, Publicity Secretary Binoy Debbarma, and Chief of Army Dhanu Koloi. In December 2014, NLFT-BM was further weakened when Commander Prabhat Jamatya walked out with more than 25 followers and large cache of arms and ammunition. The NLFT was outlawed in April 1997 under the *Unlawful Activities (Prevention) Act, 1967* following its involvement in terrorist and subversive activities, and also proscribed under the *Prevention of Terrorism Act (POTA), 2002.*

The ATTF was originally founded as All Tripura Tribal Force on July 11, 1990, by a group of former TNV terrorists led by Ranjit Debbarma who were not satisfied with the 1988 accord concluded between the TNV and the Union government. Subsequently, the outfit rechristened itself as ATTF by substituting the word "Tribal" with "Tiger" sometime in 1992. It was initially a small group of tribal extremists who operated in pockets of North and South Tripura districts. Gradually, it began mobilizing manpower by recruiting tribal youth and enhancing the firepower of its cadres, and by 1991 it had emerged as a formidable terrorist group in Tripura. For many years before the return of Awami League to power in 2009, the top leaders of both ATTF and NLFT had enjoyed safe havens in capital city of Dhaka in neighboring Bangladesh, maintained large number of camps for sheltering and training of their cadres, and forged links with other terrorist outfits and security agencies of Pakistan and Bangladesh. However, more than 1,600 cadres surrendered by March 1994, under an amnesty scheme offered by the state government. A group of ATTF cadres that did not surrender revived the ATTF. It was subsequently banned in April 1997 under the *Unlawful Activities (Prevention) Act, 1967.* Over 70 percent of the cadres of ATTF are from Debbarma community, and the rest are from Jamatia, Reang, and Tripuri communities. Furthermore, about 90 percent of the top ranking ATTF cadres are Hindus and the rest are Christians.

Many observers of the Tripura scene have commented on the militant-political nexus and alleged that while the NLFT has linkages with the Indigenous Nationalist Party of Tripura (INPT) and the Congress, the ATTF was floated by the CPI (M) to protect its tribal base (Dasgupta, 2001; Hussain, 2003a; Sahni, 2002b). Both these insurgent outfits have been used by their mentors for selective killing and intimidation of political rivals and to influence election results (Datta, 2003). Customarily, the ATTF would target leaders and supporters of Congress and its allies, while the NLFT would target the CPI (M) cadres and leaders. However, over the years these insurgent groups have consolidated their power to use violence at will and are now no longer accountable to any political sponsors or supporters (Kumar, 2003).

Both the NLFT and ATTF have developed linkages with other insurgent outfits in the northeast, operate from secure bases in neighboring countries and have the common objectives of the expulsion of *Bengali* immigrants, restoration of alienated land to tribals and the establishment of an "independent" Tripura. The NLFT has developed close linkages with the NSCN (IM) and the NDFB, while the ATTF has linkages with the ULFA, PLA and PREPAK of Manipur. An ethno-ideological divide is also discernible in the separatist groups of northeast India as groups with leftist tendencies like the ULFA or ATTF tend to stick together, while organizations more narrowly focused on ethnic concerns and united by their faith in Christianity such as NSCN and NLFT remain in the same camp (Bhaumik, 2007).

It has also been observed that while both the NLFT and ATTF profess to fight for the common "tribal" cause, they are divided on ethnic and religious lines, and there have been frequent clashes between these groups for supremacy over the tribal areas, money, and political patronage. The NLFT has mixed cadres from the Debbarma, Jamatia, and Reang tribes, while the ATTF cadres are predominantly Debbarmas. Besides this, while most of the top NLFT leaders are Christians, the top leaders of ATTF are predominantly Hindus. Such ethno-religious differences have prevented any effective tactical unity among militant outfits and also provided Indian intelligence agencies opportunity for "special political operations" to play one group against another.

In recent years, NLFT has come to notice for forging linkages with various Bru militant groups operating in Assam, Mizoram, and Tripura with a view to utilize their services for recruitment, collection of extortion money, and kidnappings from the bordering villages on India-Bangladesh border (IBB) in North district of Tripura. In return, NLFT has reportedly agreed to arrange their training and supply arms and ammunition to Bru militants. This is a new development, and the state police have taken necessary action to counter this threat by augmenting resources for intelligence generation in concerned areas, improving co-ordination with Mizoram police, and asking the local leadership of Bru refugees not to provide any assistance, shelter, or logistic help to Bru militants. These efforts have succeeded in apprehension of many militants of outlawed UDLA from Reang refugee camps in Kanchanpur sub-division of North district (*Tripura Observer*, 2012).

As mentioned earlier, the security scenario was extremely disturbed around 2000 when the state was on the brink of civil war due to escalating ethnic, political, and terrorist violence. The educational institutions and developmental works bore the brunt of terrorist violence as the teachers and officials were specifically targeted. The terrorist groups were able to indulge in large-scale abductions, extortions, and killings with impunity due to political patronage and availability of safe sanctuaries just across the border in Bangladesh. The situation was so bad that even some policemen had to pay protection money to extremists to spare their lives. Tripura became the "abduction capital" of the NER as the state with barely 8 percent of the population in the northeast suffered over 70 percent of all kidnappings in the region. The executives of the tea plantations, petty traders, contractors, and political workers became the favored targets of insurgent groups for extorting large sums of ransom. Police estimates indicated that over ₹16.3 million were collected in 2000 by different militant outfits in the state and this figure went up to ₹21.3 million in 2001 (ICM, 2007: 76). Apart from earning huge amounts of liquid cash for funding militancy, the kidnappings terrorized the *Bengali* settlers and sharpened the ethnic polarization, forcing thousands of them from the rural hinterland to relocate to safer places.[10]

According to the data compiled by the SATP, there have been a total of 3,488 casualties (2,511 civilians, 457 security person-nel, and 520 insurgents) in Tripura from 1992 till May 3, 2015

---

[10] Bengali-speaking residents of Takarjala, Kendraicherra, Prabhapur, and several other areas of West District were forced to leave their villages in 2000, and had to be resettled in newly formed cluster villages (Tripura: *Human Development Report,* 2007: 109).

(SATP 13). A gradual decline in the insurgent violence over the past decade is clearly reflected in these statistics related to extremist violence. The number of civilian fatalities that peaked in 2000 at 453 had declined to 66 in 2004. The subsequent security operations have further consolidated these gains and since then the number of civilian fatalities and extremist incidents has been remarkably low (Table 5.3), while the kidnappings have declined steadily from 62 in 2005 to 8 in 2014.

Table 5.3:

Extremist Crime in Takarjala Police Station (2000–2007)

Years	Incidents	Extremists Arrested	Extremists Killed	Extremists Surrendered	SFs Killed	Civilian Killed
2007	94	64	19	220	6	14
2008	68	44	13	325	3	10
2009	19	14	1	293	1	8
2010	30	7	–	148	2	2
2011	13	19	–	25	–	1
2012	6	12	2	13	–	–
2013	6	10	–	22	–	1
2014	8	8	–	40	2	1

Source: MHA, Annual Report, 2014–2015.

The well-conceived COIN operations have neutralized a large number of hardcore extremists and their harborers. According to Tripura police records, over 1,000 hardcore extremists have been arrested and 280 extremists killed during encounters with security forces from 2000 to 2013. The above-ground network of collaborators and harborers which supplied intelligence and logistic support to the militants has been systematically dismantled with over 2,600 arrests during the corresponding period. The present strength of NLFT is estimated to be less than 100 hardcore extremists, mostly in safe sanctuaries across the international border. The surrender of some top leaders of NLFT such as

Suran Debbarma—responsible for killing 20 TSR personnel in an ambush in August 2002—and Atharababu Halam, s/s Deputy Chief of NLFT along with several cadres to police recently has further demoralized and weakened NLFT. In the past few years, the Bangladesh Army, Rapid Action Battalion, and Border Guards of Bangladesh have destroyed several camps of northeast insurgent groups, seized large cache of arms and ammunition, and arrested many top cadres. Following such incessant pressure, s/s NLFT Chief Biswamohan Debbarma has expressed his willingness to the central government to hold talks. On the other hand, ATTF has been effectively neutralized in recent years with the arrest of its chief Ranjit Debbarma in January 2013 and surrender of its self-styled Chief of Army Staff Chitta Debbarma to Assam Rifles in December 2012. The information provided by Chitta Debbarma led to the detention of ATTF supremo Ranjit Debbarma in Bangladesh by DGFI in January 2013 and subsequent deportation to Tripura where legal proceedings have been initiated against him (*Tripura Times*, 2013). In the coming days, more northeast insurgents are likely to be deported to India by Bangladesh following the extradition treaty between these two countries in 2013. Clearly, there has been a considerable reduction in insurgent ranks over the past decade as around 2003, the NLFT had 700–800 hardcore cadres, while ATTF had an estimated strength of 500–600 hardcore elements, and both of these outfits were supported by a large network of above-ground collaborators.

Considering the history and apprehension of escalating violence in pre- and post-election period, special efforts were made during 2013 Legislative Assembly elections in Tripura to further strengthen the border security arrangements to check infiltration of insurgents from across the border by (a) opening several new camps of TSR as a second line of defense along the IBB and augmenting manpower in other camps for intensive operations; (b) shifting of some BOPs to forward locations along the IBB by BSF; and (c) improving operational co-ordination between BSF and TSR in border areas (*Tripura Times*, 2013). Consequently, the level of militant violence during 2013 Legislative Assembly elections has been much less than 2003 and 2008 Assembly elections, leading to a record turnout of voters. In the February 2013 Assembly elections, 93.57 percent of votes were cast, which is a record in the electoral history of the country. Furthermore, the percentage of female voters (93.02) exceeded the percentage of male voters (90.89), signifying women's active participation in the democratic politics as well as a peaceful atmosphere in the state (*Tripura Times*, 2013).

COIN Strategy of the Tripura State

Economic and Developmental Initiatives

In keeping with the national policy, the Tripura state has also never viewed the insurgency as a mere law and order or security problem and adopted a holistic approach toward its resolution. It has also been willing to consider any political demand within the democratic framework of the Constitution of India and made concerted efforts to resolve the problems of social, economic, and political development of the affected tribal population. The policy of the state government to address the problem of insurgency has been well summarized as follows:

> Government initiatives include attempts to restore alienated lands to tribals; rehabilitation of the *Jhumias* (shifting cultivators) through different schemes; measures for poverty alleviation; the decentralization of administration and devolution of powers to local bodies; providing employment for tribal youth in the state sector; working to protect tribal languages and cultures; strengthening friendly relations with people on the other side of the border; and attempting to convince youth that legitimate socio-political grievances can be resolved through dialogue and within the framework of the Constitution of India (*Tripura: Human Development Report*, 2007: 114).

In many conflict theaters across the country, the apparently "defeated" insurgencies have often re-emerged due to the inability of the state to consolidate their gains in the "recovered" areas through suitable policies and programs. Therefore, the re-establishment of a secure environment for civil governance, development, and welfare in areas "liberated" from insurgent activity has been an integral component of the comprehensive COIN approach implemented in Tripura (ICM, 2007: 93).

Tripura made considerable progress during the past two decades on all the three indices of human development—literacy and schooling, life expectancy, and per capita income[11]—which is in contrast to the international experience that shows that countries and regions in conflict regress rather than progress in respect of economic and social indicators of development (Stewart, 2004). Notwithstanding the pervasive culture of corruption and lawlessness in many northeast states, Tripura has earned a well-deserved reputation about the quality of its governance. In fact, E.N. Rammohan, a well-respected IPS officer from Assam cadre who also served as DG of Border Security Force and Adviser to the Governor of Manipur, has called the Left Front government as "the cleanest government in India" (Rammohan, 2005: 66). This is largely due to the personal example set by the present Chief Minister, Manik Sarkar, who leads an austere lifestyle, does not allow family or friends to interfere in administration, and does not tolerate corruption among party cadres or bureaucrats (*Tripura Times*, 2011). As per press reports, Manik Sarkar who has been the Chief Minister of Tripura since 1998 does not own a house or car, has a modest bank balance of a few thousand rupees, and donates his monthly salary to the CPI (M) party fund and in turn gets meager amount for his personal expenses. His wife retired from government service recently, and according to Manik Sarkar, his wife's pension is sufficient to sustain their modest lifestyle (*India Today*, 2012). This is in striking contrast to the situation in

---

[11] Life expectancy of 74 years for women and 71 years for men is higher than the corresponding national averages which is 61 years for males and 62.5 for females (HDR, 2007: 17); there is now near universal enrolment of children in the age group 6–14 years and the overall literacy rate is now a commendable 87.7 percent much higher than all-India literacy rate of 74.04, and the sex ratio in 2011 was 961, well above Indian average of 940 (*Census of India*, 2011).

many other states and federal government that have been rocked by a spate of scams running into billions of dollars leading to resignations and arrests of several politicians and high-ranking government officials, and a popular anti-corruption movement in the country.[12]

The targeted developmental initiatives for empowerment of tribals include a 37-point "Special package for Development of Scheduled Tribes" introduced in 2003 for accelerated development of physical infrastructure and socio-economic uplift of tribals; and a range of forest-based livelihood programs as part of its efforts to reduce the economic vulnerability of tribal people. The rubber cultivation scheme has been one of the major success stories in Tripura[13]—not a traditional rubber-growing state—and used for resettlement of both *Jhumia* tribals[14] and even some surrendered extremists.[15] Special attention has been paid for supply of drinking water, public housing, and connectivity of village roads. The state government has also taken up steps to protect and promote tribal language and culture by opening of a channel of All India Radio in Kokborok, the main tribal language in the state. Kokborok is also taught as a language in the tribal areas at the school level. In another significant initiative, the state government has constituted a separate Directorate of Kokborok and other minority languages in August 2012.

In yet another effort to ameliorate the economic hardships of *Jhumia* tribals living in interior rural areas and to insulate them from the influence of insurgents, the government has facilitated

---

[12] To get an idea of pervasive corruption and public backlash, see "Top 10 corruption scams in India" http://trak.in/tags/business/2010/11/25/top-10-corruption-scams-scandals-india and "2011 Indian anti-corruption movement" http://en.wikipedia.org/wiki/2011_Indian_anti-corruption_movement

[13] Tripura has been dubbed as the "Second Rubber Capital of India," after Kerala, by the Rubber Board, India due to the success of its pioneering efforts in rubber cultivation. "Agriculture, Rubber," at official website of Tripura government http://www.tripura.gov.in/agr3.htm, accessed on April 18, 2010.

[14] A total of 9,445 families had been *Jhumia* families had been resettled on rubber plantations till 2005 (Tripura: *Human Development Report*, 2007: 39).

[15] Each surrendered extremist of NLFT (Monto Koloi and Nayanbashi Jamatia) factions was allotted one hectare plot of rubber garden by the State government for rehabilitation purposes.

their relocation in "cluster villages" by providing basic civic and infrastructural facilities such as drinking water, sanitation, basic education, and employment under the poverty alleviation schemes. The security to these new villages has been assured by locating them close to the armed security camps. Significantly, unlike the experience in Mizoram and Nagaland, the implementation of this scheme has not generated any negative reaction among the affected citizens (Chadha, 2005: 288–290, 344–347). This is so because unlike the harsh methods adopted in some other conflict-theatres, people in the state were not forcibly evicted from their tradition habitats and resettled in these new villages. Instead, these "cluster villages" were used to resettle villagers, both tribals and non-tribals, who were driven out from their hamlets by insurgents for refusing to pay extortion money (taxes) and for not preventing the police from collecting information in the villages (*Tripura: Human Development Report*, 2007: 109).

The lack of sufficient employment opportunities for tribal youth in government or private sector is a major problem in Tripura. This issue needs to be addressed on priority to ensure that local tribal youth are not tempted by the militants' inducements due to poverty or unemployment.[16] Presently, there is a reservation of 31 percent in all government jobs for STs, and many tribal youth have found employment in rapidly expanding TSR battalions and other government departments. However, more than one lakh tribal youth still remain unemployed, and there are relatively few tribals in prestigious positions in the government, which reinforces their perceptions of disempowerment.

Special efforts are required to impart them quality education up to graduation and post-graduation so that they can compete for higher jobs. One of the reasons for their poor representation in All India Services is their inability to clear a compulsory paper in an Indian language in the Civil Services examination conducted by Union Public Service Commission, whereas the tribals of other northeast states are exempt from this paper

---

[16] A survey of 23 villages in northeast in 1993–1994 found that bulk of insurgent cadres were drawn from unemployed youth whose choice of alternate professions included "joining the underground, couriering counterfeit money and drug running" (Pillai, 2002).

(Vohra, 2011: 215). This issue needs to be suitably taken up with the central government.

Clearly, despite various positive developments much remains to be done on the development front to uplift the economic status of tribal people and improve their access to quality education, health, sanitation, drinking water, and physical infrastructure. During the course of visits to interior areas, one is appalled to see utter poverty and woeful lack of basic amenities in many interior tribal populated areas. Acute shortage of qualified teachers in large number of schools in tribal areas persists because despite considerable improvement in security scenario, *Bengali* teachers have refused to locate themselves in interior areas and happily pocket salary sitting in capital city of Agartala and pay pittance to the "proxy" teachers who are themselves barely literate. Many of the buildings constructed by the government close to TSR camps in interior areas for housing teachers lie abandoned. The dropout rate among ST students at the primary school level (classes I–V), middle school level (classes I–VIII), and high school level (I–X) was 41.5, 61.6, and 71.6 percent, respectively. The pass percentage of ST students (regular + private) in High School Examination, 2010—Annual and Supplementary Examination was only 30.4 percent, the lowest in the country. Furthermore, 93 percent of ST students who passed this examination scored below 50 percent, 5.3 percent scored between 50 and 60 percent, and only 1.7 percent scored more than 60 percent. The performance of ST students in the Higher Secondary examination in 2010 was no better. The pass percentage of ST students was only 42.9 percent, again the lowest in the country, and 89.7 percent students scored below 50 percent marks (*Statistical Profile of Scheduled Tribes in India*, 2013).

There are large inter-district disparities in various components of Human Development Index (HDI) and achievements in respect of literacy and school enrolment, life expectancy and per capita income were significantly lower in Dhalai district whose population is largely rural and tribal (*Tripura: Human Development Report*, 2007:

1–31). The status of several components of school infrastructure was extremely poor in Dhalai and North districts as compared to West and South districts.[17] Furthermore, asset poverty was acute among ST households, and as many as 75 percent of households in rural areas of Dhalai and North district did not own any asset specified in the 2001 population Census Schedule.[18] The pace of construction of roads and other infrastructure, delivery of basic civic amenities, and implementation of federal government schemes such as National Rural Employment Guarantee Act (NREGA) was very slow in remote interior areas, which are inhabited by tribal people. The Government of Tripura was aware that Dhalai was the least served on all major indicators of infrastructure provisions (*Economic Review of Tripura*, 2012–2013: 344). Such uneven pattern of socio-economic development has severely undermined the quality of life of tribal people, and urgent government action is required to reverse this trend in the interest of internal security, communal peace, and harmony. These concerns were articulated forcefully by several participants during a national seminar on "Issues of the Marginalized tribals in Tripura" organized from January 20–22, 2012 at Government Degree College, Kamalpur, Dhalai district.[19]

Political Initiatives

In pursuance of its flexible political approach, Tripura government has worked closely with the Union government and

---

[17] In 2005–2006, 32 percent of schools in Dhalai district, 16 percent in North district, and 12 percent in south district did not have even a blackboard. West district was a notable exception. Similarly, disaggregated data reveal poor facilities for drinking water, toilets, and electricity in Dhalai and north districts (HDR, Tripura, 2007: 81).

[18] The assets specified in the Census Schedule are radio/transistor, bicycle, telephone, television, and two-and four-wheel vehicles.

[19] A select list of these seminar papers is indicative of their concern: "Ethnicity and Identity conflict: A case of Marginalization in Tripura" by Lincoln Reang; "Ethnic identity movement of the indigenous tribals in Tripura" by Kalidash Brahma; "Problems and Prospects of Tribal Youth in Tripura" by L. Darlong; "Development induced displacement of indigenous people" by J. Kundu and N.K. Upadhyay; "Tribal Education and its Problems—A sociological Insight" by Ms. S. Chanda and Ms. L. Sailo; and "Marginalized Tribes and Globalization" by Manish Prasad.

encouraged negotiated settlement of conflict by holding talks with major insurgent groups. The decade-long violence unleashed by the TNV during the 1980s in Tripura was resolved through a Memorandum of Understanding in 1988 leading to surrender of 447 TNV cadres and similar agreements with NLFT (Kamini-Mantu Koloi) and NLFT (Nayanbasi) factions in 2004 led to the surrender of over 200 NLFT cadres with large number of weapons (Tripura Police website, "Farewell to Arms").[20] Recently, the state government has responded positively to overtures by NLFT's chief Biswamohan Debbarma to surrender and already two rounds of tripartite meetings have been held in Shillong and Delhi in 2015 which were attended by representatives of NLFT-BM, GOI, and the state government.

The state government has repeatedly appealed to the "misguided" youth to abjure violence, surrender arms, and join civil society. The Union government's Surrender-cum-Rehabilitation Scheme has been particularly helpful in this regard. According to SATP data, from 2000 to 2013, a total of 2,650 extremists had surrendered before the government, while the number of surrendered extremists was 2,410 from 1992 to 1999 (SATP 14). "Surrenders in Tripura, 1992–2014". Besides the attractive financial package,[21] the heat generated by aggressive COIN operations in recent years and changed attitude of Bangladesh government toward northeast rebels has also been instrumental in persuading many insurgent cadres to lay down their arms.

The revocation of *Armed Forces Special Powers Act* in May 2015 is a major political decision by the state government which is bound to positively impact tribal people's perceptions of government legitimacy. This Act was imposed in February 1997 following severe insurgent violence and since then it had covered most police stations located in rural areas generally inhabited by tribal people. Local rights groups and tribal parties such as

---

[20] Details of the Agreement are available at "Farewell to Arms" at official website of Tripura Police, at http://www.tripurapolice.nic.in/arms.htm accessed on April 13, 2010.

[21] The surrendered militants receive a monthly payment of ₹2,000, a grant of ₹150,000 and vocational training to facilitate their rehabilitation. The amount of monthly payment has been raised substantially from ₹2,000 to ₹3,500 in December 2009 by the federal government (GOI, MHA, order dated December 2, 2009).

the Indigenous Nationalist Party of Tripura and the Indigenous Peoples Front of Tripura had been demanding the withdrawal of the Act, saying it was aimed at suppressing the state's 33 percent tribal population.

Strengthening Institutions of Local Self-governance

It has been rightly observed that apart from the social and economic demands, a major issue in insurgencies is demand for participation in the political process by various groups (O'Neill, 1990: 135). In NER, despite central outlay of over 80,000 *crore* per annum for rural development, welfare and various other schemes people remain frustrated because of leakages and lack of participation of communities in planning, implementation and supervision of these programs (*NER Vision 2020*, Vol. 1: 16). However, Tripura is one of those states that has conscientiously engaged in building institutions of local self-governance for participatory planning by both tribal and non-tribal sections of the population. While the non-tribal areas have a three-tier Panchayati Raj Institutions (PRIs) at village, block and district level, the tribal areas have got TTAADC for administering themselves. The TTAADC, covering more than two-thirds of the state's tribal population and geographical area, is an extremely important institution for fulfilling the aspirations of self-administration by tribal people.[22] Since 1999–2000, the state government has further committed itself to participatory planning process through specific schemes to involve common specific participatory planning for both the rural and urban areas.[23]

Tripura government has also taken steps to strengthen the institutions of local self-governance by holding regular elections at the village, block, and district levels. In addition, the functioning

---

[22] For details about TTADC structure, responsibilities, budget and other details, see TTADC website at http://ttaadc.nic.in/album/DevMatter.html accessed on October 20, 2012.

[23] For details of implementation of Decentralized Planning in Tripura see (*Human Development Report*, 2007: 117–127). Also see Tripura government's "Approach to People's Plan," available at http://tripura.nic.in/govm2.htm accessed on October 15, 2012.

of TTAADC has been improved to meet the aspirations of self-government among the tribal people of the state. In the 2000 TTAADC elections, the ruling Left Front had lost its majority to the NLFT-backed IPFT which secured 18 of the 28 seats for which elections were held, sending shockwaves among the ruling CPI (M) party. This defeat spurred the government to pull all stops in its COIN campaign, leading to marginalization of insurgents and gradual restoration of normalcy in large parts of the state. Since then ruling Left Front has made a clean sweep of the TTAADC elections and won all the 28 seats in 2015 and 2005 and all the 27 seats in 2010 for which elections were held. The fact that the Left Front is in power in both the TTAADC and the Legislative Assembly has paved the way for better co-ordination between them and greater flow of funds to the TTAADC, enabling it to play a progressively larger role in the development of rural areas. Regarding the functioning of institutions of local self-governance in the state, the National Commission for Review of Working of the Constitution(NCRWC) has observed that the relations between these local bodies and the state government have been smooth when the same party has been in power in both the TTAADC and the state government, otherwise tensions have been generated leading to blockage of funds and other obstructions in the functioning.[24]

The impact of all these initiatives is amply reflected in the resounding success of the Left Front in all elections held in the state in recent years. In 2013, the Left Front was returned to power for the fifth consecutive time, winning 50 out of 60 Assembly seats in 2013, and Manik Sarkar became the Chief Minister for the fourth time. This was a further improvement over its impressive tally of 49 out of 60 seats in 2008 and 41 seats in the 2003 elections. In the TTAADC elections held in 2005 and 2010, between 70 and 80 percent of voters cast their votes despite insurgent threats and returned the ruling Left Front to power, thereby exposing the hollowness of the claims of insurgents of representing them (*Tripura: Human Development Report*, 2007: 125).

---

[24] For an idea of the impact of political tensions on the functioning of the TTAADC, see *Deccan Herald*, 2005.

Mobilization of People against Insurgent Violence

The crucial role of popular support in protracted insurgent warfare has been well recognized by insurgent groups and counterinsurgent across the world, and the ways in which it helps them has been aptly summarized in a Vietminh manual on guerrilla warfare:

> Without the people the guerrillas could neither attack the enemy nor replenish their forces.... The population helps us to fight the enemy by giving us information, suggesting rues and plans, helping us to overcome difficulties due to lack of arms, and providing us guides. It also supplies liaison agents, hides and protects us, assists our actions near posts, feeds us and looks after our wounded ... (cited in O'Neill, 1990: 72).

The critical role of popular support in COIN has been well documented in several studies. An extensive study conducted by Ellis (1995) that analyzed 160 "guerrilla wars" from the Scythians in 156 B.C to the invasion of the Soviets in Afghanistan (1978–1993) came to conclusion that in all successful COIN campaigns the police had gained public trust. Bayley and Perito (2010: 55) have mentioned the findings of a study-group of the U.S. Department of Defense (2006), which analyzed 34 counterinsurgencies from 1948 onwards and concluded that in all successful cases police had the popular support whereas in all unsuccessful cases, the police had failed to establish effective contact with the public and their role had been marginal, indifferent or passive. Another study conducted by Sepp (2005) also observed that suitable expansion and diversification of police coupled with police's leading role played a significant part in success of COIN efforts. Therefore, a sound strategy for any COIN campaign is to wean popular support away from insurgents (Rich et al., 1997: 8) and the most effective way to do this is by according them protection from insurgent violence. As noted by Gill (2000: 81):

> "[T]he people" are, except in rare and extraordinary circumstances, not particularly concerned with ideological niceties and just want to

get on with life. This gives a natural advantage to those who, most effectively threaten—or conversely, protect them (Gill, 2000: 81).

These observations of a veteran police officer are well supported by research findings of academics like Mason (1996) who has developed a model of rational choice theory to demonstrate that the decisions of non-elites are informed more by their "everyday concerns with economic survival and avoidance of violence than by the broader, more abstract preferences between the political doctrines of competing elites." In Tripura, by providing effective protection from insurgents, the police have been able to tilt the "shifting loyalties" in government's favor and created space for the launch of political and economic initiatives for peace and development. In the past decade, the state government has made concerted efforts to build-up peace constituency by mobilizing people through large-scale peace meetings and canvassing by its extensive network of party cadres. For example, soon after coming to power in 2003, peace meetings were held in all the 40 administrative blocks across the state during 2003 and attended by a large number of ministers, government functionaries, civil society organizations, surrendered militants, guardians, and parents of tribal insurgents. These efforts have continued since then, and form an integral part of COIN strategy. Another important facet of this COIN campaign has been effective political mobilization of women and influential Jamatia tribal community against insurgent violence. Women's empowerment—"a brake on the aggression of disillusioned males"—has been considered a central component of successful COIN strategy (Metz, 2007). In Tripura, women have played an important and highly visible role in the fight against insurgency by defying insurgents' dictates to boycott elections, and voted in large numbers in all elections. Moreover, through their active participation in various mass-based organizations and local political institutions they have helped crystallize public opinion against violence. For example, The Tripura Nari Samiti (Tripura Women Organization) has more than 400,000 members, that is, one in two adult women in the state. Women's grass-roots leadership has been a resounding success in Tripura. In the local self-governing bodies, the number of elected women exceeds the legislated quota of one-third of seats in the case of Panchayat Samitis and Zilla Parishads, and in the Village Development Committees also women are well represented (*Tripura: Human Development Report*, 2007: 122–123).[25] It was also seen that the atrocities committed by NLFT insurgents on tribal communities also backfired and galvanized the powerful Jamatia community into stiff resistance against them. In December 1999 as many as 21 *Hoda* (community council) volunteers were kidnapped *en masse* by NLFT insurgents and in September 2000, six *Hoda* members were killed at Naobari, leading to revulsion against insurgent groups' brutal tactics and a collective decision by the community leaders not to pay any "tax" to the insurgents (*Tripura: Human Development Report*, 2007: 115).

The state government has been adept in conducting information operations to gain popular support for their development work. Before the last Assembly elections, the state government had directed all important departments to prepare small attractive booklets highlighting their achievements. Subsequently, these booklets were released for free public distribution by the concerned departmental ministers during press conferences spread over several months throughout 2012. This move immensely succeeded in its aim of generating regular publicity for developmental initiatives of the government in the pre-election period and winning voters' support as seen from the results of 2013 Assembly elections. These booklets and a consolidated list of important awards and achievements of the state government have also been posted on the state government's website for greater reach among citizens.[26]

---

[25] The one-third representation of women in local self-governing bodies has been ensured through Tripura Panchayat Act, 1993, which applies to both membership and to the office of Chairperson at all levels—Gram Panchayat, Panchayat Samiti, and Zilla Parishad (*Tripura: Human Development Report*, 2007: 123).

[26] For achievements of the Tripura State, see "Tripura Marching Ahead," http://tripura. nic.in/portal/More_Info/document/Planning/Tripura%20Marching%20Ahead%20(1972-2012)%20English.pdf accessed on October 5, 2012. And for awards/achievements, see "Tripura winning Awards and Recognition,"http://tripura.nic.in/portal/More_Info/document/Planning/Tripura%20Winning%20Awards%20and%20Recognitions%20(English). pdf accessed on October 5, 2012.

The Legal Framework

The terror tactics adopted by insurgent groups pose special problems for law-enforcement agencies in democratic countries as the normal legal and judicial processes are found inadequate to cope with their criminal acts of violence. SFs face enormous difficulties in conducting searches, interrogation and collection of evidence, intimidation of witnesses, prosecutors and judges, misuse of legal provisions to jump bail and initiation of legal proceedings against those involved in COIN operations (Kumar, 2006: 67). Therefore, special legislation is enacted to counter these disadvantages and empower police and SFs to prosecute insurgents and also provides them a degree of legal immunity from harassment through court proceedings. However, a heavy-handed implementation of these provisions creates a human rights problem for the government combating insurgency/terrorism (Wallace, 2007: 454), underlining the need for using special legislation with extreme care and caution.

In Tripura, both the NLFT and ATTF have been proscribed by the GOI under the *Unlawful Activities (Prevention) Act, 1967.* In February 1997 the territorial jurisdiction under 19 police stations was declared as "disturbed areas" under the *Armed Forces Special Powers Act, 1958* (ICM, 2007: 65), and subsequently it was gradually expanded to include jurisdictions under 34 police stations in full and parts of another six police stations in 2012 (Government of Tripura, Home Department, Notification dated September 6, 2012). However, in view of the improved security scenario in June 2013 the state government reduced its territorial jurisdiction and finally revoked AFPSA in May 2015. The provisions of *National Security Act, 1980* have been invoked only against the most hardened criminals to disrupt insurgent networks, avoiding alienation of general tribal population. This discriminate use of "draconian" laws has played an important part in defeating insurgent propaganda against SFs in Tripura, unlike many other northeast states which have been periodically rocked by allegations of human rights abuses (Baruah, 2005: 20–21). The observance of human rights by police has been an important part of their reorientation process as the troops have remained disciplined and refrained from indiscriminate retaliation even under extreme provocation.[27] The records of the National Human Rights Commission (NHRC) contain very few references to the alleged violations of human rights in Tripura and a study commissioned by the NHRC (Khan and Mangathai, 2003), which questioned a number of former insurgents in Tripura found that none of them had listed "police harassment" as the reason for joining the insurgent groups. The economic, developmental, and political initiatives of the state government have been accompanied by aggressive police actions to marginalize hardcore extremist elements who have continued to perpetrate violence and refused to surrender.

Conclusion

It is a fact that insurgency in Tripura has been substantially contained over the past decade. The strategic deployment of security forces and the imaginative COIN operations since 2000 have ensured effective security cover to all sections of public and enabled the penetration of state structures in the remotest interior areas to undertake developmental tasks and deliver basic services to the citizens. The return of the Awami League to power in Bangladesh in 2009 has further boosted the prospects for peace as it has ushered the process of de-radicalization by taking strong action to rein in the Islamist extremists and arresting several militant leaders of northeast insurgent groups operating on its soil. Recent agreements signed during the visit of Prime Minister Modi to Bangladesh in June 2015 have further boosted the prospects of trade, commerce, and connectivity of the state with the rest of the country and other south Asian countries. The public endorsement of government's COIN strategy is clearly reflected in the

---

[27] The last incident of major human rights violation by the police occurred over a decade ago in 1996, when the TSR burned 94 houses and killed three people in Sidhai police station area in retaliation after one of their convoys was ambushed.

overwhelming success of ruling Left Front candidates in all elections held in the state in recent years.

Regrettably, the pattern of socioeconomic development in the state has been rather lopsided, and provision of roads and physical infrastructure, delivery of basic services, such as health, sanitation, education, drinking water, and electricity and income-generation schemes. in many interior remote areas inhabited by tribal people remains tardy. The tribal cause has also been ill-served by poor implementation of various land acts legislated to restore alienated land to tribals. Consequently, quality of life of tribals remains poor, with widespread poverty and unemployment leading to frustration and resentment against the prevailing system. This trend needs to be reversed without further delay and suitable policies devised to truly empower tribal people and address their genuine grievances so that insurgency does not resurface in the state. Therefore, in keeping with the comprehensive approach to COIN, the key to a durable peace in the state lies in a more inclusive growth and equity for the ethnic minorities in economic sphere, and ensuring that the political democracy is accompanied by a robust social democracy.

6

Police Response to Insurgency in Tripura

Introduction

Tripura had some sort of an indigenous policing system even before the establishment of British presence in 1871. In ancient times, each aboriginal tribe had its own rudimentary policing arrangement based on age-old customs and religious practices to maintain order in the society. In subsequent years, some police reforms on the lines of Muslim administrative system of Bengal were made by various kings of Tripura, but the introduction of British policing system institutionalized through the *Police Act, 1861* sounded the death knell of these traditional decentralized policing systems. The Administration Report of Captain W.L. Samuel dated July 9, 1875 submitted to the Secretary to the Government of Bengal, Political Department mentions that Tripura had only five police stations and eight outposts. The total strength of police in 1876 was 192 (Menon, 2005: 27–28). Modernization of police in this princely state started in 1905 with the separation of police and revenue functions. During this time, police administration was headed by a Superintendent of Police (SP) and the strength of police in 1907 was 233, which grew to 651 in 1945. This was supplemented by six companies of Tripura Army, which comprised 277 personnel (43 officers, 4 buglers, and 230 sepoys) in 1874–1875 (Goswami, 1996: 144). These troops were charged with the responsibility of maintaining internal security, escorts, and guarding the royal palace. The number of army personnel had declined to 227 when the First World War broke out in 1914–1915. However, during the Second World War (1939–1945), Tripura fully supported the British in their war effort and the total strength of manpower organized by the state in expansion of its forces approached 5,000 (Goswami, 1996: 28). These troops were deployed in Burma and Arakan front and earned many rewards and honors for their outstanding service.

Post-independence, the post of SP was upgraded to Inspector General of Police (IGP) in 1965 and Director General of Police (DGP) in 1987. The strength of Tripura police went up from 5,000 in 1976 to 15,000 in 2001, and exceeds 25,000 in 2015. Meanwhile, the population of Tripura has grown from 173,325 in 1901 to 640,000 in 1951, 1.5 million in 1971, 2.5 million in 1981, 3.1 million in 2001, and 3.6 million in 2011. The purpose of providing this information is to establish a proper perspective to the rapid expansion of police that has taken place in Tripura during the past few decades and also underline the tremendous growth in population during the corresponding period. In 2013, there were 636 police personnel per 100,000 people, which is significantly higher than the all-India average of 141, but lower than some other northeast states like Manipur (1,020), Mizoram (904), and Sikkim (680) (MHA, 2013).

For revenue and general administration purposes, till very recently the state was divided into four districts, that is, West, North, South, and Dhalai. However, a major administrative reorganization drive in 2011 has increased the number of districts to eight, and created four new districts namely Unakoti, Khowai, Sepahijala, and Gomati (see Table 5.2). Each district is further divided into a number of subdivisions, Community Development (CD) blocks, and revenue villages, and headed by a District Magistrate (DM) who is responsible for development administration and also maintains proper coordination with SP for maintenance of law and order. Under the DM, there are Sub-Divisional Magistrates (SDMs) and Block Development Officers (BDOs). Presently, there are 23 subdivisions, 58 blocks, and 595 panchayats in the state.

For policing, the state is headed by a Director General of Police (DGP) and assisted by Additional Director General of Police (ADGP), Inspectors General of Police (IGPs), and Deputy Inspectors General (DIGs) who look after various "civil" and "armed" police organizations.[1] Tripura Police is organized into eight districts administered by two headquarters (HQs), called "ranges", that is, the North Range and the South Range. Each range is headed by a DIG who supervises the functioning of SPs and is directly answerable to the IGP (law and order). The police districts are headed by an SP who is assisted by various officers in the rank of Additional SP, Deputy SP (DSP), Inspectors, sub-Inspectors, and other staff. While the police sub-divisions are normally headed by a DSP, the police stations are usually headed by an Inspector and outposts by a sub-Inspector. Following the massive reorganization of police during the past decade, the number of police stations has increased from 46 in 2000 to 74 in 2015, while the number of police outposts has increased from 22 to 37 during the same period. Five Government Railway Police (GRP) stations are also functional in the state at Agartala, Teliamura, Manu, Ambassa, and Dharmanagar. The reorganization and expansion of the police network continues and gradually most police posts would be upgraded to full-fledged police stations to further strengthen the police network. This denser web of police infrastructure, supported by a large number of security camps, has greatly reduced reaction time to militant incidents, improved intelligence flow, and boosted public confidence.

This chapter focuses its attention on the protracted processes of reorientation and reorganization that have enabled Tripura police to reinvent itself and emerge as an effective and credible force capable of combating insurgency and all other policing challenges. The success of this effort is reflected in the fact that Tripura police is being held as a model for other police forces in the country facing similar threats and challenges. This chapter is organized into two sections. The introductory section gives an overview of the new

---

[1] As on January 1, 2014, the total sanctioned strength of Civil Police and Armed Police was 12,898 and 14,535, respectively, and the posted strength of Civil and Armed Police was 10,441 and 13,178, respectively (GOI, MHA, BPR&D, 2014).

concept and conduct of COIN followed by an in-depth analysis of various measures taken to improve operational preparedness of police units and dominate the conflict zone.

The thrust of police strategy has been substantial augmentation of resources of police stations, increased emphasis on intelligence generation for targeted operations, deployment of large number of forces in COIN grid for operations and security of civilians and vital infrastructural projects, effective coordination among all SFs, scrupulous adherence to the rule of law and respect for human rights, and mobilization of popular resistance against extremist violence. It would be seen that a shared understanding of COIN strategy among police, administration, and the political executive coupled with allocation of requisite resources for capacity building of police have been important factors in the gradual return of normalcy, ethnic harmony, and development in the state. With the progressive marginalization of insurgent groups, democratic politics has been revived, structures and institutions of civil governance restored across the state, and a general feeling of optimism has emerged after decades of endemic violence.

The New "Concept and Conduct of CI Operation"[2]

Despite the presence of a large number of SF personnel during the 1990s, militant violence could not be contained in the state and the militants were able to indulge in large-scale extortion, kidnappings, and killing of the civilians and SF personnel at will without facing severe reprisals. There appeared to be a distinct lack of appreciation of proper theory and methodology of COIN, as the forces muddled along, learning slowly "on the job" (ICM, 2007: 9). Unsurprisingly, without a sound appreciation of an overall strategy by the senior formations, even the best of troops could not deliver the desired

---

[2] "Concept and Conduct of CI operation," Tripura Police, IGP/Armed Police, Memo dated August 7, 2000.

results.[3] Therefore, with the change in top police leadership in May 2000, the matter was re-examined at the highest operational level by the State Level Operations and Intelligence Group (SLOG) and fresh instructions were issued in August 2000 to all SFs, including TSR, through a remarkably concise and clear four page document titled "Concept and Conduct of CI Operation." This document stressed a holistic approach to COIN and sought to achieve seamless integration of civil administration, police, and SFs.

Salient Features of the New COIN Concept

The new Concept and Conduct of CI Operation document issued by SLOG in August 2000 stressed:

1. Battalion-level planning and coordination of operations and establishment of a grid of "Coy Op Bases" (COB) within the allotted area of responsibility (AOR); coordination among subunits of all SFs deployed in the battalion's AOR; and availability of one Quick Reaction Team (QRT) at each COB and battalion HQ. The new strategy also recognized the importance of junior leadership in an insurgency situation and gave maximum freedom to the company commanders in planning and executing operations within their jurisdiction; and specifically directed them to generate local intelligence, and ensure unpredictability in all operations and movements.

   The advantages of deployment of SFs in a grid are that it helps them to effectively dominate the area, influence the population, collect intelligence, and facilitate civic actions that support governance, economic development, and essential services (Banerjee, 2009: 201). Moreover, grid

---

[3] The need for proper appreciation of COIN conduct by senior formations is borne out by the fact that even the Special Task Force (STF), especially raised by the state government in 1999 from highly trained TSR troops, had to be disbanded in 2002 following a review by the then-DGP, which indicated that STF was being used by the district SPs for routine area domination instead of intelligence-led COIN operations against selected insurgent groups, resulting in sub-optimum operational output.

deployment repulses the enemy attempts to hold territory and conveys the impression that the state, and not the insurgents, has the initiative (Ladwig, III: 2009).

2. All COBs to ensure regular aggressive patrolling, ambushes, personnel and vehicle checks, and "cordon and search" operations in their AOR. Routine operations of general nature were expressively prohibited and raids on militant hideouts, snatch ops, or specific search operations were to be conducted on hard intelligence only. Small-unit operations such as sustained and aggressive patrols in guerrilla-infested zone have been found to be highly effective (O'Neill, 1990: 130). The purpose of such operations is not to seize territory, but neutralize insurgents, collaborators, sources of supply and organization. The concept of "floating coy base" was also introduced to undertake short duration operations for a few days in the unaddressed areas.

3. All SFs to organize "synergized ops" periodically as per directions of SLOG based on hard intelligence. It meant that during the specified duration of such operations maximum troops would be mobilized by them for: laying ambushes on suspected routes used by the militants, conducting maximum number of personnel and vehicle checks, "cordon and search operations," and effective sealing of infiltration prone border areas. The synergized operations proved extremely effective in disrupting the terror network as the militants could not easily escape the dragnet of hundreds of road-blocks, ambushes or "cordon and search operations," which were centrally coordinated, totally unpredictable, and organized simultaneously all over the state.[4]

4. SFs to ensure effective population and resource control measures to deny easy movement or flow of funds and resources to insurgent groups.

5. SFs to institute necessary measures to ensure camp security and protection of troops during foot or mobile patrolling.

---

[4] Senior police officer, Tripura, Field notes, Kuldeep Kumar, March 12, 2011.

6. SFs to give maximum assistance to police, administration and political functionaries to facilitate their movement in interior areas; encourage and monitor functioning of administration in tribal villages and mixed populated areas; organize civic action programs and take pre-emptive actions in conjunction with civil administration to prevent ethnic conflicts within their allotted jurisdiction.

The government officials and other agencies that are required to be in the field to implement social and economic programs are specifically targeted by the insurgents (O'Neill, 1990: 139). Hence, despite their heavy commitments for offensive operations and meager strength, TSR troops were directed to extend all possible help to such officials in facilitating their visits, programs, and projects in interior areas. The importance of such security cover to these officials was brought home starkly some time back with the kidnapping of a DM and an engineer by the Maoist insurgents in Odisha when these officials had gone to supervise developmental work in the interior areas.[5] The release of these officials could be secured by the Odisha government after several days only when it agreed to suspend operations against Maoists and released several militants holed up in various jails as demanded by insurgents.

However, mere enunciation of revised COIN concept would have never mitigated the violence unless it was effectively backed up by the operational superiority of the SFs to inflict demonstrable defeat on the insurgent groups. Soon after assumption of charge by the new Police Chief in mid-2000, a thorough review of prevalent administrative structures, operational strategies, manpower, intelligence, training, and infrastructure was undertaken and many innovative practices were introduced to make police a motivated and credible force capable of responding effectively to the multiple challenges of insurgency, ethnic and political violence, crime, and general law and order (*Tripura Observer*, 2002). Since then, a thorough administrative reorganization of

---

[5] "Patnaik seeks release of DM kidnapped by Naxals," at http://www.thenews24x7.com/news24x7national-network/963-news/7425-patnaik-seeks-release-of-dm-kidnapped-by-naxals accessed on March 19, 2011.

Tripura police has significantly enhanced police presence in most violence-affected areas by opening new police stations, outposts, and subdivisions. While only one police station and two outposts were added during the preceding decade from 1990 to 2000, as many as 28 new police stations and 15 outposts have been added during the last decade and half, bringing the number of police stations and outposts to 74 and 37, respectively. The denser web of police network has been crucial to the success of COIN operations by reducing reaction time to extremist incidents, generating better intelligence flow, and improving police-public interface. The extensive police presence has also been augmented through the establishment of over 100 Special Police Pickets (SPPs) manned by more than 3,500 civilian Special Police Officers (SPOs),[6] and a large number of village resistance (VR) parties, mostly in vulnerable areas near Indo-Bangladesh border. The public's involvement in COIN operations has succeeded in building public resistance against insurgent groups, prevented extremist movements in these areas, and freed regular troops for operational tasks. The strength of the state police force has been substantially enhanced to over 25,000 with the addition of seven new armed police battalions reflecting a transformation of the police from a defensive to offensive force.[7] An aggressive deployment policy since 2001 has ensured domination of all important hill ranges and other strategic areas by locating over 300 police camps, mostly staffed by one or two platoon outposts, and the establishment of TSR battalion HQs in the interior areas has further consolidated permanent hold of SFs over the rural hinterland. The extensive network of security camps has ensured effective security to all sections of the public, accelerated the pace of development in interior areas and restored public confidence in the government's capability to neutralize insurgent threats. In

---

[6] The SPOs are mainly deployed to provide round-the-clock security to the villages, markets, and other government establishments in thickly populated areas. Each SPP has about 30 armed SPOs under the command of a small detachment of regular police (Kumar, 2006: 53).

[7] These armed battalions are in addition to the usual 15,000–20,000 federal paramilitary troops of AR, CRPF, and BSF deployed in the state for operations and guarding the international border with Bangladesh.

Tripura, both the main components of state police—the armed police and civil police—were overhauled and worked in tandem to defeat insurgent designs. The following narration describes briefly the circumstances relating to TSR's origins, its performance and transformation in subsequent years as these battalions were earmarked to function as the lead agency in this campaign.

Tripura State Rifles

Background

As mentioned earlier, in the late 1970s Tripura was ravaged by severe ethnic and political violence unleashed by TNV. However, the two armed police battalions of the state were found grossly deficient and undisciplined to handle this full-blown insurgency. The discomfiture of the State government was further aggravated by occasional delay in the arrival of central paramilitary forces. Therefore, the inadequacy of local armed units and frequent and growing requirements in the state for police forces due to the extremist problem in the 1980s prompted the state government to raise its own force on the pattern of paramilitary forces. A memorandum signed by the Government of Tripura mentions that:

> The Tripura State Rifles is intended to provide the State government with a fully self-reliant special armed force with officers and men of specially trained calibre with a high degree of fighting fitness, proficiency, discipline, rigorous training, control and combat readiness along with communication, transport, provisioning and equipment, capable of meeting any challenge (Government of Tripura, F.6. (9)-PD/83 dated December 30, 1983).

The state government was also aware of the rampant indiscipline and politicization prevalent among some sections of Tripura police[8] and expected that the imposition of stricter disciplinary rules on the paramilitary pattern would counter this trend effectively. In brief, the main challenge was to raise a professional and impartial force that could "out-run, out-gun and out-wit" their adversaries and insulate it from the pervasive negative influences and political pressures seen in some other local police units. Accordingly, *Tripura State Rifles Act, 1983* was drafted on the lines of central paramilitary forces, passed by Tripura Legislative Assembly on May 22, 1984 and assented to by the President of India in July 1984. The form and organizational structure of TSR battalions has been carefully conceived to support their assigned functions.[9] Each battalion of TSR, headed by a commandant, has a sanctioned strength of 1,210 personnel and is well equipped with suitable weaponry, communication, transport, and other logistic/administrative support.

Since its inception, TSR units have been deployed for COIN operations, law and order duties during ethnic or political riots, VVIP visits and major festivals, elections, and natural calamities within Tripura. More recently, following considerable improvements in the security scenario, the Government of India has started deploying India Reserve (IR) battalions of the rifles for elections and other duties across the country. TSR troops have performed duties in several states across the country, including Madhya Pradesh, Chhattisgarh, Rajasthan, West Bengal, and Delhi.

---

[8] During the tenure of the first Left Front Government in the state, Tripura Non-Gazetted Police Association was formed on January 19, 1978 for the welfare of the policemen and improvement in their service conditions. However, with passage of time office bearers of the Association became politicized, undisciplined, and started interfering in administrative matters. Consequently, the Association was banned in 1988, and Tripura Armed Police (TAP) 1st and 2nd Battalions were disbanded by the government in 1992 to control police agitation (Menon, 2005: 66–67).

[9] The main tasks and roles of TSR as follows:
(a) Restoration and maintenance of law and order; (b) operations against extremists, insurgents, dacoits, and the like elements; (c) helping the authorities in dealing with disaster and natural calamity; and (d) such other tasks or duties as may be assigned by the state government, Inspector-General, Deputy Inspector-General, and the Commandant (Section 4.2 of TSR Rules).

Improving Operational Preparedness for COIN

Though TSR battalions were specifically raised on paramilitary pattern for COIN operations, they had not been very effective initially in containing the intensity and spread of militancy due to the absence of a coherent COIN strategy, lack of operational preparedness, and shortage of modern weaponry, equipment, and other logistic support. With the articulation of a new concept of COIN, necessary framework was put in place and a slew of measures were introduced between 2000 and 2002 to motivate and reorient them for their COIN role and improve their operational preparedness, culminating in a remarkable transformation of TSR within a short span of time. The following discussion is not intended to make any personality specific assessment of various Police Chiefs, but merely to note that the process of transformation, which started in 2000 with B.L. Vohra as the Police Chief has been further consolidated by successor DGPs.

Reorienting Police for COIN

First, it was observed by the then DGP that despite a very high intensity of militant violence, the police was mostly functioning in "civil" mode, visible mostly during daytime only and generating a lot of instructions and circulars but hardly making an impact on the insurgents who roamed unchallenged all over the state. Further, while the insurgents had their hideouts in remote and inaccessible jungles/hills, police presence was usually restricted to main highways and urban areas. To rectify the situation, all senior officers were directed to undertake extensive touring, conduct surprise checks, and make frequent night halts at TSR camps/ battalion HQs. The DGP himself was on the move at least 15–20 days per month visiting the remotest insurgency-affected areas, day and night, to keep abreast of developments on the ground. Frequent visits by senior officers and their encouragement resulted in a more proactive style of policing and ensured: effective night domination, compliance with operational guidelines, close super-vision of performance, prompt redress of grievances of troops, and speedy resolution of administrative problems. This also promoted a shared understanding of policing challenges between the police leadership and constabulary, which facilitated a smooth and rapid transition from a defensive to offensive role and laid the foundations for future successes. This proactive style has become ingrained in the state police culture and greatly contributed to police function-ing and positive image. Even in 2012–2013 when the insurgency had been substantially controlled, I as Additional DG and many other officers frequently traveled 20–30 km on foot in Dhalai and North district to visit TSR camps in the most interior areas.

The impact of these improvements was visible within a remarkably short period of three months (*Tripura Times*, 2000). A report prepared by GOI's Ministry of Home Affairs that had been closely monitoring the developments in the state also noted the marked improvement in the security scenario in later part of the year 2000 and observed that

> The efforts put in to contain militancy in Tripura have now started yielding results. Security forces in the State have fought back the militants and other criminal elements in a forceful way in the recent past.... The efforts of security forces have resulted in reduction in the number of incidents by extremists, drastic reduction in kidnapping, controlling of ethnic situation and generally a peaceful atmosphere.[10]

Incidentally, the immediate impact of resolute police action on terrorist violence has been mentioned elsewhere by another veteran police officer, K.P.S. Gill (2000: 76) also:

> ... it is my firm conviction that, if they are suitably empowered—politically, legally and technologically—there is not a single

---

[10] The MHA Report compared the dramatic improvement in the situation in Tripura from May 2000 to September 2000 and mentioned that in May 2000 there were 54 extremist incidents, 71 kidnappings and no killing of extremist, while in September, 2000 there were only 13 extremist incidents, 12 kidnappings and as many as 9 killings of extremists by security forces (MHA, 2000).

terrorist movement in India today that the security forces cannot control or contain within six months, and comprehensively defeat within two years.

These examples of dramatic improvement in the security situation following determined police action reinforce the central theme of the thesis that with suitable empowerment police are fully capable of tackling all challenges of internal security, including insurgency and terrorism.

Specialized Training for COIN

COIN is a form of irregular warfare that is totally different from the received training and ethos of the uniformed forces, whether police, paramilitary, or military (Gill, 2000). Hence, before induction for CI operations, troops need specialized training and orientation. The importance of such training was highlighted by the difficulties faced by the Indian Army in COIN operations in Nagaland in the 1950s, leading to establishment of Counter-Insurgency and Jungle Warfare (CIJW) school at Vairengete, Mizoram, in 1970 (Shekatkar, 2009: 20).

Though Tripura had been fighting insurgency for over a decade and half, the TSR troops had not received such specialized training in jungle warfare. Therefore, two newly raised battalions of TSR were detailed for Jungle Warfare and Counterinsurgency (JWCI) training at Indian Army's CIJW School at Vairengete in Mizoram for the first time during 2002.The exposure gained through this exercise was used to establish a small JWCI school in Tripura to impart continuous training to TSR battalions and other police units as it was not possible to obtain frequent training slots in such institutions due to the army's own heavy training commitments.[11] The jungle warfare training has been made an integral part of basic training and promotion cadre courses of TSR troops. Specialized commando and leadership training for

---

[11] Since its inception, this JWCI School has trained 2,800 trainees from different organizations including TSR, police, and paramilitary units deployed in the state (TSR, 2010: 11).

junior leaders are also organized in various reputed police and paramilitary training institutes across the country. More recently, the federal government has approved setting up of a "Counter Insurgency and Anti-Terrorist" (CIAT) School in Tripura and allocated funds for construction of infrastructure and imparting training. The CIAT-1 is being established at 3rd Battalion TSR HQ at Kachucherra by upgrading the existing JWCI School training infrastructure and constructing additional buildings/facilities. Sufficient suitable land has also been identified for establishment of a field firing range and conducting field exercises. It is expected that augmentation and upgrading of training infrastructure at CIAT School would go a long way in further enhancing the capabilities of TSR for COIN.

Second, revised standard operating procedures (SOPs) were framed regarding camp security, escorts, road opening patrols (ROPs), improvised explosive devices (IEDs) and ambushes, foot and mobile patrolling, intelligence generation, and other operational matters. These instructions were neatly compiled in an operational manual and distributed among all TSR battalions. Furthermore, troops were regularly briefed by the post commander and senior officers regarding all operational matters, and frequent surprise checks were made to ensure meticulous observance of security guidelines. Despite all these precautions, violations of such instructions have occurred occasionally due to negligence or inexperience of young troops, resulting in heavy losses through ambushes or IEDs.[12] However, it is remarkable that not even a single TSR camp, including those located in most interior areas, could be ever overrun by the insurgent groups during the past decade and half. This is truly an exceptional achievement considering frequent successful attacks on police and security camps in other parts of the country.

In this context, it is pertinent to point out that the appointment of battle-hardened officers from CRPF/BSF as commandants in

---

[12] For example, on August 20, 2002, a TSR truck was ambushed by NLFT extremists in Tripura, killing 20 TSR personnel on the spot and injuring many more. In this case, all the troops had climbed into one truck instead of traveling tactically while moving through insurgency affected areas.

particular has been extremely helpful in training and orienting TSR troops to their COIN role. Their rich experience of COIN proved especially useful during 2001–2002 when TSR first set up camps in the most remote and inaccessible areas to dominate the hinterland and launch aggressive operations against the insurgents. It has been my experience that their guidance in suitable site selection and organization of defense, establishment of proper procedures and protocols for defensive and offensive operations, and enforcement of strict discipline and restraint helped the troops in gaining confidence of tribal people and preventing or successfully repulsing all attacks on security camps.[13]

Improved Capacities for Intelligence

The importance of intelligence in COIN is well documented in the academic and professional literature, and bears no repetition. However, this intelligence has to be generated and developed by the troops on the ground through their own actions and operations (Thompson, 1967: 88–89). It has also been experienced that units and company level posts which generate their own actionable intelligence tend to do much better than units that wait for information from higher formations (Kilcullen, 2010: 32).

Hence, intelligence generation at local level was accorded a high priority and special intelligence courses were organized to reorient troops for this purpose. Voluminous intelligence was generated by patrols through systematic data collection about missing tribal youth and visual observation in insurgency affected areas, and sources were raised among tribal people by gaining their

---

[13] The importance of this observation is obvious in the backdrop of frequent successful attacks by Maoist and other insurgent groups on camps of state police and paramilitary forces all over the country, resulting in killing of troops, looting of arms/ammunition, and the consequent demoralization among security forces. For example, see "Maoists attack security camp in West Bengal; 24 Jawans killed" at http://india-news-show.blogspot.com/2010/11/maoists-attack-security-camp-in-west.html accessed on January 11, 2011 and "10 deadliest Naxal attacks in the last six years" at http://www.hindustantimes.com/10-deadliest-Naxal-attacks-in-India-in-the-last-six-years/Article1-424053.aspx accessed on January 11, 2011.

confidence through meaningful civic action programs and acting as an interface between villagers and administration for delivery of various services such as schools, dispensaries, bridges, roads, and ration shops. Suitable tribal troops within TSR battalions were identified, briefed, and sent periodically to their homes in interior areas to collect information through their network of friends and family members.[14] According to a senior police officer, "In many battalions where the commandants took personal interest, the intelligence provided by these troops often led to successful operations as these boys could not only collect valuable information but also act as guides due to their familiarity with local terrain and routes."[15] The interception of wireless communication of insurgent groups has also proved to be rich source of intelligence and many insurgents have been apprehended or neutralized through operations based on such intelligence.

The police have also gone in for major upgrades of technical capabilities for COIN operations by acquiring state-of-the-art communications monitoring equipment and procuring Geo Satellite Applications System (GSAS). The enhanced operational capabilities of the state's SFs have enabled them to undertake aggressive small-unit operations in the most inhospitable interior areas for extended periods to neutralize or capture insurgents. Moreover, the improved flow of intelligence from the general public, political cadres of the ruling CPI (M) and its affiliates, the SPOs, and the surrendered militants have all combined to dramatically augment police capabilities to launch successful intelligence-led operations against insurgent groups. These sustained offensive operations have wrested the initiative from insurgent groups and significantly reduced their potential for violence.

In many cases, the police have also launched covert operations across the border that made insurgents feel insecure and the resultant demoralization was easily exploited to cause factionalism, splits, and surrenders which effectively marginalized the major

---

[14] The latest "Revised Employment Policy" order issued by Government of Tripura, General Administration (Personnel Training) Department in August 2010 provides for 31 percent reservation for ST.

[15] Senior police officer, Tripura, *Field notes*, Kuldeep Kumar, March, 12 2011.

insurgent groups. While operational details about covert operations in the state cannot be shared here, Bhaumik (2015) has mentioned employment of Bangladeshi Mafiosi to target rebels in safe houses in Dhaka and Chittagong. Between 2002 and 2005, Tripura police and the military intelligence managed to manipulate some extremists who had not yet surrendered and used them for a series of attacks on rebel bases just inside Bangladesh across the border with Tripura (Bhaumik, 2009: xvii). According to him, this Trojan Horse model proved to be a greater success than getting rebels to surrender first and then use them against their former colleagues.

Finally, joint operations and intelligence sharing with other northeast states, especially the neighboring states of Assam and Mizoram, have been an important feature of Tripura's COIN strategy (*Hindustan Times*, 2000). Such coordinated operations have been quite useful in tackling extremist crime in bordering areas of these states and also led to seizure of biggest ever arms haul of 33 AK-47 rifles, an Light Machine Gun (LMG), and big cache of ammunition in Mizoram in March 2013 (*The Assam Tribune*, 2013). Thus, a fine mix of human and technical intelligence has driven the COIN operations of Tripura police and contributed to their success.

Improving Core Capacities of "Shoot, Move, and Communicate"

In 2000, Tripura police was not adequately equipped or resourced to handle full-blown ethnic insurgency, leading to a general lack of confidence and demoralization. There were hardly any armored vehicles or automatic weapons as most of the TSR battalions were equipped with 7.62 mm Self-Loading Rifles (SLR) and total combined holding of AK-47 rifles in the state was only 160. This sorry state of affairs prevailed due to shortage of funds for procurement of requisite expensive hardware for COIN and lack of determination among senior police leaders to overcome difficulties through innovative methods. The then-DGP initiated and vigorously pursued various proposals with the federal government to obtain requisite resources (Vohra, 2011: 94–95). The federal government's "Modernization of Police Forces scheme" was utilized to procure more number of better weapons, bullet-proof (BP) jackets and vehicles. However, even this scheme could not be relied upon to meet immediate requirement of BP vehicles, because of usual bureaucratic procedures. Therefore, it was decided to fabricate improvised BP vehicles by fitting 6 mm BP metal sheets locally in battalion workshop, and during 2000–2002, 30 jeeps and trucks were fitted with BP sheets, and provided to TSR battalions and district police. In another innovation, two-inch-thick wooden planks were fitted on the sides of 30 new commander jeeps with provision to hang BP jackets which provided additional protection to troops from extremist fire. In this way, almost 60 vehicles were modified during 2000–2002, which went a long way in raising confidence levels of TSR battalions and police. To put this in perspective, from 1996 to 1999, only eight vehicles were fitted with wooden planks, and another two vehicles were fitted with bulletproof metal sheets in the same workshop. Temporary transfer of available automatic weapons, such as AK-47 rifles was also made among various battalions and vulnerable police stations/police units to improve their response capacities. This discussion highlights the critical need for prompt and imaginative deployment of available resources to meet insurgent threats even as plans are drawn for augmentation of resources in the long term.

Over the past decade, things have improved considerably and the combined holding of TSR battalions now exceeds 2,400 AK-47 rifles, 4,200 5.56 mm INSAS rifles, and 7,500 7.62 SLRs. This is in addition to over 200 51-mm mortars, 600 LMGs, and a large number of grenades and other explosives. The central government provided an average annual allocation of ₹39.40 crores between 2000 and 2014 under the central government's scheme for "Modernization of Police Forces (MPF)."[16] The modernization of police is a continuing process and improved availability of modern arms, transport, and other equipment has

---

[16] The main objective of Police Modernization scheme is to meet the critical deficiencies identified by the Bureau of Police Research and Development (BPR&D) in a study conducted in 2000 (GOI, MHA, 2005–2006, Chapter IV).

greatly strengthened the core capabilities of TSR battalions to tackle whatever challenges remaining insurgent groups may pose. There has also been a general upgrade of all police stations and outposts, which have been constructed or renovated to include enhanced security features and provided with requisite firepower, mobility, and communications to respond effectively to challenges in their respective jurisdictions. These improvements have enabled these forward posts to play a crucial role in the COIN campaign and inflict a succession of reverses on the insurgents. The reimbursements under central Security Related Expenditure (SRE) scheme of state government's expenditure on COIN operations have also been quite useful for Tripura. The items covered under federal SRE scheme include raising of IR battalions, logistics provided to central armed forces, ex-gratia grant and gratuitous relief to victims of extremist violence, 75 percent of the cost of fuel incurred for operational purposes, honorarium paid to the Home Guards/Village Guards detailed for security purpose, and maintenance of designated camps set up for groups with whom state or central governments have entered into Suspension of Operations. The average annual allocation under SRE scheme between 2001 and 2014 has been around ₹27.73 crores (MHA, 2012–2013, 2013–2014).

Improving Manpower Capacities for COIN

The requirement of troops in COIN is huge, and the shortage of troops cannot be compensated through firepower, technology, or other resources. Given the hilly terrain, dense jungles, widely dispersed population and poor road connectivity in interior areas in the state, large number of troops are required for offensive operations to "clear" the area and permanently "hold" and dominate the conflict zone to prevent insurgents from re-concentrating or re-infiltrating (Thompson, 1967: 111–112). In this context, deployment of local forces is especially helpful in COIN due to their better cultural and situational awareness.

A very important feature of the state's COIN strategy has been the steady and substantial augmentation of its own armed battalions to combat militancy. The first TSR battalion was raised in 1984, followed by two more battalions in 1990 and 1996. The relatively slow growth of armed battalions despite an ongoing insurgency may be partly attributed to the financial constraints of a backward state like Tripura. However, since then 10 more battalions have come up as the state government has taken full advantage of central government's IRBs[17] scheme and starting from 5th TSR Battalion (IR-I) in 1997, all the newly raised units have been IRBs (TSR, 2010: 2).[18] In December 2013, the Union government has sanctioned another three IRBs for Tripura, taking the total number of TSR battalions to 15. The rapid expansion of TSR units during the last decade has added a substantial number of armed personnel to the state police and decidedly changed its character from a defensive to offensive force. The availability of large number of these highly trained and motivated troops, mostly local, has been the single most important factor in the state's COIN drive. This has also reduced the state's dependence on central paramilitary forces, which is reflected in the fact that at present only three-four CRPF battalions are deployed in Tripura, which is much less than the usual deployment of 10–15 CRPF battalions a decade ago. The raising of new armed battalions has also provided employment to large number of young tribal boys who would otherwise have been easy targets for recruitment by militant groups.[19]

---

[17] The IRBs are sanctioned by the Central government to meet the demands for additional troops by various states on the condition that the federal government may use these battalions elsewhere whenever required. Under the IRB scheme, the Central government bears the initial cost of raising IRBs while the responsibility for meeting the recurring expenditure rests with the state government (GOI, MHA, 2005–2006, Chapter II).

[18] The actual number of TSR Battalions deployed in the state at present has come down to 12, with the abolition of 4 Battalion TSR (a non-IRB) for administrative reasons. This unit has been abolished and its manpower distributed among other TSR units to fill up existing vacancies.

[19] During the course of a debate in the Parliament on December 17, 1996, the Union Home Minister mentioned that in view of acute shortage of Central forces, the states may raise their own India Reserve Battalions for security duties that would also provide employment to local youth, and prevent them from taking recourse to illegal channels for sheer survival.

Encouraging Professional Excellence

Since 2000, several measures have been instituted to encourage professional excellence, restore pride and enhance visibility and positive image of police. These include institution of Chief Minister's Medal, DGP's Commendation Disc, Policeman of the Year, observation of the Police Week, and out-of-turn promotions for outstanding achievements (Paul, 2009: 285). Before this, there were rather limited opportunities to recognize and reward outstanding professional merit as only a few personnel could be recommended for award of The Indian Police Medal (IPM) and the President's Police Medal (PPM) annually. The institution of Best TSR Battalion Trophy and organization of inter-battalion sports and shooting competitions have also encouraged professional excellence. To restore professional pride and project positive image of police, written orders were issued to all formations to ensure that policemen had smart turnout at all times while on duty, and conducted themselves with due decorum in public (DGP order dated May 29, 2002). They were also instructed to use Jai Hind[20] (Victory to the Indian nation) as a form of salutation in their interaction with the DGP or other senior officers (DGP order dated October 20, 2001). Over the years, these measures, big and small, have proved very useful in raising police morale, promoting healthy competition, and rewarding outstanding achievements of brave officers and men (Table 6.3).

A revised schedule and exhaustive format of annual inspections of TSR battalions on the paramilitary pattern has been introduced since 2001 to ensure proper monitoring and continuous evaluation of their performance. All commandants are now required to conduct a thorough inspection of their battalion every year, followed by an inspection by the DIG or IGP. The shortcomings noticed during these inspections are required to be rectified promptly by the concerned battalions and the inspection notes are put up to the DGP also for perusal and instructions.

---

[20] This salutation "Jai Hind" is commonly used in the military and paramilitary instead of "Good Morning."

As DIG/Armed Police (2000–2003), I had found this new format and schedule of regular inspections very helpful in streamlining functioning of TSR units.

While the holistic concept of COIN introduced in 2000 has essentially remained unchanged over the past decade, some operational modifications have been made by successor police chiefs as per their appreciation of prevailing situation. Thus, a Zonal Policing System was introduced in 2003 under which all local commands were placed under one TSR commandant designated as Zonal commander who in conjunction with the district SP was responsible for launching coordinated operations within his jurisdiction. An important innovation has been constitution of Special Operation Groups (SOGs) in TSR battalions to launch small-group operations based on hard intelligence. While no details can be shared regarding such covert operations, it is a fact that the SOGs, mostly comprising tribal troops, have displayed exceptional courage in such operations and succeeded in neutralizing quite a few important insurgents through operations that lasted up to a week deep inside the jungles in the harshest possible terrain and conditions.

Dominating the Conflict Zone

A growing body of academic literature has identified a lack of good governance and administrative competence as key proximate causes of the emergence of insurgent violence (Kalyvas, 2006; Fearon and Laitin, 2003). The most problematic areas are rural hinterlands and those areas with poor communication or infrastructure which may limit the government's reach. In Tripura, the predominantly hilly and jungle terrain and lack of infrastructure coupled with threat of guerrilla violence makes things extremely difficult for the civil administration. The re-establishment of government's authority in such "liberated zones" cannot be bolstered by temporary insertion of SFs, but requires carefully conceived measures to improve functioning of civil administration for delivery of basic services and establishment of law and order. This issue has been resolved satisfactorily in the state through establishment of TSR battalions' HQ and security camps in strategic interior militancy-affected areas as indicated below.

Establishment of Permanent Battalion HQs and Security Camps in Interior Areas

The first two TSR battalions raised in 1984 and 1990 were located in West Tripura district close to Agartala. Thereafter, in a significant departure from conventional wisdom the state government has taken a conscious decision to establish the HQs of many TSR units in interior areas instead of locating them close to the national highway or district HQs. While this move has posed some logistic and administrative difficulties to the affected units, it has ensured permanent penetration of SFs in interior areas, enabled the administration to implement developmental schemes and effectively secured the civilian population from the militant violence. Consequently, now the government departments and other civil institutions are able to operate freely in several parts of the state, which were earlier hotbeds of militancy. This is particularly true of units located in relatively backward Dhalai and North districts where it had been earlier difficult to provide dedicated security cover in remote areas due to hilly terrain and poor infrastructure.

Thus, in Dhalai district, the establishment of 3rd TSR Battalion HQ at Kachucherra in 1996 and 8th TSR Battalion HQs at Lalcherra in 2000 and their strategic deployment has been crucial to smooth functioning of the district administration and safety of large commercial and infrastructural projects of the ONGC, National Power Construction Corporation (NPCC), Gas Authority of India Limited (GAIL), and railways. Similarly, the establishment of 4th TSR Battalion HQs (now 13th Battalion TSR) at Subash Nagar in 1997 and its deployment in the most inaccessible and remote areas of Kanchanpur subdivision has effectively curtailed militant movement in North Tripura district. This move has also given a boost to economic activity in the state as it has become possible now to implement projects unhindered by the militant threats after a prolonged phase of insurgency and extremism.

The establishment of TSR camps in the most interior areas to dominate strategic hill features and dense forests which had long been the militant hideouts and were used as their bases for keeping kidnapped persons or committing crimes has been another key aspect of police strategy. Starting from 2001, these camps, mostly staffed by two or three platoons, have successfully undertaken offensive operations in their respective AORs and curtailed extremist movement effectively.[21] Many security camps in interior areas involved a trek of several kilometers through dense forests and rivers and lacked even basic accommodation, water, electricity, and medical facilities or logistic support. Even now TSR troops manning temporary operating bases (TOBs) continue to face severe logistic problems as these have been set up in remote jungles close to international India-Bangladesh border as a "second line of defense" to plug gaps between various border outposts manned by BSF.

With the benefit of hindsight, it is possible to appreciate the wisdom of this move, but at that point in time this decision had generated intense debate among senior police officers as many were apprehensive that such isolated camps would not be able to withstand pressure from insurgent groups. The survival and effectiveness of these interior camps in this initial phase was crucial as any major reversal at this stage would have raised concerns about the professional capabilities of TSR and the practical wisdom of setting up such isolated camps in interior areas, and, in all probability, compromised the launch of the new aggressive COIN policy. In many parts of the country, such isolated camps have been especially targeted by Maoist insurgents, leading to killing of large numbers of SFs. It is a tribute to the resilience and dedication of these troops that, despite all hardships, they have succeeded in marginalizing insurgent influence in these areas and won over the tribal people through selfless service and sacrifices.

---

[21] The interior camps set up during 2001–2002 included Panjirai and Dasaramkhamarbari in south district; Tuichakma and Ravanpara in Dhalai district; Tuisama, N.R. Para and Mitrojay para in north district; and Champahour and Nabanjoy Bari in west district.

Strategic Deployment of TSR Battalions

It has been argued that a proper response to low-level guerrilla warfare is the positioning of armed units in a large number of small posts where they can protect and mix with the local people, supported by mobile back-up and ground forces that conduct ambushes, patrols, and other offensive operations in underpopulated hinterlands (O'Neill, 1990: 130).The pattern of deployment of TSR has ensured that it meets both these requirements of protective and operational tasks. The deployment of SFs in the state is constantly reviewed by the government at the highest level in the light of fresh intelligence inputs, induction or de-induction of federal paramilitary forces, and raising of new TSR batallions. However, a review of TSR deployment pattern since 2000 reveals some consistent features.

First, population security measures have been central to the COIN campaign in Tripura. Thus, in 2000, of the 95 total camps as many as 42 performed protective tasks, 18 camps performed law and order duties, 6 camps performed ROP, and 29 camps conducted COIN operations (see Table 6.1 and Figure 6.1). Again, despite a decline in militancy, there has been no corresponding reduction in the deployment of TSR for protective tasks, and, in fact, their number has risen from 42 in 2000 to 61 in 2012 (Table 6.2 and Figure 6.2). This dedicated and expanding security cover has been crucial in garnering public support for the government by giving them assured protection from militant depredations and demoralized insurgent groups by denying them soft targets.

Second, despite significant reduction in insurgent activities in recent years, there has been no dilution in TSR's commitment for operational tasks and, in fact, the number of CI camps has steadily increased. For example, in 2000 out of the total 95 TSR camps, only 29 camps were maintained for COIN operations, while in 2012 their number has gone up to 170, which is over 65 percent of the total 262 camps (see Tables 6.1 and 6.2). This sustained pressure has ensured a progressive marginalization of insurgent capabilities and further consolidated the hold of SFs and civil administration in large parts of the state.

Table 6.1:

Pattern of Deployment of TSR Battalions (2000)

Unit	CI Ops	Nature of Duty		Law and Order	Total Camps
		Protective	ROP		
1st TSR	05	03	01	03	12
2nd TSR	03	14	0	0	17
3rd TSR	08	06	02	04	20
4th TSR	03	09	02	05	19
5th TSR	08	0	0	03	11
6th TSR	02	10	01	03	16
Total	**29**	**42**	**06**	**18**	**95**

Source: Tripura Police.

Figure 6.1:

Pattern of Deployment of TSR Battalions (2000)

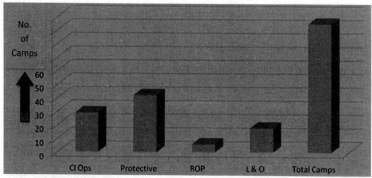

Source: Tripura Police.

Table 6.2:

Pattern of Deployment of TSR Battalions (2012)

Name of Unit	CI Ops	Protective/ Security	Railway Duty	Escort Duty	ROP Duty	Total
1st Battalion TSR	16	1	0	1	0	18
2nd Battalion TSR	9	4	3	0	1	17
3rd Battalion TSR	14	1	7	0	1	23
5th Battalion TSR	21	0	0	0	0	21
6th Battalion TSR	17	5	3	0	0	25

Continued Table 6.2

208 Police and Counterinsurgency

Continued Table 6.2

Name of Unit	CI Ops	Protective/ Security	Railway Duty	Escort Duty	ROP Duty	Total
7th Battalion TSR	11	8	0	0	2	21
8th Battalion TSR	14	3	0	0	8	25
9th Battalion TSR	18	3	0	2	1	24
10th Battalion TSR (ONGC)	0	22	0	0	1	23
11th Battalion TSR	10	8	0	0	1	19
12th Battalion TSR	23	0	0	0	0	23
13th Battalion TSR	17	6	0	0	0	23
Total	**170**	**61**	**13**	**3**	**15**	**262**

Source: Tripura Police.

Figure 6.2

Pattern of Deployment of TSR Battalions (2012)

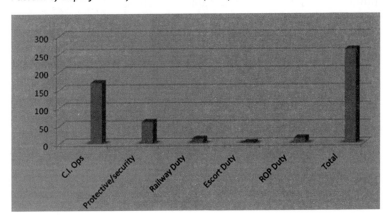

Source: Tripura Police.

However, a significant change is discernible in the operational deployment of troops. When militancy was at its peak from 2000 to 2005, there were several security camps manned by two or three platoons (60–90 persons) as the troops were required to be posted in sufficient numbers in these interior areas for effective area domination, operations, and camp security. But with the decline in militancy in recent years, security camps are usually manned by only the strength of one platoon now and, in fact, many camps have the posted strength of only 20–25 men.[22] For illustration, in June 2002 TSR 3rd Battalion maintained as many as six interior camps (total 12 posts) with three platoons strength at Ravanpara, Karamcharra, Khasiapunji, Tuichakma, Dulubari, and Kachucherra for COIN operations in highly militancy affected areas of Dhalai district, whereas now it is deployed at 23 locations with one platoon or less strength. Such examples can be multiplied from other battalions also. This strategy of thin deployment has enabled the TSR battalions to establish more number of camps for round-the-clock security to larger number of people and instill confidence in them.

Third, the deployment of troops for infrastructural projects has gone up considerably during the last decade which indicates the high importance accorded by the state to such projects, which are considered vital for the economic development of the state as also improved availability of manpower resources accruing from larger number of TSR battalions (see Table 6.3). Thus, apart from providing one full TSR battalion for protection of ONGC installations, operations and their personnel, these troops are also deployed for protection of Power projects, GAIL, and railway security. The crucial role played by TSR in extension of railway line to Agartala deserves special mention in view of its vital importance to economic development of the state, stiff resistance by insurgent groups, and the enormous physical and operational challenges successfully tackled by them.

Operational Achievements

A summary of major achievements by TSR battalions during the past decade is a testimony to the efficacy of new concept, strategies, and tactics of COIN in successfully disrupting and dismantling complex network of insurgent outfits and their collaborators and criminals as mentioned below:

---

[22] This is a major departure from the practice of paramilitary forces which normally deploy not less than one coy.

Table 6.3:

Summary of Achievements of TSR Battalions (2000–2012)

Sl. No.	Type of Success	2k	01	02	03	04	05	06	07	08	09	10	11	12	Total
1.	No. of Encounters	21	27	25	63	95	73	49	36	29	06	07	4	03	438
2.	Extremists Killed	16	10	11	25	33	13	14	09	14	0	0	0	01	146
3.	Extremist Arrested (listed/unlisted)	29	70	34	105	79	35	11	32	24	05	0	0	01	425
4.	Collaborators Arrested (listed/unlisted)	261	210	168	260	321	198	111	87	26	12	07	02	08	1,671
5.	No. of Weapons Recovered	65	33	32	48	79	39	42	47	63	24	17	09	28	526
6.	Kidnapped Persons Rescued	21	15	10	14	06	05	06	12	4	0	0	0	0	93
7.	Permanent Warrantee Arrested	10	78	85	125	64	66	61	27	20	17	05	07	08	573

Source: Tripura Police.

A review of the operations conducted by TSR battalions over the past decade indicates that most of these have involved encounters between small contingents of SFs and extremist groups leading to the killing or arrest of a small number of extremists, harborers, or other hardened criminals, rescue of kidnapped persons, and recovery of weapons. These operations were driven by intelligence mostly generated by TSR units from their own operations, sources or local recruits, and sometimes information provided by local police station or intelligence agencies.

The success of these small unit operations validates the observation of Thompson that:

> In an insurgency it is not the major operations that defeat the insurgents. It is a high rate of contact in minor operations, based on good intelligence and resulting perhaps in only one or two kills to each contact. These soon add up.... Good intelligence leads to more frequent and more rapid contacts. More contacts lead to more kills. These in turn lead to greater confidence in the general population, resulting in better intelligence and still more contacts and kills (Thompson, 1967: 111–112).

Such fusion of operation and intelligence has been found highly effective in neutralizing middle level of planners, facilitators, and operators and disrupting their networks of terror (Kilcullen, 2010: 4).[23] TSR's COIN operations did not involve high-tech weapons, airpower, or surveillance as seen in most ongoing COIN operations waged by the United States in Afghanistan, Pakistan, and Iraq.[24] However, lack of high-tech equipment was never perceived as an insurmountable handicap and may, in fact, have contributed to operational successes by facilitating better appreciation of ground realities and close interaction with affected population through constant foot patrolling in vulnerable areas. This assertion gets support from observation of Galula (1964: 32), who has

---

[23] Kilcullen (2010: 4) has used the term F3EA to describe "Find, Fix, Finish, Exploit, Assess" phases of such intelligence-led operations.

[24] In fact, high technology may lead to unintended collateral damage, killing innocent civilians, and further complicate the situation as has happened many times in case of drone attacks by the U.S.-led coalition forces in Pakistan and Afghanistan.

mentioned that because such conflicts basically require infantry soldiers, rather than modern air, sea, or ground components, therefore, "... the less sophisticated the counterinsurgent forces, the better they are."

Finally, most of these operational successes have entailed meticulous planning, passion, and courage on the part of officers and troops engaged in this COIN drive over the past many years. Some of these operations have involved exceptional daring, innovation, and resourcefulness on the part of junior leaders. However, as details of covert operations by the SOG cannot be shared, some case studies are presented in Part three of this book to demonstrate how many of the aforementioned reforms and tactics have enhanced TSR's COIN capabilities and effectiveness, and highlight TSR's professionalism, concern for safety of innocent citizens, and an aversion to inflict any "collateral damage" even when conducting offensive operations.

Civic Action Programs

COIN has been called "armed social work" (Kilcullen, 2006) and well-conceived civic action programs have played a positive role in several COIN campaigns, including Tripura. The poor tribals in many interior areas have been the worst victims of insurgency as the civil administration had been finding it difficult to provide even the basic amenities due to threat of insurgents. The SFs in Tripura have, therefore, moved to fill this gap and undertaken a wide range of Civic Action programs such as blood donation camps, health camps, free distribution of medicines, blankets, and mosquito nets, renovation and construction of hospitals, community halls, pre-recruitment training to boys for joining SFs, and assistance to civil administration in organizing administrative camps in interior areas. These initiatives have been very helpful to the SFs in building good rapport with the tribal people living in remote areas, and facilitated in turning the tide against insurgents. The positive impact of these civic action programs would be illustrated through an in-depth case study of a police primary school established by 5th Battalion TSR at its HQs at Daluma in a remote corner of South District in Tripura (see Chapter 8).

Psychological Operations

The purpose of psychological operations or PSY OPS has been well summarized as:

> Mobilizing public support by explaining to them the justification of own cause; insulating people against insurgent propaganda; align the support of neutral population to one's own side or at least to dissuade them from supporting the enemy's cause (Schleifer, 2003: 50).

PSY OPS are also helpful in inducing surrenders among insurgents by stressing their declining fortunes and promises of amnesty, security, and material benefits (O'Neill, 1990: 145). However, sometimes democracies engaged in counterinsurgencies fight shy of employing these methods because of sinister connotations associated with this term. In a major departure from their conventional approach, Tripura police have used PSY OPS to undercut the recruitment base of insurgent groups in tribal areas through large-scale public screening of documentary films and performances by cultural troops in interior villages to highlight atrocities of militants; lavish lifestyle of top insurgent leaders and the hardships suffered by the lower insurgents/common tribal people; futility of the so-called "cause"; and adverse effects of militancy on developmental activities. The SFs through active cooperation of village-level leaders have been able to persuade family members of many insurgents to convince some misguided youth to abjure violence and surrender before government. In some cases, appeals by family members were broadcast on the state radio channels also to give wide publicity. All these measures have had considerable positive impact on common people, leading to negligible fresh recruitment, increased surrenders, and splits among insurgent groups as well as growing public resistance and revulsion against this culture of violence and hatred propagated by insurgent groups.

Coordination among Civil-paramilitary and Security Forces

Finally, excellent coordination between police and other paramilitary forces and with civil authorities has been critical to the success of COIN operations. Historically, in most conflict theatres friction between various forces operating within a multi-force environment has undermined operations. However, in Tripura, systematic multi-layered institutional mechanisms have been established at the state, district and the sub-divisional level to ensure continuous operational coordination. The State-level Coordination Committee (SLCC), chaired by the Chief Secretary, and comprising senior officers of the police, paramilitary, and other security agencies is the apex body in the state for all policy matters relating to COIN campaign. The operational coordination at the top is secured through SLOG, comprising senior police, paramilitary, and security agency officers. The real-time operational coordination between Forces is secured through District-level Operations and Intelligence Group (DLOG). As per state government orders issued in 1998, both SLOG and DLOG were directed to meet as often as necessary, including daily, if required at a location convenient to members of the Group. The Sub-Divisional Police Officers (SDPOs) also hold periodic meetings with the representatives of SFs to resolve local problems and ensure continuous operational coordination. The success of these institutional mechanisms is assured through informal interaction and personal rapport among the senior officers. And lastly, over the last decade the Chief Minister himself has been holding weekly law and order meeting regularly every Monday with the DGP, Chief Secretary, and other senior officers, and periodic review meetings with the district officials all over the state to keep himself abreast of the latest developments and secure compliance of instructions issued by the government. Such close monitoring of ground situation by the top political executive and sustained commitment of necessary resources over the years has ensured proper implementation of the state government's "comprehensive" strategy, leading to a steady improvement in governance and security in the state.

Conclusion

The above discussion focusing on evolution and remarkable transformation of Tripura police for their COIN role complements the political, economic, diplomatic, and other non-kinetic strategies of the government and demonstrates how integration of police strategies with the comprehensive strategy of the government has succeeded in isolating insurgent groups from the common law-abiding citizens, re-established primacy of the rule-of-law, and facilitated delivery of basic services and security to all citizens.

The comprehensive COIN strategies of the state have led to retrogression of insurgency and gradual return of normalcy in the state. This is reflected in repeal of ASFPA, declining trends of violence, inability of insurgent groups to subvert democratic elections, increased public and private investment in industrial projects and business, and a general relaxed demeanor of common people. Besides this, an increased flow of high-grade intelligence from common people and the failure of insurgent groups to replenish cadres are also indicative of COIN success. Another indicator is a shift in policing priorities from control of insurgency to Road Traffic Accidents (RTA) and Crime Against Women (CAW) articulated by the DGP Tripura in August 2013 ("Chief's Message," August 2013 http://www.tripurapolice.nic. in/chiefMsg.htm).[25] On an average, one person dies daily in the state in road accidents, and almost 70 percent of the police effort is focused on keeping the roads and women safe. The improved

---

[25] The rate of total cognizable crime committed against women in 2013 was 89.75—the second highest in the country after Assam (MHA, 2013: 385).

security situation is amply reflected in statistics related to extremist violence. Remarkably, from 2010 till 2014, on an average only one civilian and one SF have been killed in insurgent violence. At the peak of insurgency in 2000, the corresponding figure was 453 civilians and 16 SF casualties (SATP 12 and Vohra, 2011: 144). However, at the peak of insurgency, the state police considered increasing number of community celebrations of Durga Puja (a major religious festival of the Hindus in Tripura) in defiance of the insurgents' threat to boycott Hindu festivals and growing public revulsion against insurgent violence reflected in popular refusal to pay "taxes" as the clearest indicators of declining hold of insurgents among civil population.

The improved efficiency and effectiveness of the state police was evident in their successful handling of urban terrorism attempted by ATTF through five serial bomb blasts in Agartala city on October 1, 2008, which injured 76 persons and spread panic throughout the state. The state CID successfully cracked the case in less than 3 months with the arrest of many local ATTF militants and their accomplices and unearthed the role of other northeast militant outfits and some foreign agencies in this case. In April 2015, four militants have been sentenced to life imprisonment for their involvement in Agartala serial bomb blast case. The successful investigation and prosecution of this case has effectively nipped the militant plans to revive militancy through urban guerrilla warfare in the state. The loyalty of the local tribal troops has been an important factor in this success, and barring some isolated acts of desertion the insurgent influences have spectacularly failed to subvert the force.

7

Discussion and Conclusion

Introduction

This concluding chapter ties different strands of the two dominant themes of this study pertaining to the radical transformation of police in Tripura and the efficacy of the comprehensive approach to COIN, which has immensely succeeded in marginalizing insurgent influences in the state, not only in terms of their diminished capacities for indiscriminate violence, but more importantly, their complete political irrelevance to and isolation from their purported support bases in the indigenous population. That this task could be accomplished within the democratic framework of the country and with complete respect for the human rights of the tribal population speaks volumes about the astuteness of the political approach in Tripura. This achievement is all the more significant in the backdrop of persistent violence in several other neighboring states in the northeast that has severely impaired the functioning of their institutions for governance, security, and democratic politics, leading to conditions of "durable disorder" and "democracy deficit." Tripura has also managed to significantly reduce poverty and promote economic development, even as situation has worsened in many neighboring states (Chakravarty, 2012). Apparently, peace and development go together. To put these main themes of this research in their proper perspective, this chapter is divided into two sections. The first section presents the main insights from this research, while the concluding second section makes an assessment of Tripura police's capabilities for meeting future policing challenges.

Insights from COIN in Tripura

It is commonly mentioned that there is no "silver bullet," magic mantras, or universal COIN strategies, tactics, or techniques. This is due to the fact that the permutation and combination of factors that give rise to insurgencies in any given conflict theater are virtually endless, and also because the COIN success or failure can be caused by a variety of different mechanisms. However, this is not to say that lessons, ideas, or strategies from one campaign cannot be transferred to another case with profit. Indeed, the COIN leaders have a moral obligation to learn proper lessons from the past campaigns to avoid tremendous unnecessary costs imposed on society by enormous wastage of resources, efforts and lives, and a fractured polity and society (ICM, 2007: 9). The following discussion presents some of the "best practices" in COIN recommended by various experts, theorists, and practitioners before proceeding to the specific insights from Tripura's COIN campaign.

Austin Long (2006) has presented lessons from five decades of RAND COIN research and made recommendations for current and future COIN. Briefly stated, these are: (a) organization for COIN must be improved to ensure unity of effort between the political and military components of the government, and improved coordination between the police, civil administration, and military down to the tactical level; (b) institution of suitable amnesty and reward programs to persuade insurgents to surrender or provide intelligence, and provision of effective protection to informers and surrendered enemy personnel; (c) effective border security to deny external support or cross-border sanctuaries; and (d) pacification of smaller political units, that is, villages and neighborhoods through a combination of local security and development programs rather than grandiose national projects. David Kilcullen

(2010: 3–4), a well-known Australian soldier-scholar, has observed that there are only two fundamentals of COIN: (a) a clear understanding in detail of "what drives the conflict in any given area or with any given population group," and (b) "to act with respect for local people, and putting the well-being of non-combatants above everything else—even—in fact, especially—ahead of killing the enemy." Lieutenant General Peter Leahy, the Chief of Australian Army, in his "Introduction" to the Special Edition of Australian Army Journal titled *Counterinsurgency* has recommended: (a) discriminate use of force to support a clearly defined political objective; (b) fusion of the political and military leadership of the COIN campaign at the highest level; and (c) winning the trust and respect of the indigenous people (Leahy, 2008). The latest edition of the *U.S. Counterinsurgency Field Manual* (2007) also does not differ in any significant way from these recommendations. According to K.P.S. Gill (2000), a veteran Indian police officer, success in COIN requires (a) "a clarity of purpose, unflagging determination and, critically, an unqualified sense of moral authority" to overcome the crisis of confidence among government functionaries; (b) a radical transformation of internal SFs to create necessary skills, knowledge, attitude, and infrastructure; and (c) suitable mechanisms to ensure accountability of the political executive, the civil administration, and the judiciary.

Finally, R. Scott Moore (2007), a U.S. soldier-scholar, has made a detailed analysis of nearly 60 COIN campaigns and recommended a set of tasks across six functional categories for effective resolution of insurgency: (a) establish and maintain security; (b) provide humanitarian relief and essential services, including rebuilding of essential infrastructure; (c) establish governance; (d) sustain economic development; (e) support reconciliation; and (f) foster social change. Historically, presence of some critical enablers that cut across all tasks has been essential for effective execution of COIN strategy, and must be integrated into each task. These enablers are clear goals, civil–military unity of purpose, integrated intelligence, legitimacy—both inside and outside the conflict zone—selective and appropriate use of force as per situation, and a vigorously executed integrated strategy. According to Moore (2007):

> Successful counterinsurgency results from a long-term, continuous, and integrated civil-military strategy carried out by soldiers and civilians operating side by side, that builds lasting social, political, and economic stability in a state or region while resolving the underlying causes that led to insurgency. Nothing less achieves success.

Apparently, the basic principles of COIN are not in doubt and a certain level of consistency is seen in the available literature concerning "best practices." But the key questions are which lessons or ideas can be borrowed and how they might be adapted under somewhat dissimilar circumstances, given the rigidity of bureaucratic structures that impede organizational learning. In this context, Gray (2007) has rightly observed that one of the main tasks before the COIN leaders is "to persuade our institutions to change their preferred behavior while being alert to the possibility that institutional, strategic, and public cultures may not permit necessary adjustments." The travails of some major powers in various COIN theaters across the world are indicative of the immense difficulties involved in implementing apparently simple COIN principles in the field situation.

With this highly selective overview of the literature on effective COIN strategies, we now proceed to examine Tripura's COIN campaign to gain some insights into "COIN in the real world" (Haines, 2009).[1] The first cluster of lessons derives from the policing aspects of this campaign, and the second cluster of lessons derives from the comprehensive nature of the political strategy adopted by the state. While the lessons derived from empowering the police to function as the lead agency for COIN in violently divided conflict-driven societies would definitely illuminate some new aspects of policing, some other lessons may appear common. However, Clausewitz advises that "everything in strategy is very simple, but that does not mean that everything is very easy" (Clausewitz, 1976: 178, quoted in Gray, 2008: 394).

---

[1] "Coin in the real world" is a paper by David R. Haines in which he observes that the "best practices" COIN prescriptions by the rich Western world do not factor in the resource constraints and other institutional and structural weaknesses in the middle-power countries such as India.

Policing Aspects of COIN in Tripura

Building Comprehensive Police Capacities Is Essential for COIN Success

Conventional responses to severe and escalating insurgent violence have usually involved recourse to deployment of military or paramilitary units, and marginalized the role of local police in COIN due to a variety of reasons such as superiority of military's "hardware, training, discipline, and integrity as compared to presumed subversion of loyalty of local troops, politicization, corruption, and inferiority in operational preparedness" (Gill, 2000: 85–86). Tripura's experience demonstrated that these disadvantages are not inherent in police and can be definitely overcome with superior leadership; and that presumption of divided loyalties or unreliability of local police was entirely unfounded. In fact, the SOGs that went deep inside insurgent-dominated territory were formed mostly of local tribal troops, while civil police staff comprising a mix of tribal and Bengali police personnel dealt impartially and effectively with communal and political violence. The operational successes of SOGs in neutralizing insurgents through small unit operations in tribal hinterlands suggest distinct advantages of employing local forces.

Tripura's campaign also confirms that investing in building local police capacities is an extremely efficient, reliable, and economical way of dealing with insurgent violence. Self-reliance is essential because adequate capacities have to be made available urgently within the time frame of conflict and decentralized across the conflict zone to enable the first responders to pre-empt or respond promptly to incidents in their respective jurisdictions (Sahni, 2009b, 2010a). In Indian setting, states cannot be certain of enough federal forces on long-term basis as their availability keeps fluctuating from time to time due to political and administrative contingencies, calculations, and constraints of the federal government. For example, all army units and substantial number of border guarding BSF battalions were withdrawn from Tripura in 1999 in the wake of Kargil War despite strong objections from the state government, leading to major escalation in violence. It is also a fact that despite deployment of large number of paramilitary battalions, actual manpower available on ground is much less as substantial part of their manpower is consumed for non-operational tasks that are required for providing administrative, logistic, communication, and miscellaneous support functions. On the other hand, local armed battalions and civil police are able to spare larger component of manpower for operational tasks in a more flexible deployment pattern as they are less constrained by central SOPs.[2]

The shortage of federal forces turned out to be a blessing in disguise for Tripura police as this compelled the state government to be self-reliant and take determined action to empower local police for effectively countering various challenges (The Statesman, 2000). To this end, concerted efforts were made to align resource capacities with insurgent challenges on an urgent basis through inter-unit transfers of available modern weapons, diversion or hiring of additional vehicles, and bullet-proofing of vehicles locally, even as a protracted process of capacity building was underway through federal government's "Modernization of Police Forces" scheme. Accelerated growth of armed battalions helped substantially in augmenting manpower resources for COIN, while the employment of SPOs and VR parties served to mobilize popular resistance against insurgent violence, provided crucial local intelligence and helped in isolating insurgents from local population. Empowerment of "small commanders" is a key aspect of this process of capacity building for successful COIN effort, and reorientation and retraining of troops, especially junior leaders, have been given a very high priority. Consequently, over the past decade the state's dependence on federal forces for law and order and operational purposes has come down drastically, which is reflected in the

---

[2] For instance, paramilitary forces like Assam Rifles, CRPF, and BSF are generally deployed in company-level strength, while Tripura's TSR battalions have been frequently deployed at platoon level or even lesser strength.

deployment of only three to four CRPF battalions in 2013 as against 14 battalions in 2001.

Police-Primacy, Intelligence, and Police-led Operations

Effectiveness of COIN efforts has been frequently compromised by lack of coordination or disunity between civil and police/military authorities, and friction between local police and federal forces (Gill, 2000). Examples abound from recent campaigns in Afghanistan and Iraq to Assam and Kashmir in India. This issue has acquired special relevance for present COIN campaign in Tripura as in addition to local police, the state has usually got deployment of 15,000–20,000 troops of various paramilitary forces for COIN operations, guarding of international border with Bangladesh and other internal security (IS) duties. This matter has been resolved by devising suitable institutional mechanisms that unambiguously declare supremacy of political executive leadership and civil authority at the state level for overall direction and policy formulation, while responsibility for operational matters is vested in civil police. These institutional mechanisms have been reinforced by the personal rapport and cooperative attitude of the top police leadership.

In Tripura, federal security forces deployed for COIN in a particular district conduct their COIN operations to support the District Superintendent of Police who is responsible for law and order in his jurisdiction. Effective coordination mechanisms have been built at the state and local levels to ensure synchronization of responses. The local police have been able to effectively lead COIN operations due to their improved operational preparedness and tremendous capacities for intelligence generation through wide variety of trusted relationships with local communities, and a vast network of contacts and sources supplemented by surrendered extremists and SPOs. The armed battalions have also generated actionable intelligence through operations, tribal recruits, and technical interception of insurgents' communication. Acquiring capabilities to strike at rebel camps across the border has been an important feature of police strategy. The intelligence-led operations have also led to discriminate use of force against recalcitrant guerrillas, and avoided alienation among ethnic communities.

Another important dimension of local police deployment has been the ethnic composition of local forces. The armed battalions of the state have a balanced mix of tribal and non-tribal troops, recruited from within and outside the state. Adequate care has been taken to ensure sufficient representation from interior areas of the state, once considered stronghold of insurgent outfits, by holding recruitment rallies in those far-flung areas. Members of the ST comprise almost one-third of TSR battalions. This balanced composition has prevented overreaction by troops during operations and saved indigenous people from excesses by SFs. All efforts have been made to avoid "collateral damage" to innocent civilians. Furthermore, the fact that TSR armed battalions have been raised, trained, and equipped like paramilitary forces has contributed immensely to their over-all discipline and professionalism. In nutshell, all these measures have helped in defeating insurgent propaganda against SFs, provided invaluable allies among indigenous people to the government, and weaned tribal youth away from insurgent influences by giving them government jobs, guns, and uniform, effectively trumping any offer that could be made by insurgent groups. Therefore, the TSR model of armed battalions can be useful to governments fighting ethnic insurgencies as it effectively combines various advantages of paramilitary forces and local forces.

Focus on the Civilian Population as the Center of Gravity

The importance of popular support has been recognized by insurgent leaders and counterinsurgents alike.[3] COIN is "a competition with the insurgent for the right and the ability to win the hearts, minds,

---

[3] According to Taber (2002): Without the consent and active aid of the people, the guerrilla would be merely a bandit, and could not survive long. If, on the other hand, the counterinsurgent could claim the same support, the guerrilla would not exist, because there would be no war, no revolution.

and acquiescence of the population" (Kilcullen, 2010: 4). The evidence amassed on guerrilla battlefields on three continents over three decades indicates that civilian support is the most essential element of successful guerrilla operations (Fall, 1967: 345). The non-combatant civilians function as guerrilla's "camouflage, his quartermaster, his recruiting office, his communications network, and his efficient, all-seeing intelligence service" (Taber, 2002: 12). Research suggests, and field officers confirm, that providing effective security to people from insurgent violence on permanent basis is essential for enlisting popular support for government's COIN effort (Galula, 1964; Gill, 2000; Kilcullen, 2006; Mason, 1996; Moore, 2007). The deployment pattern of SFs over the past decade suggests that population-centric measures have been central to COIN in Tripura. Even during the worst period of violence in 2000, of the 95 total camps, as many as 42 performed protective tasks, while only 29 conducted COIN operations. Further, there has been no dilution of TSR's deployment for protective tasks even after considerable improvement in security scenario, and the number of protective camps has steadily increased to 61 in 2012. This dedicated security to threatened populations has been helpful in mobilizing popular support for government efforts and is a key aspect of successful COIN in Tripura. This deployment is in line with the observation of COIN experts that in most COIN campaigns "the force devoted to establishing order will be both larger in numerical terms than the forces dedicated to field combat and more aligned to political aspects of a 'heart-and-minds' concept of operations" (Quinlivan, 1995).

The destruction of "non-violent discourses" and its replacement with socially constructed "war-discourses" has been considered as one of the most significant precipitating factor in armed civil conflicts (Jackson, 2004: 63–64). Therefore, another effective way of countering insurgency is to mobilize popular support by replacing insurgents' idea—the "popular objective"—with an "alternative idea" through a consistent narrative that addresses the root cause of the problem rather than addressing the outer manifestations of insurgency through direct action (O'Neill, 2008). Over the years, Tripura government has succeeded in promoting its alternative narrative of "peace through development" and created a solid peace constituency through large-scale peace meetings, effective political mobilization of women and influential Jamatia community, devolution of powers to local bodies, and encouraging "misguided" youth to renounce violence (*Tripura Human Development* Report, 2007: 103–127).

Effective Domination of Conflict Zone Is Essential for COIN Success

The first rule of deployment in COIN is "Be there" (Kilcullen, 2010: 35). Permanent deployment in the conflict zone, rather than sporadic raids from outside, is essential to win popular support by providing dedicated security cover to people and ensure their safety from reprisals from insurgents. In absence of this, no amount of civic works, developmental or welfare initiatives can persuade people to risk their lives by opposing extremists (Krepinevich, 1986: 12). While no standard formulae can provide useful guide to tie-down ratios in guerrilla warfare, the level of COIN forces has to be large enough to provide effective security to the population, and has very little to do with the actual number of guerrillas as under favorable conditions even small number of guerrillas can cause substantial violence to effectively dent government's authority, and undermine development and governance programs (Fearon and Laitin, 2003). The violence unleashed by Tripura's main insurgent groups such as the TNV, NLFT, and ATTF for over three decades certainly supports this point as none of these groups had more than 1,000–1,500 hardcore cadres at their peak.[4]

According to modern COIN thinking, a troop density of 20–25 counterinsurgents for every 1,000 density in an AOR is considered

---

[4] Internationally also, there are several cases that prove this point. For example, in Cyprus more than 40,000 British troops were unable to suppress 300 Greeks in the EOKA (National Organization of Cypriot Struggle) militarily even after a five-year counterinsurgency campaign (Fall, 1965), and the Irish Republic Army that probably never consisted of more than 1,000 active cadres could not be defeated by the armed forces of the U.K.

the minimum troop density required for effective COIN (CFM, 2007: 22–23). In keeping with this logic, a heavy presence of SF personnel in the state has been maintained even as there has been a steady erosion of insurgents' numbers and capabilities. Thus, the total number of TSR battalions and paramilitary battalions deployed in the state has risen to 37 in 2013 (TSR-12, CRPF-3, AR-4, BSF-18) as against 35 in 2001 (TSR-8, CRPF-14, AR-4, BSF-9). The thin deployment of TSR scattered all over the state in over 250 small camps of platoon strength augmented with over 100 SPO camps has significantly reinforced population security. Currently, the small state of Tripura has a total of over 700 such defended locations if we add the number of all security camps, locations held by police stations, police outposts, border outposts, and battalion HQs of police and paramilitary forces (Vohra, 2011: 178).

The establishment of large number of protective and operational camps across the state including the most inaccessible remote areas and strategic hill ranges has eliminated all "safe havens" for insurgent groups. This massive deployment of SFs in COIN grid has supplemented and supported a dense network of police stations, outposts and SPO camps, leaving no scope for insurgents to intimidate, induce or mobilize support among indigenous people. Moreover, the permanent presence of SFs has facilitated restoration of civil administration and other institutions of governance and democratic polity in "recovered" areas. Construction of roads, bridges, schools, dispensaries, and other infrastructure for delivery of basic services has created local stakeholders in the developmental process, further diminishing insurgents' capacities to mobilize people.

Border security is considered an important component of comprehensive COIN strategy to deny foreign sanctuaries and support to insurgent groups (Long, 2006). In Tripura also strengthening of security along the 856-km international border with Bangladesh has played a crucial role in curtailing infiltration and free cross-border movement of insurgent groups, smugglers and illegal immigrants, leading to reduction in extremist violence and smuggling of arms, drugs and fake currency. Over the past decade while the number of central paramilitary CRPF battalions deployed for law and order has gone down substantially, the number of BSF battalions in the state has been doubled from nine in 2001 to 18 in 2013, thereby reducing the distance between each BOP to only three to 4 km from an average of earlier 10 km. Furthermore, through central funding substantial progress has been made regarding fencing, flood-lighting, and construction of border roads along the Indo-Bangladesh border. As per GOI records, 782 km of the total sanctioned 848 km border has been already fenced, 642 km of the sanctioned 718 km border area has been covered by floodlighting, and 992 km of the sanctioned 1,182 km roads have been constructed along the border (MHA, 2013–2014, Chapter III). Recent deployment of TSR troops in more vulnerable areas along this international border as "the second line of defense" is aimed to plug remaining loopholes in border security and successfully frustrated insurgents' plans to disrupt 2013 Assembly elections.

Outstanding Leadership for Success in COIN

Successful COIN efforts have been usually associated with strong and professional leaders. Recent research (Moyar, 2009) suggests that outstanding leadership is so critical to the success of COIN that it may be proper to consider COIN as "leader-centric" warfare. The main leadership attributes for success in COIN include adaptability and flexibility (USA, IDA, 2005), tremendous initiative to invigorate all aspects of COIN—military as well as non-military, absolute integrity in all personal and professional dealings, dedication, and fearlessness (McClellan, 1966). Realizing centrality of the position of the DGP, at the peak of violence around 2000–2003 the state government was especially careful in selecting officers for this position and did not restrict its choice of officers from within the state only. Considering the largely passive and reactive nature of policing and their inability in the past to check this rising tide of violence, the government's decision to entrust police with this responsibility amounted to a tremendous leap of faith in the new police chief, B.L. Vohra, who assumed the charge of DGP, Tripura in May 2000 and vindicated the faith reposed in him by successfully turning the much-maligned Tripura police into a highly motivated offensive force during his eventful two-year tenure (*Tripura Times,* 2000). He proved to be "the man" to execute government's "plan."[5] DGP Vohra was followed by another capable officer, Mr G.M. Srivastava, who neutralized the insurgent challenge effectively in the decisive phase of COIN during his tenure from September 2003 to February 2007 by aggressive policing and constituting SOGs for covert operations. These operational achievements have been further consolidated in subsequent years by successive officers.

Re-establishment of the Rule of Law Is Essential to Demonstrate the Integrity of Governments' Response

In India's northeast several insurgencies have lost their ideological coherence, and established strong nexus with local politicians, policemen, and bureaucrats to siphon off large amounts of developmental funds, and ensure protection of their own criminal operations (Sahni, 2002a). Some commentators have located roots of increased ethnic and communal violence, and lawlessness in NER to federal policies that privilege local ethnic militias and autocrats in consolidating their power, and overlook their violent deeds and corrupt practices in exchange for protection of critical infrastructure, vital installations, and federal forces (Lacina, 2009a, 2009b). A strong political–militant nexus in northeast states, including Tripura, has also been frequently cited as reason for escalating violence in the region. Therefore, restoration of law and governance, disruption of underground economy of insurgents, and strengthening of institutions of criminal justice system shall be central to any COIN strategy. In highly divided violent societies, it is also essential that law-enforcement agencies take firm action against the

---

[5] Field Marshal Montgomery emphasized the importance of leadership after a series of debacles in tackling the insurgency. In his letter to the Colonial Secretary Alfred Lyttelton, Montgomery wrote, "We must have a plan. Secondly, we must have a man" (quoted by Mathur, 2011).

terrorist/insurgent groups belonging to the majority community. Any perceived complicity, laxity or biases by police in prosecuting such criminals from the majority community could lead to a loss of confidence in the impartiality of the government and facilitate recruitment for extremist groups. In Tripura, firm and prompt handling of pro-Bengali militant organization UBLF increased confidence of tribal people in the integrity of the government. The role of DGP was crucial in this case, and even in the face of stiff political opposition in 2000 special care was taken to post a competent SP in the sensitive West district who was perceived as impartial by both the communities as he did not belong to the resident tribal or non-tribal population groups (Vohra, 2011: 17–18). Over the past decade and half, state police have booked miscreants, criminals, and militants of all hues, irrespective of their ethnic or political affiliations, leading to improved law and order situation and restoration of normalcy in large parts of the state. The lesson from this COIN is that re-establishment of rule-of-law and integrity of response is essential to earn legitimacy.

COIN Is Not a High-Tech Warfare

COIN is the war of the foot-soldier; hence, the high-tech equipment, armored vehicles, helicopters, and other paraphernalia of conventional forces have a limited role in COIN. Historically in COIN operations primitive armies have been more successful than technologically advanced forces (Galula, 1964: 32). Kilcullen (2010: 36) has scathingly compared the tendency of some troops to drive around in armored convoys as "day-tripping like a tourist in hell," and observed that such movement degrades situational awareness and creates more dangers for troops. In Tripura, significant achievements have been secured by lightly armed small units of SOGs in covert operations behaving like guerrillas during the most decisive phase of battle from 2000 to 2005. Furthermore, troops of armed battalions have been living in close proximity to civilians in areas of intense conflict and provided effective security through protective patrols, collection of intelligence, and liaison with local leaders and other SFs.

However, this is not to deny that appropriate technology can be an important force-multiplier. Technical interception of insurgent groups' wireless communication, bullet-proof jackets, headgear and vehicles, and NVDs (night vision devices) are all useful to the SFs in their operations. The insight from this campaign is that the absence of expensive military hardware is definitely not an insurmountable problem in COIN. This is confirmed by my experience of supervising TSR Battalions which have done exceedingly well in neutralizing insurgents' influence in their respective AORs by adhering to basics of good policing and without much high-tech gadgetry. Thompson (1967: 171) has the last word: "The only two prerequisites and enduring assets for counterinsurgency are brains and feet. These are entirely human. The side which has its feet on the ground at the right time and in the right place will win."

Lessons from the Comprehensive Strategy

Much quantitative literature on civil wars is centered on rebels— their motivations, capacities, or opportunities—and tends to treat the state merely "as an arena where actors either seek to maximize their wealth (greed) or rectify an inequitable system (grievance)" (Sobek, 2010). However, astute political commentators have long recognized the crucial impact of state structures and capacities of state organizations on social revolutions (Skocpol, 1979). Recent research on fragile or weak states reinforces this notion by conceptualizing state as the primary unit of analysis, and suggests that an effective functional state needs to have, at the minimum, three fundamental properties: authority, legitimacy, and capacity (ALC), also loosely translated as security, justice, and jobs (Carment and Samy, 2012). From this perspective, comprehensive approach for effective state-building would require the state to exercise its sovereignty in such a manner that the government not only has a monopoly of power within its territorial boundaries, but also exhibits functional legitimacy of its conduct and is able to meet the basic human needs of all people under its jurisdiction (Louise, 1995). In brief, the comprehensive approach to effective state building requires that:

(a) leaders must ensure they have institutions to provide adequate services to the population; (b) leaders must find ways to properly channel ethnic, social, and ideological competition that will otherwise erode the effectiveness of weak institutions even more; and (c) leaders must find a way to overcome the cumulative effects of poverty, over-population, rural flight, and rapid urbanization and environmental degradation that can otherwise overwhelm a vulnerable state's capability to function (Carment and Samy, 2012).

The following discussion covers various important lessons that can be distilled from Tripura's comprehensive COIN strategy.

Firm Political Resolve Is Essential for Success in COIN

No COIN strategies can ever have a chance of success in the absence of firm political resolve which unambiguously demonstrates the government's determination to join the battle with "vigor, deter-mination, and skill" (Sonderlund, 1970). The neutralization of Khalistan terrorism in Punjab was possible largely because of clear political mandate from the leadership to mount an all-out offensive (Gill, 1999). Similarly, a clear political mandate for offensive oper-ations and commitment of all requisite resources—material, politi-cal, administrative, and economic—over the protracted period of conflict has been the key to success of COIN in Tripura. It has also helped that there has been no change in the political dispensation and the present Chief Minister, Manik Sarkar, has continued to supervise and guide the COIN effort since March 1998.

The strength of the Indian democracy is evident from the fact that this state which is being ruled by the Left Front since 1993, with CPI (M) as its main constituent, has continued to get substantial resources and support from the federal government over the years despite frequent changes in the composition of ruling coalition parties at the center. The diplomatic initiatives of the federal government have led to improved relations with neighboring Bangladesh since the return of Awami League to power in 2009, leading to denial of sanctuaries to insurgent outfits and better trade relations. Similar diplomatic initiatives have led to improved relations with other neighboring countries such as Myanmar, Bhutan, and Nepal and assisted the COIN operations against northeast insurgents.

Fight the Strategy of Insurgent, Not the Insurgent

Sun Tzu recommends that the best alternative in war is to attack the enemy's strategy. The next best is to attack his alliances, and the least preferred option is to attack the enemy (Sun Tzu quoted in Mahnken and Maiolo, 2008: 51). The challenge for those in leadership positions is to figure out enemy's strategy. Underlining the importance of correct assessment, Clausewitz (1976: 88) in his classic, *On War*, has noted that the most crucial strategic question confronting the statesman and the commander is "the kind of war on which they are embarking; neither mistaking it for, nor trying to turn it into, something that is alien to its nature." At the turn of the millennium, the political leadership and the new police chief of Tripura were confronted with the same question as they faced escalating militant, ethnic, and political violence which had brought the state to "the brink of civil war" (Chakravarti, 2000). The political fortunes of the ruling Left Front government and credibility of the state police depended on an objective and accurate assessment of the challenges and formulation of suitable strategy to effectively tackle the problem at hand.[6] After a thorough study of the situation, the government formulated a holistic approach which focused on (a) protecting social, economic, and cultural interests of tribal people (*Human Development Report,* 2007: 114); and (b) "the re-establishment of a secure environment for governance and development, and not just a victory over, or elimination of, the insurgency... as the goal of the campaign" (ICM, 2007: 93). In Tripura, the success of COIN has emanated

---

[6] The ruling Left Front government was defeated in the TTAADC elections in 2000 due to militant violence and feared that it could lose power in the State if the militants were again able to intimidate voters in the forthcoming Assembly elections scheduled in 2003. Incidentally, this reconfirms Thucydides' famous triptych of "fear, honor, and interest" as the primary motives for political behavior, including war (Strassler et al., 1996: 43).

from this comprehensive strategy that has ensured political marginalization of insurgent groups, and their isolation from their potential support base among indigenous people. Following the defeat of ruling Left Front in the TTAADC elections in 2000 owing to intimidation of tribal people by insurgent groups, the state government has resolved to deny them such opportunities in future and committed enormous efforts and resources for this purpose.

More specifically, insurgents' strategies to win elections through intimidation have been effectively checked through establishment of security camps in interior areas; insurgents' designs to provoke communal or ethnic riots have been frustrated through denial of soft-targets among non-tribal population, and active promotion of a "culture of peace" at all forums; insurgents' isolation from indigenous people has been secured through systematic dismantling and disrupting insurgents' network of sympathizers, supporters, and collaborators by diligent police action; "re-grouping" of villages near security camps to deny enemy access to resources among tribal populations; and finally taking effective measures to restrict or cut-off their access to sanctuaries across the international borders through federal government's diplomatic channels, border-fencing, and "covert actions." The impact of these strategies is reflected in the fact that the pro-militant parties have not been able to defeat the ruling Left Front again during the past decade and failed to capture political power.[7]

Restoration of Governance Is Essential for Success in COIN

The absence of effective governance and rule-of-law has been held to be proximate causes for the emergence of insurgent violence in several conflict theatres. In India, this is borne out by the spread of Maoist violence in conditions of "security, administrative, and

---

[7] In this context, observations of Guevara are very pertinent that where a government has come into power through some form of popular vote and maintains a semblance of constitutional legality, guerrilla warfare cannot flourish because the possibilities of peaceful struggle have still not been exhausted (Guevara, 2007: 8)

political vacuum" that exist in vast rural hinterlands across the country (Sahni, 2010c). On the other hand, successful counterinsurgents make determined efforts and investments over a protracted period in development, social justice, education, and health to actively promote people's welfare and pre-empt conditions that could potentially generate discontent (O'Neill, 2008). Bernard Fall (1965) has put it succinctly arguing that a government which is losing to insurgents "is not being out-fought, but out-administered."

In Tripura, sustained efforts have been made to restore governance, develop rural infrastructure and expand the network of police stations and police posts in interior areas. The effectiveness of these programs is indicated by the index of human development in Tripura, which has improved from 0.32 in 1993–1994 to 0.61 in 2009–2010 (on a scale of 0–1), corresponding to a moderate level of achievement. Considering the persistent violence since the 1980s, its achievements on all the three indices of human development—literacy and schooling, life-expectancy, and per-capita income—have been quite remarkable (*Human Development Report of Northeast States,* 2014). The efforts to deliver governance at their door-step by organizing frequent "administrative camps" have been especially helpful in establishing government's legitimacy to govern, and earned popular support. The latest figures released by federal Planning Commission in 2012 indicate substantial decrease in reduction of poverty in Tripura from 40 percent in 2004–2005 to 14 percent in 2011-2012. The state government is also making efforts to bridge rural–urban divide by creating better infrastructure for health, education, transport, irrigation, and markets in the rural areas (*Frontline,* 2014).

Finally, the restoration of normalcy in large parts of the state has also boosted investor confidence and accelerated growth of large developmental and infrastructural projects. Recent trade agreements between India and Bangladesh have further improved prospects of bilateral trade and re-establishment of the historical links between Tripura and Bangladesh. In this regard, signing of Bangladesh, Bhutan, India, and Nepal (BBIN) Motor Vehicle Agreement and creation of National Highways &

Infrastructure Development Corporation Limited (NHIDCL) for executing critical road projects in border areas is also significant as it will promote regional integration through mutual cross-border movement of passengers and goods through road transport in the sub-region. All this augurs well for Tripura, and will effectively integrate the economy of Tripura with the rest of India and other countries in the region. In fact, it will make Tripura the "Gateway to the North-East" and will give a great boost to the state economy.

Don't Demonize Insurgents, Win Them Over

In a democracy, restoration of peace is facilitated by reconciliatory gestures by the government toward its rebellious citizens. Government schemes that offer amnesty and a chance for them to reintegrate in society are also a cost-effective way to separate the rank and file from hardcore insurgents (Ladwig III, 2009: 58). Furthermore, all insurgents are not hardcore extremists, irrevocably opposed to the government, and many insurgents can be induced through financial incentives or politically swayed to switch sides (Ladwig III, 2009: 46). However, the effectiveness of such amnesty and reward programs critically depends on state's ability to protect informants and surrendered enemy personnel (Long, 2006). Operationally, surrendered extremists provide valuable intelligence, and in some cases can be used to hunt down their former comrades. Such "cats"[8] were employed successfully in Punjab to hunt down several top terrorists (Mahadevan, 2008). Similarly, between 2002 and 2005, Tripura police and military intelligence in Tripura were able to win over many extremists who had not yet surrendered and used them to good effect to attack rebels inside Bangladesh (Bhaumik, 2009: xvii).

In keeping with its political approach to insurgency, Tripura government has provided generous incentives for rehabilitation

---

[8] This is the term used by Punjab Police to describe use of specially recruited infiltrators and systematically turned captured terrorists as intelligence assets for tracking down listed terrorists (Mahadevan, 2007).

of surrendered extremists and treated them as "misguided youth" rather than criminals. The SFs, executive, and political workers have also played a crucial role in persuading families of extremists to get their family members to surrender. A scrupulous observance of human rights by police has also helped in persuading many extremists to surrender. According to data maintained by SATP, there have been over 2,600 surrenders in the state from 2000 to 2014 (SATP 14). However, it is also a fact that many times surrendered extremists have rejoined insurgent group or failed to generate adequate income despite vocational training in rehabilitation camps. Apparently, there is ample scope to improve operation of such relief and rehabilitation schemes.

Conclusion

A review of the COIN campaign in Tripura over the last decade would indicate inherent superiority of the "comprehensive" or "political" approach over the "military" approach in dealing with ethnic insurgencies and supports Horowitz's (1985) view that such conflicts are better resolved through a combination of electoral politics, redistribution of economic resources, and military campaigns rather than through military means alone. It is also the case that techniques adopted by the western nations in their COIN campaigns abroad are not at all suitable for democratic nations in dealing with internal conflicts as they tend to further alienate the citizens (Ahmad, 1982: 260; Jafa, 2001: 250). More to the point are the techniques of political accommodation, enlightened political and socio-economic reforms, and ameliorative measures practiced by the developed countries such as the United Kingdom, Canada, and Italy in resolving ethnic conflicts within their own countries (Singh, 2008: 58). This research suggests the need to defeat insurgencies at the *political* level by an imaginative response to the legitimate demands and aspirations of the very social groups the insurgents seek to mobilize

(Wilkinson, 1977:47).[9] The Chief Minister of Tripura, Manik Sarkar, in an interview recently (*Frontline,* 2014) clearly articulated the broad-based approach of the state government by observing that it comprised political, administrative, and ideological dimensions to overcome the extremist challenge. According to the Chief Minister, the ideological issues raised by the extremists were countered and debunked ideologically; political questions were answered politically, administration was geared for development work; and SFs were deployed to tackle hardcore extremists.

In 2007, a research project sponsored by federal government's BPR&D to undertake an in-depth study of special challenges to policing in Tripura had identified some areas where improvement was required for boosting the capacities of the state police for COIN. It had, inter-alia, stressed the need for increased funding for intelligence gathering and transportation; better arms, light bullet-proof vests, and improved health care facilities; provision of improved clothing, protection, and packaged food during operations; improved training facilities; better coordination with federal paramilitary forces; equity between local police and paramilitary forces in basic facilities; management of SPOs; better border management; and improvement in the conviction rate of extremist cases (ICM, 2007: 239–246).

Though there is no denying that facilities available to state police personnel are not at par with CPMFs due to dearth of financial resources, sustained efforts to professionalize police through systemic reforms are being made. In compliance with the directions of the Supreme Court of India, Tripura government has enacted "*The Tripura Police Act,* 2007" which provides for fixed tenures to the DGP and other key functionaries such as District SP or Officer-in-Charge of police station. This Act also provides for a "State Police Board" to frame policy guidelines and establish criteria

---

[9] Good examples of this method of heading off a potentially long civil war include Italian government's handling of the German-speaking province of South Tyrol, U.K.'s "Devolution Package" to Scottish and Welsh demands and Canada's accommodation of aboriginals and Quebec issue (Puri, 2002: 301–311). A more recent example of similar political accommodation is the recent referendum in 2014 to ascertain Scotland's future in the United Kingdom.

for efficient policing; review and evaluate police performance; and examine complaints from police personnel about being subjected to illegal orders. Another significant feature of this Act is the establishment of a "Police Accountability Commission", headed by a retired High Court Judge, to inquire into public complaints against police personnel. Such provisions are designed to prevent arbitrary transfers of key personnel and enable them to perform their tasks without fear or favor, while simultaneously ensuring that they do not misuse or abuse their power. However, these are still early days and full impact of these new initiatives is yet to be felt on the ground, and much more is required of police and political leadership to translate these ideals into reality.

The diplomatic initiatives of the federal government with neighboring countries have also contributed to curbing insurgent influences in the region. The return of the Awami League to power in Bangladesh in January 2009 has had a positive impact on the security situation in the NER as it has taken strong action against several Indian insurgent groups operating from its soil. More deportations of other northeast insurgents to India by Bangladesh are expected following the extradition treaty between these two countries. Analyzing the reasons for endemic violence and unrest in the NER, K.P.S. Gill, the veteran police officer credited with effectively crushing Khalistan militancy in Punjab, had observed:

> The core of the crisis, not only in Manipur, but also throughout the region, is the inability of the States to develop, equip and maintain a viable apparatus to execute their own law and order responsibilities. This weakness is exacerbated when a change of political dispensations and continuous politicisation of the police undermines discipline and effectiveness (Gill, 2001b).

The fact that the present Left Front government has been continuously in power since 1993 and lent unqualified support to police leadership to build a robust and impartial "apparatus" for internal security duties goes a long way in explaining the success of COIN operations in Tripura (ICM, 2007: 100). The state police is now fully geared-up to root out extremism which, according to DGP, Tripura, is in its "residual phase".[10]

There is extensive literature and empirical research that suggests that resolution of such ethnic conflicts is greatly facilitated through political accommodation rather than military victories. The state government has made efforts to empower the institutions of self-governance in the state and enhanced allocation of funds for rural development to win the "hearts and minds" of tribal people. However, a lot more needs to be done to make TTAADC a truly autonomous and powerful institution capable of serving as a vehicle for the expression and fulfillment of the aspirations of the tribals for self-government. Strong government interventions are required to improve tribal people's chances of employment and quality of life; otherwise the current pattern of development based on massive industrial projects is likely to further heighten economic inequities in the state, fuelling discontent and disaffection.

Considering the magnitude of poverty, hunger, and unemployment among rural people, especially tribals, there is a strong case for simultaneously strengthening agricultural sector and rural infrastructure in northeast states for equitable growth (Bhattacharjee and Saravanan, 2012). More specifically, this involves (a) massive investments to improve the quality of physical infrastructure, drinking water, health and sanitation, education, and technical training in rural areas to improve their chances of employment and quality of life; (b) introduction of better agricultural practices and productivity, establishment of agricultural credit institutions, arrangements for secure storage, marketing and transportation of agricultural produce (Bhattacharjee and Saravanan, 2012); (c) creating stakeholders in development by redistribution of land to landless farmers (Bhaumik, 2007), sincere implementation of laws for restoration of alienated land to tribals, and promoting forest-based livelihood programs. In Cuba, comprehensive agrarian reforms and reforms of the mining sector were cornerstone of Fidel Castro's policy to redress genuine grievances of peasants

---

[10] "Tripura to use satellites to track terrorists," http://daily.bhaskar.com/article/tripura-to-use-satellites-to-track-terrorists-1548065.html accessed on February 11, 2011.

and workers in Cuba in the 1960s (Guevara, 2007: 95). A greater focus on sustainable and equitable natural resource management, within a framework of greater devolution of powers and participatory development planning will greatly improve quality of life of tribal population (Bakshi et al., 2015).

At this point, tribal people appear to be almost reconciled to their minority status realizing that it is not possible to alter the demographic composition of Tripura by sending non-tribal immigrants to Bangladesh or other parts of the country. The harsh reality of electoral politics also leaves them with no other alternative, but to cooperate and move forward with their non-tribal leaders.[11] However, it is also a fact that the issues of marginalization of their ethnic identity, culture, development-induced displacement, poor education, and social and economic disempowerment continue to agitate tribals.[12] The pace of agrarian reforms and the implementation of all land related Acts has been extremely tardy, and no significant restoration of land to tribals has taken place over the past many decades (Agrawal, 2010). Therefore, the state government would be well advised to take advantage of its current secure political position, retrogression of insurgency and cordial relations with neighboring Bangladesh to take some bold decisions to redress legitimate and perceived grievances of minority tribal population for further consolidation of peace.

Aspiration toward ownership of land has been held to be the main economic aim of insurgencies in underdeveloped countries, and restoration/redistribution of land to disadvantaged sections through agrarian reforms shall be part of government's comprehensive policy (Guevara, 2007). Subir Bhaumik (2007), a well-known political commentator on India's northeast, has

---

[11] In the 60-member Legislative Assembly, 20 seats (one-third seats) are reserved for tribals, which is in accordance with their population percentage in the state. Some of the tribal MLAs are ministers too. However, in the political arena, these numbers are insufficient to drive major pro-tribal policy changes in the government.

[12] For details, see proceeding of National Seminar on "Issues of the Marginalized Tribals in Tripura," January 20–22, 2012, organized by Government Degree College, Kamalpur, Dhalai district, Tripura. This seminar was sponsored by UGC, NERO & ICSSR, NEC, Shillong.

suggested decommissioning of 10 MW Gomati Hydel project to reclaim more than 45 sq. km of fertile land presently submerged under water, and its distribution among landless tribals whose lands were acquired by the state government for this project. This seems to be a feasible proposition following the recent commissioning of 726 MW Palatana power project in Tripura. Such a gesture from the government would send a very positive signal to tribal people and facilitate in ushering genuine peace. Historically, some form of compromise or reconciliation between the opposing elements of society has been necessary for long-term resolution of insurgency (O'Neill, 2008). Research suggests that resolution of ethnic conflicts is facilitated by "democratic leaders with inclusionary, accommodating strategies" (Kohli, 1997).

In brief, sincere and concerted efforts by majority community to empower indigenous people and ensure their socio-cultural, economic, and political integration would go a long way in forging reconciliation between these communities. Changing these entrenched social and economic structures may seem like a tall order, but as noted by Moore (2007), nothing short of this guarantees success in establishing long-term stability.

To conclude, the Indian experience of COIN in Tripura emphatically proves inherent advantages and superiority of local police forces and a comprehensive approach in dealing with ethnic insurgencies in developing democratic countries. The Tripura model of development and COIN has succeeded in reducing poverty and violence within a democratic framework, and can be emulated, with suitable modifications, by other states in India, as well as other developing democratic countries across the world. It is hoped that this study of Tripura police's experiences has generated sufficient new understandings of the topic itself and enhanced the broader literature and knowledge base on COIN.

PART THREE

8

Full Spectrum COIN: Some Case Studies

Case Study One: Recovering "Liberated Zones" from Insurgents

The following case study of Takarjala area describes in detail the integration of various COIN strategies and tactics to politically and physically neutralize insurgent groups in one of their so-called "liberated zones." As DIG/Armed Police (2000–2003), I was responsible for CI Ops by TSR battalions and was closely associated with implementation of various government policies and decisions that led to re-establishment of civil authority and governance in this troubled area.

Background

At the turn of the Millennium, there were several areas in the state that were effectively dominated by the insurgent groups, and were considered "safe zones" or "liberated zones" by them as police and security forces were in no position to challenge them owing to paucity of manpower, firepower, and lack of proper direction from police and political leadership. One such "liberated zone" was Takarjala, located at a distance of only 26 km from the capital city of Agartala, which had been badly affected by the insurgent

246 Police and Counterinsurgency

violence unleashed by the NLFT and ATTF. This area had great political significance and symbolic value too as it was located close to TTAADC HQ, which is entrusted with the responsibility of implementing various developmental programs in tribal-majority areas. The fact that the NLFT insurgents had successfully captured the TTAADC through intimidation and violence against civilians and ruling CPI (M) cadres, and installed their front political organization Indigenous People's Front of Tripura (IPFT) in power in the TTAADC elections held in 2000 made this area particularly challenging for political leadership and one of the "hottest spots" for security forces.

Takarjala P.S. has an area of 167 sq. km, 15 revenue villages, and about 56,000 people, of which over 80 percent are tribals. Around the year 2000, in Takarjala area the insurgents had almost complete freedom of movement and could commit all sorts of heinous crimes with impunity. The civil administration had collapsed completely, all developmental activities had come to a standstill, and no government offices, schools, and hospitals functioned in Takarjala as the employees and contractors had deserted the area for fear of militants, and the place looked like a "ghost town" (Vohra, 2011: 176). The insurgents freely extorted money from the local farmers, traders, and specifically targeted non-tribal people to drive them away from TTAADC areas and create ethnic divide among tribal and non-tribal communities. Following such intimidation and ethnic cleansing, hundreds of non-tribal families were compelled to leave their homes and habitats in Takarjala and surrounding villages and were resettled in newly formed "cluster villages" (*Tripura: Human Development Report, 2007*: 109). Subsequently, the insurgent groups, both NLFT and ATTF, started targeting ordinary tribals, members of Village Development Councils and TTAADC residing in Takarjala, Jampuijala, and adjoining areas for extortion, leading to exodus (*The Telegraph*, 2005). The ruling CPI (M) leaders and cadres, both men and women, were also targeted by NLFT insurgents to demoralize them and dissuade them from undertaking political activities. These terror tactics by insurgent groups ensured that the ruling CPI (M) lost the TTAADC elections in 2000, and a newly floated IPFT captured the TTAADC with the support of NLFT insurgents (*Oriental Times*, 2000).

The following account by Ms Bayjanti Koloi, a CPI (M) MLA, gives a fair idea of insurgent terror in Takarjala around the year 2000:

> Women then began to receive threats from activists of the NLFT to stop all political activities. In the ADC areas, tribal and non-tribals lived together. However, the NLFT is targeting non-tribals and forcing them to leave. Tribals were stopped from selling rice to non-tribals. If a tribal woman wore a sari or a bangle she was stopped and threatened (AIDWA, 2000, quoted in *Tripura: Human Development Report, 2007*: 110).

A grim reminder of the extremists' atrocities today is the Khumpui (meaning a small flower) Community Hall in Ashigar village in West district named after a baby of 6 months who was killed brutally by the NLFT insurgents in 2002 as her father was a CPI (M) worker (Chattopadhyay, 2014). By all accounts, there was an acute crisis of sovereignty as (a) the state was not able to meet the demands of human security, political security, and economic security; and (b) there was a vacuum of state authority characterized by failure of institutional authority to reach all parts of the sovereign territory (Louise, 1995). And true to the pattern of violence in the state, maximum violence occurred in 2000 and 2003 when elections for the Autonomous District Council (ADC) and Legislative Assembly, respectively, were held (Lacina, 2009a). However, the extremist violence had significantly declined by 2005 and no extremist case has been registered since 2007, indicating effective neutralization of insurgent capabilities and domination of security forces.

Police Strategy

With the assumption of charge by the new police chief in May 2000, a fresh assessment was made of all possible options to counter insurgent violence in the state, and it was decided that police shall focus their meager resources on the "hottest spots" first, wherever these may be, and boldly confront the insurgent groups to bolster their own confidence and restore people's faith in law enforcements' capabilities. After due deliberations at the highest level, it was decided to recover Takarjala from militants and re-establish rule-of-law and civil administration on priority basis because of its crucial political significance (Vohra, 2011: 176). The process was kick-started by a meeting at Takarjala where the Chief Minister accompanied by the Chief Secretary and Director General of Police patiently listened to the local representatives' complaints centering on absence of security, administration, and development. Following this meeting, it was decided to reinstall civil administration in this area by providing effective security cover to government employees and offices in Takarjala. For this purpose, government employees were daily transported from Agartala to Takarjala and back under police escort in a bus. Though government employees had strong reservations and apprehensions about their security initially, the Chief Secretary was able to convince them of the necessity of re-establishing state authority and governance in the area (Vohra, 2011: 176).

Meanwhile, the police also intensified COIN operations in the area and capabilities of local police station were suitably enhanced through a gradual process of augmentation of manpower, intelligence, firepower, transport, and other logistics. The availability of additional TSR troops from newly raised 7th Battalion TSR who had undergone training at the army's famed CIJW School at Vairengete (Mizoram) in 2002 was of great help. The number of TSR posts was increased steadily from only two in 2000 to seven in 2012 by establishing some new posts and completely replacing CRPF in Takarjala P.S. area. This is significant because soon after coming to power in the TTAADC, the IPFT had started a virulent propaganda against TSR by branding it as "anti-tribal" force and demanded that this should be disbanded by the state government (Chaudhuri, 2000). To further bolster the presence of TSR in this area, construction of 7th Battalion TSR HQ at nearby Jampuijala village was started in May 2003 by stationing one platoon initially; gradually more and more troops were concentrated as the barracks and other infrastructure became available. The Battalion HQ was formally shifted to its permanent location in July 2010.

However, it is a fact that initially the security forces did find it very tough to break the stranglehold of insurgent groups as they did not receive cooperation from most of the local tribal people who had been either intimidated or convinced by insurgents' propaganda that they would be tortured and harassed by security forces during COIN operations. To further compound their woes, the 7th TSR Battalion lost 20 troops and their weapons including a LMG, 17 SLRs, wireless sets and ammunition in a deadly ambush at Hirapur village under Takarjala P.S. jurisdiction on August 20, 2002. Remarkably, there were no reprisals from the TSR against innocent civilians after this ambush. This was in stark contrast to some previous incidents where the security forces had gone on a rampage after suffering similar losses. This self-restraint went a long way to dispel propaganda against the TSR, and the security forces were able to gradually win over the confidence of public through discriminate use of force, and their courteous behavior, selfless service, and sacrifices. Meanwhile, insurgent groups were neutralized through relentless operations and as the security situation improved, there was better inflow of intelligence from political cadres of ruling CPI (M) cadres, civilians, and other sources, leading to further operational successes. Thus, through sustained and targeted actions, insurgent groups' capabilities for indiscriminate violence, "taxation" and recruitment were significantly blunted by 2006, and after that there has been no extremist case registered in Takarjala P.S.

The improved security situation has led to revival of political activities, increased voters' confidence and since 2005 people have been able to vote freely without intimidation from insurgent groups (*Oneindia*, 2008). In the past decade, the ruling Left Front has swept away all political opposition in tribal-majority TTAADC areas by winning all the seats for which elections were held, thus exposing the hollowness of insurgent claims of representing tribal people and ensuring their complete political marginalization and irrelevance.

The restoration of normalcy has given a fillip to developmental activities in the area. From a "ghost town" only a decade ago,

Takarjala has been now transformed into a vibrant town with vastly improved infrastructure of roads, schools, colleges, hostels, hospitals, markets, and government offices. Its famous eco-park attracts tourists from all parts of the state, and the TTAADC is able to function freely without fear of insurgents. In and around Khumulung, the HQ of TTAADC, an Industrial Training Institute (ITI) and a degree college has been already established and a large polytechnic college is coming up. These all-round achievements in security and governance have confirmed the soundness of state's comprehensive approach to COIN, leading to replication of these strategies in other areas with similar success in subsequent months and years. However, despite all this, there is no sense of complacency in the police and civil administration circles as the Chief Minister himself continues to pay close attention to security situation to prevent repeat of 2,000 TTAADC defeat of the ruling CPI (M) party (*Northeast Today*, 2012).

Finally, it is also interesting to note some striking similarities between the strategies successfully adopted by police in Tripura and those employed by the U.S. Army in one of its most successful COIN operations in Ramadi in Iraq.[1] Major Neil Smith and Colonel Sean Macfarland who were deployed with the 1st Brigade of the 1st Armored Division, the "Ready First Combat Team" during 2007 have described in detail how they went about recovering this "liberated zone" from the insurgents (Smith and Macfarland, 2008). The success of "Anbar Awakening" has been attributed by them to the following methods: focused lethal operations; securing the populace through forward presence; co-opting local leaders; developing competent host nation security forces; creating a public belief in rising success; and developing human and physical infrastructure.

The Ready First Combat Team paid a heavy price for securing Ramadi and during the course of 9 months in 2007, 85 soldiers, sailors, and Marines were killed and over 500 wounded (Smith and Macfarland, 2008). However, in the absence of appropriate

---

[1] According to Smith and Macfarland (2008), the Ramadi model has been suitably adapted and used by other army formations in Anbar region of Iraq and elsewhere also in the War on Terror.

political strategies, many of the gains secured by the US forces in this area have been nullified in subsequent years (Pampinella, 2012). The striking similarities of strategies and tactics adopted by security forces in Takarjala (India) and Ramadi (Iraq) and the heavy price paid by them in life and blood for recovery of "liberated zones" confirm that while some COIN strategies may look deceptively simple, implementing them is far from easy. The physical and operational difficulties of conducting COIN operations in such "liberated zones" are enormous and may not be easily comprehended by those unfamiliar with such conflicts. It is to the credit of these security forces that despite enormous hardships, they have succeeded in creating conditions in which political and developmental initiatives could be conceived and implemented leading to glimmers of hope of long-term resolution of the problem of insurgency.

Case Study Two: "Winning Hearts and Minds"

Civic Action Programs: Establishment of a Primary School by 5th Battalion TSR

The HQ of 5th Battalion TSR is located at Daluma in Amarpur sub-division of South Tripura district under Birganj P.S. at a distance of about 7 km from Amarpur and 102 km from Agartala, the capital of Tripura. In mid-1990s, Daluma and adjacent areas of Birganj and Nutanbazar Police Station had witnessed a number of kidnappings, murders, and ambush of security forces by the extremists. In keeping with its policy of locating the TSR battalions in interior insurgency-affected areas, the state government decided to establish the HQ of 5th Battalion TSR at Daluma to check the insurgent activities. This battalion was raised in April 1997, became fully operational in September 1998, and was initially deployed for COIN operations in South district in camps at Jatanbari, Sarbong, and Karbook in Amarpur sub-division and at Rashiyabari in Gandacherra sub-division, which were all severely affected by insurgency. The battalion was allotted 128 acres of land for office, residential buildings and training activities at Daluma and construction by the State Public Works Department commenced from November 1999. At this time, one platoon (about 30–35 persons) of this battalion was stationed at the location for security of the laborers, contractors, and surrounding areas. Apparently, establishment of security camps right in the middle of their stronghold was taken as a challenge by extremists and provoked immediate retaliation from them. It is also a fact that at that time most tribal villagers appeared to be hostile or neutral at best to security forces as they were led to believe by insurgent propaganda that security forces were anti-tribal and out to commit horrendous atrocities on them in the name of COIN operations. The local people were instigated, intimidated, and threatened not to cooperate with the security forces. Thus, the security forces did not receive any local intelligence and the insurgent groups could continue to move freely in interior areas and inflict severe casualties on this battalion and other security forces.

The first major attack after deployment of this battalion took place on July 10, 1999 when five riflemen of 5th TSR were killed at Tukumbari (22 km from Daluma HQ) under Karbook P.S. in an ambush. Barely a month later, on August 20, 1999, one more rifleman of 5th TSR was killed near Paharpur (8 km from Daluma HQ) at Nutanbazar in an attack on the Road Opening Party (ROP) by the extremists. The insurgents were so emboldened by these successes that by next year they could attack even senior police officers passing through these areas. The convoy of the Additional Superintendent of Police of South District was ambushed at Paharpur (scene of an earlier ambush) on June 17, 2000 in which five police personnel were seriously injured. The extremists also made concerted efforts to intimidate the laborers and contractors to stop the construction work of battalion HQ and fired at Daluma TSR camp two months later on August 15, which is the Independence Day of India. The enquires into these incidents revealed tacit support of neighboring villagers to insurgent groups and made it clear that immediate and effective neutralization of insurgents in this sector was essential for smooth construction of the Battalion campus, safety of the troops and security of public at large. It was also realized by police leadership that this task demanded a more nuanced COIN strategy and could not be accomplished without support of local population. For this purpose, security forces were required to immediately find a way to win over local people by addressing some of their most pressing needs and concerns. The challenge was to make an offer which could not be refused by the local tribal people despite insurgent propaganda against forces.

After a very careful assessment of the ground situation, it was felt that police–public interface could be best promoted through establishment of a primary school at Daluma in the battalion HQ. Due to worsening security scenario, a large number of schools (about 30 percent, according to conservative estimates) in the interior areas had been severely affected and many had either closed down or were functioning irregularly. Many teachers did not attend the school regularly due to extortion, intimidation and threat to their life from insurgents. In some of the worst affected areas, the drop-out rate of tribal students had gone up to 90 percent and the entire education system in the hills of Tripura had collapsed (Chakravarti, 2000). The fears of teachers for their lives were not baseless. Writing in 2004, Hussain reported that during the past 7 years, around 20 teachers had been killed, and at least 35 kidnapped during the same period by rebel armies for ransom (Hussain, 2004). In all probability, a large number of such crimes would not have been reported to the police for obvious reasons. The collapse of education system was causing serious worry to parents as their children were not able to get good education and appeared an easy target for recruitment by insurgent groups.[2] After due consideration of various options, the police leadership felt that many local tribals would gladly avail this chance to give their children a decent education in a safe environment despite adverse propaganda and intimidation by insurgents. To make

---

[2] Children Bunk Class, Join Terror School in India's Northeast, Syed Zarir Hussain, *One World South Asia*, July 28, 2004.

this offer further irresistible, the package included free tuition, textbooks, refreshments, medical treatment through unit doctor and school transport at nominal rates. The basic philosophy was that the enrolment of each child would translate into addition of one family on the side of TSR and demonstrate public faith in the security forces. After careful consideration of all available inputs, setting up of a primary school was included in the Annual Civic Action Program of TSR units and the Commandant of the unit was encouraged to take initiative and set up this school immediately from available resources. In the event, police assessment proved correct and the 5th battalion TSR opened an English-medium *Veerta Bandhuta* ("Bravery and Friendship," the motto of TSR) primary school on January 1, 2001 with 77 children (37 boys and 40 girls) in KG-I, KG-II, and Class I by converting three semi-permanent barracks made of bamboo walls and tin roofs into improvised classrooms. Every effort was made to provide a good learning environment to young children by decorating the classrooms with charts and posters, providing proper furniture for classrooms, free school uniforms, books and stationery, as well as a small playground in the unit campus. The children were also given some refreshments during school hours and a weekly medical check-up was done by the medical officer of the unit. The service of a TSR school bus was extended up to Nutanbazar (20 km from Daluma), which was within operational responsibility of the unit, to build rapport with local people who are predominantly tribal.

A conscious decision was taken by police leadership at the very beginning to make it a model school and no efforts were spared for this purpose. Initially, four educated unemployed local youth were appointed as teachers at the monthly salary of ₹1,500 and one maid was engaged to look after young children at ₹1,000 per month. In addition, two educated TSR personnel were also engaged as teachers to facilitate bonding of children with security forces.

Fortunately, the Unit Commandant K.C. Pandit, an ex-BSF officer, had an exceptionally long tenure of 5 years (1998–2003) and took keen interest in developing the school. (Incidentally, I also had a long tenure of over three years as DIG/TSR (2000–2003) supervising these TSR battalions.) His personal rapport with the concerned government officials proved crucial in flow of additional resources from the Tribal Welfare Department, Education Department, and District Administration. While the initial grants by the Tribal Welfare Department helped in paying part of the honorarium to teachers and free textbooks to students, South District administration helped in constructing a computer education-cum-recreation center and procurement of two computers for the school.

In the year 2005, that is, within four years after establishment of the school, the Directorate of School Education, Government of Tripura after being fully satisfied that the school was following all prescribed norms, granted formal recognition to the school and also included it in the mid-day meal program. Subsequently, it has also been included in Sarva Siksha Abhiyan ("Education for All" program), an important initiative of the Union Government, whereby additional posts of teachers, infrastructure, and regular financial assistance has been assured to this school. This school has been upgraded to Senior Basic standard now with 10 teachers and functions from a proper building that has adequate number of class rooms, play ground, staff room, and an office for Headmaster.

All these efforts have helped in the development of the school and swelled the number of students from the initial 77 to around 200. The school campus has arrangements for about 30–35 very young children also (aged below 3–4 years) who are looked after by a lady teacher and her assistant. The school has already earned a good name for the quality of education being imparted and its young students often end up winners in local competitions. Apart from academic and cultural activities, the national integration of these children also receives special attention. The daily singing of national anthem and participation in the Republic Day, Independence Day, and other such functions has helped in inculcating patriotic feelings among the students.

In the initial years, the administration of the school was run by a School Development Committee, which was headed by the Commandant and comprised some school teachers, an educationist, and representatives of the neighboring village councils. In addition, a six-member Mother–Teacher Association (MTA) was also formed to assist the smooth running of the school. However, some changes have been made in this school's administration after its take-over by the state government, and currently the school administration is being run by an Education Committee comprising Chairman of West Daluma village, school Headmaster, and some local village council members.

The sincere efforts and hard work of successive commandants and keen interest taken by senior officers in establishing and developing the school has generated tremendous goodwill for the TSR not only in the surrounding areas but all over the district. More crucially from the security angle, the daily risk of ambush on ROP troops every morning got immediately reduced as their movement was carefully synchronized with the school bus timings. Earlier, the extremists had been able to lay overnight ambush for TSR troops when they proceeded to take up positions along the 8 km stretch of Daluma–Jharjharia road in the morning for keeping it safe for vehicular traffic. Now the presence of large number of students and their guardians all along the highway for availing the school bus leaves no scope for the insurgents to lay ambush or spring any surprises on the security forces moving on this route in the morning. The improved police–public interface has generated good intelligence inflow and ensured that information regarding the presence of insurgent groups is conveyed to TSR promptly.

After establishment of the school, there has been no attack on TSR personnel and extremist crime in local Birganj P.S. has drastically declined due to increased number of arrests of hardcore extremists and their collaborators since 2000. According to South Tripura district Police records, during 1994–1999, a total of 33 civilians were killed and 123 kidnapped as against 15 civilian casualties and 27 kidnappings between 2000 and 2005 in Birganj P.S. jurisdiction, with almost half of these crimes occurring in 2000. The decline is still more dramatic when we see that from 2001 to 2005, there have been only eight civilian fatalities and four kidnappings. On the other hand, while the police could arrest less than 10 hardcore extremists from 1994 to 1999, 72 hardcore extremists were arrested from 2000 to 2005. More crucially, insurgents have failed to make any fresh recruitment from the neighboring villages.

In recent years, with the improvement of security scenario many new English medium schools have opened in nearby areas where people can enroll their children, and are no longer solely dependent on this school. However, this school has succeeded in its objective of forging and strengthening bonds between local tribal people and TSR at a very difficult time. Apart from running this school, the battalion has also taken up other civic action programs to further strengthen their bonding with local people. The Unit Medical Officer has been treating local villagers during the course of his visits to TSR camps in interior areas. Health camps, administrative camps, and blood donation camps are also organized in conjunction with civil administration and full security cover is extended for construction of the roads and other civil works in interior areas. Strict observance of the human rights during the COIN operations has also helped in allaying the fears of local people. The students of this school have an excellent chance of developing as loyal citizens as they receive decent education, interact with the disciplined troops of the unit on a daily basis, and witness the all-round development being undertaken in their area through the coordinated efforts of various government agencies.

This case study highlights how a carefully conceived Civic Action program has been able to achieve immediate operational objectives and also turned into a successful social engineering initiative in the long run. It would be perhaps best to conclude this case study with the observation of a TSR commandant of this unit who during an interaction (June 2006) with me remarked that:

> This battle against the insurgents was won with the cooperation of villagers who did not fight the extremists directly but by sending their children to the "Veerta Bandhuta School" they made their intentions clear. In fact, they made it so clear that today Daluma and the neighbouring villages have become largely free from the militants and enjoying a peaceful life.

Case Study Three

Rescue Operation for Release of a Railway Engineer[3]

Introduction

One of the major reasons for Tripura's economic backwardness in the post-independence period has been its poor physical infrastructure, especially in terms of rail and road links. The lack of connectivity has severely affected movement of men and materials between Tripura and other parts of the country as well as within the state itself, hampering growth of trade, businesses, and employment. As mentioned earlier, post-independence Tripura was linked with rest of India through a meter gauge rail link at Dharmanagar (North district) in 1964, which was extended to Kumarghat (length 45 km) in 1989 and further up to Manughat (length 21 km) in 2003. However, extension of railway line beyond this point to Agartala was considered particularly challenging both from the engineering point of view and the security angle as the railway track had to pass through Atharamura, Longtarai, and Baramura hill ranges, which were the stronghold of insurgent groups. Therefore, ensuring physical security of railway officials, contractors, and workers as well as their machinery from the insurgents was considered crucial for smooth construction of railway line, and TSR was entrusted by the state government with this onerous responsibility. The first post for railway protection was established by 6th Battalion TSR at Swapanabari (Teliamura) in December 2003 and gradually strengthened by other posts at 41 Miles, Sukdebpara, and Mungiakami. Similarly, security of Longtarai range was entrusted to 8th Battalion TSR and 3rd Battalion TSR, while Baramura range was placed under the charge of 1st Battalion TSR and 10th Battalion TSR. As apprehended, concerted efforts were made by the insurgent groups to disrupt construction of railway line by committing several incidents

---

[3] This account is based on the written information provided by the office of the Commandant 6th Battalion. TSR dated October 15, 2010. For this successful rescue operation, L. Darlong, Commandant; Badal Debbarma, Assistant Commandant; Samar Debnath, Havildar; and Rabindra Kaloi, Rifleman of 6th Battalion. TSR were awarded "President Police Medal for Gallantry" in the year 2010.

to demoralize project officials and spread panic.[4] However, all these incidents were tactfully handled, security arrangements were reviewed, and COIN operations were intensified in adjoining areas to flush out insurgents from these jungles. Despite enormous hardships, over the next 5 years (2003–2008) TSR ensured effective security cover to this construction project, and the train was flagged off from Agartala railway station on October 5, 2008 (TSR, 2010: 13–14). Work is now underway to extend this railway line to Udaipur (Gomati district) and there are plans to further extend this rail link to the southernmost corner of the state in Sabroom in South district, which would facilitate trade with Bangladesh.

During the last few years, TSR deployment has been further strengthened along the vulnerable sections of railway line and currently 13 TSR posts of various units are operating to ensure uninterrupted railway operations round-the-clock. The resilience of these troops and their dedication in braving difficult living conditions, harsh terrain, and operational challenges posed by insurgent groups has won appreciation from the political leadership, project officials, and citizens. The extreme lengths to which TSR could go to discharge this responsibility would be apparent from the rescue mission mounted for release of a kidnapped railway engineer narrated as follows.

Rescue Operation

On April 26, 2008 at about 11:15 hours Debabrata Das, a Section Engineer, went to a railway worksite under Mungiakami P.S., Teliamura sub-division of West district to supervise the progress of railway works where 60–70 laborers were employed every day. He went up to Mungiakami by vehicle and from Mungiakami to the worksite on foot. Around 12:15 hours, a heavily armed group of NLFT extremists (7/8) led by Karna Debbarma stormed the worksite, caught hold of Debabrata Das and and dragged him toward the jungles. The extremists also shot dead Dhirendra Debnath, a

---

[4] Two officials and one driver of a construction agency were kidnapped when TSR was in the process of establishing its first post at Swapanabari, and a cashier and a driver were kidnapped in the last week of December 2003 from Swapanabari. One TSR rifleman of 3rd Battalion. TSR was killed at Tuikarma while conducting ROP, and two TSR riflemen were killed near S.K. Para (Dhalai district).

mason from Teliamura, who obstructed the extremist group from taking away the engineer. Following this incident, all the laborers fled from the railway worksite out of fear. Subsequent enquiries revealed that the extremists had engaged one of the laborers for passing information about movement of the security forces and railway officials to them. Apparently, the leakage of information had facilitated abduction of this railway officer. During his captivity, Mr Das was frequently moved to different inaccessible locations in the Atharamura and Petramura hill ranges to avoid detection by security forces. The extremists initially demanded ₹5 million ransom for his release, but later increased the price to ₹10 million.

Following this incident, the security forces launched several operations of 3–6 days duration in the neighboring dense forests where the militants' presence was suspected, but there was no breakthrough nor was there any clue about the presence of any extremist group. However, the SFs persisted in their efforts and activated all their channels to obtain reliable intelligence leads. Finally, on June 3, 2008, a 72-hour Encirclement, Raid, and Search Operation was organized on the basis of secret information provided by two surrendered extremists, which proved to be the turning point in this case. Mr L. Darlong, a tribal officer and Commandant of 6th Battalion TSR, accompanied by one Coy of TSR personally led the rescue operation. The TSR contingent despite facing heavy rain and extreme hardships in rugged terrain destroyed and overran several hideouts in deep jungles, as identified by the surrendered militants. This enabled them to engage the militants in a gun battle on the second night, which confirmed the presence of extremists in the area. On the third day, when the operation was about to be called-off as per the original program, Commandant Darlong took extra initiative and decided to extend the duration of the said 72-hour operation to the adjoining hill areas situated in the eastern side about 7/8 km from the terminating point. The name of the place was locally known as Chibukhar (den of snakes) and it was covered with thick vegetation making it extremely difficult to reach and there was no human habitation within a radius of 12 km. The commandant and his men proceeded toward the hostile hills without paying any heed to the hardships and difficulties. On reaching the place, the operational parties could see that the only approach to the targeted area lay along the stream, which was full of slippery and fungous rocks, with many subordinate rivulets. The commandant divided the troops into several small groups in order to cover all possible approaches and proceeded toward the interior most jungle areas.

On June 5, 2008 at about 14:20 hours, while the troops were advancing toward the target zone, one of the operational parties led by the Commandant was fired upon by a group of heavily armed militants. The TSR troops also retaliated and when exchange of fire was going on, Commandant Darlong along with his group scaled an extremely difficult and slippery slope of the hill and moved toward the extremists. The heavy exchange of fire continued for about 15 minutes. Meanwhile, screams were heard from the deep gorge, followed by burst of fire by extremists from their automatic weapons. The Commandant and his subordinate officers kept on firing, taking cover of huge boulders and again heard a screaming sound of the railway engineer pleading for help. Due to effective TSR fire, the extremists were compelled to retreat taking cover of big stones, thick vegetation, and undulating terrain, leaving behind the kidnapped railway officer. Subsequently, Mr Das was recovered from a cave. He looked very weak, lean, and thin with long unshaved beard. During this operation, the troops showed exemplary restraint and discipline in the face of extreme provocation by insurgents as indiscriminate firing could have seriously injured or killed the hostage.

Mr Das had experienced uncertainty, with extreme stress and strain for about 41 days in insurgents' captivity and was mentally prepared to breathe his last in the jungles before he was rescued by TSR contingent. Mr Debabrata Das subsequently revealed that there were four armed guards with him at the time of encounter who had tried to drag him along with them but since he was extremely weak, he could not keep pace with them. Therefore, he was left behind in a cave under the heap of gigantic stones. In this rescue operation, Commandant Darlong along with his subordinate officers displayed a very high degree of courage, commitment, and professionalism for which he and his team of officers were awarded the highly coveted President's Police Medal for Gallantry in 2010.

Conclusion

The successful culmination of this rescue mission reflects favorably upon the carefully conceived protracted process of capacity building of TSR battalions over the past decade and provides some insights into the reasons for TSR's effectiveness in neutralizing insurgent groups. First, it speaks volumes about the motivation, initiative, determination, and personal leadership qualities exhibited by the unit commander in leading this difficult operation; second, the fact that the commander continued to pursue leads in this case for over 40 days until he could accomplish this task indicates his determination, resourcefulness, and ability to generate actionable information through multiple channels including surrendered extremists; third, the fact that the commander and his troops could operate in the jungle for several days and during their encounter resorted to highly controlled fire to avoid injuries to the kidnapped person indicates a high degree of professionalism. A less trained contingent could have opened heavy fire to inflict casualties on the insurgents and inadvertently killed the hostage, nullifying the objective of the whole mission. Fifth, there is no evidence that civilian population was harassed at any point in this operation to obtain leads or punish suspected collaborators. Sixth, the fact that the operational commander was a young and dynamic tribal officer well versed with the local situation reinforces the importance of local forces in COIN. Finally, prompt recognition of this operational achievement by the state and federal governments through highly prestigious President's Gallantry Medal to the commandant and his subordinate officers suggests an encouraging atmosphere highly conducive of performance of such conspicuous acts of courage.

This astute policy of simultaneous unrelenting focus on operational effectiveness, population security, and development has paid rich political dividends to the ruling CPI (M) party, which has continued to consolidate its political hold since coming to power in 1993 and earned the people's endorsement for its COIN campaign through sustained efforts to improve governance and economic development.

Case Study Four: Avoiding "Collateral Damage" in CI Ops

An Encounter with NLFT Extremists on July 22, 2012, Leading to Killing of an Armed Extremist

The paramount concern for innocent human lives and strict adherence to the principle "do no harm" is also reflected in a recent special operation by TSR troops, which led to the killing of an NLFT extremist after a fierce encounter and recovery of an AK-47 rifle, 2 hand-grenades, 50 rounds of live ammunition, and some extortion notices.[5] In this operation, a 21-member TSR operational group led by a TSR Subedar was conducting a special operation from Ratan Nagar TSR camp since July 18, 2012, when they received information from the wife of a police source that three armed NLFT extremists had come to her mother's hut to take food. The location is near Border Pillar 2272 located close to international India–Bangladesh border and about 15 km northeast from Ratan Nagar TSR camp and 36 km from Rashiyabari P.S. The place is surrounded by vast jungle and devoid of human habitation except some *Jhumia* (shifting cultivation) tribal people.

On receipt of the information, the party leader divided the troops into two groups—a striking group and a cut-off group—and advanced toward the hideout. As the Ops party reached close to the target, they noticed the presence of some ladies inside the house and also saw an armed extremist performing sentry duty in front of the house. During the course of a personal interview, the TSR party commander informed me that despite confirmed presence of three extremists, he refrained from firing at the hut to avoid civilian casualties and waited for an opportune moment when the group was retreating toward Bangladesh border.[6] In the ensuing

---

[5] Reference Rashiyabari P.S. case no. 06/12 under section 148/149/120(B)/ 353/307/384 IPC & 25 (1-B)/27 of Arms Act, 10/13 ULA (P) Act. The deceased extremist was subsequently identified as Bahijoy Tripura, 35 years, resident of Taraban Colony, Haripur under Gandacherra Police Station.

[6] Personal interview with TSR Subedar, Agartala, September 28, 2012.

encounter, two extremists managed to escape under the cover of thick jungle and one extremist was killed. For their exemplary courage and professionalism, all the troops were suitably rewarded. This particular operation demonstrates an intuitive understanding of fundamentals of COIN warfare by TSR troops, which, is "to act with respect for local people, putting the well-being of non-combatant civilians ahead of any other considerations, even—in fact, especially—ahead of killing the enemy" (Kilcullen, 2010: 4).

The above case studies underline the strength of professional training and human rights orientation imparted to troops engaged in COIN operations that has established the reputation of this people friendly force as the ultimate fighter. These examples also provide a stark contrast to the frequent reports of heavy "collateral damage" inflicted by the United States and its allies in neighboring Pakistan, Afghanistan, and Iraq, leading to strong resentment against these forces (Sewall, 2007: xxv–xxvi).

Case Study Five: Teliamura Police Sub-division

A Case Study of Civil Police Initiatives in Combating Insurgency

Introduction

The traditional responsibilities of police have been maintenance of law and order, and detection and investigation of crime. However, in recent years maintenance of internal security has become a crucial aspect of policing in India due to threats posed by insurgent groups, terrorism, organized crime, and religious fundamentalist groups. This is especially true of policing in India's northeast due to presence of extensive and porous international borders and a large number of insurgencies supported and manipulated by foreign powers seeking to weaken India (Ganguly and Fidler, 2009: 2). The issue of "human security" in violent conflict zones, first emphasized by the UN Development Program (UNDP, 1994), has added another dimension to these existing policing challenges.[7] The displacement of populations, loss of livelihood, brutal physical violence, psychological trauma, and a wide range of other material and physical deprivations are routinely experienced by people living in such violent societies. The extremist violence in Tripura severely impacts on all these three dimensions of security and provides a concrete example of how terrorism and insurgency feed on underdevelopment and, in turn, create circumstances of insecurity that impede advances in human development (*Tripura: Human Development Report*, 2007: 103). Therefore, the COIN strategy of Tripura government emphasizes that this vicious cycle of underdevelopment and insurgency has to be broken through economic and social development (*Tripura: Human Development Report*, 2007: 114). In this strategy, the role of police and security forces is to subdue violence by neutralizing insurgent threats and create necessary space for political and developmental initiatives. This philosophy is clearly reflected in the new police strategy being implemented in the state since August 2000.

As mentioned earlier, at the turn of the millennium, the security scenario in Tripura was extremely disturbed as the ruling CPI (M) had been defeated in the TTAADC elections in which voters were widely believed to have been coerced by the insurgent groups, leading to escalating ethnic, political, and terrorist violence. The educational institutions and developmental works bore the brunt of terrorist violence as the teachers and officials were specifically targeted.

Teliamura police sub-division, comprising three police stations in the erstwhile West Tripura district (now constituent of the newly created Khowai district), presents a representative case study of the successful police drive in the state, which has effectively contained persistent militant, political, and ethnic violence, and restored near normalcy in most parts of Tripura. This chapter is organized into three sections. The first section contains general information about Teliamura sub-division and West Tripura

---

[7] Human security emphasizes the importance of ensuring "security of all people everywhere in their houses, in their jobs, in their streets, in their communities, and also in their environments" (Haq, 1998).

district,[8] and background of violence in Teliamura sub-division. The second section analyzes the patterns of extremist violence in this sub-division and comprises police station-specific statistical data (2000–2011) pertaining to extremist incidents and police action in this sub-division, and the "Action Plan for Counterinsurgency" of West district for 1997, that is, before the launch of current phase of radical transformation. The third section presents the main components of the revised police strategy and its implementation in Teliamura sub-division.

This case study supports the assertion that a permanent solution to the problem of insurgent/terrorist violence lies in "the restoration, strengthening, and extension of the permanent institution for the maintenance of law and order—the police station", and temporary allocations of armed battalions, paramilitary and "special" forces usually lead to only temporary respite from militant violence (Gill, 1994: 127–131 and Sahni, 2013). Furthermore, integration of security strategies with developmental, welfare, and other service agencies of the state government remain the most effective strategy to defeat insurgent terrorism (Sahni, 2005a).

Violence in Teliamura Sub-division

General Information about Teliamura Sub-division

Teliamura police sub-division was created in 1997 with Teliamura and Kalyanpur police stations, and Mungiakami P.S. established in 2007, was added subsequently to this sub-division. According to P.S. records, Teliamura P.S. is the largest in the sub-division and covers about 122,200 persons, followed by Kalyanpur P.S. with about 75,000 persons, and Mungiakami P.S. with approximately 17,000 persons in its jurisdiction. Furthermore, while both Teliamura and Kalyanpur have mixed populations, Mungiakami is almost exclusively tribal populated area. This sub-division has a significant presence of tribal people and in September 2008 out of an estimated population of 182,461, members of the ST

---

[8] Both Teliamura and Khowai were police sub-divisions of West district till recently, and Khowai became a separate district only in January 2012. Therefore, crime data for this case study have been taken up to December 2011 only.

community comprised 69,999, which is about 38 percent of the total population in Teliamura sub-division. According to revenue records (*Teliamura, Teliamura Subdivisional Profile at a Glance,* 2008), this sub-division has an area of 537.34 sq. km, of which 367.58 sq. km lies in the TTAADC area and the remaining 169.76 sq. km is in non-ADC area. As per 2011 *Census of India,* males constitute 51 percent of the population and females 49 percent. Teliamura has an average literacy rate of 93.7 percent, which is much higher than the national average of 74 percent. Teliamura town is located on the National Highway (NH-44) about 45 km from Agartala, capital of Tripura.

Till 2011 Teliamura sub-division was part of West Tripura district, and became a constituent of the newly formed Khowai district very recently following the latest round of reorganization. The undivided West Tripura district comprised five sub-divisions, that is, Sadar (Central), Bishalgarh, Sonamura, Khowai, and Teliamura (see Figure 8.1). The importance of this district for both political and developmental purposes can be realized from the fact that the undivided West district had as many as 29 of the total 60 Assembly constituencies; 10 of the 28 ADC constituencies for which elections are held; the sole Municipal Council; and four of the 12 *nagar panchayats.* Consequently, this area has been the site of intense political and ethnic rivalry as also violence perpetrated by major extremist groups over the past few decades which would be clear from the following discussion.

On the political front, it has three Assembly constituencies— Kalyanpur–Pramodnagar, Teliamura, and Krishnapur (ST constituency). While the CPI(M) has complete domination in tribal areas, both the major political parties, that is, the CPI (M) and INC are evenly matched in Teliamura and Kalyanpur constituencies, which is reflected in the results of the last Assembly elections held in 2013.[9] Among other political parties, *Amra Bengali* and BJP are also active in this sub-division. The resultant power struggle and highly

---

[9] In 2013 Assembly elections for Krishnapur constituency, which is reserved for Scheduled Tribes, the CPI (M) secured a landslide victory with 58.32 percent votes polled by total 31,215 electors. However, it faced stiff competition in other two constituencies of this sub-division. In Kalyanpur–Pramodnagar Assembly constituency, the CPI (M) candidate polled

competitive ethno-centric politics has often led to ethnic and political riots and fuelled extremism in the state (Upadhyay, 2005).

Background of Violence in the Teliamura Sub-division

While discussing the background of political and ethnic unrest in the state, Paul (2009: 33) has traced its origins to the resettlement of Bengali migrants in interior tribal compact areas. He has mentioned that in West Tripura district, a large number of Bengali migrants were provided land and settled by the Congress government led by Sachindra Lal Singh at various places, including Kalyanpur, Khowai, Mandai, Takarjala, and Jampuijala.[10] Apparently, the idea was to ensure presence of pro-Congress voters in tribal compact areas dominated by Communist Party of India. However, this move proved disastrous and created a serious rift between these two communities, particularly after the demographic changes that accelerated further in 1971,[11] as uneven economic competition with relatively developed Bengali community, alienation of land to non-tribal people, and shrinkage of land for shifting cultivation brought about a radical change in the socio-economic and cultural life of tribals and posed a grave existential threat to them. According to Datta ("Preface" in Paul, 2009: xv):

> Relegation to the status of minority community had ensured the banishment of the tribals from the core of political power; economic marginalization had cast a shadow over their survival while cultural decimation threatened to wipe off their identity.

This sense of insecurity among the tribals was exploited by various political parties, which resorted to strong ethnic rhetoric and a competitive "tribalism" to protect and create respective vote

---

19,755 votes as against 15,975 votes polled by INC candidate, while for Teliamura Assembly constituency, the CPI (M) candidate polled 18,357 votes and INC candidate polled 17,044.
[10] Sachindra Lal Singha was the Chief Minister of Tripura from 1963 to 1972 (Tripura Year Book, 2010: 103).
[11] In 1971, there was massive influx of people from East Pakistan into bordering Indian states, including Tripura, following crackdown of Pakistan Army to quell the struggle for independence launched by Sheikh Mujib.

banks. And as the situation worsened further, it needed only a spark for ethnic conflagration (Paul, 2009: 33–34). This spark was provided by the introduction of the TTAADC Bill in the Assembly by the CPI (M) government in 1979, which provided for 68.10 percent area of the state for 30.50 percent of the population, mainly tribal but including non-tribal too (Menon, 2005: 14). This Bill provoked a strong reaction from the non-tribal Bengalis who perceived a threat to their land holdings and organized themselves under the banner of *Amra Bengali,* a militant Bengali political party. Thus an atmosphere of mutual distrust developed among these two communities, which was exploited by some political parties to engineer ethnic riots during 1979 and 1980 for electoral gains.[12]

The political tug-of-war was played out first in Teliamura where a major communal riot erupted on June 9, 1979 when the Left Front's call for a massive rally at Kamraj Field to show its strength in favor of ADC was opposed by the *Amra Bengali* party, which asked all Bengalis to oppose it with all their might. Heavily armed supporters of CPM and *Amra Bengali* clashed with each other at Teliamura, which resulted in the death of three persons in police firing. At Moharcherra, located beside Khowai-Teliamura road, the Amra Bengali activists set fire to the house of a tribal CPM supporter, Samprai Debbarma, in Moharcherra market and killed him along with his wife and children. According to Paul (2009: 74–75), the killing of Samprai Debbarma and his family was the turning point as hitherto clashes that could be termed as "political" took on ethnic color. The subsequent rioting in the next 24 hours left 18 people dead, both tribals and non-tribals, 300 injured, and more than 500 houses gutted in fire. The following year witnessed far more serious riots in West Tripura district in 1980 at Guliraibari, Mandai, Lembucherra, and Amarendra Nagar in which hundreds of people—both tribal and non-tribal—were killed and hundreds of thousands were rendered homeless.[13]

---

[12] For an overview of various political developments leading to ethnic divide and rioting during 1979 and 1980, see Paul (2009), particularly Part Two, "The Widening Divide" (65–98).

[13] According to official sources, a total number of 1,439 people (both tribals and non-tribals) were killed and 315,000 (both tribal and non-tribal) were affected in June 1980 riots (Menon, 2005: 14).

These communal passions were again triggered after an interregnum of almost 17 years in December 1996 when a squad of ATTF attacked a thickly populated Bengali locality, Bazaar Colony, under Kalyanpur P.S. on December 13–14, 1996, killing 24 persons and injuring 18 others (Paul, 2009: 183). In February 1997, there were several incidents of communal/ militant violence in Khowai sub-division,[14] which threatened to spill over in the entire West Tripura district and prompted the government to promulgate *Armed Forces Special Power Act, 1958* and several police station areas, including Khowai, Kalyanpur, Teliamura, Takarjala, and Sidhai P.S. were declared as "disturbed areas" under this Act. The situation could be controlled only with the deployment of army in the state. However, the withdrawal of all the three army battalions deployed for CI Ops and sizable number of BSF troops guarding the international border with Bangladesh from Tripura in 1999 in the wake of Kargil War with Pakistan had drastic consequences for COIN (ICM, 2007: 89). The security scenario continued to worsen for some more time until police got its act together and came up with its new strategy to effectively combat insurgency.

Patterns of Extremism in Teliamura Sub-division

The present phase of insurgency that began with the emergence of NLFT and ATTF in the early 1990s has been marked by brutal large scale massacres of non-tribal people and burning of their villages, and attacks on security forces, as perpetrated by the TNV militants in the 1980s. However, unlike earlier groups, both NLFT and ATTF have also resorted to large-scale kidnappings of non-tribal people which brought them huge liquid cash to finance their operations, compelled the Bengalis to move out from the interior areas and frequently provoked large scale communal flare ups (Bhaumik, 2009: 139).

Another important feature of extremist crime has been the targeted violence against political workers and voters to influence

---

[14] For details of militant attacks and ethnic violence in Tripura during the second phase of militancy in 1990s, see Paul (2009), particularly, part IV, "Shadow of Gun Returns", (155–292).

election results. For example, the TTAADC elections in 2000 and Assembly elections in 2003 were marred by severe violence. In the three months preceding the TTAADC elections in 2000, there were 176 extremist incidents, with 100 persons killed, another 86 injured, and 172 persons abducted, including 12 relatives of candidates abducted in the month prior to elections. This allowed the pro-militant Indigenous National Party of Tripura to dominate the elections (ICM, 2007: 85). The Assembly elections in February 2003 also witnessed heightened extremist violence leading to the deaths of 56 persons in the state between January 1 and March 11, 2003, including 44 civilians, six insurgents, and six security force personnel (SATP, 15). The obstruction of normal political process and more targeted violence against civilians has been a distinct feature of insurgent violence in northeast (Lacina, 2007) and the pattern of electoral violence in 2000 and 2003 in West Tripura confirms this trend.

Police Station-wise Number of Extremist Cases in Teliamura Sub-division (2000–2011)[15]

Table 8.1:

Number of Extremist Cases in Teliamura Police Station (2000–2011)

| Year | Extremist Cases | Killed | | Kidnapped |
		Civilians	SFs	
2000	19	14	0	13
2001	03	02	0	01
2002	04	03	0	09
2003	22	31	2	04
2004	04	0	0	0
2005	03	0	0	01
2006	10	06	1	16
2008	02	0	0	02
2010	0	0	0	0

Continued Table 8.1

[15] For consistency, the Extremist Crime data here has been restricted up to 2011 for West Tripura district and its police stations in Teliamura sub-division (that is, before the latest administrative re-organization in Tripura in 2012).

Continued Table 8.1

| Year | Extremist Cases | Killed | | Kidnapped |
		Civilians	SFs	
2011	0	0	0	0
Total	72	56	3	46

Source: West Tripura District Police.

Table 8.2:

Number of Extremist Cases in Kalyanpur Police Station (2000–2011)

| Year | Extremist Cases | Killed | | Kidnapped |
		Civilian	SF	
2000	32	51	0	06
2001	11	13	0	07
2002	08	03	0	04
2003	14	22	0	05
2004	09	03	1	01
2005	04	09	0	01
2006	01	0	0	01
2007	05	01	0	02
2008	02	0	0	0
2009	01	0	0	0
2010	0	0	0	0
2011	0	0	0	0
Total	87	102	1	27

Source: West Tripura District Police.

Table 8.3:

Number of Extremist Cases in Mungiakami Police Station (2007–2011)

| Year | Extremist Cases | Killed | | Kidnapped |
		Civilian	SF	
2007	06	0	0	1
2008	06	1	0	1
2009	02	0	0	0
2010	0	0	0	0
2011	0	0	0	0
Total	14	01	0	02

Source: West Tripura District Police.

Figure 8.1:

Map of West Tripura District (Old)

Source: http://westtripura.gov.in/forms/west.pdf

Disclaimer: This figure is not to scale. It does not represent any authentic national or international boundaries and is used for illustrative purpose only.

Figure 8.2:

Number of Extremist Cases in Teliamura Police Station (2000–2011)

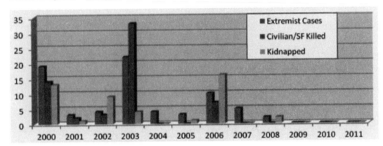

Source: West Tripura District Police.

Figure 8.3:

Number of Extremist Cases in Kalyanpur Police Station (2000–2011)

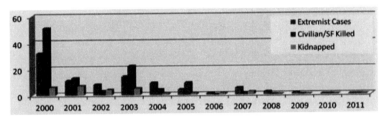

Source: West Tripura District Police.

Figure 8.4:

Number of Extremist Cases in Mungiakami Police Station (2007–2011)

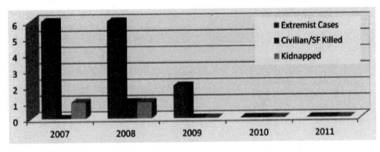

Source: West Tripura District Police.

Table 8.4:

Extremist Crime Data for West Tripura District (2000–2011)

Year	2000	2001	2002	2003	2004	2005	2006	2007	2008	2009	2010	2011
Extremist Cases	146	82	92	162	89	48	46	55	35	07	0	0
Civilians Killed	92	62	50	125	29	16	05	06	06	0	0	0
SFs Killed	03	09	29	25	16	05	04	04	0	0	0	0
Persons Kidnapped	137	11	51	62	24	30	25	11	10	02	0	0
Extremists Killed	05	27	15	36	37	09	12	17	04	0	0	0
Encounters/Ambushes	11	17	22	54	38	28	29	28	12	04	0	0
Arrest of Hardcore Extremists	09	28	30	61	58	34	18	21	32	03	0	02
Collaborator Arrested	177	201	125	287	192	133	73	27	19	08	0	02

Source: West Tripura District Police.

Table 8.5:

Extremist Crime Data for Tripura State (2000–2012)

Year	2000	2001	2002	2003	2004	2005	2006	2007	2008	2009	2010	2011	2012
Extremist Incidents	449	187	196	305	184	115	102	113	80	24	22	12	15
Civilian killed	192	134	93	184	55	30	13	14	07	08	0	01	0
SFs Killed	16	31	42	39	47	11	14	07	03	01	02	0	0
Persons Kidnapped	427	123	145	178	92	62	43	59	32	07	29	24	10
Extremists Killed	31	24	31	50	54	23	27	21	17	0	0	0	02
Encounter/Ambush	89	48	50	84	76	53	57	45	28	08	10	0	03
Arrest of hardcore Extremist	259	233	57	128	101	61	67	39	77	15	07	06	17
Arrest of Harborers/Collaborators	519	208	258	594	330	263	147	157	63	19	08	09	21

Source: SCRB, Tripura Police.

Figure 8.5:

Extremist Crime Data for West District (2000–2011)

(A)

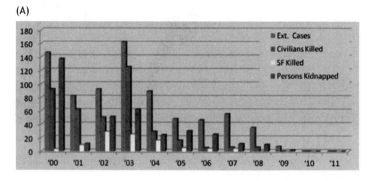

(B)

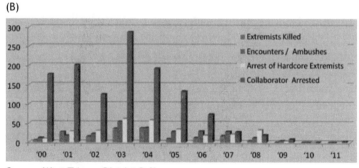

Source: West Tripura District Police.

Figure 8.6:

Extremist Crime Data for Tripura State (2000–2012)

(A)

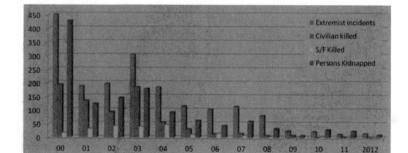

(B)

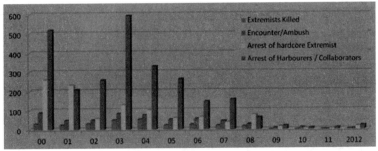

Source: SCRB (State Crime Record Bureau), Tripura Police.

Action Plan for CI Ops (1997)

An "Action Plan for Counterinsurgency" prepared by West Tripura district police in 1997 suggested the following measures to curtail rising extremist violence (West Tripura Police, 1997):

1. The officers-in-charges (OC) of six most extremist affected police stations in West Tripura district, that is, Khowai, Kalyanpur, Teliamura, Jirania, Sidhai, and Takarjala shall take full responsibility for collection of specific intelligence concerning the presence and movement of extremist groups, extremist hideouts, and collaborators in their respective jurisdiction;

2. The OCs of Khowai, Kalyanpur, Teliamura, Jirania, Sidhai, and Takarjala shall identify ethnically sensitive villages and ensure suitable action to prevent or reduce ethnic tension promptly in their jurisdiction as these places have history of ethnic violence. Failure to take proper preventive action leads to ethnic riots and contributes directly to extremism;

3. The senior police officers, that is, SDPO, Additional SP and District SP shall play a more active role in COIN operations and promptly muster requisite troops from their own resources on receipt of specific 'A' grade information. These senior officers shall also plan effective joint operations to nab the insurgents moving between the jurisdiction of two police stations, sub-divisions, or districts;

4. The security forces such as TSR, CRPF, and AR shall raise their own sources for obtaining actionable information, and ensure effective domination of vulnerable areas to boost public confidence, familiarize themselves with the topography of the area, and verify the presence of actual residents;

5. The police shall reactivate the existing village resistance (VR) parties and raise new VR parties to boost their morale and bring people closer to the security forces. The VRs comprising people from different communities shall be armed with spears, torch lights, and whistles, and encouraged to provide information concerning the presence and movement of extremists in their area;

6. Police and security forces shall pay serious attention to prevent kidnappings in their area and in case of any such incidents, they should promptly pursue extremists and put stops on their anticipated routes of retreat.

Apparently, these eminently sensible measures suggested in the Action Plan could not be implemented effectively on the ground for the next few years and insurgent groups continued to perpetrate violence with impunity. The reasons for this below-par police performance during this period can be largely attributed to absence of a coherent COIN strategy and lack of adequate wherewithal with the police to combat extremism. As mentioned earlier, the withdrawal of sizable number of army and BSF troops in 1999 further handicapped the police response.

Action Taken against Extremists and Collaborators under Teliamura Sub-division (2000–2011)

In Teliamura sub-division, the impact of this coherent strategy is reflected in the large number of killings, arrests, and surrenders of extremists and their collaborators as also decline in registration of extremist cases as shown in the tables below:

An index of gradual marginalization of insurgent groups during the last decade is provided in the number of extremist cases registered in various police stations in Teliamura sub-division. From the police records, it is seen that while 133 extremist cases were registered in Teliamura sub-division from the year 2000 to 2005, the number of extremist cases declined to only 40 during 2006–2011. Significantly, no extremist case was registered in any police station in Teliamura sub-division during 2010 and 2011 (Tables 8.6, 8.7, 8.8 and 8.9 and Figures 8.6, 8.7, 8.8 and 8.9).

From the available crime data, it is seen that in Teliamura sub-division at the peak of insurgency from 2000 to 2005, 28 extremists were killed, and 122 extremists and 167 collaborators were arrested, while the corresponding figures for 2006–2011 are only two extremists killed, and five extremists and 53 collaborators arrested (see Tables 8.6, 8.7, and 8.8 and Figures 8.6, 8.7, and 8.8). This clearly indicates that insurgency had been substantially controlled in this sub-division by 2005. Furthermore, according to the state police records, from 2000 to 2011, over 250 extremists from Teliamura sub-division had surrendered due to sustained pressure exerted by the police and security forces.

Table 8.6:

Action Taken against Extremists and Collaborators under Teliamura Police Station (2000–2011)

Sl. No.	Year	No. of Extremists Arrested	No. of Collaborators Arrested	No. of Extremists Killed
1.	2000	27	03	02
2.	2001	07	10	02
3.	2002	07	21	03
4.	2003	16	36	05
5.	2004	15	08	02
6.	2005	03	09	02
7.	2006	0	18	0
8.	2007	0	05	0
9.	2008	0	01	0
10.	2009	0	0	0
11.	2010	0	0	0
12.	2011	0	0	0
	Total	**75**	**111**	**16**

Source: West Tripura District Police.

Table 8.7:

Action Taken against Extremists and Collaborators under Kalyanpur Police Station (2000–2011)

Sl. No.	Year	No. of Extremists Arrested	No. of Collaborators Arrested	No. of Extremists Killed
1.	2000	15	06	01
2.	2001	08	11	03
3.	2002	05	02	02
4.	2003	06	38	03
5.	2004	11	12	03
6.	2005	02	11	0
7.	2006	0	06	01
8.	2007	05	04	0
9.	2008	0	04	0
10.	2009	0	01	0
11.	2010	0	0	0
12.	2011	0	0	0
	Total	**52**	**95**	**13**

Source: West Tripura District Police.

Table 8.8:

Action Taken against Extremists and Collaborators under Mungiakami Police Station (2000–2011)

Sl. No.	Year	No. of Extremists Arrested	No. of Collaborators Arrested	No. of Extremists Killed
1.	2007	0	12	0
2.	2008	0	02	01
3.	2009	0	0	0
4.	2010	0	0	0
5.	2011	02	0	0
	Total	**02**	**14**	**1**

Source: West Tripura District Police.

Figure 8.7:

Action Taken against Extremists and Collaborators under Teliamura Police Station (2000–2011)

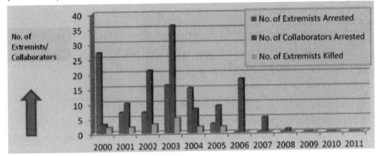

Source: West Tripura District Police.

Figure 8.8:

Action Taken against Extremists and Collaborators under Kalyanpur Police Station (2000–2011)

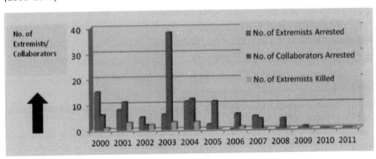

Source: West Tripura District Police.

Figure 8.9:

Action Taken against Extremists and Collaborators under Mungiakami Police Station (2000–2011)

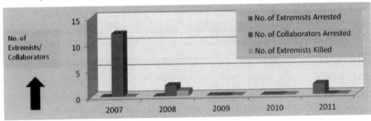

Source: West Tripura District Police.

Table 8.9:

Force-wise Summary of Deployment in Teliamura Sub-division (2000–2011)

Sl. No.	Year	CRPF	TSR	AR	Miscellaneous District Armed Reserve (DAR)/HG/SPO
1.	2000	11 Coy	4 Coy	-	50 Men
2.	2001	11 Coy	4 Coy	-	80 Men
3.	2002	9 Coy	3 Coy	-	150 Men
4.	2003	10 Coy	3 Coy	-	150 Men
5.	2004	9 Coy	4 Coy	-	120 Men
6.	2005	12 Coy	7 Coy	1 Coy	170 Men
7.	2006	12 Coy	7 Coy	-	160 Men
8.	2007	9 Coy	9 Coy	-	150 Men
9.	2008	11 Coy	9 Coy	1 Coy	225 Men
10.	2009	9 Coy	10 Coy	1 Coy	190 Men
11.	2010	10 Coy	11 Coy	1 Coy	180 Men
12.	2011	08 Coy	12 Coy	1 Coy	145 Men

Source: Tabulated from data provided by West Tripura District Police.

Figure 8.10:

Force-wise Summary of Deployment in Teliamura Sub-division (2000–2011)

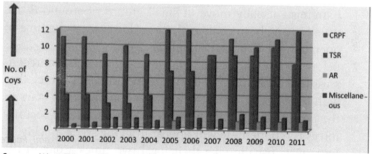

Source: West Tripura District Police.

Counterinsurgency Planning for Teliamura Sub-division

The COIN strategy for Teliamura sub-division included several measures: analysis of the modus operandi of insurgent groups; comprehensive upgrades of police stations' capabilities to combat whole range of challenges in their respective jurisdictions;

deployment of substantial security forces for area domination, CI Ops and security of population and vital installations; mobilization of people through their appointment as SPOs and enlistment in VR groups; coordinated operations by SFs; and extension of all possible help to civil administration and political workers to facilitate their movement in interior areas.

Analysis of the Modus Operandi of Extremists

"Know thy enemy and know yourself: in a hundred battles you will not be in peril" is one of the most famous aphorisms of Sun Tzu, the great strategist (Sun Tzu quoted in Mahnken, 2008: 51). In the present context, the comprehensive assessment of police vulnerabilities and resources (know yourself) was complemented by gathering all possible information about the insurgent groups (know thy enemy). This information, collected through multiple channels, revealed many important details about modus operandi of extremist groups which facilitated proper planning of CI Ops (*District Intelligence Document*, West Tripura district, 2000). Some of the more important points of operational relevance were:

1. Extremists usually move in small groups of around 8–10, usually at night in civilian clothes. However, at the time of operation they put on camouflage dress.
2. Before conducting operation, some of them conduct reconnaissance of the proposed area of operation in plain clothes with small arms, while the uniformed armed party stays in the nearby jungle areas. In case the movement of security forces is reported, they disappear from the scene quickly.
3. Extremists usually take their meal two times a day in the early morning and early evening in abandoned *jhum* huts in the jungle. They prefer meat and dry fish with rice.
4. In jungle they sleep over polythene sheets and maintain distance of 200–300 yards from each other. They also put guards all around the halting place.
5. They visit different villages in the first week of every month to collect subscriptions.

6. They frequently change the location of kidnapped persons and generally confine them in remote inaccessible jungle areas in temporary sheds.
7. Some gang members occasionally visit different towns by passenger vehicles in plain clothes.
8. Generally, the extremists halt in the adjoining areas of two police stations and sometimes crossover into Bangladesh.

Strengthening of the Police Stations

A P.S. symbolizes the presence of the administration and is the place from where the OC carries out all his functions for maintenance of public order, and for prevention and detection of crime. As the pattern of extremist crime suggests, by the year 2000 the character of insurgency in Tripura had become highly criminalized and comprised gruesome acts of violence, kidnappings, and extortion. Frequently, extremist violence provoked ethnic riots, communal tension, or political disorder in the sub-division, stretching meager resources of the local police stations to their limits and frustrating them. Therefore, capacity building of police stations was accorded a very high priority in police strategy. This strategy had been employed successfully earlier in Punjab during the 1990s and has been used more recently in Andhra Pradesh also (Sahni, 2009b). The distinguishing feature of this police strategy is proper identification of the vulnerabilities of, and then empowering, the police station to deal with the whole range of problems (ICM, 2007: 17). Selective enhancement of the capacities of police stations is also a far more efficient and cost-effective method of capacity building than raising federal paramilitary units (Gill, 1994).[16] In Tripura also, comprehensive upgrades of police capabilities of most vulnerable police stations, including Teliamura and Kalyanpur P.S. were made on an urgent

---

[16] According to Gill (1994):

The cost of enhancing 500 police stations would about equal the sums required to form twenty to thirty new paramilitary battalions. Moreover, in a battalion of a thousand men, those available operationally would be about 400, on the other hand, in a police station of 100 men, in a crisis, except for four or five, the rest can fan out in the operational area.

basis to provide substantial resources—manpower, mobility, weaponry, and communications— as indicated as follows:

1. Augmentation of Manpower

In Teliamura sub-division, both Teliamura and Kalyanpur P.S. were categorized as "A" category police stations due to severe extremist violence and sanctioned additional number of civil officers and constables. In 1999, both Teliamura and Kalyanpur had the sanctioned strength of only three sub-inspectors, three assistant sub-inspectors, three Head Constables and 30 Constables each, which was considered quite insufficient to meet their requirements. Therefore, in 2000, the sanctioned strength of both these police stations was revised upwards to six Sub-inspectors, six Assistant Sub-inspectors, five Head Constables, and 50 constables. Furthermore, the post of Officer-in-Charge of both Teliamura and Kalyanpur police stations was upgraded from Sub-inspector to Inspector and due care was taken to post motivated and competent officers for these difficult charges.[17]

Mungiakami P.S., which was opened in 2007, is headed by a Sub-inspector and has the sanctioned strength of two Sub-inspectors, two Assistant Sub-inspectors, three Head Constables, and 40 constables. This strength is considered adequate for its present requirement and reflects an improvement in crime and security situation in its jurisdiction.

2. Augmentation of Transport

The shortage of suitable transport in P.S. is a major handicap for CI Ops as it severely hampers the mobility of police officials and security forces. A detailed assessment of availability and requirement of transport in 2000 by West Tripura district police had indicated major shortfalls and noted that as against the projected requirement of three light vehicles, one medium vehicle, and one heavy vehicle per extremist-affected police station, the availability of transport was much less. Moreover, many of the available

---

[17] Statement of sanctioned and posted strength of Teliamura, Kalyanpur, and Mungiakami Police Stations (2000–2010). (Courtesy: West Tripura District police).

vehicles were too old and unfit for operational tasks. As a result, many times, the police staff had to rush to the place of occurrence of a major violent incident in a single vehicle only, thus exposing themselves to the ambush/attack from the militants. Underlining the critical importance of police infrastructure, the then-SP (West) had observed that, "Unless the police stations were equipped properly to react to the calls of people, we will keep on fighting a losing battle" (*District Intelligence Document*, West Tripura District, 2000).

Starting in 2000, concerted efforts were made to substantially improve mobility in all highly vulnerable police stations on a priority basis by temporarily diverting vehicles from other police stations/ units, or hiring of private vehicles to meet their urgent operational requirements. Thus, both Teliamura and Kalyanpur had as many as three to five additional vehicles for extended periods to deal effectively with challenges of extremism, ethnic riots, and law and order problems during the peak of insurgency. The ready availability of adequate transport boosted the confidence of police officers as they were able to mount intensive mobile patrolling of vulnerable areas, check fixed pickets, and foot patrols in their jurisdiction and immediately rush to the place of incidents in sufficient numbers.

Meanwhile, some augmentation of police transport was also made through MPF scheme of the federal government. Over the years, there has been a considerable improvement and lack of transport has ceased to be a constraint in all police stations. According to Tripura police records, in 2011 West Tripura district had 224 vehicles of various categories, which is more than double its holdings in 1999.[18] As a result, most police stations have got at least three vehicles, which is adequate for their present requirements.

3. Procurement of Sophisticated Arms

Around the year 2000, Tripura police's lack of modern weapons severely affected its capacity to launch aggressive operations against insurgents who were armed with sophisticated automatic weapons. The deficiency in arms and equipment in the state is

---

[18] Tripura Police, "Statement of holding of Departmental vehicles of Tripura Police, March 2011."

clearly visible in the following partial data relating to requirement and availability of arms in 2001–2002 (Menon, 2005: 40):

a. AK-47 Rifles: Requirement-2609; Availability-418
b. Carbines: Requirement-2120; Availability-1207
c. INSAS Rifles: Requirement-1000; Availability-200

The gravity of the situation can be realized from the fact that in 1999, West Tripura district police, with strength of over 2000 persons in all ranks, had only seven AK-47 Rifles and 425 7.62 mm SLR Rifles, and a majority of its policemen were equipped with .303 Rifles.

To overcome this problem in the short run in 2000–2001, a temporary diversion of small number of AK-47 rifles was made from some TSR units to the extremism-affected police stations and it was stressed that these weapons were not to be issued to any individual officers such as OCs/circle inspectors/SDPOs, but were meant to be used exclusively for operations only. Over the years, the situation has gradually improved and all the three police stations in Teliamura sub-division have been issued adequate supplies of modern weapons such as AK-47 rifles, 5.56 INSAS rifles, and 7.62 SLRs to meet their operational requirements.

The improved position of West Tripura district is reflected in its current holding (2012), which includes 109 AK-47, 220 5.56 INSAS rifles, 1652 7.62 SLRs, and over 900 carbines, pistols and revolvers. It also has some .303 rifles, which are mostly distributed among non-extremist affected police stations and SPOs in the West Tripura district.

4. Improvement in Communication Network

Before 2000, both Teliamura and Kalyanpur P.S. had wireless communication with a Control Room at Agartala. These police stations had also been provided with telephone connection to keep in touch with various civil, paramilitary and other agencies. During operations, the troops were also provided with limited number of wireless handsets. However, it was observed that the insurgent groups were able to intercept police communication which compromised the security operations and endangered lives of troops. This problem was resolved through strict enforcement of communication security protocols and provision of scrambling facility to prevent leakage of information to insurgent groups. Furthermore, for better communication among security forces, a Joint Control Room (JCR) was established in Teliamura with wireless sets of all security forces operating in the area. These arrangements ensured proper coordination and prompt sharing of information between police and paramilitary forces and effectively prevented cross-firing among them. The introduction of mobile telephone network in Tripura in recent years has further facilitated communication among police, security forces and civilian contacts/sources residing in remote interior areas, resulting in improved intelligence and prompt response from security forces.

Strengthening the Leadership at Sub-divisional Level

The implementation of new COIN concept and strategies demanded capable and courageous leadership at the SDPO level whose main job was to plan and execute operations along with other security forces operating in his sub-division. This centralization of multi-force operations in the office of SDPO proved to be a highly effective strategy as it led to increased coordination and intelligence sharing between police and security forces in the field and enhanced their operational efficiency.

From 1997 when a new police sub-division was created, the responsibility for planning of operations was assumed by SDPO, Teliamura. This was necessary as it was observed that the extremists often preferred to establish their hideouts or strike at the border of two police stations or two districts as they knew that this would lead to some confusion regarding territorial jurisdiction and prevent prompt reaction from the police station. In such cases, the role of the SDPO was crucial as he was able to mobilize requisite forces from various resources in his jurisdiction promptly, and, if necessary, could also liaise with the concerned district SP/Additional SP for additional forces.

The command of Teliamura sub-division was given to capable officers who had a proven track record in handling extremism and tough law and order situations. Further, they were also given sufficiently long tenures, which ensured continuity and effective implementation of the CI strategy and prevented unnecessary disruptions. The incumbency chart of SDPO Teliamura reveals that during the most severe phase of violence over a period of nine years between April 1997 and September 2006, two SDPOs held the charge for over four years each.[19] This continuity of command of these experienced and courageous officers has been an important factor in the success of CI Ops in this sub-division.

The fact that apart from planning of operations, SDPO Teliamura himself started leading the operations also gave a tremendous morale boost to the security forces and resulted in an increased number of encounters, killing or surrenders of extremists. In this context, Gill (2001: 45) has rightly noted that "... even the finest men cannot be asked to risk their lives for a leader who will not lead from the front." To date, it is now a well-established practice in the state police that in all major operations that are not solely for the purpose of area domination, the leadership role is played by the SDPO or the OC of the concerned police station, or by some senior officer of the concerned security force.

Augmentation of Security Forces in Teliamura Sub-division

In view of the rugged terrain and uneven spread of population, with myriad detached settlements and homesteads, the requirement of troops for CI Ops and effective domination of terrain is huge in Tripura. Galula (1964: 32) has observed that a ratio of 10 or 20 to one between the counterinsurgent and the insurgent is common, but even that may not be sufficient in all cases. In Tripura, the state government has made concerted efforts to increase the level of local forces by recruiting larger numbers of civil and armed police personnel, and mobilizing the civilian population by enlisting them as SPOs and Home Guards (HGs). These are supplemented by federal paramilitary forces such as Assam Rifles, BSF, and CRPF.

---

[19] B.K. Nag held the charge of SDPO, Teliamura from April 1, 1997 to March 26, 2001 and Shankar Debnath held the charge from September 28, 2001 to September 15, 2006.

There are two significant features of deployment of security forces in Teliamura sub-division. First, there has been a marked increase in the total quantum of security forces, particularly local forces, over the past decade. In 2000, total deployment in this sub-division was about 15 Coys comprising 11 Coys of paramilitary CRPF, four Coys of TSR, and one platoon of DAR, while a decade later in 2011, total deployment had increased to 21 Coys, including eight Coys of CRPF, one Coy of Assam Rifles, and 12 Coys of TSR (Table 8.9 and Figure 8.10). This substantial deployment is further supplemented with 145 persons of HG, SPOs, and DAR, which yields another one Coy in strength. Thus, while the overall force level has increased by one and half times in Teliamura over the past decade, there has been a threefold increase in the deployment of local forces, mainly resulting from the accelerated raising of several new TSR battalions.

Second, the number of security camps has almost doubled from 29 in 2000 to 55 in 2011 (Table 8.10 and Figure 8.10), which has been possible due to augmentation of troops as also relatively thin deployment of TSR personnel in platoon or less strength. The deployment of TSR reflects a substantial economy and efficiency of force as even the platoon posts are entrusted with the responsibility of covering several villages within a radius of 3–5 km or more, besides ensuring their own post-protection from extremist attacks.

Table 8.10:

Summary of Operational Deployment of Security Forces in Teliamura Sub-division (2000–2011)

Sl. No.	Year	Total Camps	CI Ops	Protective Camps	Miscellaneous ROP/Railway Protection, etc.
1.	2000	29	06	14	09
2.	2001	30	06	15	09
3.	2002	26	08	13	05
4.	2003	26	08	13	05

Continued Table 8.10

Continued Table 8.10

Sl. No.	Year	Total Camps	CI Ops	Protective Camps	Miscellaneous ROP/Railway Protection, etc.
5.	2004	31	11	17	03
6.	2005	38	13	24	03
7.	2006	36	12	21	03
8.	2007	40	14	22	04
9.	2008	47	20	23	04
10.	2009	45	20	21	04
11.	2010	52	24	20	08
12.	2011	55	27	16	12

Source: Tabulated from data provided by West District Police.

It is a common observation that the center of gravity in COIN is the civilian population. Therefore, gaining and maintaining popular support, or at least, acquiescence, must be the primary objective of all civil and military efforts: all else is secondary. As a result, providing for the security for the civilian population is the key to success of COIN effort. In an insecure environment government programs have no chance to win popular support unless the people are convinced that the government has the ability to secure them from reprisals of the extremists. Krepinevich (1986: 12) has put it neatly: "The people will not expose themselves to support the regime merely because government troops have temporarily occupied the area and dug a well." The deployment in Teliamura sub-division has been made to meet this critical requirement of dedicated security for civilian population.

A review of the operational deployment (2000–2011) in ethnically sensitive Teliamura sub-division indicates a marked preference for deployment of security forces for protection of vulnerable people followed by a gradual increase in deployment for CI Ops as per the availability of troops. Thus, in 2000 out of the total 29 camps in Teliamura sub-division, as many as 14 were deployed for protection of vulnerable people, and only six camps conducted CI Ops. Furthermore, despite gradual restoration of normalcy in the state, there has been no dilution of this commitment and, in fact, the number of protective camps has risen marginally from 14 in 2000 to 16 in 2011 (Table 8.10 and Figure 8.11). This sustained focus on population security has proved crucial in securing the general population from extremist attacks, and has prevented ethnic backlash in sensitive Teliamura sub-division. By providing effective security from militant violence, the police have also been able to tilt the "shifting loyalties" in favor of government and wean popular support away from the insurgents.

Second, it is also noticed that this protective deployment has been complemented with operational deployment for CI Ops as there can be no permanent strategy of defense in such conflicts. Hence, there has been a steady rise in deployment of security forces for offensive operations also resulting from a gradual improvement in manpower resources. Third, improved manpower has also allowed the government to provide dedicated security to crucial infrastructural projects such as railways, which is considered vital to the economic development of the state. Thus, the number of CI camps has increased from only six in 2000 to 24 in 2011 and currently there are as many as seven camps providing dedicated security to the railway (see Table 8.9 and Figure 8.11).[20] While enhanced commitment for CI deployment has effectively neutralized insurgent groups, dedicated security cover to major developmental projects has choked off avenues of extortion by extremists and consequent decline in their capacities for recruitment, and acquisition of arms and ammunition and operations. In brief, the wide network of security camps and availability of a very substantial, dispersed but coordinated force at the disposal of civil police officers have greatly contributed to the success of the COIN drive (ICM, 2007: 119).

---

[20] In Teliamura subdivision, seven camps for protection of railways are located at: Tunnel and Waximalam (Teliamura P.S.), and Swapanabari, 41 miles, Sukhdeb para, Mungiakami and Abhimohanbari (Mungiakami P.S.).

Figure 8.11:

Summary of Operational Deployment of Security Forces in Teliamura Sub-division (2000–2011)

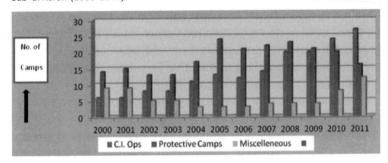

Source: West Tripura District Police.

Effective Area Domination

To curtail the free movement of extremists and check escalating militant violence, comprehensive area domination exercises are undertaken by security forces in their respective jurisdiction. This involves patrolling mixed population areas; thorough search of extremist infested areas; effective road opening, ensuring night domination through foot patrols and vehicular mobiles; arresting over-ground harborers, collaborators, and other hostile elements; and maintaining close watch over all important markets, which may be frequented by the villagers from the interior areas, extremists, or their sympathizers.

The effective domination of mixed populated areas in ethnically highly sensitive Teliamura and Kalyanpur Police Stations has often enabled police to discover latent tensions and reduce or resolve them through peace meetings or other appropriate methods, while the aggressive patrolling by police and security forces has effectively curtailed insurgent movement, instilled confidence in the common people, and greatly facilitated SF operations through better familiarization with the local topography and residents.

Intelligence-based Operations

Intelligence plays a crucial role in CI Ops as it ensures economy and efficiency of Force, and prevents excesses against innocent civilians.

Being a local force, police are well placed to collect local intelligence due to their extensive presence all over the area, and vast network of trusting relationships, contacts, informers, and sources among communities developed over the years (Gill, 2000). Consequently, their local connections and knowledge are a key source of human intelligence (HUMINT) that is essential for the success of CI Ops:

> Intelligence operations that help detect terrorist insurgents for arrest and prosecution are the single most important practice to protect a population from threats to its security. Honest, trained, robust police forces responsible for security can gather intelligence at the community level (Sepp, 2005: 9).

As part of the new strategy, the police station and SFs have been assigned a pivotal role in generating operational intelligence through their own sources, and are also held squarely responsible for any lapses in this regard. The main intelligence tasks related to extremist activity include identification of (a) vulnerable villages, security camps and road-stretches; (b) communally sensitive villages; (c) hardcore extremists; (d) over-ground collaborators; and (e) preparation of suitable contingency plans and SOPs to respond to extremist incidents. For collection of this vital information, police and SFs have raised new sources from the deep interior areas through civic action programs or VR groups; used surrendered or arrested extremists/collaborators; and developed contacts in mixed populated areas.

By the end of 2000, through much painstaking hard work, Teliamura and Kalyanpur P.S. were able to prepare a fairly accurate profile of extremist activities in their respective jurisdictions. A total of about 20 places in Teliamura P.S. and 50 places in Kalyanpur P.S. were identified as most frequented by extremists; and another list of about 140 hardcore extremists and 15 harborers/collaborators in Teliamura P.S. and about 70 hardcore extremists and 35 harborers/collaborators in Kalyanpur P.S. was prepared for targeted action (*District Intelligence Document*, West Tripura District, 2000). These lists are regularly updated and circulated among concerned security forces and other agencies for suitable action.

The new strategy effectively reversed the then prevalent practice of downward flow of information from the state or district level to the police stations and ensured that all actionable leads were promptly followed up at the local level without any loss of time. This was essential because the insurgents were highly mobile and seldom stayed at any place for more than a few hours. In subsequent years, with improved intelligence flow and constitution of SOGs, it became possible to launch small group operations targeting specific groups of militants. These operations were usually carried out by TSR troops who were accompanied by some police representative from the local P.S.

Action against United Bengali Liberation Front

In violently divided societies, the violence perpetrated by the extremist groups belonging to the majority community and its handling by the law-enforcement agencies is of crucial importance in legitimizing the authority of the state. The complicity, laxity or perceived biases of police in prosecuting the insurgents belonging to the majority community can irreparably harm the COIN efforts by alienating the minority communities.

In Tripura, following a series of brutal targeted attacks against non-tribal people in the late 1990s, a militant Bengali organization, United Bengali Liberation Front (UBLF), emerged in 1999 in Khowai-Teliamura sub-divisions to indulge in retaliatory attacks against tribal people, which vitiated the communal harmony in West Tripura district (Paul, 2009: 253). In 2000, the UBLF killed 35 tribals and was also implicated in a number of abductions, extortions, arson, and bombings targeting tribal people (SATP 16). The UBLF was banned by the government of Tripura and the outfit was effectively neutralized within two years by police with the arrest of its top leaders and other workers. The prompt, firm, and impartial handling of this terrorist outfit belonging to majority community went a long way in shaping the attitude of tribal people toward the government and increased their confidence in police.

Targeted Action against Collaborators

The crucial role of collaborators and sympathizers in insurgent warfare has been aptly summarized in a Vietminh manual on guerrilla warfare as follows:

> The population helps us to fight the enemy by giving us information, suggesting rues and plans, helping us to overcome difficulties due to lack of arms, and providing us guides. It also supplies liaison agents, hides and protects us, assists our action near posts, feeds us and looks after our wounded (cited in O'Neill, 1990: 72).

Therefore, it is important for police to sever the links between insurgents and the populace. As the CFM (2007: 41) notes, "it is easier to separate an insurgency from its sources and let it die, than to kill every insurgent." One of the better ways to achieve this task is to develop a good intelligence network that allows for identification and elimination of the insurgents' support network (Ganguly, 2009: 56). It has been rightly observed that "the mere killing of insurgents, without the simultaneous destruction of their infrastructure, is a waste of effort because their subversive organization will continue to spread and all casualties will be made good by new recruits" (Thompson, 1996: 118).

In keeping with this principle, apart from targeting hardcore extremists, the police also launched a concerted drive against the collaborators and over-ground sympathizers to disable or weaken the intelligence network of the militants. The success of this drive was ensured by dramatic improvements in intelligence gained from secret sources and interrogation of arrested and surrendered extremists as a result of which a large number of collaborators were identified and apprehended, while many of them fled abroad. The extremists, by now, had realized that the villages were no longer safe havens for them as the police were targeting their collaborators also. This simultaneous focus on neutralizing hardcore extremists as well as their collaborators gave a major setback to the extremist groups. As a changed strategy, police now started keeping a sharp watch over marketing activities of the local public on market days. And if any person was observed making any suspicious bulk purchases, he was questioned, and many times it was revealed that the person was making purchases for some extremist group. Some extremists were forced to come out of their hideouts in desperation and were arrested, while others felt that it was better to return to their bases across the border rather than die of hunger in jungles. As per state police records, over 1,200 collaborators were arrested from 2000 to 2010 in West Tripura district, of which 220 collaborators were from Teliamura sub-division alone. These large-scale arrests of collaborators have effectively disrupted local networks of militant support and made their operations increasingly difficult.

Special Police Officers and Village Resistance Groups

In COIN, it is important to arm and train those elements of the population that are willing to defend themselves against the insurgents to build small pockets of resistance (Sarkar, 1998: 86). This move helps to separate the insurgents from the civilian population and shrinks the political space in which the insurgents can operate because citizens' militias establish a government presence in the village (Ganguly, 2009: 52). However, their effectiveness would depend whether they are perceived as a disciplined force, or commit excesses against the people (O'Neill, 1990: 130).

The appointment of SPOs, provided under the *Police Act, 1861* has been a standard practice in many other insurgency affected states such as Punjab and Jammu and Kashmir. However, though Tripura had been facing insurgency for several decades, the SPOs were first recruited in 2001, given arms and deployed for guarding vulnerable villages or markets near their place of residence.[21] A number of pickets were established all over Tripura with a sanctioned strength of 30 SPOs each who were armed with .303 rifles. An armed component of DAR was also posted at each such picket to give them confidence, guard them from extremist attacks and discipline them. Maintaining proper discipline among such armed civilians is vitally important to ensure that they do not misuse their new status for personal vendetta.

---

[21] A provision for appointment of SPOs has been now incorporated in *The Tripura Police Act, 2007* (Section 8) which explicitly provides for appointment of "able-bodied and willing persons between the age of 18–40 years" as SPOs.

In Teliamura sub-division, the first SPO camp was established under Kalyanpur P.S. in 2001. Over the years many more SPO camps have come up and in 2010, SPOs were deployed at nine locations in Teliamura sub-division, with a posted strength of about 240.[22] Besides this, the government has also sanctioned the attachment of SPOs, usually one or two, with many paramilitary camps to provide vital local intelligence. According to most police officers, deployment of SPOs has been useful in providing a better flow of local intelligence, building public resistance against insurgents, and preventing kidnappings/raids by extremists in these areas. At the peak of insurgency, the OCs of Teliamura and Kalyanpur were also tasked with reviving and raising new VR parties in vulnerable villages. These VR groups were provided spears and whistles by the police and frequently contacted by them during night patrolling. However, most of these VR parties have now become defunct with the gradual restoration of normalcy and fencing of international Indo-Bangladesh border.

Psychological Operations in Teliamura Sub-division

An important strategy for countering the insurgency in Tripura has been to undercut the support base of militant groups among tribal people and secure their support for the government through a wide range of psychological operations. These objectives were achieved by exposing common people to the realities behind the mask of the extremist leaders through large-scale screenings of video films and distribution of leaflets, banners and cassettes of songs in local Kokborok language bearing anti-extremist messages, which highlighted the atrocities of militants, the lavish lifestyle of militant leaders, and adverse effects of militancy on development projects. The screening of films was usually organized in public grounds during festivals, market days, or other occasions when mass gatherings of people from interior areas were expected. This single initiative has had a profound impact on the psyche of young tribal people, dissuading them from joining the extremist groups.

The SDPO and OCs of police stations along with the political workers of the ruling CPI (M) party and civil administration have

---

[22] Six of these SPO camps were located in Teliamura P.S. jurisdiction, and the remaining three were in Kalyanpur P.S. jurisdiction.

played an active role in effectively propagating the government's "surrender-cum-rehabilitation" policy by holding frequent meetings with the village elders and family members of insurgents to persuade them to convince the militants to surrender and join the mainstream. In this context, the humanitarian approach of the police has also played an important role in persuading the extremists to surrender as they could see their erstwhile colleagues enjoying a normal life without any harassment by the police. The absence of reprisals from police against guerrillas who come over to the government side has been considered one of the key aspects to maximize "uptake" of amnesty programs (Ladwig III, 2009: 58).

The local police and security forces also interacted closely with tribal people during patrolling in interior areas and projected their local problems to the civil administration for speedy resolution and also helped the civil administration in organizing administrative camps and health camps in interior areas. Even now despite considerable improvement in the situation, there is no complacency in this drive and police continue to provide effective security cover to civil administration and public representatives in organizing administrative-cum-health camps and undertaking visits to interior areas to supervise development works/hold political meetings or celebrating. The police also provide security at all venues where large congregations are expected to celebrate major religious festivals of both the main communities.

Conclusion

This case study has attempted to showcase the remarkable processes of sustained strengthening of police capacities in Teliamura sub-division over the past decade that have effectively restored the integrity of police stations and made them fully capable of responding to whole range of policing challenges in their respective jurisdictions. The security forces have been able to establish "resilient, full-spectrum control" in their respective jurisdictions to gain popular support which, according to Kilcullen's theory of competitive control is the key to successful COIN (Kilcullen, 2010: 152).[23]

In recent years, of the three police stations in Teliamura sub-division, movement of small militant groups of NLFT has been reported sometimes from Mungiakami P.S. But due to strategic deployment of security forces and aggressive operations, these elements have not been able to commit any major incident so far. However, the broader aim of this police-led strategy has been "recovery" of vulnerable areas and restoration of civil authority and governance in "disturbed areas" to usher peace and development in the state (Sahni, 2005). The improved situation is reflected in a steady decline in militant violence, conduct of peaceful elections, and prevalence of communal harmony in this ethnically sensitive sub-division. Furthermore, there has been negligible recruitment of extremist groups from this sub-division in recent years, and continuous stream of surrenders reflects general public disillusionment with extremist goals. The implementation of development schemes in TTAADC areas of this sub-division, mostly inhabited by tribal people, has also led to a visible all-round improvement in rural infrastructure—roads, schools, hospitals—and renewed people's faith in government's capacity to provide effective security and undertake development programs (ICM, 2007: 131–135). In brief, this case study provides some meaningful insights into actual implementation of a complex strategy over the past decade leading to empowerment of police and marginalization of tribal extremists under a democratic set-up.

---

[23] According to Kilcullen (2010), the essence of theory of competitive control is: In irregular conflicts, the local armed actor that a given population perceives as most able to establish a normative system for resilient, full-spectrum control over violence, economic activity, and human security is most likely to prevail within that population's residential area (Kilcullen, 2010: 152).

Appendix

Data Highlights: Scheduled Tribes of Tripura

Census of India, 2001

The total population of Tripura in 2001 Census has been 3,199,203. Of these 993,426 persons are STs constituting 31.1 percent of the total population. The state has registered 16.4 percent decadal growth of ST population in 1991–2001. There are nineteen (19) notified STs in the state.

Population: Size & Distribution

1. Tripura, the main ST in the state from which the state has earned its name 'Tripura,' alone accounts for more than half of the total ST population of the state (54.7 percent). Riang (16.6 percent), Jamatia (7.5 percent), Chakma (6.5 percent), Halam (4.8 percent), Mag (3.1 percent), Munda (1.2 percent), Any Kuki Tribe (1.2 percent), and Garoo (1.1 percent) are the other major STs in terms of population. Along with Tripura they constitute about 97 percent ST population of the state (Statement-1). The rest of the STs are small in population size.

Statement-1: Population and proportion of major STs, 2001 census

SL. No.	Name of the Scheduled Tribe	Total Population	Proportion to the Total ST Population
1.	All Scheduled Tribes	993,426	100%
2.	Tripura	543,848	54.7
3.	Riang	165,103	16.6
4.	Jamatia	74,949	7.5
5.	Chakma	64,293	6.5
6.	Halam	47,245	4.8
7.	Mag	30,385	3.1
8.	Munda	12,416	1.2
9.	Any Kuki Tribe	11,674	1.2
10.	Garo	11,180	1.1

2. The STs in the state are predominantly rural (97.4 percent). One third of the total ST population of the state is living in West Tripura district (39 percent), followed by South Tripura (29.1 percent), Dhalai (16.7 percent), and North Tripura (15.1 percent). Dhalai district, however, has recorded the highest proportion (54 percent) of ST population.

Sex Ratio

3. As per 2001 Census, sex ratio of the ST population is 970, which is below the national average for STs (978). The Jamatia has recorded the highest sex ratio of 996 among the major STs. On the other hand comparatively low sex ratio has been recorded among Munda (950), Chakma (951), and Riang (962).

4. The child sex ratio (0-6 age group) for the STs in the state (981) is higher than the corresponding aggregated national average (973). It is important to note that while Jamatia has recorded a high overall sex ratio, the child sex ratio (958) among them is comparatively low. This situation is just the opposite among Chakma.

Literacy and Educational Level

5. Among all STs, 56.5 percent of the population has been recorded as literate, which is higher than the national average for STs (47.1 percent). The male literacy rate of 68 percent and female of 44.6 percent show high gender disparity in literacy.

6. Any Kuki Tribe with 73.1 percent literacy rate is well ahead of other major STs. The Tripura has recorded literacy rate of 62.1 percent with male and female literacy rate of 81.9 percent and 63.8 percent respectively. On the other hand more than half of the population among Munda, Riang, and Chakma are illiterate (Statement-2).

Statement-2: Literacy rate among major STs

SL. No.	Name of the Scheduled Tribe	Literate Rate (7 years and above)		
		Total	Male	Female
1.	All Scheduled Tribes	56.5	68.0	44.6
2.	Tripura	62.1	73.7	50.2
3.	Riang	39.8	51.8	27.3
4.	Jamatia	60.2	72.5	47.9
5.	Chakma	47.6	59.5	35.0
6.	Halam	56.1	67.5	44.5
7.	Mag	51.4	61.6	40.9
8.	Munda	33.6	43.8	22.8
9.	Any Kuki Tribe	73.1	81.9	63.8
10.	Garo	66.8	75.3	58.3

7. Among all STs, 62.7 percent of the children in age group 5–14 years have been attending schools or any other educational institutions. Any Kuki Tribe have recorded the highest (77.6 percent) and Munda the lowest (36.7 percent) percentage attending schools or any other educational institutions.

8. As regards level of education, merely 9.5 percent of total literates among STs are having educational level of Matric/

Secondary and above. Among the major STs, Tripura have 10.5 percent of their total literates as matriculates, while among Munda (4 percent), Riang (5.7 percent), and Mag (6.5 percent) this percentage is low.

Work Participation Rate (WPR)

9. In 2001 Census, 42.7 percent of the ST population has been recorded as workers, which is lower than the aggregated national average for STs (49.1 percent). Of the total workers, 69.6 percent have been recorded as main workers and 30.4 percent as marginal workers. WPR of 37.5 percent among females is slightly lower than that of males (47.6 percent). Gender wise disparity, however, is paramount in case of main workers; 86.5 percent among males and only 47.5 percent among females have been recorded as main workers (Statement-3).

Statement-3: Distribution of total, main and marginal workers among STs

T/M/F	Percentage of Workers		
	Total Workers	*Main Workers*	*Marginal Workers*
Total	423,851(42.7%)	294,980 (69.6%)	128,871(30.4%)
Male	240,239(47.6%)	207,708 (86.5%)	32,531 (13.5%)
Female	183,612(37.5%)	87,272(47.5%)	96,340 (52.5%)

10. Individual ST wise Jamatia have recorded the highest WPR (48.7 percent). On the other hand it is the lowest among Riang (39.2 percent).

Category of Workers

11. Agriculture is the mainstay of economic activities among the STs in Tripura. Among all STs, 45.9 percent of the total

main workers have been recorded as cultivators and 29.7 percent agricultural labourers.

12. The Riang are predominantly involved in cultivation with the highest of 64.9 percent of their total main workers as cultivators among the major STs. On the other hand it is the lowest among Munda (12 percent).

Marital Status

13. The distribution of ST population by marital status shows that 54.3 percent is never married, 41.9 percent currently married, 3.3 percent widowed, and 0.6 percent divorced/separated.

14. The percentage of widowed population among Garoo (4.4 percent) and Munda (4.1 percent) is considerably high. As regards the divorced/separated population, Mag have recorded the highest 1.1 percent, while Chakma the lowest at 0.3 percent among the major STs (Statement-4).

Statement-4: Percentage distribution of population by marital status among major STs

SL. No.	Name of the Scheduled Tribe	Never Married	Currently Married	Widowed	Divorced/ Separated
1.	All Scheduled Tribes	54.3	41.9	3.3	0.6
2.	Tripura	54.0	42.1	3.4	0.5
3.	Riang	55.0	41.3	2.9	0.8
4.	Jamatia	51.8	44.5	3.1	0.6
5.	Chakma	54.9	42.2	2.7	0.3
6.	Halam	56.0	40.2	3.3	0.4
7.	Mag	55.8	39.2	3.8	1.1
8.	Munda	54.3	40.9	4 1	0.6
9.	Any Kuki Tribe	55.2	40.9	3.3	0.7
10.	Garo	54.1	40.8	4.4	0.7

15. Among all STs, 1.4 percent of the total females below 18 years–the minimum legal age for marriage–have been returned as ever married. The Munda have recorded the highest 1.9 percent ever married females below the stipulated age for marriage.

16. The ever married males below 21 years–their minimum legal age for marriage–constitute 1.7 percent of their total population. The Riang have recorded the highest 2.3 percent ever married males in this category, closely followed by Jamatia (2 percent). It is the lowest among Garoo (0.9 percent).

Religion

17. Of the total ST population 80.1 percent are Hindus, 10 percent Christians, 9.6 percent Buddhists, and only 0.2 percent Muslims.

Note

1. Data for this Appendix has been obtained from Census of India, 2001. http://censusindia.gov.in/Tables_Published/SCST/dh_st_tripura.pdf

Bibliography

Government of India (GOI)

Census of India, 2001.
Census of India, 2011.
Ministry of Development of Northeast Region, Human Development Report of Northeast States, 2014.
Millennium Development Goals: India Country Report 2014, Social Statistics Division, Ministry of Statistics and Programme Implementation, Government of India.
Ministry of Development of Northeast Region, *Annual Report*, 2005–2006.
Ministry of Home Affairs (MHA), *Annual Report*, 2001–2002.
———, *Annual Report*, 2005–2006.
———, *Annual Report*, 2009–2010.
———, *Annual Report*, 2010–2011.
———, *Annual Report*, 2012–2013.
———, *Annual Report*, 2013–2014.
———, *Annual Report*, 2014–2015.
———, "Amendment in Surrender-cum-rehabilitation scheme for North Eastern States to increase monthly stipend from Rs. 2000 to 3,500 p.m. to each surrenderee for a period of one year," dated December 2, 2009.
———, "Crime in India: 1991," National Crime Records Bureau.
———, "Crime in India: 2008," National Crime Records Bureau.
———, "Crime in India: 2011," National Crime Records Bureau.
———, "Crime in India: 2013," National Crime Records Bureau.
———, "Report on Situation in the State of Tripura (2000)," http://www.satp.org/satporgtp/countries/india/states/tripura/documents/papers/situation_in_state_tripura.htm.
———, "Data on Police Organizations in India (as on 1.1.2014)," Bureau of Police Research and Development (BPR&D), http://www.bprd.nic.in/showfile.asp?lid=1047.
———, "Statistical Profile of Scheduled Tribes in India (2013)," Statistics Division.
Ministry of Tribal Affairs (2013), "Statistical Profile of Scheduled Tribes in India," Statistics Division.
National Police Commission (NPC), "Policing in the North-East" (1981), http://www.satp.org/satporgtp/countries/india/document/papers/policing_ne__may_1981.htm.
Northeast Region (NER): Vision 2020, Volume 1, http://tripura.nic.in/portal/More_Info/document/central/NE%20Vision.pdf.

Planning Commission (1997). The Shukla Commission Report, Transforming the North East—High Level Commission Report.

Speech of Prime Minister of India at the Chief Ministers' Conference on Internal Security on February 1, 2011 in New Delhi, http://www.satp.org/satporgtp/countries/india/document/papers/2011/pmspeechjan.htm.

Government of Tripura

Directorate of Economics and Statistics, Planning (Statistics) Department, *Economic Survey* (2004–2005).

———, *Economic Review of Tripura* (2005–2006).

Directorate of Economics and Statistics, Planning (Statistics) Department, *Economic Review of Tripura* (2010–2011).

———, (2012–2013).

———, (2013–2014).

Directorate of Economics and Statistics, Planning (Statistics) Department, *Statistical Abstract* (2010–2011).

Dr. N.C. Nath (1999) *Sri Rajmala*, Tribal Research Institute, Agartala.

General Administration (P&T) Department, "*Revised Employment Policy,*" Memorandum dated August 18, 2010.

Home Department, Notification ("Disturbed Areas") dated September 6, 2012.

R.G. Singh and Arun Debbarma (Eds), E.F. Sandy's compiled *History of Tripura*, Tripura State Tribal Cultural Research Institute and Museum, Third reprint, July 2008.

Sub-Divisional Officer, Teliamura subdivision, West District, "*Sub-Divisional Profile at a Glance: Administrative Report, Teliamura, 2008.*"

Teliamura subdivision, *Final Result Sheet*, Elections to the Tripura Legislative Assembly, 2008.

The Tripura Police Act, 2007, http://tripurapolice.nic.in/TripuraPoliceAct2007.pdf

Tripura at a Glance, 2011–2012.

Tripura: Human Development Report (2007) (New Delhi).

Tripura State Rifles Act, 1983.

Tripura State Rifles (Recruitment), Rules, 1984.

Tripura State Rifles (Discipline, Control, Conditions etc.), Rules, 1986.

Tripura Police Documents

"Chief's Message," Message of DGP, Tripura (August 2013), Tripura police website: http://www.tripurapolice.nic.in/chiefMsg.htm

DGP, Tripura order dated October 20, 2001.

———, Tripura order dated May 29, 2002.

IGP (Armed Police), "Concept and Conduct of CI Operation," August 7, 2000.

Police HQ, "Pattern of Deployment of TSR battalions (2000)."

————., "Pattern of Deployment of TSR battalions (2012)."

————., "Summary of Achievements of TSR battalions (2000–2012)."

"*Prerana*" (2012), Special issue of Tripura police to mark 150th anniversary of the Indian Police.

Special Branch, "Surrender of Extremists in Teliamura Subdivision (2000–2010)."

State Crime Record Bureau, "Extremist Crime data for Tripura State (2000– 2012)."

Tripura State Rifles (TSR): Silver Jubilee Special issue (2010), Tripura police website (http://www.tripurapolice.nic.in/Silverjubilee.pdf).

Tripura police website (http://www.tripurapolice.nic.in/).

Tripura State Rifles

1st Bn. TSR, *Visitors' Book*, entry of P.K. Sharma, Commandant, dated March 12, 1984.

————, entry of A. Jayapaul, Assistant Commandant, dated January 28, 1985.

————, Address of General K.V.K. Rao (Retd), former Governor of Nagaland, Manipur and Nagaland to the Passing Out Parade of 1st Battalion TSR on April 11, 1986 at Battalion HQ., Agartala, Tripura.

Commandant 2nd Bn. TSR, "Year-wise details of fabrication of BP Vehicles at BP Workshop 2nd Bn. TSR' (1996–2002)."

Commandant 6 Bn. TSR, "Deployment of 6 Bn. TSR (2000–2010)."

————, "Operational Achievements of 6 Bn. TSR (2000–2010)."

————, "Police station wise achievements of 6 Bn. TSR (2000–2010) in Teliamura Subdivision."

West Tripura District Police

SP, West District (1997), "*Action Plan for Counter-Insurgency, West Tripura District.*"

———— (2000), "*District Intelligence Document.*"

————, "Extremist Crime Data for West Tripura District (2000–2011)."

————, "Summary of Deployment of Security Forces in Teliamura Subdivision (2000–2011)."

————, "Kalyanpur P.S.: Extremist Crime Statistics (2000–2011)."

————, "Number of extremist cases in Kalyanpur P.S. (2000–2011)."

————, "Action taken against extremists and collaborators under Kalyanpur P. (2000–2011)."

————, "Number of extremist cases in Mungiakami P.S. (2000–2011)."

————, "Action taken against extremists and collaborators under Mungiakami P.S. (2000–2011)."

————, "Number of extremist cases in Teliamura P.S.(2000-2011)."

SP, West District, "Action taken against extremists and collaborators under Teliamura P.S. (2000–2011)."
———, "Sanctioned and Posted strength of Teliamura P.S., Kalyanpur P.S., and Mungiakami P.S. (2000–2010)."

Miscellaneous

Commonwealth Human Rights Initiative (CHRI/2011), Better Policing Series-India, "*Police reform debates in India*," http://www.scribd.com/doc/267856/police-reform-debates-in-india

Department of Defence, USA, Institute for Defense Analyses (2005), *Learning to Adapt to Asymmetric Threats* (Project leader: John C.F. Tillson).

RAND Corporation Report (2006), *On "Other" War: Lessons from Five Decades of RAND Counterinsurgency Research* (Author: Austin Long).

——— (2007), *War by Other Means: Building Complete and Balanced Capabilities for Counterinsurgency* (Authors: David C. Gompert and John Gordon IV).

——— (2009), *Preparing and Training for the Full Spectrum of Military challenges: Insights from the Experiences of China, France, the United Kingdom, India and Israel* (Authors: David E. Johnson, Jennifer D.P. M., Roger Cliff, M. Wade Markel, Laurence Smallman, Michael Spirtas).

Report of Commission on Centre-State Relations (2010), Vol. V, *Internal Security, Criminal Justice and Centre-State Cooperation.*

Report of Independent Commission on Policing for Northern Ireland (1999).

Report of Law Commission of Canada (2006).

Report of Dutch Police "Police in Evolution" (2006).

Report of the Secretary-General on the implementation of the Naples Political Declaration and Global Action Plan Against Organised Transnational Crime, E/CN.15/1996/2, April 4,1996, United Nations Economic and Social Council, Commission on Crime Prevention and Criminal Justice, Fifth session at Vienna, May 21–31,1996, Section F, Para 18.

Index, 2014, The Global Hunger.

The Global Terrorism Index, 2014.

The UN Human Development Index, 2013, http://hdr.undp.org/en/content/human-development-report-2013-media-toolkit

The U.S. Army /Marine Corps Counterinsurgency Field Manual: U.S. Army Field Manual no. 3–24 (2007) (Chicago: The University of Chicago Press).

United States Departments of the Army and the Air Force, *Military Operations in Low Intensity Conflict,* Field manual 100-20/ Air Force Pamphlet 3-20 (Washington, DC: Headquarters, Departments of the Army and Air Force).

United Nations Development Programme (UNDP), *Human Development Report, 1994* (New York).

Secondary Sources

Adhikari, O.S. (1982), *The Problem of indebtedness among the tribals in Sadar Subdivision of Tripura* (Agartala: Directorate of Research, Department of Welfare for Scheduled Tribes and Scheduled Castes).

Agrawal, P.K. (2010), *Land reforms in states and union territories in India* (New Delhi: Concept Publishing Company).

Ahluwalia, V.K. (2012), 'Strategy and tactics of the Indian Maoists,' *Strategic Analysis*, Vol. 36, No. 5, pp. 723–734.

Ahmad, Eqbal (2006), *The selected writings* (New York: Columbia University Press).

Ahmad, Eqbal (1982), "Revolutionary warfare and counterinsurgency". In Gerard Chaliand (Ed.) *Guerrilla strategies: A historical anthology from the long march to Afghanistan* (Berkeley: University of California Press).

Ahuja, Pratul and Ganguly, Rajat (2007), "The fire within: Naxalite insurgency violence in India," *Small Wars and Insurgencies*, Vol. 18, No. 2, pp. 249–274.

All India Democratic Women's Association (AIDWA) (2000), *Women against terrorism: The Tripura experience* (New Delhi: AIDWA).

Andreas, Peter and Price, Richard (Fall 2001), "From war fighting to crime fighting: Transforming the American national security state," *International Studies Review*, Vol. 3, No. 3, pp. 31–52.

Arnold, David (1986), *Police power and colonial rule* (Delhi: Oxford University Press).

Art, Robert J. and Richardson, Louise (Eds.) (2007), *Democracy and counterterrorism: Lessons from the past* (Washington, D.C.: United States Institute of Peace Press).

Atwan, A.B. (2006), *The secret history of al-Qaeda* (London: Saqi Books).

Austin, Dennis (1994), *Democracy and violence in India and Sri Lanka* (London: Pinter Publishers).

Azam, Jean-Paul and Bhatia, Kartika (2012), "*Provoking insurgency in a Federal State: Theory and application to India*" (Toulouse School of Economics, Working Paper Series, 12–329), fr.eu/sites/default/files/medias/doc/wp/dev/wp_tse_329.pdf.

Bajaj, Kamlesh (2014), "Cyberspace: Post-Snowdon," *Strategic Analysis*, Vol. 38, No. 4, pp. 582–587.

Bajpai, Kanti P. and Pant, Harsh V. (Eds) (2013), *India's national security: A reader* (New Delhi: Oxford University Press).

———. (Eds.) (2013a), *India's foreign policy: A reader* (New Delhi: Oxford University Press).

Bakshi, Sanchita, Chawla, Arunish, and Shah, Mihir (January 3, 2015), "Regional disparities in India: A moving frontier," *Economic and Political Weekly*, Vol. 50, No. 1, pp. 44–52.

Banerjee, Dipankar (2009), "The Indian army's counterinsurgency doctrine," in Ganguly, S. and Fidler, D. P. (Eds) *India and counterinsurgency: Lessons learned* (London: Routledge).

Baruah, Sanjib (2005), *Durable disorder: Understanding politics of northeast India* (New Delhi: Oxford University Press).

——— (2009), "Introduction," in Baruah, Sanjib (Ed.) *Beyond counterinsurgency: Breaking the impasse in northeast India* (New Delhi: Oxford University Press).

Basumatary, Jaikhlong (2014), *Quest for peace in Assam: A study of the Bodoland movement*, Manekshaw Paper No. 44, Centre for Land Warfare Studies (New Delhi: KW Publishers).

Bayley, D.H. and Perito, R.M. (2010), *The police in war: Fighting insurgency, terrorism and violent crime* (London: Lynne Rienner Publishers).

Beckett, Ian (Ed.) (1988), *The roots of counter-insurgency: Armies and Guerrilla warfare* (London: Blandford Press).

——— (2001), *Modern insurgencies and counter-insurgencies: Guerrillas and their opponents since 1750* (London: Routledge).

——— (March 2005), "The future of insurgency," *Small Wars & Insurgencies*, Vol. 16, No. 1, pp. 22–36.

Beede, R. Benjamin (2008), "The roles of paramilitary and militarized police," *Journal of Political and Military Sociology*, Vol. 36, No. 1, pp. 53–65.

Beers, Jason H. (2007), *Community-oriented policing and counterinsurgency: A conceptual model*, a Master's thesis, U.S. Army Command and General Staff College, Fort Leavenworth, Kansas.

Bengelsdorf, C., Cerullo, M., Chandrani, Y. (Eds.) (2006), *The selected writings of Eqbal Ahmad* Foreword by Noam Chomsky (New York: Columbia University Press).

Bhatia, Bela (2005), "The Naxalite movement in central Bihar," *Economic & Political Weekly*, Vol. 40, No. 15, pp. 1536–1549.

Bhatia, Michael V. (2005), "Fighting words: Naming terrorists, bandits, rebels, and other violent actors," *Third World Quarterly*, Vol. 26, No. 1, pp. 5–22.

Bhattacharjee, Giriraj (October 22, 2012), "Assam: Another tenuous peace," *South Asia Intelligence Review*, Vol. 11, No. 16, http://www.satp.org/satporgtp/sair/Archives/sair11/11_16.htm#assessment2, accessed on November 30, 2015.

Bhattacharjee, S.R. (1989), *Tribal insurgency in Tripura: A Study in the Exploration of Causes* (New Delhi: Inter-India Publications).

Bhattacharjee, S. and Saravanan, R. (2012), "Poverty in natural prosperity: Can agriculture bring the renaissance in North-East India?" In Kashyap, Shivendra Kumar, Pathak, Awadhesh, and Papnai Gaurav (Eds), *Saving humanity: Swami Vivekananda perspective* (pp. 260–274), Uttarakhand: Vivekananda Swadhyay Mandal, G.B. Pant University of Agriculture and Technology.

Bhattacharya, Suchintya (1992), *Genesis of tribal extremism in Tripura* (New Delhi: Gyan Publishing House).

Bhaumik, Pradyot (2012), "People's police system in ancient indigenous society," in "*Prerana*," Special issue of Tripura Police magazine.

Bhaumik, S. (1996), *Insurgent crossfire: North-east India* (New Delhi: Lancer).

——— (February 2002), "Disaster in Tripura," *Seminar*, No. 510, pp. 68–71, Delhi.

——— (2004), Ethnicity, ideology and religion: Separatist movements in India's northeast, http://www.apcss.org/Publications/Edited%20Volumes/ReligiousRadicalism/PagesfromReligiousRadicalismandSecurityinSouthAsiach10.pdf.

——— (2007), "*Insurgencies in India's northeast: Conflict, co-option & change,*" Working Paper No. 10 (Washington: East-West Centre).

——— (2009), *Troubled periphery: Crisis of India's north east* (New Delhi: SAGE Publications).

——— (2009a), "Jihad or Joi Bangla: Bangladesh in Peril." In Saikia, J and Stepanova, E. (Eds) *Terrorism: Patterns of internationalization* (New Delhi: SAGE Publications).

Bhaumik, S. (June 13, 2015), "Army's trans-border raid in Myanmar: Interrogating the claims," *Economic and Political Weekly*, Vol. L, No. 24, http://www.epw.in/reports-states/army%E2%80%99s-trans-border-raid-myanmar.html.

Blair, Sir Ian (2007), "Surprise news: Policing works," *Police Practice and Research*, Vol. 8, No. 2, Special Issue–"Reshaping Policing: Ideas in Action," pp. 175–182.

Bowman, Bradley L. (2007), "U.S. grand strategy for countering Islamist terrorism and insurgency in the 21st century." In James J.F. Forest (Ed.) *Countering terrorism and insurgency in the 21st century*, (Vol. 1, pp. 29–55, Westport: Praeger Security International).

Boyle, Michael J. (2010), "Do counterterrorism and counterinsurgency go together?" *International Affairs*, Vol. 86, No. 2, pp. 333–353.

Bradley, David and Nixon, Christine (October–December 2009), "Ending the 'dialogue of the deaf': Evidence and policing policies and practices. An Australian case study," *Police Practice and Research*, Vol. 10, Nos. 5–6, pp. 423–435.

Brodeur, Jean-Paul (2007), "High and low policing in Post-9/11 Times," *Policing: An International Journal of Police Strategies and Management*, Vol. 1, No. 1, pp. 25–37.

Brogden, M.E. (1987), "The emergence of the police-the colonial dimension," *British Journal of Criminology*, Vol. 27, No. 1, pp. 4–14.

Bryman, Alan (2006), "Paradigm peace and the implications for Quality," *International Journal of Social Research Methodology*, Vol. 9, No. 2, pp. 111–126.

Business Standard (2011), "India 134th in global Human Development Report," November 03, New Delhi.

Byman, Daniel L. (Fall 2006), "Friends like these: Counterinsurgency and the war on terrorism," *International Security*, Vol. 31, No. 2, pp. 79–115.

Calese, Gary D. Major (2005), *Law enforcement methods for counterinsurgency operations*, A monograph, U.S. Army Command and General Staff College, Fort Leavenworth, Kansas.

Carment, David and Samy, Y. (October 2012), "State fragility: Country indicators for foreign policy assessment," *The Development Review: Beyond Research*, Vol. 1, No. 1, pp. 94–112.

Cassidy, Robert H. (2004). "Back to the street without joy: Counterinsurgency Lessons from Vietnam and Other Small Wars," *Parameters*, Vol. 34, No. 2, pp. 73–83.

———. (2006). "The long small war: Indigenous forces for counterinsurgency," *Parameters*, Vol. 36, No.2, pp. 47–62.

Cassidy, Robert M. (2008), *Counterinsurgency and the global war on terror* (Stanford: Stanford Security Studies).

Cederman, Lars-Eric, Wimmer, Andreas and Min, Brian (2010), "Why do ethnic groups rebel: New data and analysis," *World Politics*, Vol. 62, No. 1, pp. 87–119.

Celeski, Joseph D. (2009), "Policing and law enforcement in COIN—The thick blue line," JSOU Report 09-2 (Florida, USA: The JSOU Press).

Chadha, Vivek (2005), *Low intensity conflicts in India: An analysis* (New Delhi: Sage Publications).

Chakravarti, Mahadev (July 22, 2000), "Tripura's ADC elections, 2000: Terror tactics win," *Economic and Political Weekly*, Vol. 35, No. 30, pp. 2615–2617.

——— (2005), "Insurgency and human security in Tripura: Past and present," Background Papers commissioned for Tripura: Human Development Report, 2007, Government of Tripura, http://planningtripura.gov.in/THDR/backgroundreport/Insurgency%20 and%20Human%20Security.pdf.

Chakravarty, Manas (March 22, 2012), "The Tripura model and other thoughts on the poverty numbers," *live mint*, E-Paper, http://www.livemint.com/Opinion/fAvT3RCQi89dd3ngDsParM/The-Tripura-model-and-other-thoughts-on-the-poverty-numbers.html.

Chakraborty, Dipannita (2004), *Land Question in Tripura* (New Delhi: Akansha Publishing House).

Chakraborty, S. (April 11, 2010), "Tripura Congress gets smart," *The Statesman*, http://www.thestatesman.org/index.php?option=com_content&view=article&id=32504 6&catid=52.

Chakravarti, Mahadev (2000), "Tripura's ADC Elections, 2000: Terror Tactics Win," *Economic and Political Weekly*, Vol. 35, No. 30, July 22, pp. 2615 -2617.

Chalk, Peter (Winter 1995), "The liberal democratic response to terrorism," *Terrorism and Political Violence*, Vol. 7, No. 4, pp. 10 -44.

Chalk, Peter and Rosenau, William (2004), *Confronting the "Enemy Within": Security intelligence, the police, and counterterrorism in four democracies* (Santa Monica, CA: RAND Corporation).

Chandran, D. Suba (2012), "Prospects for autonomy in Jammu and Kashmir," in Rajat Ganguly (Ed.) *Autonomy and ethnic conflict in South and South-East Asia* (London and New York: Routledge).

Chattopadhyay, S.S. (August 22, 2014), "Tripura: Road to progress," *Frontline*.

Chaudhuri, Kalyan (May 27-June 09,2000), "A victory at gun-point," *Frontline*, Vol. 17, No. 11, http://www.frontline.in/static/html/fl1711/17110390.htm.

Chima, Jugdep S. (2014), "The Punjab police and counterinsurgency against Sikh militants in India: The successful convergence of interests, identities, and institutions." In Ganguly, Sumit and Fair, C. Christine (Eds.) *Policing insurgencies: Cops as counterinsurgents* (New Delhi: Oxford University Press).

Chomsky, N. (2007), *Hegemony or survival: America's quest for global domination* (NSW, Australia: Allen and Unwin), https://7chan.org/lit/src/Chomsky,_Noam_-_Hegemony_or_survival.pdf.

Choudhary, Rohit (2009), *Policing: Reinvention strategies in a marketing framework* (New Delhi: Sage Publications India).

Clarke, R.V., and Newman, G.R. (2007), "Police and prevention of terrorism," *Policing*, Vol. 1, No. 1, pp. 9 -20.

Clausewitz, Carl von (1976), *On War*, Ed. and translated. Michael Howard and Peter Paret (Princeton: Princeton University Press).

Clegg, I., Hunt, R., and Whetton, J. (2000), *Policy guidance on support to policing in developingcountries* (Swansea, UK: Centre for Development Studies, University of Wales).

Cline, Lawrence E. (2006), "The insurgency environment in northeast India," *Small Wars and Insurgencies*, Vol. 17, No. 2 (June), pp. 126 -147.

Cohen, S. (Spring 2003), "Why do they quarrel? Civil-military tensions in LIC situations," in *The Review of International Affairs*, 2/3, pp. 21 -40.

Collier, Paul (2000), "Doing well out of war: An economic perspective," in Berdal, Mats and Melone, David H. (Eds) *Greed & grievance: Economic agendas in civil wars* (Boulder & London: Lynne Rienner Publishers).

Commonwealth Human Rights Initiatives (2001), *Police reform debates in India*, http://www.humanrightsinitiative.org/publications/police/PRDebatesInIndia.pdf.

Cordner, Gary and Shain, Cynthia (2011), "The changing landscape of police education and training," *Police Practice and Research*, Vol. 12, No. 4, pp. 281 -285.

Dahrendorf, R. (1959), *Class and class conflict in industrial society* (Stanford: Stanford University Press).

Das, Dilip K., and Verma, Arvind (1988), "The armed police in the British colonial tradition: The indian perspective," *Policing: An International Journal of Police Strategies and Management,* Vol. 21, No. 2, pp. 354–367.

Das, Samir Kumar (2007), *Conflict and peace in India's northeast: The role of civil society,* Policy Studies 42, East West Center, Washington.

Das, N.K. (2009), "Identity politics and social exclusion in India's Northeast: The case for re-distributive justice," *Bangladesh e-Journal of Sociology,* Vol. i, No. i.

Dasgupta, A. (December 18, 2001), "Tripura's brutal *Cul de Sac,*" *Himal South Asian,* Vol. 14, No. 12 ((Nepal: South Asian Trust).

Dasgupta, Jyotirindra (1997), "Community, authenticity, and autonomy: Insurgence and institutional development in India's northeast," *The Journal of Asian Studies,* Vol. 56, No. 2(May), pp. 345–370.

Dash, S. (September 8, 2008), "Nagaland: Extortion dynamics," *South Asian Intelligence Review,* Vol. 7, No. 9, http://www.satp.org/satporgtp/sair/Archives/7_9.htm#assessment2.

———— (June 29, 2009), "Manipur: Timorous transformations," *South Asia Intelligence Review,* Vol. 7, No. 51, http://www.satp.org/satporgtp/sair/Archives/7_51.htm#assessment2.

———— (November 16, 2009a), "Manipur: The persistence of despair," *South Asia Intelligence Review,* Vol. 8, No. 9, http://www.satp.org/satporgtp/countries/india/states/manipur/index.html.

Datta, S. (February 3, 2003), "Tripura: A bloody prelude to elections," *South Asia Intelligence Review,* Vol. 1, No. 29 (February), http://www.satp.org/satporgtp/sair/Archives/1_29.htm#assessment2.

———— (2009), "Preface" in Paul, Manas (Ed.) *The eyewitness: Tales from Tripura's ethnic conflict* (New Delhi: Lancer Publishers & Distributors).

Davar, Kamal, Lt. General (2012), "Next generation defence reforms," *India Defence Review,* Net Edition, August 21, http://www.indiandefencereview.com/spotlights/next-generation-defnce-reforms/

Davis Mike (1992), "Understanding L.A.: The new urban order," in *USA: A look at Reality* (Hyattsville, Maryland: Equal Justice USA/ Quixote Center).

Debray, Regis (1967), "*Revolution in the revolution: Armed struggle and political struggle in Latin America*" Bobbe Ortiz, trans. (New York: Monthly Review Press).

Deccan Herald (January 7, 2005), "HC issues show-cause notice in dissolution of Tripura ADC case."

———— (July 28, 2013), "Nearly 1,100 IPS vacancies across the country."

Deka, Kaushik (2012), "Defender of the last bastion," *India Today,* October 5, http://indiatoday.intoday.in/story/tripura-chief-minister-manik-sarkar-keeps-left-front-flag-high/1/223587.html.

DNA, Daily News & Analysis (December 22, 2012), "Insurgency on the wane in Tripura."

Dreze, Jean and Sen, Amartya (November 14, 2011), "Putting growth in its place," *Outlook,* http://www.outlookindia.com/article.aspx?278843#.TrYr7ppjwso.

———— (2013), *An uncertain glory: India and its contradictions* (London: Allen Lane, Penguin Group).

Duyvesteyn, Isabelle (September 2008), "Exploring the utility of force: Some conclusions," *Small Wars & Insurgencies,* Vol. 19, No. 3, pp. 423–443.

Dziedzic, Michael and Stark, Christine (2006), *Bridging the security gap: The role of the centre of excellence for stability police units in contemporary peace operations*, Briefing Paper, USIP, Washington, DC, June.

Economic Survey, Assam, 2013–2014, http://www.planassam.info/economic_survey_assam_13-14/Economic_Survey_%202013-14.pdf.

Ellis, J. (1995), *From the barrel of a gun* (London: Greenhill Books).

Emsley, Clive (1999), "The origins of the modern police," *History Today*, Vol. *49*, No. 4, pp. 8–14.

Enloe, C.H. (1976), "Ethnicity and militarization: Factors shaping the roles of police in third world nations," *Studies in comparative International Development*, Vol. *11*, No. 3, p. 25.

———— (1978), "Police and military in Ulster: Peace-keeping or peace-subverting forces," *Journal of Peace Research*, Vol. *15*, No. 3, pp. 243–258.

Epifanio, Mariaelisa (2011), "Legislative response to international terrorism," *Journal of Peace Research*, Vol. *48*, No. 3, pp. 399–411.

Epstein, David G. (1968), "The police role in counterinsurgency efforts," *The Journal of Criminal Law, Criminology and Police Science*, Vol. *59*, No. 1, Northwestern University School of Law, pp. 148–151.

Esteban, J., Mayoral, L., and Ray, D. (2012), "Ethnicity and conflict: Theory and facts," *Science*, Vol. *336*, No. 6083, p. 858.

Ezrow, Natasha M. and Frantz, Erica (2013), *Failed states and institutional decay: Understanding instability and poverty in the developing world* (London: Bloomsbury).

Fair, C.C. (2009), "Lessons from India's experiences in the Punjab," in Ganguly, S. and Fidler, D. P. (Eds) *India and counterinsurgency: Lessons learned* (London: Routledge).

Fair, C.C. and Ganguly, S. (Eds) (2014), *Policing insurgencies: Cops as counterinsurgents* (Oxford: University Press).

Fall, Bernard (April 1965), "The theory and practice of insurgency and counterinsurgency," *Naval War College Review*, pp. 21–38.

Fearon, J.D. and Laitin, D. (Autumn 2000), "Violence and the social construction of ethnic identity," *International Organization*, Vol. *54*, No. 4, pp. 845–877.

————. (2003), "Ethnicity, insurgency and civil war," *American Political Science Review*, Vol. *97*, No. 1, pp. 75–90.

Fitzsimmons, Michael (June 2008), "Hard hearts and open minds? Governance, identity and the intellectual foundations of counterinsurgency strategy," *Journal of Strategic Studies*, Vol. *31*, No. 3, pp. 337–365.

Ford, Matthew Charles (2012), "Finding the target, fixing the method: Methodological tensions in insurgent identification," *Studies in Conflict & Terrorism*, Vol. *35*, No. 2, pp. 113–134.

Frontline (August 22, 2014), "We are bridging the rural-urban divide," an interview with Tripura's Chief Minister Manik Sarkar, Agartala, India.

Fuller, Gary (1995). "The demographic backdrop to ethnic conflict: A geographic overview," in *The challenge of ethnic conflict to national and international order in the 1990s: Geographic perspectives* (pp. 151–154), Washington, D.C.: Central Intelligence Agency.

Galula, David, (1964), *Counter-insurgency warfare: Theory and practice* (London: Pall Mall Press).

Ganguly, Rajat (2012), "Introduction: Is autonomy a solution or an obstacle to resolving ethno-national conflicts?" in Rajat Ganguly (Ed.) *Autonomy and ethnic conflict in south and south-east Asia* (London and New York: Routledge).

Ganguly, S. (2009), "Slow learning: Lessons from India's counterinsurgency in Kashmir," in Ganguly, S. and Fidler, D.P. (Eds) *India and counterinsurgency: Lessons learned* (London: Routledge).

Ganguly, S. and Fidler, D.P. (Eds) (2009), *India and counterinsurgency: Lessons learned* (London: Routledge).

———— (Winter 2010), "India and Eastphalia," *Indian Journal of Global Legal Studies,* Vol. 17, No. 1, pp. 147–164.

Gateway House (January 13, 2012), "Bangladesh: A passage through Tripura."

Ghosh, P.S. (2006), "Challenges of peace building in India's northeast: A holistic perspective," in Hussain, Wasbir (Ed.) *Order in chaos* (Guwahati/Delhi: Spectrum Publications).

———— (2006a), "Socio-political trends in southern Asia: Security implications for India," *Faultlines: Writings in Conflict & Resolution,* Vol. 17, pp. 73–104.

Ghosh, S.K. (1992), "The district police and public order," in Roy, J.G. (Ed.) *Policing a district* (New Delhi: Indian Institute of Public Administration).

Gill, K.P.S. (1994), "The dangers within: Internal security threats," in Bharat Karnad (Ed.) *Future imperilled: India's security in the 1990s and beyond* (New Delhi: Viking).

———— (1997), *The knights of falsehood* (Delhi: Har- Anand Publication).

———— (May 1999), "End game in Punjab: 1988–1993," *Faultlines: Writings on Conflict and Resolution,* Vol. 1, http://www.satp.org/satporgtp/publication/faultlines/volume1/ Fault1-kpstext.htm.

———— (2000), "Tackling terrorism in Kashmir: Some lessons from recent history," in M.L. Sondhi (Ed.) *Terror and political violence: A source book* (Delhi: Har-Anand Publications).

———— (2001), "Introduction," in Gill, K.P.S and Sahni, A. (Eds) *Terror and containment: Perspectives on India's internal security* (New Delhi: Gyan Publishing House).

———— (2001a), "Technology, terror and a thoughtless state," in Gill, K.P.S. and Sahni, A. (Eds) *Terror and containment: Perspectives on India's internal security* (New Delhi: Gyan Publishing House).

———— (June 30, 2001b), "Managing NE: More foresight needed," *Pioneer.*

———— (August 13, 2012), "Demographic Invasion," *Outlook.*

———— (October–December 2012a), "Observations on India's state and central intelligence apparatus." In The intelligence bureau: The first 125 years' a special issue of *The Indian Police Journal,* Vol. LIX, No. 4, (Delhi: Bureau of Police Research & Development).

———— (December 29, 2014), "Assam: Cyclical butchery," *South Asia Intelligence Review,* Vol. 13, No. 26.

Goldenberg, S. (1992), *Thinking methodologically* (New York: Harper Collins).

Gonzalez, Roberto (2009), *American counterinsurgency: Human science and the human terrain* (Chicago: Prickly Paradigm Press).

Goodhand, Jonathan (2000), "Research in conflict zones: Ethics and accountability," *Forced Migration Review* 8, No. 4, pp. 12–16, http://law.wustl.edu/Library/cdroms/ refugee/data/FMR%5CEnglish%5CFMR08%5CFmr8.4.pdf.

Gordon, Sandy (2008), "Policing terrorism in India," *Crime, Law and Social Change,* Vol. 50, Nos. 1–2, pp. 111–124.

Goswami, Debabrata (1996), *Military history of Tripura (1490 to 1947)* (Agartala: Tripura State Tribal Cultural Research Institute and Museum).

Goswami, Uddipana (2007), *International displacement, migration, and policy in Northeastern India* (Washington: East-West Center).

Graham, Stephen (2010), *Cities under siege: The new military urbanism* (London: Verso).

Gray, Colin S. (Winter 2007), "Irregular warfare: One nature, many characters," *Strategic Studies Quarterly,* pp. 35–57.

———— (2008), "Why strategy is difficult," in Mahnken, T.G. and Maiolo, J.A. (Eds) *Strategic studies: A reader* (New York: Routledge).

Gray, Colin S., Wirtz, James J., Baylis, John (2013), *Strategy in the contemporary world,* Fourth edition (Oxford: Oxford University Press).

Greenhill, K.M. and Staniland P. (2007), "Ten ways to lose at counterinsurgency," *Civil Wars,* Vol. *9,* No. *4,* pp. 402–419.

Gregory, Derek (2011), "The everywhere war," *The Geographical Journal,* Vol. *177,* No. 3 (September), pp. 238–250.

Grey, Jeff (2008), "Australia's counterinsurgencies: A brief history," *Australian Army Journal,* Vol. *V,* No. 2, pp. 17–26.

Guevara, Ernesto "Che" (2007), *Guerrilla warfare* (California, USA: BN Publishing), originally published in 1960.

Gurr, T. (1970), *Why men Rebel* (Princeton: Princeton University Press).

Hagan, F.E. (1993), *Research methods in criminal justice and criminology* (New York: Macmillan Publishing Company).

Haines, David R. (2009), "Coin in the real world," *Parameters,* Vol. *38,* No. 4, pp. 43–59.

Hansen, W., T. Gienanth, and R. Parkes (2006), *International and local policing in peace operations,* in report of the 8th International Police Workshop. (Berlin: Centre for International Peacekeeping (ZIF).

Harkavy, R.E. and Neuman, S.G. (2001), *Warfare and the Third World* (New York: Palgrave).

Haq, Mahbub-ul, (Fall/Winter 1998), "Human rights, security and governance," *Peace & Policy, Journal of the Toda Institute of Global Peace and Policy Research,* Dialogue of Civilisations for World Citizenship, Vol. *3,* No. 2.

Heickero, Roland (2014), "Cyber terrorism: Electronic jihad," *Strategic Analysis,* Vol. *38,* No. 4, pp. 554–565.

Hendrix, Cullen S. (2010), "Measuring state capacity: Theoretical and empirical implications for the study of civil conflict," *Journal of peace Research,* Vol. *47,* No. 3, pp. 273–285.

Herman, T. (2001), "The impenetrable identity wall: The study of violent conflicts by 'insiders' and 'outsiders,'" in Smyth, M. and Robinson G. (Eds) *Researching violently divided societies: ethical and methodological issues* (New York: United Nations University Press), pp. 77–92.

Hill, J. B. (2010), "Conflict policing: Policing in a time of war," *International Criminal Justice Review,* Vol. *20,* No. 4, pp. 384–397.

Hill, Stephen and Beger, Randall (2009), "A paramilitary policing juggernaut," *Social Justice,* Vol. *36,* No. 1, pp. 25–40.

Hindustan Times (August 11, 2013), "Army Chief wanted to hit Pak hard, LoC battle rages."

———— (November 06, 2000), "N-E States unite against militancy."

Hocking, Jenny (Spring 1988), "Counterterrorism as counterinsurgency: The British experience," *Social Justice,* Vol. *15,* No. 1, pp. 83–97.

Hoffman, Bruce (1998), *Inside terrorism* (New York: Columbia University Press).

Hoffman, Frank G. (2005), "Small wars revisited: The United States and non traditional wars," *Journal of Strategic Studies*, Vol. *28*, No. 6 (December), pp. 913–940.

Horowitz, Donald (1985), *Ethnic groups in conflict* (Berkeley: University of California Press).

Horowitz, S. and Sharma, D. (2008), "Democracies fighting ethnic insurgencies: Evidence from India," *Studies in Conflict and Terrorism*, Vol. *31*, No. 8, pp. 749–773.

Hsia, Timothy K. (2008), "Law enforcement professionals and the army," *Army*, July 2008. Reprinted in *JIIM Training Newsletter*, March 2011, Center for Army Lessons Learned, USA.

Human Security Report, Human Security Centre. (2005), *War and peace in the 21st century* (New York: Oxford University Press).

Huntington, Samuel (1968), *Political order in changing societies* (New haven, CT: Yale University Press).

Huntington, S.P. (1962), "Introduction," in Franklin M. Osanka (Ed.) *Modern Guerrilla warfare: Fighting communist Guerrilla movements, 1941–1961* (New York: The Free Press).

Hussain, Wasbir (December 22, 2003), "Going for the Kill," *South Asian Intelligence Review*, Vol. 2, No. 23, http://www.satp.org/satporgtp/sair/Archives/2_23.htm#assessment1.

——— (August 18, 2003a), "Tripura: In the rebels' firing line," South Asian Intelligence Review, Vol. 2, No. 5, http://www.satp.org/satporgtp/sair/Archives/2_5.htm.

——— (February 2006), "Insurgency in India's northeast: Cross-border links and strategic alliances," *Faultlines: Writings on Conflict and Resolution*, Vol. 17, http://www.satp.org/satporgtp/publication/faultlines/volume17/wasbir.htm.

——— (2006a), "Insurgency Sans borders: An analysis of separatist insurrections in India's northeast," in Hussain, Wasbir (Ed.) *Order in Chaos: Essays on Conflict in India's Northeast and the Road to Peace in South Asia* (Guwahati/Delhi: Spectrum Publications).

Ibrahim, Azeem (Winter 2004), "Conceptualisation of Guerrilla Warfare," *Small Wars & Insurgencies*, Vol. *15*, No. 3, pp. 112–124.

Inbar, E. (2003), *Democracies and small wars* (London: Frank Cass).

India Today (October 10, 2012), "Defender of the last bastion."

——— (December 17, 2012), "The paranoid state."

——— (January 7, 2013), "The angry Indian: Newsmaker 2012," www.indiatoday.in.

India Today Group (2014), "Mood of the nation poll."

India Today (May 4, 2015), "Fake naxal scam."

Institute for Conflict Management (ICM) (2007), "*Project report on insurgency and special challenges to policing in India's northeast: A case study of Tripura police*" submitted to The Bureau of Police Research and Development, Government of India, New Delhi.

IW (November 2006), "Policing society in counterinsurgency," *IW Message of the Month*.

Jackson, Richard (2004), "The social construction of internal war," in Richard Jackson (Ed.) *(Re) Constructing cultures of violence and peace* (Rodopi: Amsterdam and New York), pp. 61–77.

Jackson and Lyon (2002), "Policing after ethnic conflict: Culture, democratic, democratic policing, politics and the public," *Policing: An International Journal of Police*, Vol. 25, No. 2, pp. 221–241.

Jafa, V.S. (August 1999), "Administrative policies and ethnic disintegration: Engineering conflict in India's northeast," *Faultlines: Writings on Conflict and Resolution*, Vol. 2, http://www.satp.org/satporgtp/publication/faultlines/volume2/Fault2-JafaF.htm.

————— (2001), "Counterinsurgency Warfare: The Use and Abuse of Military Force," in K.P.S. Gill and A. Sahni (Ed.) *Terror and Containment: Perspectives of India's Internal Security'* (New Delhi: Gyan Publishing House).

Jefferson, Tony (1990), *The case against paramilitary policing* (Philadelphia: Open University Press).

Jeffries, C.J., Sir (1952), *The colonial police* (London: Parrish).

Johnson, S. (1806), *A dictionary of the English language* (London: Published by printed for J. Johnson et al).

Jones, S.G., Wilson, J.M., Rathmell, A., and Riley, K.J. (2005), *Establishing law and order after conflict* (Santa Monica, CA: RAND Corporation).

Kalyanraman, Sankaran (2003), "The Indian way in counterinsurgency," in Inbar, E.(Ed.) *Democracies and small wars* (London: Frank Cass Publishers), pp. 85–100.

Kalyvas, S.N. (2006), *The logic of violence in civil war* (Cambridge University Press).

Kanwal, Gurmeet and N. Manoharan (January 2009), "Countering urban terrorism in India," Centre for Land Warfare Studies, Issue Brief No. 6, pp. 1–6, http://www.claws.in/images/publication_pdf/779343069_CLAWSIssuebrief,No.6,2009.pdf.

————— (May 14, 2012), "India's counter terrorism policies are mired in systemic weaknesses," *Institute of Defence Studies and Analyses.*

Kaplan, Robert D. (February 1994), "The coming anarchy," *The Atlantic Monthly,* Vol. 273, No. 2, pp. 44–76.

Kapoor, Rajesh (2010), "Revolution in military affairs and counterinsurgency in India," Working Paper No. 2, Centre for land Warfare Studies, http://www.claws.in/Revolution-Military-Affairs.pdf.

Kelling, G.L. and Bratton, W.J. (2006), "Policing terrorism," *Civic Bulletin* 43 (New York: Manhattan Institute).

Kelling, G.L. and Moore, Mark H. (September 1988), *The evolving strategy of policing*, Paper presented at Harvard University's John F. Kennedy School's Executive Session on Policing.

Kennedy, David (April 2010), "Hope and despair," Police *Practice and Research,* Vol. 11, No. 2, pp. 166–170.

Khan, M.H. and Mangathai, R.A. (2003), *Human rights in Tripura* (Mussoorie: LBS National Academy of Administration).

Khangchian, Veronica (December 12, 2011), "The vanity of hope," *South Asia Intelligence Review,* Vol. 10, No. 23.

————— (January 23, 2012), "India: Meghalaya: Festering wounds," *South Asia Intelligence Review,* Vol. 10, No. 29.

————— (April 16, 2012a), "Naga factionalism escalates," *South Asia Intelligence Review,* Vol. 10, No. 41.

Kilcullen, David (2000), "The Political Consequences of Military Operations in Indonesia 1945-99: A fieldwork analysis of the political power-diffusion effects of guerrilla conflict," PhD Dissertation, Politics, Australian Defence Force Academy, UNSW.

————— (Winter 2006), "Counterinsurgency *redux*," *Survival,* Vol. 48, No. 4, pp. 111–130.

————— (2009), *The accidental Guerrilla: Fighting small wars in the midst of a big one* (Carlton North, Australia: Scribe Publications).

————— (2010), *Counterinsurgency* (Carlton North, Australia: Scribe Publications).

Kiras (2007), "Irregular warfare: Terrorism and insurgency," in Baylis, John, Wirtz J. James, and Gray, Colin S. (Eds) *Strategy in the Contemporary World* (Oxford University Press), pp. 163–190.

Kiszely, Sir John (Lieutenant General) (December 2007), "Post-modern challenges for modern warriors," *The Shrivenham Papers*, No. 5.

Kitson, Frank (1971), *Low-intensity operations: Subversion, insurgency and peacekeeping* (London: Faber and Faber).

Knutsson, Johannes (April 2010), "Nordic reflections on the "dialogue of the deaf," *Police Practice and Research*, Vol. 11, No. 2, pp. 132–134.

Kohli, Atul (May 1997), "Can democracies accommodate ethnic nationalism? Rise and decline of self-determination movements in India," *The Journal of Asian Studies*, Vol. 56, No. 2, pp. 325–344.

Kraska, Peter. B (February 1997), "Militarizing American police: The rise and normalization of paramilitary units," *Social Problems*, Vol. 44, No. 1, pp. 1–18.

Kraska (2007), "Militarization and policing Its relevance to 21st century police," *Policing*, Vol. 1, No. 4, pp. 501–513.

Kratcoski, Peter (May 2004), "Police education and training in a global society: Guest editor's introduction," *Police Practice and Research*, Vol. 5, No. 2, pp. 103–105.

Krepinevich, A.F. (1986), *The army and Vietnam* (Baltimore: Johns Hopkins University Press).

Kumar, B.B. (2007), *Problems of ethnicity in the north-east India* (New Delhi: Concept Publishing Company).

Kumar, Kuldeep, *Counterinsurgency operations in Tripura (India) since 2000*, unpublished Master's thesis, Department of Criminology, Leicester University, UK.

Kumar, Praveen (July 2003), "Tripura: Beyond the insurgency: Politics nexus," *Faultlines: Writings on Conflict & Resolution*, Vol. 14, http://www.satp.org/satporgtp/publication/faultlines/volume14/index.html.

——— (2003a), "Tripura: Lethal strikes from external bases," *South Asia Intelligence Review*, Vol. 1, No. 43, http://www.satp.org/satporgtp/sair/Archives/1_43.htm.

——— (July–September 2004), "External linkages and internal security: Assessing Bhutan's operation all clear," *Strategic Analysis*, Vol. 28, No. 3, Institute for Defence Studies and Analyses, pp. 390–410.

Lacina, Bethany (September 8–10, 2005), "Rebels as lobbyists: A political theory of asymmetrical insurgency," Paper presented at the *Third European Consortium for Political Research General Conference, Budapest*.

——— (July–September 2007), "Does counterinsurgency theory apply in northeast India," *India Review*, Vol. 6, No. 3, pp. 165–183.

——— (2009a), "Rethinking Delhi's northeast India's policy: Why neither counterinsurgency nor winning hearts and minds is the way forward," in Baruah, S. (Ed.) *Beyond counter-insurgency* (pp. 329–342), New Delhi: Oxford University Press.

Lacina, Bethany (2009b), "The problem of political stability in northeast India: Local ethnic autocracy and the rule of law," *Asian Survey*, Vol. 49, No. 6, pp. 998–1020.

Ladwig, W.C., III (2009), "Insights from the northeast," in Ganguly, S. and Fidler, D.P. (Eds) *India and counterinsurgency: Lessons learned* (pp. 45–62), London: Routledge.

Lakshman, K and Jha, S.K. (2003), "India-Bangladesh: Restoring sovereignty on neglected borders," *Faultlines: Writings on Conflict and Resolution*, Vol. 14, http://www.satp.org/satporgtp/publication/faultlines/volume14/Article7.htm.

Laws, S. (2003), *Research for development: A practical guide* (New Delhi: Vistaar Publications).

Leahy, Peter, Lt. General (Winter 2008), "'Introduction' to 'counterinsurgency,'" Special edition of *Australian Army Journal*, Vol. V, No. 2, pp. 9–16 (Land Warfare Studies, Australia).

Lenoir, J.C.P. (1779), *M'emoire sur la Police en France, et Particulierement sur la Police de Paris, Presente a la Reine de Naples* (second version), Document Manuscript, University Library of Cambridge, Rare Books Department, Paris, Classmark–Add. 4651.

Liang, Qiao and Xiangsui, Wang (2002), *Unrestricted warfare* (Panama city: Pan American Publishing Company), originally published in 1999 By China's People Liberation Army, Beijing.

Libicki, Martin C., David C. Gompert, David R. Frelinger, and Raymond Smith (2007), *Byting back: Regaining information superiority against 21st century insurgents* (Santa Monica: Rand).

Liddel-Hart, Basil (1943), *Thoughts on war* (London: Faber and Faber).

Lintner, Bertil, "Bangladesh: A cocoon of terror," *Far Eastern Economic Review*, Hong Kong, April 4, 2002, pp. 14–17.

Long, Austin (2006), *On other war: Lessons from five decades of RAND counterinsurgency research* (Santa Monica, CA: Rand).

Louise, Christopher (1995), The social impacts of light weapons availability and proliferation, *United Nations Research Institute for Discussion Paper (UNRISD-59)*, United Nations Research Institute for Social Development.

Lutterbeck, Derek (2004), "Between police and military: The new security agenda and the rise of gendarmeries," *Cooperation and Conflict: Journal of the Nordic International Studies Association*, Vol. 39, No. 1, pp. 45–68.

Madhab, J. (February 1999), "North-east: Crisis of identity, security and underdevelopment," *Economic and Political Weekly* (Mumbai), Vol. 34, No. 6, pp. 320–322.

Mahadevan, Prem (2008), "The Gill doctrine: A model for 21st century policing," in *Faultlines: Writings in Conflict & Resolution*, Vol. 19, http://www.satp.org/satporgtp/publication/faultlines/volume19/Article1.htm.

———— (2009), *The politics of rebellion*, Research Paper No. 134, http://www.rieas.gr/images/rieas134.pdf.

———— (2012), *The politics of counterterrorism in India: Strategic intelligence and national security in South Asia* (London: I. B. Tauris).

Mahajan, Neeraj (2012), "The collusion: Politico-business nexus," *g files*, November 2012, Vol. 6, No. 8, http://gfilesindia.com/Contents/pdfMagazine/Nov2012/Default.html.

Mahapatra, D. (August 13, 2012), "How illegal immigrants morphed into an invaluable vote-bank," *Times of India*, http://articles.timesofindia.indiatimes.com/2012-08-13/india/33181550_1_illegal-migrants-illegal-migration-aggression.

Mahnken, T.G. and Maiolo, J.A. (Eds) (2008), *Strategic studies: A reader* (New York: Routledge).

Manning, Peter K. (March 2005), "The study of policing," *Police Quarterly*, Vol. 8, No. 1, pp. 23–43.

Manwaring, Max G. (2002), "The new global security landscape: The road ahead," *Low-intensity Conflict & Enforcement*, Vol. 11, Nos. 2–3, pp. 190–209.

Mao Tse-Tung (1961), *On Guerrilla warfare*. Translated by Samuel B. Griffith Foreword by Captain B.H. Liddel Hart (London: Cassell).

———— (1967), *Selected military writings of Mao Tse-Tung* (Beijing: Foreign Language Press).

Marighella, Carlos (1969), *Mini-manual of the urban Guerrilla*, http://www.socialhistoryportal.org/sites/default/files/raf/0719730000_0.pdf.

Markon, Jerry (December 5, 2010), "Tension grows between Calif. Muslims, FBI after informer infiltrates mosque," *Washington Post*.

Markowski, Stefan, Koorey, Stephanie, Hall, Peter, and Brauer, Jurgen (2008), "Channels of small-arms proliferation: Policy implications for Asia-Pacific," *The Economics of Peace and Security Journal*, Vol. 3, No. 1, http://www.stonegardeneconomics.com/pubs/2008_Markowski_Koorey_Hall_Brauer_EPSJ_v3n1.pdf.

Marks, Thomas A. (2003), "Urban insurgency," *Small Wars & Insurgencies*, Vol. 14, No. 3, pp. 100–157.

Marwah, V. (2009), "India's counterinsurgency campaign in Punjab," in Ganguly, S. and Fidler, D.P. (Eds) *India and counterinsurgency: Lessons learned* (pp. 89–106), London: Routledge.

Mason, David T. (1996), "Insurgency, counterinsurgency, and the rational peasant," *Public Choice*, Vol. 86, pp. 63–83.

Mathur, Anant (January 10, 2011), "Secrets of COIN success: Lessons from the Punjab campaign," *Faultlines: Writings on Conflict and Resolution*, Vol. 20, http://www.satp.org/satporgtp/publication/faultlines/volume20/Article2.htm.

Mazumdar, Arijit, (2013), "Left-wing extremism and counterinsurgency in India: The 'Andhra model,'" *Strategic Analysis*, Vol. 37, No. 4, pp. 446–462.

McAdam, Doug, Tarrow Sidney, and Tilly, Charles (2001), *Dynamics of contention* (Cambridge: Cambridge University Press).

McClellan, George B. (1966), "Observations on police leadership," *The Journal of Criminal Law, Criminology, and Police Science*, Vol. 57, No. 3, pp. 354–355.

McCuen, John J. (1966), *The art of counter-revolutionary war* (Harrisburg, PA: Stockpole Books).

McCulloch, Jude (2001), *Blue army: Paramilitary policing in Australia* (Victoria: Melbourne University Press).

——— (2001a), "Paramilitary surveillance: S11, globalization, terrorists & counter – terrorists," *Current Issues in Criminal Justice*, Vol. 13, No. 1, pp. 23–35.

McDuie-Ra, Duncan (2009), "Vision 2020 or Re-vision 1958; the contradictory politics of counterinsurgency in India's regional engagement," *Contemporary South Asia*, Vol. 17, No. 3, pp. 313–330.

McMaster, H.R. (2008), "On war: Lessons to be learned," *Survival*, Vol. 50, No. 1, pp. 19–30.

Menon, N.R.M. (Ed.) (2005), "*Criminal justice India series, volume XII, Tripura, 2003*," National University of Juridical Sciences, Kolkata (New Delhi: Allied Publishers Pvt. Limited).

Merton, R. (July 1972), "Insiders and outsiders: A chapter in the sociology of knowledge," *American Journal of Sociology*, Vol. 78, No. 1, pp. 9–47.

Metz, Steven (2007), "New challenges and old concepts: Understanding 21st century insurgency," *Parameters*, Vol. 37, No. 4, p. 20.

Metz, Steven and Raymond Millen (2004), *Insurgency and counterinsurgency in the 21st century: Reconceptualising threat and response* (Carlisle Barracks, PA: U.S. Army War College).

Miklian, Jason (2011), "Revolutionary conflict in federations: The Indian case," *Conflict, Security & Development*, Vol. 11, No. 01, pp. 25–53.

Mishra, T.N. (2007), *Barrel of the gun: The Maoist challenge and Indian democracy* (New Delhi: Sheridan Book Company).

Mitra, D.M. (2007), *Understanding Indian insurgencies: Implications for counterinsurgency operations in the Third World*, U.S. Army war College, The Letort Papers.

Mockaitis, Thomas R. (2008), *The "New" terrorism: Myths and reality* (Stanford, CA: Stanford University Press).

Mohan, C.R. (2006), "India and the balance of power," *Foreign Affairs*, Vol. 85, No. 4, http://proquest.umi.com.ezproxy.lib.monash.edu.au/pqdlink?Ver=1&Exp=04-19-2016&FMT=7&DID=1058765521&RQT=309&cfc=1.

Mohanty, Tushar Ranjan (December 07, 2009a), "Assam: Watershed transformations," *South Asian Intelligence Review*, Vol. 8, No. 22, http://www.satp.org/satporgtp/sair/Archives/sair8/8_22.htm#assessment2.

——— (February 2, 2009b), "Tripura: Steady gains," *South Asian Intelligence Review*, Vol. 7, No. 30, http://www.satp.org/satporgtp/sair/Archives/7_30.htm#assessment2.

Moore, R. Scott (2007), "The basics of counterinsurgency," *Small Wars Journal*, http://smallwarsjournal.com/documents/moorecoinpaper.pdf.

Moyar, Mark (2009), *A question of command: Counterinsurgency from the civil war to Iraq* (New Haven: Yale University Press).

——— (Winter 2010), "Leadership in counterinsurgency," *The Fletcher Forum of World Affairs*, Vol. 34, No. 1, pp. 135–146.

Mukherjee, Anit (2013), "Failing to deliver: Post-crises defence reforms in India, 1998-2010," in Bajpai, Kanti P. and Pant, Harsh V. (Eds) *India's national security: A reader* (New Delhi: Oxford University Press).

Mukerjee, Jhumpa (2014), *Conflict resolution in multicultural societies: The Indian experience* (New Delhi: SAGE Publications).

Murayama, Mayumi (April 8–14, 2006), "Borders, migration and sub-regional cooperation in eastern South Asia," *Economic and Political Weekly*, Vol. XLI, No. 14, pp. 1351–1359.

Muzzatti, Stephen L. (2005), "The police, the public, and the post-liberal politics of fear: Paramilitary policing post 9/11," in James F. Hodgson and Catherine Orban (Eds) *Public policing in the 21st century: Issues and dilemmas in the U.S. and Canada* (New York: Criminal Justice Press).

Nagl, John A. (2002), *Counterinsurgency lessons from Malaya and Vietnam: Learning to eat soup with a knife* (Westport: Praeger).

Nanda, Prakash (2012), "Turmoil in Bodoland," *Indian Defence Review*, July 26, 2012, net edition, http://www.indiandefencereview.com/news/turmoil-in-bodoland/

Nardi, Dominic J. (Winter–Spring 2008), "Cross–border chaos: A critique of India's attempts to secure its Northeast tribal areas through cooperation with Myanmar," *SAIS Review of International Affairs*, Vol. XXVIII, No. 1, pp. 161–171.

Nepram, B. (2001), "The origin and impact of small wars and insurgencies in the Northeast," *Himalayan and Central Asian Studies*, Vol. 5, Nos. 3–4, p. 56.

Nepram, B. (2004), *Gun wars and drug deaths in South Asia*, A talk delivered at a seminar hosted by South Asia Partnership, Canada and CPCC Small Arms Working Group.

Newman, Graeme R. and Clarke, Ronald V. (2008), *Policing and terrorism: An executive guide*, US Department of Justice, Office of Community Oriented Police Services (COPS), Washington, DC-20530.

Ngaihte, T. (2014), "Beyond the Indo-Naga talks: Some reflections," *Strategic Analysis*, Vol. 38, No. 1, pp. 25–30.

Nibedon, Nirmal (1985), *Night of the Guerrillas* (New Delhi: Lancer Books).

Northeast Today (April 15, 2012), "2000 TTADC fearing Manik Sarkar."

Oetken, J.L. (2009), "Counterinsurgency against Naxalites in India." In Ganguly, S and Fidler, D.P. (Ed.) *India and counterinsurgency: Lessons learned* (pp. 127–151), London: Routledge.

Omotola, Shola J. (September–October 2012), "Legitimacy crisis and 'popular uprisings' in North Africa," *Strategic Analysis*, Vol. *36*, No. 5, pp. 713–719.

O'Neill, Bard E. (1990), *Insurgency & terrorism: Inside modern revolutionary warfare* (Virginia: Brassey's, Inc).

O'Neill, Lieutenant Colonel Mark (Winter 2008), "Back to the future: The enduring characteristics of insurgency and counterinsurgency," *Australian Army Journal*, Vol. V, No. 2, pp. 41–56.

Oneindia (February 24, 2008), "Takarjala votes without fear."

Oneworld South Asia (July 28, 2004), "Children bunk class, join terror school in India's northeast," Syed Zahir Hussain.

Operation Enduring Freedom, icasualties, http://icasualties.org/oef/. *Oriental Times* (May 22–June 6, 2000), "IPFT captures TTADC: When ballot bows before bullet," Vol. 2, No. 47–48.

Osaghae, E. and Robinson, G (2005), "Introduction," in Porter, E., Robinson G., Smyth, M., and Schnabel, A. (Eds) *Researching conflict in Africa: Insights and experiences* (Tokyo: United Nations University Press).

Outlook (January 10, 2012) "President's Colour for Tripura Police," Agartala.

Oxford Advanced Learner's Dictionary (2000), A.S. Hornby, Sixth edition (Oxford University Press).

Paget, J. (1967), *Counterinsurgency campaigning: Techniques of Guerrilla warfare* (New York: Walker and Co.).

Pampinella, Stephen (2012), "Hegemonic competition in intrastate war: The social construction of insurgency and counterinsurgency in Iraq's al-Anbar Province," *Studies in Conflict & Terrorism*, Vol. *35*, No. 2, pp. 95–112.

Patankar, V.G. (2009), "Insurgency, proxy war and terrorism in Kashmir," in Ganguly, S. and Fidler, D.P. (Eds.) India *and counterinsurgency: Lessons learned* (London: Routledge).

Paterson, Craig (August 2011), "Adding value? A review of the international literature on the role of higher education in police training and education," *Police Practice and Research*, Vol. *12*, No. 4, pp. 286–297.

Paul, Manas (2009), *The eyewitness: Tales from Tripura's ethnic conflict* (New Delhi: Lancer Publishers & Distributors).

Paul, T.V. (October-December 2013), "Why has the India-Pakistan rivalry been so enduring? Power asymmetry and an intractable conflict," *Security Studies*, Vol. *15*, No. 4, pp. 600–630.

Petraeus, David H (January–February 2006), "Learning counterinsurgency: Observations from soldiering in Iraq," *Military Review*, p. 45, http://www.au.af.mil/AU/awc/awcgate/milreview/petraeus1.pdf.

Phanjoubam, P. (2002), "Ethnicity, identity & conflict." In *Faultlines: Writings on Conflict and Resolution*, Vol. *10*, http://www.satp.org/satporgtp/publication/faultlines/volume10/Article5.htm.

Piazza, James A. (2010), "Terrorism and party systems in the states of India," *Security Studies*, Vol. *19*, No. 1, pp. 99–123.

Pickering, S., McCulloch, J., Wright-Neville, D. (2008), *Counter-terrorism policing: Community, cohesion and security* (New York: Springer).

Pillai, S.K. (October 2002), "Insurgencies in northeast India," in *Aakrosh*, Vol. 5, No. 17, pp. 31–52.

Pimlott, John (1988), "The British experience," in Beckett, Ian (Ed.) *The roots of counter-insurgency: Armies and Guerrilla warfare* (pp. 17–38), London: Blandford Press.

Poffenberger, Mark (2006), *Forest sector review of northeast India,* Background paper No. 12, Community Forestry International, Santa Barbara, CA, USA.

Ponterotto, Joseph G. (2006), "Brief note on the origins, evolution, and meaning of the qualitative research concept 'Thick Description,'" *The Qualitative Report*, Vol. 11, No. 3 (September), pp. 538–549, http://www.nova.edu/ssss/QR/QR11-3/ponterotto.pdf.

Porch, Douglas (May 2011), "The dangerous myths and dubious promise of COIN," *Small Wars and insurgencies,* Vol. 22, No. 2, pp. 239–257.

Prakash, Arun (2012), "National security reforms: Ten years after the Kargil Committee Report," *USI National Lecture 2012,* delivered on December 5, 2012 at USI, New Delhi, http://www.usiofindia.org/Article/?pub=Journal&pubno=590&ano=1384.

Press Trust of India (June 13, 2012), "Govt. mulls options to fill up 3,400 vacancies," http://www.greaterkashmir.com/news/2012/Jun/13/govt-mulls-options-to-fill-up-3-400- vacancies-in-ias-ips-ifos-51.asp.

Pritchett, Lant (2009), *Is India a Flailing state? Detours on the four lane highway to modernization*, HKS Faculty Research Working Paper Series RWPO9 -013 (John F. Kennedy School of Government-Harvard University).

Puri, H.K. (2002), "Ethno-national politics: Some lessons from Canada," in Singh, G. (Ed.) *Ethno-nationalism and the emerging world (Dis)order* (New Delhi: Omsons Publications).

Quinlivan, James T. (Winter 1995), "Force requirement in stability operations," *Parameters,* pp. 59–69), http://www.carlisle.army.mil/usawc/Parameters/Articles/1995/quinliv.htm.

Rajgopalan, R. (Spring 2000), "Restoring normalcy: The evolution of the Indian army's counterinsurgency doctrine', *Small war and Insurgencies*, Vol. 11, No. 1, pp. 44–68.

Rajagopalan, Swarna (2008), *Peace accords in northeast India,* policy studies (Washington: East-West Center).

Ramana, P.V. (2002), "'Networking' the northeast: Partners in terror," *Faultlines: Writings in Conflict and Resolution,* Vol. 11, http://www.satp.org/satporgtp/publication/faultlines/volume11/Article6.htm.

Rammohan (2002), "Manipur: A degenerated insurgency," *Faultlines: Writings on Conflict and Resolution,* Vol. 11, http://www.satp.org/satporgtp/publication/faultlines/volume11/Article1.htm.

Rammohan, E.N. (2005), "Insurgency in the northeast-Tripura," *Agni*, Vol. 8, No. 1, pp. 60–69.

Ransley, J. and Mazerolle, L. (August 2009), "Policing in an era of uncertainty," *Police Practice and Research,*Vol. 10, No. 4, pp. 365–381.

Rao, B.V. (January 1–15, 2013), "Govern us, please govern us!" *Governance Now.*

Ravi, R.N. (January 23, 2014), "Nagaland: Descent into chaos," *The Hindu.*

Government is complicit in communal violence," May 8, 2014, Rediff.com.

Reddy, Sanjeev P.L. and Reddy, Shekar P.C. (2007), *Peace and development in northeast: A virtuous spiral* (New Delhi: Mittal Publications).

Reiner, R. (2000), *The politics of the police*, 3rd Edition (Oxford: Oxford University Press).

Richman, Daniel C., "The changing boundaries between federal and local law enforcement," in Charles M.F. (Ed.), National Institute of Justice 2000 series, *Boundary changes in criminal justice organizations* (Vol. 2, pp. 81–111), Washington D.C.: National Institute of Justice, http://citeseerx.ist.psu.edu/viewdoc/download?doi=10.1.1.207.4289&rep=rep1&type=pdf.

Rich, P.B. and Stubbs, R. (1997), *The counterinsurgent state: Guerrilla warfare and state building in the twentieth Century* (London: MacMillan Press Ltd.).

Routray, B.P. (May 01, 2006a), "Manipur: The state abdicates," *South Asian Intelligence Review*, Vol. 4, No. 42, South Asia Terrorism Portal, http://www.satp.org/satporgtp/sair/Archives/4_42.htm#assessment2.

———— (July 24, 2006b), "India's northeast: Long shadows of subversion," *South Asian Intelligence Review*, Vol. 5, No. 2, South Asia Terrorism Portal, http://www.satp.org/satporgtp/sair/Archives/5_2.htm#assessment2.

Routray, B.P. (November 27, 2006c), "Nagaland: The frozen theatre of 'Peace,'" *South Asia Intelligence Review*, http://www.satp.org/satporgtp/sair/Archives/5_20.htm#assessment1.

———— (June 18, 2007a), "Manipur: Extortion rules," *South Asia Intelligence Review*, Vol. 5, No. 49, http://www.satp.org/satporgtp/sair/Archives/5_49.htm#assessment2.

———— (October 15, 2007b), "Manipur: Nexus again," *South Asia Intelligence Review*, Vol. 6, No. 14, South Asia Terrorism Portal, http://www.satp.org/satporgtp/sair/Archives/6_14.htm#assessment2.

Routray, B.P. (November 17, 2008a), "Epitome of police ineptitude," *South Asian Intelligence Review*, Vol. 7, No. 19, South Asia Terrorism Portal, http://www.satp.org/satporgtp/sair/Archives/7_19.htm#assessment1n.

———— (June 09, 2008b), "Nagaland: Beginning of an end?" *South Asia Intelligence Review*, Vol. 6, No. 48, http://www.satp.org/satporgtp/sair/Archives/6_48.htm#assessment2.

Roy, H. and Dastidar, S.G. (2011), "Dynamics of economic growth: A study of some selected Indian states," *Asian Journal of Business and Economics*, Vol. 1, No. 1, pp. 1–44.

Rowe, Michael (2006), "Following the Leader: Front-line narratives on police leadership," *Policing: An International Journal of Police Strategies and Management*, Vol. 29, No. 4, pp. 757–767.

Sachdeva, G. (2000), "India's northeast: Rejuvenating a conflict-driven economy," *Faultlines: Writings on Conflict and Resolution*, Vol. 6, http://www.satp.org/satporgtp/publication/faultlines/volume6/Fault6-GSach-F.htm.

———— (2013), "Economic consequences of conflicts in northeast India," in V.R. Raghavan (Ed.) *Consequences of long-term conflicts in northeast India* (New Delhi: Vij Books Pvt. Ltd.).

Sahni, A. (2001), "Social science and contemporary conflicts: The challenge of research on terrorism," *Faultlines: Writings on Conflict and Resolution*, Vol. 9, http://www.satp.org/satporgtp/publication/faultlines/volume9/Article5.htm.

———— (2001a), "The terrorist economy in India's north east: Preliminary explorations," *Faultlines: Writings on Conflict and Resolution*, Vol. 8, http://www.satp.org/satporgtp/publication/faultlines/volume8/Article5.htm.

Sahni, A. (2002a), "Survey of conflicts and resolutions in India's north-east," *Faultlines: Writings on Conflict and Resolution,* Vol. 12, http://www.satp.org/satporgtp/publication/faultlines/volume12/Article3.htm.

———— (2002b), "Tripura: The politics of ethnic terror," *South Asia Intelligence Review,* Vol. 1, No. 6, http://www.satp.org/satporgtp/sair/Archives/1_6.htm#assessment2.

———— (November 3, 2003), "India-Pakistan : Another swing of the Pendulum," *South Asia Intelligence Review,* Vol. 2, No. 16.

———— (2005), "Naxalism: The retreat of civil governance," *Faultlines: Writings on Conflict and Resolution,* Vol. 5, http://www.satp.org/satporgtp/publication/faultlines/volume 5/Fault5-7asahni.htm

———— (2005a), "Counterinsurgency success," *South Asia Intelligence Review,* (August 29, 2005).

———— (2008), "Strategic vastu shastra," *South Asia Intelligence Review,* Vol. 7, No. 24 (December 22), http://www.satp.org/satporgtp/sair/Archives/7_24.htm.

———— (2008a), "Foreword," *Faultlines: Writings on Conflict and Resolution,* Vol. 19, http://www.satp.org/satporgtp/publication/faultlines/volume19/Foreword.htm.

———— (2009), "The peacock and the ostrich," *South Asia Intelligence Review,* Vol. 8, No. 7 (August 24), http://www.satp.org/satporgtp/sair/Archives/sair8/8_7.htm#assessment1.

———— (2009b), "National responses to terrorism," *National Security Paper-2009,* United Services Institute, http://satp.org/satporgtp/ajaisahni/09AS-11London.htm.

———— (2009c), "Capacity and Infirmity in Counter-terrorism," Outline Presentation at the afternoon debate at Committee Room 3, The House of Lords on Terrorism, democracy and the rule of law—Can democracy and the rule of law fight terrorism effectively?' http://www.satp.org/satporgtp/ajaisahni/09AS-11London.htm.

———— (2009d), "Counter-terrorism and the 'flailing state,'" *Eternal India,* Vol. 1, No. 5, http://satp.org/satporgtp/ajaisahni/09AS-7EtInd.htm.

———— (2009e), "*Global terrorism in an age of uncertainty,*" Presentation at the seminar on "War against global terror" by Centre for Joint Warfare Studies Dr. D.S. Kothari Auditorium, New Delhi on April 15, 2009, http://satp.org/satporgtp/ajaisahni/09AS-14CJOWS.htm.

———— (2010), "The threat within: Strengthening internal security mechanisms," *USI National Security Lecture, 2010* on December 15, 2010, http://www.satp.org/satporgtp/ajaisahni/10AS-usi.htm#1.

———— (2010a), "Counter-insurgency: Some myths and principles," Presentation at the *40th All India Police Science Congress on June 2, 2010,* http://satp.org/satporgtp/ajaisahni/2010/presantionjune2.htm.

———— (2010b), "Where the buck stops," *Indian Express,* May 28.

———— (2010c), "India's Maoists and the dreamscape of 'Solutions,'" http://satp.org/satporgtp/ajaisahni/10AS-3Seminar.htm.

———— (2012), "The northeast: Troubling externalities," *South Asia Intelligence Review,* Vol. 10, No. 38 (March 26), http://www.satp.org/satporgtp/sair/Archives/sair10/10_38.htm

———— (2013), "Naxalism: The retreat of civil governance." In Bajpai, Kanti P. and Pant, Harsh V. (Eds) *India's national security: A reader* (New Delhi: Oxford University Press).

Sahni, A. (June 30, 2014), "Rousing a crippled giant," *SAIR Weekly Assessments & Briefings*, Vol. *12*, No. *52*, http://www.satp.org/satporgtp/sair/Archives/sair12/12_52.htm #assessment1.

Sahni, A. and Routray, B.P. (August 29, 2005a), "Counter-insurgency success," *South Asia Intelligence Review, Weekly Assessments & Briefings*, Vol. *4*, No.7, http://satp.org/satporgtp/sair/Archives/4_7.htm#assessment1.

Saikia, Jaideep (2000), "The ISI reaches east: Anatomy of a conspiracy," *Faultlines: Writings on Conflict and Resolution*, Vol. *VI*, http://www.satp.org/satporgtp/publication/faultlines/volume6/Fault6-JSaikia-F.htm.

———— (2004), *Terror Sans Frontiers: Islamist militancy in northeast India* (New Delhi: Vision Books).

———— (2009), "Circle of design: 'Proxy Wars' in north east India." In Saikia, Jaideep, and Stepanova, Ekaterina (Eds) *Terrorism: Patterns of internationalization* (New Delhi: SAGE Publications).

Saikia, Pahi (2011), "Political Opportunities, Constraints, and Mobilizing Structures: An Integrated Approach to Different Levels of Ethno-Political Contention in North-East India," *India Review*, Vol. *10*, No. 1, pp. 1–39.

Salmoni, Barak A., Hart, Jessica, McPherson, R., and Winn, Aidan Kirby (Spring 2010), "Growing Strategic leaders for future conflict," *Parameters*, Vol. *40*, No. 1, pp. 72–88.

Sarkar, B. (1998), *Tackling insurgency and terrorism: Blueprint for action* (New Delhi: Vision Books).

Schleifer, R. (2003), "Democracies, limited war and psychological operations," in Inbar, E. (Ed.) *Democracies and small wars* (London: Frank Crass).

Schnabel, A. (2005), "Preventing and managing conflict: The role of the researcher," in Porter, E., Robinson G., Smyth, M., and Schnabel A (Eds) *Researching conflict in Africa: Insights and experiences* (Tokyo: United Nations University Press), pp. 24–43.

Sen, Amartya (1973), *On economic inequality* (Oxford: Clarendon Press).

Sen, Gautam (2013), IDSA Comment, Nagaland: Political and Economic Assessment, http://www.idsa.in/idsacomments/NagalandPoliticalandEconomicAssessment_gsen_100613.html.

Sepp, K. (2005), "Best practices in counterinsurgency," *Military Review*, Vol. *85*, No. 3, pp. 8–12.

Sewall, Sarah (2007), "Introduction," *The U.S. Army/Marine Corps Counterinsurgency Field Manual: U.S. Army Field Manual No. 3–24* (Chicago: The University of Chicago Press).

Shearing, Clifford and Marks, Monique (2011), "Being a new police in the liquid century," *Policing*, Vol. *5*, No. 3, pp. 210–218.

Shekatkar, D.B. (2009), "India's counterinsurgency campaign in Nagaland," in Ganguly, S. and Fidler, D.P. (Eds) *India and counterinsurgency: Lessons learned* (London: Routledge), pp. 9–27.

Singh, Chandrika (2004), *North-east India: Politics & insurgency* (New Delhi: Manas Publications).

Singh, G. (1984), "Socio-economic bases of the Punjab crisis," *Economic & Political Weekly*, No. 1, pp. 42–47.

Singh, K.S. (1992). *People of India: An introduction*, Vol. *1*, National Series, Anthropological Survey of India (Calcutta: Seagull Books).

Singh, Prakash (May 2000), "An Indian assessment: Low–intensity conflicts and high intensity crime," *Faultlines: Writings on Conflict and Resolution*, Vol. 5, pp. 125–152, http://www.satp.org/satporgtp/publication/faultlines/volume5/Fault5-10psingh.htm.

———— (January–March 2002), "Management of India's north-eastern borders," *Dialogue*, Vol. 3, No. 3, pp. 57–70.

———— (2008), "India's northeast: The frontier in ferment," *Joint Special Operations University (JSOU) Report 08–4* (Florida: The JSOU Press).

———— (October–December 2012), "Internal Security Challenges—Gravity, Manifestations and Responses," *USI Journal*, Vol. CXLI, No. 586, http://www.usiofindia.org/Article /?pub=Journal&pubno=586&ano=858.

Singh, Tej Pratap (2005), "The Tripura insurgency: Socio-economic, political and external dimensions," *South Asian Survey*, Vol. 12, No. 2, pp. 287–305 (New Delhi/London: Sage Publications).

Sinha, S.K. (2002), "Violence & Hope in India's northeast," *Faultlines: Writings on Conflict and Resolution*. Vol. 10, http://www.satp.org/satporgtp/publication/faultlines/volume10/Article1.htm.

Sinha, S.P. (2007), *Lost opportunities: Fifty years of insurgency in the north-east and India's response* (New Delhi: Lancer Publishers).

Skocpol, Theda (1979), *State and social revolutions: A comparative analysis of France, Russia and China* (Cambridge: Cambridge University Press).

Skogan, Wesley and Frydal, Kathleen (2004) (Eds), "Executive Summary," *Fairness and Effectiveness in Policing: The Evidence*, Committee to Review Research on Police Policy and Practices (National Research Council).

Sloan, Steven (1999), "The changing face of insurgency in the post-cold war era: Doctrinal and operational implications." In A.J. Joes (Ed.) *Saving democracies: US intervention in threatened democratic states* (Westport CT: Praeger).

Small Arms Survey (2001), *Profiling the problem* (Oxford: University Press).

Smith, Neil (Major) and Sean, Macfarland (Colonel) (March–April 2008), "Anbar awakens," *Military Review*.

Smyth, M. (2005), "Insider-outsider issues in researching violent and divided societies," in Porter, E., Robinson, G., Smyth, M., and Schnabel, A. (Eds) *Researching conflict in Africa: insights and experiences* (Tokyo: United Nations University Press), pp. 9–23.

Sobek, David (2010), "Masters of their domains: The role of state capacity in civil wars," *Journal of Peace Research*, Vol. 47, No. 3, p. 267–271.

Sollom, A.H. (1962), "Nowhere yet everywhere," in Franklin Mark Osanka (Ed.) *Modern Guerrilla warfare: Fighting communist Guerrilla movements, 1941–1961* (New York: The Free Press of Glencoe).

Sonderlund, W.C. (December 1970), "An analysis of Guerrilla insurgency and Coup d'Etat as techniques of indirect aggression," *International Studies Quarterly*, Vol. 14, pp. 355–360.

South Asia Terrorism Portal (SATP1), "Punjab: Annual fatalities in terrorist related violence 1981-2015," http://www.satp.org/satporgtp/countries/india/states/punjab/data_sheets/annual_casualties.htm.

South Asia Terrorism Portal (SATP2), "India assessment-2014," http://www.satp.org/satporgtp/countries/india/index.html.

South Asia Terrorism Portal (SATP 3), "India fatalities 1994–2014," http://www.satp.org/satporgtp/countries/india/database/indiafatalities.htm.

South Asia Terrorism Portal (SATP 4), *"Fatalities in terrorist violence, Jammu and Kashmir, 1988–2015,"* http://www.satp.org/satporgtp/countries/india/states/jandk/data_sheets/annual_casualties.htm.

South Asia Terrorism Portal (SATP 5), *"Fatalities in left wing extremism, 2005–2015,"* http://www.satp.org/satporgtp/countries/india/maoist/data_sheets/fatalitiesnaxal05-11.htm.

South Asia Terrorism Portal (SATP 6), *"Cumulative fatalities by conflict theatres, 2005–2015,"* http://www.satp.org/satporgtp/countries/india/database/Cumulative_Fatalities.htm.

South Asia Terrorism Portal (SATP 7), *"Assam: Insurgency related killings, 1992–2015,"* http://www.satp.org/satporgtp/countries/india/states/assam/data_sheets/insurgency_related_killings.htm.

South Asia Terrorism Portal (SATP 8), *"Nagaland: Insurgency related killings,"* 1992–2015, http://www.satp.org/satporgtp/countries/india/states/nagaland/data_sheets/insurgency_related_killings.htm.

South Asia Terrorism Portal (SATP 9), *"Internecine clashes in Nagaland since 2001,"* http://www.satp.org/satporgtp/countries/india/states/nagaland/data_sheets/internecine.htm.

South Asia Terrorism Portal (SATP 10), *"Nagaland assessment 2010,"*.http://www.satp.org/satporgtp/countries/india/states/nagaland/assessment_2010.htm.

South Asia Terrorism Portal (SATP 11), *"Nagaland assessment 2014,"* http://www.satp.org/satporgtp/countries/india/states/nagaland/assessment_2014.htm.

South Asia Terrorism Portal (SATP 12), *"Manipur: Insurgency related killings 1992–2015,"* http://www.satp.org/satporgtp/countries/india/states/manipur/data_sheets/insurgency_related_killings.htm.

South Asia Terrorism Portal (SATP 13), *"Tripura: Insurgency related killings 1992–2015,"* http://www.satp.org/satporgtp/countries/india/states/tripura/data_sheets/insurgency_related_killings.htm.

South Asia Terrorism Portal (SATP 14), "Surrenders in Tripura since 1992," http://www.satp.org/satporgtp/countries/india/states/tripura/data_sheets/surrender.htm

South Asia Terrorism Portal (SATP 15), "Tripura Assessment, year 2003," http://www.satp.org/satporgtp/countries/india/states/tripura/assessment_2003.htm

South Asia Terrorism Portal (SATP 16), "Terrorist Groups- UBLF," http://www.satp.org/satporgtp/countries/india/states/tripura/terrorist_outfits/ublf.htm

Srivastav, N. (2006), "Industrial development in the north eastern states of India: The case of service industries," *The ICFAI Journal of Indian Economics*, Vol. 3, No. 4, pp. 60–69.

Staniland, Paul (2013), "Kashmir since 2003: Counterinsurgency and the paradox of 'Normalcy,'" *Asian Survey*, Vol. 53, No. 5, pp. 931–957.

Statewatch (June–August 2000), "EU global policing role: How non-military crises management will contaminate Justice and home affairs," *Statewatch Bulletin* 10.

Stead, Jonathan (2010), *Indian national security: Misguided men and guided missiles* (New Delhi: K W Publishers Pvt. Ltd.).

Stewart, Frances (2004), *"Development and security,"* Working Paper 3, Centre for Research on Inequality, Human Security and Ethnicity, CRISE, University of Oxford, http://preparingforpeace.org/.

Strassler, Robert B. and Crawley, Richard (Eds) (1996), *The landmark Thucydides: A comprehensive guide to the Peloponnesian War* (New York: The Free Press).

Subramaniam, Arjun (2012), "Challenges of protecting India from terrorism," *Terrorism and Political Violence*, Vol. *24*, No. 3, pp. 396–414.

Subramanian, K.S. (2007), *Political violence and the police in India* (London: SAGE Publications).

Subramanian, S. (July 7–12, 2014), *Meeting the LWE challenge-success of Odisha police*—a case study, circulated by the author at the National Police Academy, Hyderabad during a Seminar on National Security.

Taber, Robert (2002), *The war of the flea: The classic study of Guerrilla warfare*. Foreword by Bard E. O'Neill (Virginia: Potomac Books Inc), Originally published in 1965, New York: L. Stuart.

Tellis, Ashley J. (2005), *"India as a new global power: An action agenda for the United States,"* http://www.carnegieendowment.org/files/Tellis.India.Global.Power.FINAL4.pdf.

The Asian Age (August 11, 2013), "Despots and puppets: Some democracy this."

———— (August 19, 2013), "CBI, NIA at loggerheads in Ishrat case."

The Assam Tribune (March 9, 2013), "Major arms haul in Mizoram," Guwahati.

The Economic Times (January 16, 2013), "India engaged in 'war-mongering': Hina Rabbani Khar," New Delhi.

———— (January 13, 2013), "Delhi gangrape case: Dikshit slams Delhi police for insensitive approach," New Delhi.

———— (August 10, 2013), "Tripura party joins statehood bandwagon."

———— (August 222014), "Home Minister Rajnath Singh orders new 'anti-Maoist doctrine' to wipe out Naxal menace."

———— (May 16, 2015), "Border Infrastructure: Modi government driving strategic projects with radical changes."

———— (May 19, 2015), "States turn a blind eye to citizen's complaints: Nearly 1.2 lakh grievances remain unattended."

The Economist (June 15–21, 2013), "Secrets, lies and America's Spies," Vol. *407*, No. 8840 (London).

The Hindu (July 9, 2012), "ONGC starts releasing natural gas to Palatana Power Project."

———— (January 31, 2014), "ULFA's Paresh Barua sentenced to death in Bangladesh," http://www.thehindu.com/news/international/south-asia/ulfas-paresh-barua-sentenced-to-death-in-bangladesh/article5634460.ece.

The Indian Express (July 10, 2013), "Supreme Court verdict on convicted MPs, MLAs: Political parties push for reforms."

The Institute for Conflict Management (2007), *"Project report on insurgency and special challenges to policing in India's northeast: A case study of Tripura police"* submitted to The Bureau of Police Research and Development, Govt. of India, New Delhi.

The Statesman (October 14, 2000), "Right remedy: Tripura Police doing a commendable job," Vol. *CXXXIV*, No. 243, Editorial.

———— (February 16, 2012), "India shining?"

The Telegraph (November 6, 2000), "Tripura Police refurbish image."

———— (August 19, 2005), "Rebels force exodus," http://www.telegraphindia.com/1050819/asp/northeast/story_5128137.asp.

———— (February 26, 2011), "TSR indiscipline irks Tripura government," http://www.telegraphindia.com/1110226/jsp/northeast/story_13636413.jsp.

———— (March 20, 2012), "Poverty rises in northeast, declines in Tripura, Arunachal."

———— (January 19, 2013), "Reading and arithmetic skills decline," Calcutta.

The Times of India (July 13, 2012), "At least 31% of MPs, MLAs have criminal cases against them."

——— (November 2, 2012), "Tripura to own stake in fertilizer plant," Kolkata edition.

——— (December 23, 2012), "11 militants surrender in Tripura," Guwahati edition.

——— (January 5, 2013), "Tripura rebel leaders held in Bangladesh," Guwahati edition.

The Times of India (June 22, 2013), "President Pranab Mukerjee commissions first unit of Palatana Power project."

——— (July 24, 2013), "IB officer Rajinder Kumar under CBI lens for another Gujarat encounter case."

——— (August 2, 2013), "Four statehood demands lead to large-scale violence in Assam."

——— (August 5, 2013), "Home Ministry flooded with demands of more than twenty states."

——— (August 6, 2013), "Now, Kukis jump on to statehood bandwagon."

——— August 11, (2013), "Bihar police guns don't fire at Khudiram homage," Patna edition.

——— (April 12, 2015), "Why it doesn't pay to be a small farmer."

Thompson, Robert (1967), *Defeating communist insurgency: Experience from Malaya and Vietnam* (London: Chatto and Windus).

Thyne, Clayton (2006), "ABCs, 123s, and the golden rule: The pacifying effect of education on civil war 1980-1999," International Studies Quarterly, Vol. *50*, No. 4, pp. 733–754.

Time Magazine (April 20, 2015), "Black lives matter."

Toft, I.A. (Summer 2001), "How the weak win wars: A theory of asymmetric conflict," *International Security*, Vol. *26*, No. 1, pp. 93–128.

Tripura, Biswaranjan (December 2013), "Tribal question in Tripura: Dialogue between its past and present," *Journal of Tribal Intellectual Collective India*, Vol. 1, No. 2, pp. 38-50.

Tripura Observer (November 6, 2000), "State police to get automatics, night vision device soon. 'Policeman of the year' on December 3."

——— (December 8, 2001), "Top cop hopeful brighter days ahead."

——— (July 3, 2002), "B L Vohra, the Chief who revived Tripura police."

——— (November 3, 2012), "3 Mizo Ultras netted," Agartala.

Tripura Times (November 7, 2000), "Transformation of Tripura police," Editorial.

——— (November 27, 2011), "Leave corruption or crumble: Manik tells party comrades," Agartala.

——— (December 7, 2012), "Rebel leader surrenders," Agartala.

——— (January 24, 2013), "ATTF supremo sent to jail," Agartala.

——— (January 24, 2013), "BSF, TSR to work together."

——— (January 25, 2013), "Extradition treaty with B'desh cleared," Agartala.

——— (February 17, 2013), "Record turnout in state," Agartala.

Sekhar Datta, Tripura Year Book (2013), (Agartala: Tripurainfo publications).

Tripura Year Book (2010), (Agartala: Tripurainfo publications).

Upadhyay, Archana (2009), *India's fragile borderlands: The dynamics of terrorism in north east India* (London: I.B. Tauris).

Upadhyay, R. (2005), "*Tripura bleeds—In the crossfire of mainstream political parties and virulent ethnic conflict*," South Asia Analysis Group, Paper No. 1613, http://www.southasiaanalysis.org/%5Cpapers17%5Cpaper1613.html.

Urdal, Henrik (2008), "Population, resources and political violence: A sub-national study of India 1956-2002," *Journal of Conflict Resolution*, Vol. 52, No. 4, pp. 590–617.

Vadlamannati, K C (2011), "Why Indian men rebel? Explaining armed rebellion in the northeastern states of India, 1970-2007," *Journal of Peace Research*, Vol. 48, No. 5, pp. 605–619.

Varshney, A. (2002), *Ethnic conflict and civic life: Hindus and Muslims in India* (Delhi: Oxford University Press).

Verghese, B.G. (2004), *India's north east resurgent: Ethnicity, insurgency, governance, development* (New Delhi: Konark Publishers).

Verghese, B.G. (2008), *Rage, Reconciliation and Security: Managing India's Diversities* (New Delhi: Penguin Books India).

Verma, Arvind (2014), "The police and India's Maoist insurgency," in Fair, C.C. and Ganguly, S. (Eds.) *Policing insurgencies: Cops as counterinsurgents* (Oxford: University Press).

Vohra, B.L. (2011), *Tripura's bravehearts* (New Delhi: Konark Publishers).

Walhert, Matthew H. (2007), "The failed state." In James J.F. Forest (Ed.) *Countering terrorism and insurgency in the 21st century* (Vol. 2, pp. 93–108), Westport: Praeger Security International.

Wallace, Paul (2007), "Countering terrorist movements in India: Kashmir and Khalistan." In Robert J. Art and Louise Richardson (Eds) *Democracy and counterterrorism: Lessons from the past* (Washington D.C.: United States Institute of Peace Press).

Ward, Michael, Greenhill, Brian D., and Bakke, Kristin M. (2010), "The perils of policy by p-value: Predicting civil conflicts," *Journal of Peace Research*, Vol. 47, No. 4, p. 363–375.

Weimann, G. (2006), *Terror on the Internet: The new arena challenges* (Washington DC.: US Institute of Peace).

Wilkinson, Paul (1977), *Terrorism and the liberal state* (London: Macmillan).

———— (2001), *Terrorism versus democracy: The liberal state response* (London: Frank Cass Publishers).

Williams, Kristina (May 2011), "The other side of COIN: Counterinsurgency and community policing," *Interface: A journal for and about social movements*, Vol. 3, No. 1, pp. 81–117.

Wolfendale, Jessica (2006), "Terrorism, security, and the threat of counterterrorism," *Studies in Conflict & Terrorism*, Vol. 29, No. 7, pp. 753–770.

Woolcock, M.J.V. (1998), *Social theory: Development policy and poverty alleviation: A comparative-historical analysis of group-based banking in developing countries*, an unpublished PHD thesis, Department of Sociology at Brown University, Providence, Rhode Island.

World Development Indicators, 2011, http://data.worldbank.org/country/india.

Zala, Benjamin and Rogers, Paul (2011), "The 'Other' Global Security Challenges," *The RUSI Journal*, Vol. 156, No. 4, pp. 26–33.

Zedner, L. (2009), *Security* (New York: Routledge).

ZeeNews (January 15, 2013), "Spl. anti-Naxal force for Bihar, Jharkhand, Odisha, Chhattisgarh," http://zeenews.india.com/news/nation/spl-anti-naxal-force-for-bihar-jharkhand-odisha-chhatisgarh_823109.html.

Index

About the Author

Kuldeep Kumar is a senior Indian Police Service officer with a rich blend of operational experience and keen interest in police research. During his three decades of policing career, he has held several challenging assignments in state police, the Intelligence Bureau, and the Central Industrial Security Force, and served with distinction in the insurgency-prone states of Tripura, Assam, and Jammu and Kashmir. He is a recipient of the Indian Police Medal for Meritorious Service and Police (Internal Security Service) Medal, and has secured the highly competitive Australia Leadership Awards (ALA) scholarship for research on counterinsurgency in Australia. He holds postgraduate degrees in Politics from Monash University, Australia; Security and Organizational Risk Management from Leicester University, United Kingdom; and English Literature from Kurukshetra University, India. He has qualified the FBI National Academy program at Quantico, Virginia (USA) and has also attended numerous other training programs in India and abroad. Presently, Kuldeep Kumar is posted as the Chief Vigilance Officer in a major public sector undertaking in New Delhi.